Anglo-Saxon
Settlements

Anglo-Saxon Settlements

Edited by
Della Hooke

Basil Blackwell

Copyright © Basil Blackwell Ltd, 1988

First published 1988

Basil Blackwell Ltd
108 Cowley Road, Oxford, OX4 1JF, UK

Basil Blackwell Inc.
432 Park Avenue South, Suite 1503
New York, NY 10016, USA

British Library Cataloguing in Publication Data
Anglo-Saxon settlements.
   1. Anglo-Saxons.   2. Human settlements –
Great Britain   3. Great Britain – Antiquities
I. Hooke, Della
941.01   DA152.2
ISBN 0–631–15454–X

Library of Congress Cataloging in Publication Data
Anglo-Saxon settlements/edited by Della Hooke.
   p. cm.
   Includes index.
   ISBN 0-631-15454-X
   1. Great Britain – History – Anglo-Saxon period, 449–1066.   2. Anglo-Saxons – England – History.   3. England – Antiquities.   4. England – Historical geography.   5. Land settlement – England – History.
   I. Hooke, Della.
DA152.A727 1988
942.01–dc19

87–26930
CIP

Typeset in 11 on 13 pt Caslon
by Joshua Associates Limited, Oxford
Printed in Great Britain by
Butler and Tanner Limited, Frome

Contents

List of Figures

vii

List of plates

List of Tables

List of Contributors

JOHN BLAIR is a Fellow and Praelector of The Queen's College, Oxford

JENNIFER BOURDILLON is a Research Fellow in the Faunal Remains Unit, Department of Archaeology, at the University of Southampton

MARGARET GELLING is an Honorary Reader in the School of History, University of Birmingham

DAVID N. HALL is Fenland Field Officer for Cambridgeshire Archaeological Committee

RICHARD HALL is Deputy Director of the York Archaeological Trust for Excavation and Research

HELMUT HILDEBRANDT is a Professor in the Geographisches Institut, Universität Mainz

DAVID HILL is Staff Tutor in Archaeology in the Department of Extramural Studies, University of Manchester

RICHARD HODGES is a Lecturer in the Department of Archaeology and Prehistory, University of Sheffield

DELLA HOOKE is a Research Fellow in the Department of Geography, University of Birmingham

HANS-JÜRGEN NITZ is a Professor in the Geographisches Institut, Universität Göttingen

TIM TATTON-BROWN was formerly Director of the Canterbury Archaeological Trust

TIM UNWIN is a Lecturer in the Department of Geography at the Royal Holloway and Bedford New College, University of London

PETER WARNER is a Lecturer in the Department of History at Homerton College, Cambridge

TOM WILLIAMSON is a Lecturer at the Centre of East Anglian Studies, University of East Anglia

Acknowledgements

The author and publisher are grateful to the following for kind permission to reproduce material: Suffolk Record Office for plate II, Berkshire County Council and Clyde Surveys Ltd. for plate XVI, York Archaeological Trust for plates XXXVI–XXXVIII. The cover photograph and plates VI, VIII, IX, XV, XVII, XVIII, XIX, XX, XXVII, XXVIII and XXIX were taken by Della and Christopher Hooke, plates I and III by Peter Warner, plates IV and VII by John Blair, plate V by Geoff Dowling, plates X–XIII by Tim Unwin, plate XIV by David Hall, plates XXI and XXII by Brian Horne, plates XXIII–XXVI by Ben Taylor and XXX–XXXV by Tim Tatton-Brown. Figure 12.3 is based upon a manuscript map of the late Dr O. August with the kind permission of Mrs August and figure 12.4 upon the published maps of O. August with the permission of the Akademie der Wissenschaften der DDR, Zentralinstitut für Alte Geschichte und Archäologie, Berlin (East Germany). The British Academy generously funded travel incurred by Professor Dr H.-J. Nitz and Professor Dr H. Hildebrandt in attending the 1986 seminar.

Introduction:
Later Anglo-Saxon England

DELLA HOOKE

Then they sent to Angel; ordered [them] to send more aid and to be told of the worthlessness of the Britons and of the excellence of the land.

C. Plummer (ed.), *The Anglo-Saxon Chronicle*

Britain is rich in grain and timber; it has good pasturage for cattle and draught animals, and vines are cultivated in various localities. There are many land and sea birds of various species, and it is well known for its plentiful springs and rivers abounding in fish.

Bede, *Venerabilis Baedae Opera Historica*

Although a far-flung piece of the late Roman Empire, Britain was obviously an attractive spectacle to the Anglo-Saxons of the fifth and subsequent centuries, seeking new lands first to plunder and subsequently to settle, and to the Scandinavian settlers of the ninth century who followed them. It was equally as attractive to the Normans of the late eleventh century who were attempting to extend their own dominions.

By late Anglo-Saxon times, the country appears to have been supporting a flourishing economy. Contemporary documents suggest that mixed farming prevailed and many of the intensively developed parts of Roman Britain continued to support thriving agriculture. There seems to have been some shrinkage in the areas under cultivation in some regions, such as the chalklands of southern England, but here, as in other regions, pastoralism may have increased in importance and woodland, too, was widely exploited as stock pasture. The strength of the rural economy is shown by its ability, in late Anglo-Saxon times, to support an increasing number of urban centres, which served as cultural and religious foci and as centres of government and trade. Under Alfred, in particular, learning and literature had been fostered and English achievements were recognized throughout continental Europe. The Normans were attracted by, and came to, a country of relatively sophisticated cultural standards. It is quite obvious

I

that the part of England surveyed by the new Norman lords immediately prior to 1086 was not of their own creation. William I sent his officials

all over England into every shire to ascertain how many hundreds of 'hides' of land there were in each shire, and how much land and live-stock the king himself owned in the country, and what annual dues were lawfully his from each shire. He also had it recorded how much land his archbishops had, and his diocesan bishops, his abbots and his earls . . . and what or how much each man who was a landholder here in England had in land or in live-stock, and how much money it was worth. So very thoroughly did he have the inquiry carried out that there was not a single 'hide', not one virgate of land, not even – it is shameful to record it, but it did not seem shameful to him to do – not even one ox, nor one cow, nor one pig which escaped notice in his survey.[1]

Many areas had suffered a temporary setback at the time of the Conquest, but the wealth recorded by the survey was derived essentially from practices that had evolved over some six hundred years of Anglo-Saxon rule. The situation thus revealed may be seen as 'the Anglo-Saxon achievement' rather than that of any new regime.

The Anglo-Saxons themselves had not settled in an empty and un-developed land. Although they may initially have been attracted to these shores by prospects of loot and plunder, they found a land that was farmed and fertile enough to warrant mass migration from their continental home-lands, one that had been immensely rich and productive under former Roman rule. Whatever the effects of the Anglo-Saxon conquest, and however calamitous this may have been for the British people, Britons certainly remained in the majority in the western parts of the island at least and, everywhere, the landscape that had evolved must have influenced sub-sequent development to a marked degree. Indeed, the search for 'con-tinuity' has dominated much of the literature over the last ten to fifteen years, with many scholars, including the late Professor H. P. R. Finberg, suggesting that earlier traditions permeated many aspects of Anglo-Saxon territorial organization and Anglo-Saxon institutions.[2] This focus has only recently been counterbalanced by Professor Alan Everitt's discussion of the role of the 'Jutes' in the colonization of the kingdom of Kent.[3] It may, indeed, be queried whether ethnicity had a great deal of influence upon the economic and settlement patterns of the countryside. It is not, however, the early period which forms the subject of the present book. In the novo-

---

[1] *The Anglo-Saxon Chronicle. Two of the Saxon Chronicles Parallel*, edited by C. Plummer (Oxford, 1892–9), p. 216.

[2] For instance, see papers in H. P. R. Finberg, *Lucerna: Studies of Some Problems in the Early History of England* (Leicester, 1964).

[3] A. Everitt, *Continuity and Change: The Evolution of Kentish Settlement* (Leicester, 1986).

centenary year of Domesday, attention has been concentrated upon the years leading up to the compilation of *Domesday Book* itself.

Domesday Book gives a picture of England at a given time, but in reality it reveals a landscape that is a palimpsest of many periods, a society in evolution.[4] It was with this view in mind that the Historical Geography Research Group of the Institute of British Geographers agreed to convene a seminar on 'The Historical Geography of Early Medieval England' in the summer of 1986, to be held immediately prior to the main conference held at Winchester which celebrated the novocentenary of the *Domesday Book*. The papers in the present volume are those presented at this 'pre-Domesday' seminar, which took place at the University of Birmingham. Archaeologists, historians and geographers were assembled and brought to the seminar the multi-disciplinary approach that has made such an impact upon the study of Anglo-Saxon England in recent years. Throughout the seminar, too, the great debt owed to the pioneering work carried out into the geographical interpretation of the contents of the *Domesday Book* by the geographer, Professor H. C. Darby, in the *Domesday Geographies*, was also clearly apparent.[5]

Fashions of interpreting historical events change, both according to the state of knowledge of the discipline and to the ideas of the time, and whereas a seminar held in the 1960s or 1970s might have been expected to express 'continuity' as a major theme, it is striking how many of the papers presented here place the emphasis upon *change*. This is not, however, necessarily a return to ideas concerning possible changes wrought by the incoming Anglo-Saxons in the fifth century (however catastrophic events at that time may have been), ideas that permeated the writing of most scholars of Anglo-Saxon history earlier this century, but changes that took place later in the Anglo-Saxon period and apparently established much of the regional framework of later, medieval England. New farming methods appear to have developed in certain parts of England and these had a profound effect upon the landscape and upon social organization in the community. As a result, field and settlement patterns changed dramatically in these areas, while, in others, relict systems were incorporated to a more marked degree in subsequent patterns of land use. In yet others, a shrinkage in the amount of cropped land seems to be indicated, accompanied often by an extension of the land devoted to the grazing of animals or allowed to revert to woodland.

In a volume of this nature, no attempt can be made to present an overall pattern of late Anglo-Saxon England, even from the aspect of historical

---

[4] Unless otherwise stated, references to the *Domesday Book* in the papers in this volume are to the 1783 Record Commission edition.

[5] H. C. Darby (ed.), *The Domesday Geography of England*, vols 1–7 (Cambridge, 1952–77).

geography alone. (A forthcoming volume in a series *A New Blackwell's Historical Geography of England*, under the general editorship of Derek Gregory and Richard Smith, will cover a more extensive area and a wider field of study.) Instead, the papers here represent some of the latest thinking in the subject and disseminate views which will undoubtedly contribute to the future of the study. It will be interesting to reassess the situation in a few years time. With the emphasis upon later *Anglo-Saxon* England, it is perhaps not surprising that so many contributors chose to report on the situation prevailing in eastern, central and southern England, the region which not only had been most intensively settled first by these people, but which lay open to subsequent influences from the Continent. In these regions, too, largely because of surviving pottery evidence, Anglo-Saxon settlement sites can most readily be identified. In contrast, the north and west are not well represented and it is to be hoped that future scholars will redress this imbalance. It is in these areas, perhaps, that more ancient systems of territorial and economic organization may be expected to survive.

Several authors deal with aspects of territorial organization in late Anglo-Saxon England and review the evidence for the antiquity of the administrative divisions then in use. Even the major folk-group regions of the early Anglo-Saxon kingdoms are not of proven antiquity, but are perhaps the type of division most likely to have been rooted in a more distant past, while the multiple estate, in spite of its apparent occurrence in both the Celtic and English parts of the country, has also recently become the subject of much debate.[6] In the formative years of the Anglo-Saxon period, 'kingdoms' and lesser tribal groupings were subject to both amalgamation and subsequent fragmentation as the more formal administrative divisions of the period were established. While the hundred is known to have been an administrative unit of central Wessex, its antiquity has been doubted and many have seen it as a unit that emerged in the formative years of the Danish invasions. Again, however, much older land groupings may have been involved in the subsequent compilation of the new administrative units. The ecclesiastical organization of the Christian Church also emerged at a time when early kingdoms were still in existence and the establishment of ministers to serve specific *parochiae* could also help to preserve early territorial groupings. A knowledge of the location of such early ministers may also help to identify 'central places' and those 'central areas' that continued to be the core areas of later administrative arrange-

[6] N. Gregson, 'The multiple estate model: some critical questions', *Journal of Historical Geography*, 11 (1985), pp. 339–51; G. R. J. Jones, 'Multiple estates perceived', *Journal of Historical Geography*, 11 (1985), pp. 352–63.

ments.[7] In the south-west, it has been demonstrated that the Christian Church, established there by the sixth century, may indeed have formalized early estate groupings and that in this region internal subdivisions were in due course to influence the delineation of parish boundaries.[8]

It is abundantly clear, however, that a study of territorial units cannot be divorced from an understanding of the contemporary geographical environment. In several parts of the country, the larger folk regions often seem to have included both intensively settled zones and less developed regions of more marginal land. The latter may have been used initially as areas of seasonal grazing, but later often supported a more pastoral economy, complementing the resources of the more heavily cultivated zones. This arrangement can be shown in some regions to underlie the arrangement of multiple estates which possessed outliers in upland or woodland regions.[9] On a smaller scale, when major units became fragmented into the smaller estate units of later Anglo-Saxon England, often on a township level, it was necessary that each unit should possess the type of land necessary for at least a degree of self-sufficiency, even if this entailed the addition of detached parcels of land lying distant from the home manor.

In recent decades, several scholars have argued for the antiquity of even minor boundaries and some have suggested that these may have been established in a pre-Anglo-Saxon context.[10] Others have thought that minor boundaries might represent a form of land division that occurred in the early years of the Anglo-Saxon 'takeover', and yet others feel that the estate fragmentation expressed in parish and township boundaries was relatively late in many regions. Boundary demarcation, however, reflects the type of estate unit that arises from the social organization of a region and this is hardly likely to have been identical in eastern England, an area subject to Anglo-Saxon and Danish incursions, with demarcation in areas further west, in some parts of which minor land units of sixth-century date can be recognized.[11] Minor boundaries, whether those of Romano-British villa estates or lesser farming units, obviously existed, but, even if these were traceable, their relevance to the later parish boundaries of eastern

[7] D. Hooke, 'Territorial organisation in the Anglo-Saxon West Midlands: central places, central areas', in E. Grant (ed.), *Central Places, Archaeology and History* (Sheffield, 1986), pp. 79–93.

[8] S. M. Pearce, 'The early church in the landscape: the evidence from north Devon', *Archaeological Journal*, 142 (1985), pp. 255–75.

[9] D. Hooke, 'Early units of government in Herefordshire and Shropshire', in D. Brown, J. Campbell and S. C. Hawkes (eds), *Anglo-Saxon Studies in Archaeology and History*, 5 (Oxford, forthcoming).

[10] D. Bonney, 'Early boundaries in Wessex', in P. J. Fowler (ed.), *Archaeology and the Landscape: Essays for L. V. Grinsell* (London, 1972); D. Bonney, 'Early Saxon burials and boundaries in Wiltshire, *Wiltshire Archaeological and Natural History Magazine*, 61 (1960), pp. 25–30; C. Taylor, *Dorset* (London, 1970), pp. 51–75.

[11] For instance W. Davies, '*Unciae*: land measurement in the *Liber Landavensis*', *Agricultural History Review*, 21 (1973), pp. 115–17.

England can with some justification be questioned.[12] Even within the area of one pre-Conquest county different situations may have prevailed, and Gelling has argued for the antiquity of a major territorial unit based upon the Iron Age focus of Blewbury in Berkshire,[13] whereas it is difficult to detect any early boundaries in the Vale of the White Horse (see chapter 6 below). It is clear that no one answer will suffice for the whole of the country. Even within the relatively restricted area of Suffolk, Dr Peter Warner suggests a complicated situation in which some ancient boundaries may have survived, while other land units were regrouped to fit changing administrative requirements. This theme is picked up again by Dr John Blair, who refers to the fragmentation of early minster *parochiae*.

Settlement studies are equally in a state of flux. The recent archaeological evidence from eastern England, much of it in the form of pottery scatters, seems to reveal the prevalence of a dispersed settlement pattern in early Anglo-Saxon England more akin to the preceding Romano-British period than that of later times. Loose clustering may have occurred earlier, but at some time around the eighth century increasing nucleation seems to have taken place, ultimately giving rise to planned settlements. Again, such a development may only have been a characteristic of the regions later to be dominated by nucleated villages. The pottery evidence is not available for the West Midlands, but a similar process seems to have taken place in the south-eastern parts of that region and in many other parts of lowland Britain.[14]

The trend towards settlement nucleation appears to have been linked with changes in agrarian organization, for the introduction of a form of open-field agriculture seems to have been a stimulus to settlement planning. This is discussed in this volume by David Hall in relation to the Northamptonshire evidence. He suggests that the medieval field systems were often established by 1086, the land in the open fields possibly laid out to correspond to the hidage assessment of each vill. I offer some evidence of the type of earlier field systems that may have influenced field layout in parts of southern England, where there is less evidence of the strongly formalized systems now recognized in parts of eastern England, but more documentary evidence of a type of open-field organization. Different, and perhaps older, patterns of infield and outfield, detected in the Welsh Border and probably also recognizable in the West Midlands, seem to have

---

[12] P. T. H. Unwin, 'Townships and early fields in north Nottinghamshire', *Journal of Historical Geography*, 9 (1983), pp. 341–6.

[13] M. Gelling, *Signposts to the Past: Place-Names and the History of England* (London, 1978), pp. 192, 196–204.

[14] D. Hooke, 'Village development in the West Midlands', in D. Hooke (ed.), *Medieval Villages: A Review of Current Work*, Oxford University Committee for Archaeology, Monograph No. 5 (Oxford, 1985), pp. 125–54.

little place in the grand reorganization of fields in eastern England.[15] On the other hand, ancient field patterns depicted by Dr Tom Williamson in Essex, and noted by other scholars elsewhere in the country, are a reminder that the typical open-field system did not bring change to all regions, even in eastern England, and that older elements in the landscape can and do persist.

There is space, too, to consider whether open-field farming may not everywhere have been the dramatic innovation it was once considered, although 'introduction' and 'reorganization' are words which dominate the literature. It involved a number of separate components which included the layout of the fields and the nature of landholding within them. Some aspects of the arrangement may have already been present before large-scale changes took place and in some regions, at least, its emergence may have been a more gradual process.[16] Its fullest development seems, however, to have been closely related to the estate fragmentation that was taking place in the Anglo-Saxon period. This was most decisive in intensively developed areas of high resource potential and it was in these areas that the classic medieval open-field landscapes were to evolve.

Much of the early documentation, not least that of the *Domesday Book*, concerns the wealth to be derived from arable cultivation, but several papers indicate the predominance of a mixed-farming economy in late Anglo-Saxon England, even in major crop-growing areas. The withdrawal of cultivation from some types of marginal land, including both chalk uplands and valley-land, may have been accompanied by increased pastoral activity, and the continued success of animal husbandry is noted by Jennifer Bourdillon in her discussion of the bone evidence from Saxon Hamwic.

The countryside was able to support a growing network of towns and markets and, like many rural settlements, urban centres were subject to a degree of formalized planning which influenced subsequent development. Attempts to show continuity of urban function and occupation from late Roman times have often foundered, in spite of determined effort, but the concept of the town as the right and proper place for administrative functions, whether lay or ecclesiastical, was not lost. Dr John Blair shows how the foundation of an Anglo-Saxon minster, often at or near a *villa regalis*, frequently led to the establishment of a market and encouraged urban growth. The influence of trade on urban development was a significant factor and is exemplified in Tim Tatton-Brown's discussion of the

[15] R. T. Rowley, 'Medieval field systems', in L. Cantor (ed.), *The English Medieval Landscape* (London, 1982), pp. 36–8.

[16] D. Hooke, 'Early forms of open-field agriculture in England'. Paper presented at the Stockholm symposium of the Permanent European Conference for the Study of the Rural Landscape, September 1987 (Stockholm, forthcoming); M. Aston, *Interpreting the Landscape: Archaeology in Local Studies* (London, 1985), pp. 120–37.

trading *wīcs* of Kent and in Dr Richard Hall's exposition of pre-Domesday York. Dr David Hill notes the coming together of those functions that would ultimately lead to true urban status.

In late Anglo-Saxon England there was considerable and continuous interchange of ideas between Britain and the Continent and many of the changes that occurred in England can also be identified in many regions of western and central Europe. Although similarities in settlement and field patterns can be recognized, however, the changes on the Continent often took place in quite different historical circumstances and an exploration of the essential differences between regions may be as revealing as the study of apparent similarities. It is, however, essential that such comparisons should be made. Here the contributions of Professor Dr Hans-Jürgen Nitz, Professor Dr Helmut Hildebrandt and Dr Richard Hodges are invaluable in setting the study within a wider, continental context. Dr Tim Unwin also briefly examines the Scandinavian evidence, but finds the German parallels more influential. The planned field systems of north Germany in the later Carolingian period described by Professor Dr Nitz offer much food for thought, although the detailed examination of the documentary evidence carried out by Professor Dr Hildebrandt suggests that the situation was much more complicated than is immediately apparent. Dr Richard Hodges examines some of the forces that may have led to change in this period.

Although the advent of new peoples has traditionally been seen as the prime instigator of economic change, this must now, as in earlier periods, be questioned. Far-reaching changes in farming techniques, settlement patterns, and even political ideals could readily be transmitted by cultural exchange and at no time in history were these islands ever isolated from outside influence. Rarely, however, were foreign systems adopted without adaptation. New ideas could, equally, develop in Britain and ancient systems might influence innovations in quite a different way here compared with on the Continent. Response to the natural environment was also an important if not overriding factor in the development of settlement patterns and field systems. The situation prevailing in late Anglo-Saxon England was exceedingly complex. While some major trends can be detected in this country, Britain has always been noted for the variation of its regional landscapes and only continued detailed studies will allow a full evaluation to be made of some of the issues raised in the present volume. It is hoped that this book may offer a stimulus to further enquiry.

1

Pre-Conquest Territorial and Administrative Organization in East Suffolk

PETER WARNER

Introduction

In Suffolk, as in many other counties, we face the most elementary questions when looking at pre-Conquest administrative boundaries. How old are they? And to what territories do they relate? To what extent do they represent a palimpsest of earlier administrative structures? Above all, how reliable is the Domesday survey as a source for the interpretation of administrative boundaries in the county? The last question is fundamental and must be addressed first and foremost before any other discussion can follow.

The staccato lines of the Domesday survey contain many minor errors and omissions, and they also deliberately subsume minor irregularities and regional differences, particularly within manor and vill. Indeed, it is likely that where anomalies are found at lower levels in the survey, it is because they have escaped deliberate attempts at subsuming or editing by those who compiled the Domesday returns. However, irregularities evident in higher levels of administrative boundaries could not be so easily subsumed or omitted, for they were more closely related to the structure of the survey itself; to omit or subsume a detached portion of a hundred might lead to the exclusion of a significant entry and so give rise to a serious administrative error. The regional differences and irregularities evident in administrative boundaries recorded in the Domesday survey can be regarded as significantly more reliable and comprehensive than those anomalies recorded within the same survey at the level of manor and vill. The *Domesday Book*, particularly volume 2, can therefore be regarded as a reasonably reliable source for the study of early administrative boundaries.

In Suffolk the rank order of administrative boundaries is complex, with the great ecclesiastical liberties of Ely and Bury St Edmunds forming two

This chapter is based in part on P. M. Warner, 'Blything hundred: a study in the development of settlement AD 400–1400 (unpublished Ph.D. thesis, University of Leicester, 1982), ch. 5.

9

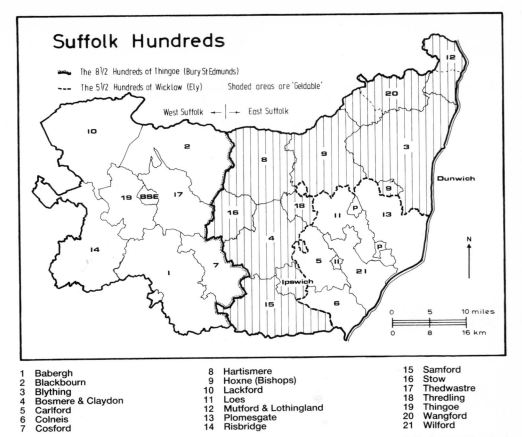

FIGURE I.I *Suffolk hundreds*

quite separate and distinct administrative districts or shires, both of pre-Conquest origin (figure 1.1). The hundredal pattern within these shires has a markedly different configuration; suffice it to say that there are many irregularities within the hundredal pattern of the county and an explanation must be attempted.

The County

The separate counties of Norfolk and Suffolk are a continual reminder that they were once a united territory. Considering the obvious geographical divide formed by the rivers Ouse and Waveney, the division of this extensive area came surprisingly late.[1] The earldom of East Anglia was not divided between the two counties until some time after the Norman Conquest,[2] while the sheriffs were also shared down to the sixteenth century.[3] An ecclesiastical division is evident much earlier, however, with two sees first appearing in about AD 673, following the Synod of Hertford, but there is no indication of their diocesan territories before the reign of Edgar.[4]

The late surviving institutional unity of the two counties of Norfolk and Suffolk bears a striking resemblance to what must once have been the territory of the early East Anglian kingdom; a territory derived ultimately from the pre-Roman tribal district of the Iceni, which, remaining intact as a *territorium* administered from *Venta Icenorum* during the Roman period, was eventually taken over by the early East Anglian kings in the late sixth century. Internal boundaries, such as those of the great ecclesiastical private hundreds and shires, which pre-date the county boundary, should therefore be seen in relation to the wider territory of the East Anglian kingdom rather than its late subdivisions, the two counties of Norfolk and Suffolk.

The fenland of west Norfolk, which acts as a natural boundary to the Icenian territory on the west, is a continuation of a boundary formed by the river Granta and the series of East Cambridgeshire hillforts[5] (the largest of which is Wandlebury), extending either side of the Cam valley and reaching from the fen edge into north-west Essex.[6] Fox and Rainbird Clarke saw the whole of the southern part of Suffolk as Trinovantian territory,[7] but recent excavations at Burgh-by-Woodbridge, undertaken by the Suffolk Archaeological Unit, have revealed a massive late Iron Age fortification overlain by later Roman building material. This fort, constructed on the north side of a tributary of the river Deben and there-fore clearly defending the East Anglian territory behind it, together with a

[1] The charter purporting to be Alfredian, once used as evidence for an early division between the counties, was exposed as a forgery by Hart in 1966; C. F. Hart, *The Early Charters of Eastern England* (Leicester, 1966), p. 40.

[2] H. M. Chadwick, *Studies on Anglo-Saxon Institutions* (Cambridge, 1905), p. 177; H. S. Cumming, 'On the kings of East Anglia', *Journal of the British Archaeological Association*, 21 (1865), pp. 22–31; J. R. Planche, 'The earls of East Anglia', *Journal of the British Archaeological Association*, 21 (1865), pp. 91–103; F. M. Stenton, 'The East Anglian kings of the seventh century', in P. Clemoes (ed.), *The Anglo-Saxons: Studies Presented to Professor B. Dickins* (Darmstadt, 1959), pp. 394–402.

[3] N. Scarfe, *The Suffolk Landscape* (London, 1972), p. 42.

[4] D. Whitelock, 'The conversion of the eastern Danelaw', *Saga-Book of the Viking Society*, 12 (1945), pp. 159–76.

[5] H. C. Darby, 'The Fenland frontier in Anglo-Saxon England', *Antiquity*, 8 (1934), pp. 185–201.

[6] C. Fox, *The Archaeology of the Cambridge Region* (Cambridge, 1923), pp. 134–40.

[7] C. Fox, 'The distribution of Man in East Anglia 2300 BC–50 AD', *Proceedings of the Prehistoric Society of East Anglia*, 7 (1933), pp. 149–66; R. Rainbird Clarke, *East Anglia* (London, 1960), p. 98; E. A. Martin, 'Burgh-by-Woodbridge', note *re*. Archaeology in Suffolk, *Proceedings of the Suffolk Institute of Archaeology*, 32 (1975), pp. 322–3.

FIGURE 1.2 *East Anglia*

similar one at Clare and possibly another at Sudbury, represent the military dispositions intended to defend a southern Icenian boundary, along the line of the Stour valley, linking up with the Granta forts (see figure 1.2). Much later, with the rise of Mercia, lands on the west of the East Anglian kingdom in what is now Cambridgeshire may have been lost.[8] Thus it may be seen that the Icenian territory corresponds closely to the area of the two

[8] C. Hart, *The Hidation of Cambridgeshire*, University of Leicester, Department of English Local History Occasional Paper, 2nd ser., 6 (Leicester, 1974), p. 10; J. N. L. Myres, *The English Settlements* (Oxford, 1986), p. 185.

counties of Norfolk and Suffolk, but it must remain uncertain to what extent the ancient 'folk' of the East Anglian kingdom reflects a pre-Roman tribal origin.

Norman Scarfe has argued for a degree of post-Roman survival in the form of 'Icen' as a tribal name in place-names such as Icklingham, Ickworth and the pre-historic Icknield Way.[9] This theory, although very attractive, is open to criticism. It has been suggested that these names derive not from the tribal name of the Iceni, but from *Icelings*, the dynastic name of the Mercian kings whose territory they bordered on the west.[10] There are also serious etymological problems concerning Scarfe's hypothesis, which are to be discussed in a forthcoming paper by McConchie.[11] However, these problems do not detract from the essential character of the Icenian territory and its close geographical relation to the Anglo-Saxon kingdom of East Anglia; a degree of continuity might reasonably be expected within the territory, if not in place-names, then at least in some of its administrative subdivisions, such as the more ancient hundreds and shires with their meeting-places and landscape foci.

How old are the minor administrative subdivisions listed in the Domesday survey and to what extent do they reflect earlier institutions, particularly those of pre-Danish origin? Anomalies in the Suffolk county boundary are well known to Domesday scholars.[12] But to what extent can such anomalies be taken as an indication of antiquity? Surprisingly, they do not seem to have caused insurmountable difficulties to medieval administrators. There were attempts at rationalization and it was probably desirable that higher-order boundaries, such as county and shire, should correspond with the lower-order boundaries of hundred and vill. Thus it is normal to find multi-functional boundaries that serve county, shire, hundred and vill; in many cases these also coincide with major topographical features such as rivers and arterial roads.

It would seem that the Domesday and later evidence for anomalies in the county boundary cannot be taken as an indication of antiquity; indeed it is argued here that such anomalies in the multi-functional boundaries of

---

[9] N. Scarfe, 'The place-name Icklingham: a preliminary re-examination', *East Anglian Archaeological Reports*, 3 (Norwich, 1976), pp. 127–34.

[10] Myres, *English Settlements*, p. 185.

[11] R. McConchie and D. M. E. Gillam, 'The place-name Icklingham: the Icenian dream', Department of English Language, University of Wollongong, Australia (forthcoming). I am grateful to Rod McConchie for allowing me to read this paper in advance of publication.

[12] On the southern county boundary, Bures lay partly in Suffolk and partly in Essex; Nayland lay in Essex, but was geldable in Suffolk. To the north, Diss, a Norfolk vill, lay outside its county in the Suffolk hundred of Hartismere; *The Kalendar of Abbot Samson of Bury St Edmunds and Related Documents*, edited by R. H. C. Davis, Camden Society, 3rd ser., 84 (London, 1954), p. xliv. Until the Divided Parishes and Poor Law Amendment Act of 1876, a large part of the parish of Mendham lay over the river Waveney in Norfolk extending as far as Harleston: Warner, 'Blything hundred', pp. 121–2, fig. 28.

Suffolk and Norfolk are an indication that the process of piecemeal administrative rationalization, following the division into two counties, had not had time to run its course by 1086.

The Liberties and Shires

The two great liberties of St Edmund and St Etheldreda have left an indelible mark on the administrative boundaries of the county of Suffolk. Most obvious is the one-time county of West Suffolk, once the liberty of St Edmund. Less well known is the district called the *Geldable*, an oddly formed territory composed out of the remaining hundreds not included in the two great liberties (see figure 1.1).

The eight and a half hundreds which comprise the liberty of St Edmund are first mentioned as 'belonging to Thinghog' in a charter of AD 1044, from which time they belonged to Bury St Edmunds.[13] The eight and a half hundreds, which comprise Babergh, Blackbourn, Cosford, Lackford, Risbridge, Thedwastre, Thingoe, and the town of Bury St Edmunds itself (which counted as a hundred and a half), are probably older than the eleventh century, but they may not be much more than a generation earlier. However, the small, but central hundred of Thingoe clearly once shared its name with the group of hundreds as a whole; it could therefore be the mother-hundred of the entire territory of West Suffolk.

Historians are generally agreed that the medieval administration based on hundreds in East Anglia was essentially a post-Danish imposition, but that it overlay a much earlier system of hundreds and shires, the meeting-places and boundaries of which were, in some cases, reused, so that an element of continuity from earlier times can occasionally be detected.[14] The original meeting-place of all eight and a half hundreds was one of a group of four mounds, called '*Thinghogo*', which lay at the junction of Thedwastre, Bury St Edmunds and Thingoe hundreds; the 'thing' place-name element meaning 'an assembly' here might suggest a Scandinavian origin for this composite group of hundreds.[15]

The boundary of Bury St Edmunds may have been established from AD 945, but there is some uncertainty about the authenticity of its charter bounds.[16] However, the *banleuca*, marked by four crosses, was probably firmly established when the abbey and town were granted extensive

---

[13] C. Hart, *Early Charters*, p. 70.

[14] H. M. Cam, *Liberties and Communities in Medieval England* (London, 1963), pp. 88–9; J. R. Morris, *The Age of Arthur: A History of the British Isles from 350–650* (London, 1973), pp. 491–5.

[15] O. S. Anderson, 'The English hundred names', *Acta Universitas Lundensis*, 30 (i) (1934), pp. 95–6.

[16] Hart, *Early Charters*, pp. 54–8.

privileges by Cnut.[17] Edmund's body was said to have been found incorrupt in AD 915 and was translated to Bury in AD 925 or before.[18] The general indication is that the division of what is now West Suffolk into the eight and a half hundreds was a substantially post-Danish creation; their place-names, which give away few clues, indicate an origin no earlier than the ninth century. But the whole territory, centred on the meeting-place of Thingoe, could be substantially earlier, either Danish or pre-Danish in origin.

The five and a half hundreds of Wicklaw, part of the liberty of St Etheldreda, present a very different picture. Their comparatively small size and their disjointed appearance makes them distinctive; for example, Loes had one, and later two, detached portions,[19] while Parham half-hundred lay in two small parts (see figure 1.1). So contrasting is this boundary pattern with other parts of Suffolk it demands an explanation.

The territory of Wicklaw as a whole contains sufficient archaeological and etymological evidence to suggest a degree of continuity with the Roman past. The original meeting-place of Wicklaw may have been a site near the Manor of Wicklows, known as Gallows Hill, near Wickham Market (see figure 1.3). Gelling has argued for the 'wick' element in these place-names being a Latin loan-word, suggestive of some degree of contact between Latin word-users and early Anglo-Saxon settlers.[20] An extensive late Roman site has been excavated in the neighbouring parish of Hacheston.[21] Isolated finds of Anglo-Saxon material within the Wicklaw territory at places such as Waldringfield, Butley, Parham and Rendlesham suggest that it was the focus of early settlement; while the ship-burial site at Sutton Hoo, overlooking the river Deben, and its counterpart at Snape, overlooking the river Alde, suggest a wealthy aristocratic Anglo-Saxon presence by the late sixth century (see figure 1.3).[22] A cluster of late Roman hoards containing gold and silver coins of the Emperor Theodosius (AD 379–95) and some of Honorius (AD 393–423), from Little Bealings, Butley, Orfordness, Sutton Hall, Woodbridge and Tuddenham St Matin,

[17] Ibid., pp. 63–6.

[18] D. H. Farmer, 'Some saints of East Anglia', in M. Barber, P. McNulty and P. Noble (eds), *East Anglian and Other Studies Presented to Barbara Dodwell*, Reading Medieval Studies, 11 (Reading, 1985), p. 41.

[19] Woodbridge seems to have been added to Loes hundred after 1086. D. Symor (ed.), *Woodbridge in Suffolk: A Tribute* (Ipswich, 1934), p. 15: 'for fiscal reasons, Woodbridge with Earl Dallingho was taken from Wilford Hundred to form part of the Loes Hundred'.

[20] M. Gelling, 'English place-names derived from the compound *wīchām*', *Medieval Archaeology*, 11 (1967), pp. 87–104; M. Gelling, 'Latin loan-words in Old English place-names', in P. Clemoes (ed.), *Anglo-Saxon England*, vol. 6 (1977), pp. 1–14. The 'camp' element in Campsey Ash may be another example, likewise Bulcamp near Blythburgh.

[21] A. Selkirk, 'The native towns of Roman Britain', *Current Archaeology*, 52 (1976) for September 1975, pp. 134–8.

[22] M. O. Carver, *Bulletin of the Sutton Hoo Research Committee*, 1 (April 1983), p. 10, fig. 4.

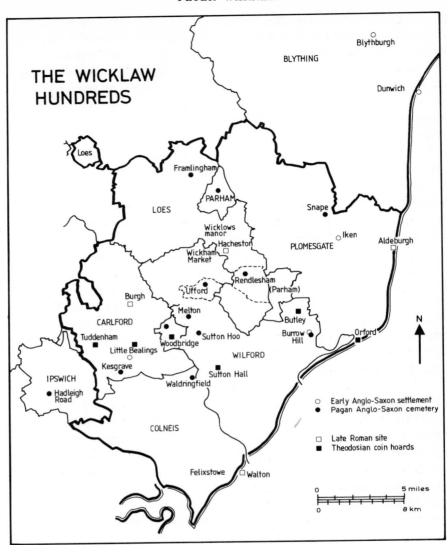

FIGURE 1.3 *The Wicklaw hundreds*

lies at the centre of the Wicklaw territory; Felixstowe, the parish which contained the late Roman shore-fort of Walton, now eroded by the sea, also has a substantial fourth-century coin series (see figure 1.3).[23]

These hoards cluster in the Deben, Butley and Alde river heartlands, behind the Roman shore-fort of Walton; such hoards in themselves suggest discontinuity, a point which needs emphasis, but at the same time they indicate a wealthy late Roman presence. The picture presented by the Wicklaw territory as a focus for wealth in the late Roman and early Anglo-

[23] I. E. More, 'Roman Suffolk', *Proceedings of the Suffolk Institute of Archaeology*, 24 (1947), pp. 172–5.

Saxon period is an interesting one, and although we may never know exactly what happened between the time of Honorius and the ship-burial at Sutton Hoo, we may reasonably ask what the source of that wealth might have been. More than likely it was land, probably the rich hinterland of those east-coast river valleys where the lighter sandy soils mixed with the loams of the clay plateau, land which was later to contribute so much towards the building of the great church at Ely.

Historical Background

The liberty of St Etheldreda was established when the monastery at Ely was refounded as a Benedictine house by Bishop Ethelwold; the five and a half hundreds of *Wicklawan* are first mentioned in Edgar's charter of AD 970.[24] Clearly this peculiar pattern of hundredal boundaries in East Suffolk was already in existence by that date; it cannot be explained away as a post-Danish phenomenon, so markedly different is it from the pattern of hundreds in West Suffolk. But is it significantly earlier, and if so, how can the hiatus of documentation caused by Danish occupation be bridged, albeit a period substantially less than the 'century of pagandom' described by Lethbridge?[25]

Miller in his scholarly work on the Abbey and Bishopric of Ely suggested that the lands that comprised the tenth-century refoundation, even the two hundreds of the Isle of Ely itself, bore little relation to the foundation established by St Etheldreda and her successors in the years following AD 673 (Plate I). Although he concludes that 'there is no inherent improbability in the supposition that the island [of Ely] may have been the endowment which St Etheldreda conferred', and that the liberty may have been made up of 'more than one original part',[26] he discounts a traditional story from the twelfth-century Ely chronicles which refer to the 'dower' of St Etheldreda being the Isle of Ely, a territory described by Bede as a *regio* of about six hundred hides in the province of the East Angles.[27] These lands were believed to have been acquired as a 'morning gift' from Etheldreda's first short-lived husband, Tonbert, prince of the South Gyrwe in or before AD 654/5.[28] Miller carefully points out discrepancies between the story as told by Bede and that told by the twelfth-century chroniclers; he insists

---

[24] E. Miller, *The Abbey and Bishopric of Ely* (Cambridge, 1951), pp. 8–15; Hart, *Early Charters*, p. 59.

[25] Whitelock, 'The conversion of the eastern Danelaw', pp. 159–76.

[26] Miller, *Abbey and Bishopric of Ely*, pp. 8–15.

[27] Bede, *Ecclesiastical History*, in *Venerabilis Baedae Opera Historica*, edited by C. Plummer, 2 vols (Oxford, 1896), IV, 19.

[28] *Liber Eliensis*, edited by E. O. Blake. Camden Society, 3rd ser., 92 (London, 1962), p. liii, fn. 6; Miller, *Abbey and Bishopric of Ely*, pp. 8–9.

PLATE I: *Ely Cathedral*
© Peter Warner.

'there is no direct link (possibly no link at all) between the region of the South Gyrwe and the medieval liberty of the Isle of Ely, or even between St Etheldreda's dower and the endowment which King Edgar conferred upon the monastery of Ely'.[29]

Whitelock has argued for a greater degree of ecclesiastical continuity on the more important early East Anglian monastic sites, minimizing the effects of Danish influence and pointing towards a continuing tradition of monastic survival.[30] There is also evidence to suggest that the boundary structure of the liberty, particularly the five and a half hundreds of Wicklaw, pre-dated that 'deliberate remodelling of administrative geography', which is supposed to have universally affected East Anglia following the reconquest of Danish territory by the West Saxon kings.[31]

Arguments for continuity in the essential boundary structure of the liberty before AD 970 are complex, but nevertheless persuasive. Most important is the link between Etheldreda and the East Anglian royal house. Her position as a princess, the daughter of King Anna of East Anglia, must be considered very carefully when looking at her marriage arrangements, which are likely to have been politically expedient where the acquisition of land was concerned.[32] Anna's predecessor, the saintly King Sigbert and his kinsman, Egric, were killed in battle by Penda, the pagan king of Mercia, a fate Anna himself was to suffer in AD 654.[33] Therefore any marriage that involved the acquisition of land on, or close to, the Mercian boundary at this time would be charged with more than usual political significance; indeed, the death of Tonbert and the acquisition of the Isle of Ely by the East Anglian royal house in AD 654/5 may well have provoked renewed attacks by Penda.

Miller makes the important point that from later evidence it would seem that the boundary between East Anglia and Mercia passed through the territory of the Isle: 'Scattered references' he says, 'seem to imply that sometimes, at least, in the seventh and eighth centuries the boundary between East Anglia and Mercia may have cut right across the Isle – leaving the "island" of Ely on the one side and Thorney and Whittlesey . . . on the other'.[34] The strategic and military importance of the Isle is well supported by events in the later eleventh and twelfth century when it was used as a base for insurgency, first by Hereward the Wake and later by Geoffrey de Mandeville; the point being that whoever held the Isle of Ely

---

[29] Miller, *Abbey and Bishopric of Ely*, p. 15.
[30] Whitelock, 'The conversion of the eastern Danelaw'.
[31] F. W. Stenton, *Anglo-Saxon England* (Oxford, 1943; 3rd edn, 1971), p. 298.
[32] Farmer, 'Some saints of East Anglia', p. 33.
[33] Bede, *Venerabilis Baedae Opera Historica*, III, 18.
[34] Miller, *Abbey and Bishopric of Ely*, p. 14; H. C. Darby, 'The Fenland frontier in Anglo-Saxon England', pp. 194–6.

was in a strong position to attack the mainland territories on either side: Mercia to the west, and East Anglia to the east. Thus it can be seen that Etheldreda's marriage, probably when she was very young, to Tonbert, a prince of the South Gyrwe, and the acquisition of the Isle through morning gift, was a crucial political move, a move made between warring nations where nuptual happiness counted for very little.

According to Bede, Etheldreda preserved her virginity through a second marriage to the young King Egfrid of Northumbria, until she was able to retire from worldly affairs and establish her monastery at Ely in AD 673, which was at that time, according to Bede, a part of East Anglia.[35] To Bede, who knew nothing about the association between Ely and St Etheldreda's dower, nor of the political significance attached to her first marriage, the Isle was simply 'in the province of the East Angles' and 'in a district surrounded on all sides by sea and fens', highly appropriate for an early monastic establishment.[36] Ely, it would seem, had never been more than a part of the territory of the South Gyrwe and its cession to East Anglia was probably of little significance by the time Bede was writing his ecclesiastical history in the early eighth century, before the days of Offa.[37]

Bede's statement that Ely comprised a territory of approximately 600 hides may be no more than an assumption on his part that it corresponded with the whole of the territory of the South Gyrwe, rated as 600 hides in *The Tribal Hidage*. Miller uses this statement as confirmation of Bede's ignorance about the Isle being part of Etheldreda's dower and therefore at variance with the later chroniclers. However, it should be pointed out that Bede delighted in his knowledge of hidation, particularly that of remote islands: he quoted the hidation of Thanet, in the kingdom of Kent, Anglesey and the Isle of Man, and of course Iona;[38] his reference to the hidation of Ely should not be seen as a statement of absolute accuracy, but as a point made to impress his aristocratic audience. It is possible therefore to reconcile any apparent discrepancy there may be between Bede's account of the foundation of Ely and that given by later chroniclers; it seems highly likely that the territorial unity of the Isle, so evident in later years, dates from the time of Etheldreda's first marriage and the acquisition of this important border outpost by the kingdom of East Anglia.

It is possible that the Wicklaw territory may also have formed part of the original endowment of Ely. At least it is highly likely that Etheldreda would have had access to property somewhere within the heartlands of her father's kingdom as well as the Ely lands, situated on the frontier, given to her in dower by Tonbert. The Wicklaw territory contains of course the

---

[35] Bede, *Venerabilis Baedae Opera Historica*, IV, 19.
[36] Miller, *Abbey and Bishopric of Ely*, p. 12.
[37] Bede, *Venerabilis Baedae Opera Historica*, I, 25; II, 9; III, 4.
[38] *Liber Eliensis*, p. 18; Warner, 'Blything hundred', pp. 75–81.

famous ship-burial at Sutton Hoo, but the earliest Christian kings of the East Anglian dynasty were buried well away from Sutton Hoo and its associated *villa regalis* near Rendlesham. Sigbert was probably buried in or near to the monastery he founded and from which he was dragged, probably Beodricksworth (Bury St Edmunds), while King Anna, we are reliably informed by the *Liber Eliensis*, was enshrined at another royal vill, Blythburgh.[39] By the time of Etheldreda's first marriage it is likely that the old *regio*, centred on a royal site somewhere near Rendlesham and corresponding perhaps with the Wicklaw territory, with its ancestral royal burial ground at Sutton Hoo, was redundant and new Christian centres were being used. It can only be suggested here that this old territory of Wicklaw would have made a very suitable marriage portion for the daughter of a Christian king, such as Anna, who may have wished to distance himself from his pagan ancestors.

The links between lands that formed the liberty of St Etheldreda and the East Anglian royal house, with its saintly cults, of which Etheldreda was herself the leading light, are useful historical clues for the interpretation of what must surely be some of the earliest Anglo-Saxon boundaries in the county. Such clues must be seen side by side with the archaeological and etymological evidence for the antiquity of Wicklaw; together they offer circumstantial evidence for a degree of territorial and administrative continuity. But now we must look at the internal evidence within the hundredal boundary structure for further clues concerning the origin of Wicklaw and its anomalous administrative pattern.

Hundreds, Half-Hundreds and Ferdings

There were twenty-five hundreds, half-hundreds and double hundreds mentioned in the Domesday survey for Suffolk. Some of these, such as Lothing and its neighbouring half-hundred of Lothingland, should really be regarded as one, whereas others, such as Blackbourn and Bradmere, are really double hundreds, like the double hundred of Babergh.[40] Although there were minor changes, for example the tiny half-hundred of Parham was to disappear by the thirteenth century and the hundred and a half of Samford became a single hundred, and there were one or two changes of name, the hundreds of 1086 are much the same as those listed in the Hundred Rolls of 1274. Indeed the essential framework of the Domesday Suffolk hundreds, as in so many other counties, was to remain the basic

---

[39] *Liber Eliensis*, p. 18; Stenton, 'East Anglian kings', p. 397, fn. 2; Warner, 'Blything hundred', pp. 75–81.

[40] B. A. Lees, 'Introduction to the Suffolk Domesday', in *The Victoria History of the County of Suffolk*, vol. 1, edited by W. Page (London, 1911), pp. 358–9.

pattern of local administration until the reorganization of local government in 1894.

The picture of Domesday hundreds and half-hundreds is further complicated by fractions of hundreds. A ferding, or quarter hundred, is mentioned at South Elmham in Suffolk; ferdings are also found at Ludham (Norfolk), Huntingdon and Wisbech (Cambridgeshire), which is referred to by the *Liber Eliensis* as a 'quarter part of the Hundred of the Isle' [of Ely].[41] It is important to note that the ecclesiastical authorities utilized this hundredal subdivision for their own administrative convenience, in much the same way as they utilized the hundredal pattern for the boundaries of deaneries. Thredling hundred or the 'Trelling of Claydon', being a third of Claydon hundred, does not appear until 1188. In 1274 it was classified as a half-hundred. Anderson observed that Thredling was often mentioned together with the five and a half hundreds of Wicklaw, which it adjoined.[42] He concluded that the reason why it had been upgraded into a separate hundred was that it belonged to the franchise of the Abbey of Ely and was not under the same jurisdiction as the rest of Claydon hundred. The financial advantages to Ely of upgrading fractions of hundreds into full hundreds need hardly be emphasized.

At Wilford hundred, in Wicklaw, recent research has brought to light a heathen place-name close to the hundredal meeting-place of Wilford Bridge, less than a mile from Sutton Hoo. The medieval field-name, 'harrough pightle', can be pin-pointed by the abuttals of a sixteenth-century survey to a hilltop site coinciding with the position of the gallows above Wilford Bridge, as marked on a map of 1601 (plate II). The 'harrow' element is one of a recognized group of heathen place-names, meaning a temple or shrine. It is an established fact that some of our earliest English hundredal meeting-places coincide with sites of heathen association and also with places of execution, as attested in the names of hundreds such as Wodneslawe (Bedfordshire), and Gallow hundred (Norfolk).[43] It would seem therefore that the hundredal meeting-place of Wilford was a particularly interesting and early one, relating perhaps to a pre-Christian cadastre at the heart of the Wicklaw territory.

There is an extraordinary disparity between the size of some hundreds

[41] E. Miller, *Abbey and Bishopric of Ely*, pp. 32–3, 144; F. M. Stenton, 'St Benet of Holme and the Norman Conquest', *English Historical Review*, 37 (1922), p. 227; R. H. C. Davis (ed.), *The Kalendar of Abbot Samson*, p. xxlx; *Liber Eliensis*, p. liii, fn. 6. The ferdings of East Anglia are quite distinct from the ferdings of the West Midlands: D. Hooke, *The Anglo-Saxon Landscape: The Kingdom of the Hwicce* (Manchester, 1985), pp. 76–7.

[42] S. Anderson, 'English hundred names', p. 91; W. G. Arnott, *The Place-Names of the Deben Valley Parishes* (Ipswich, 1946), p. 2; Lees, 'Introduction to the Suffolk Domesday', p. 358; G. C. Homans, 'The Frisians in East Anglia', *Economic History Review*, 2nd ser., 10 (1957), p. 197.

[43] P. M. Warner, 'The Sutton parish survey', in M. O. Carver (ed.), *Bulletin of the Sutton Hoo Research Committee*, 3 (July 1985), pp. 16–21.

PLATE II: *Wilford Bridge shown on John Norden's map of Bromeswell, 1600/01. The hundredal gallows stood on the hill beside the approach road to the bridge.*
© Suffolk Record Office V5/22/1.

within the county, so that a small hundred such as Stow, comprising approximately 22,000 acres, is but a fraction of one of the larger hundreds, such as Blything, containing over 87,000 acres.[44] Indeed the single hundred of Blything is substantially larger than the 71,000 acres of the double hundred of Babergh. Although differences in soil quality may account for the large size of Breckland hundreds such as Lackford and Blackbourn (approximately 83,000 and 66,000 acres respectively), it cannot account for the very small size of hundreds on the comparable Sandling soils of the east coast such as Wilford and Colneis (31,500 and 17,000 acres approximately). There must be other reasons for the unusually small size of the Wicklaw hundreds.

In contrast, however, Blything hundred is by far the largest hundred in East Suffolk; it dwarfs its southern neighbours in the Wicklaw territory (see figure 1.1). The name Blything means simply the people of the river Blyth; the river is central to the hundred (see figure 1.3); furthermore its northern and southern boundaries coincide with minor streams, both called 'Hundred River'.[45] Similar hundredal territories with names linked to river dwellers have been noted recently by Dymond at Loddon and Happing hundreds in Norfolk.[46] The hundredal meeting-place was the royal vill of

[44] Acreages given in this paragraph are taken from White's 1844 *Directory of Suffolk* and are only an approximation for the purpose of this exercise.

[45] Warner, 'Blything hundred', p. 110.

[46] D. Dymond, *The Norfolk Landscape* (London, 1985), pp. 67–8.

Blythburgh, important from the mid-seventh century as a place of veneration for the body of King Anna (plate III).[47] In 1086, when the main manor of Blythburgh was royal demesne, the judicial precedence of Blythburgh over its near neighbour, the port and borough of Dunwich, is clearly stated; also there was no money-changer at Dunwich, but only at Blythburgh. Although Dunwich was the site of the first East Anglian see established under St Felix in AD 630, in origin it was probably no more than a coastal trading *wīc* supplying the more important royal centre upstream at Blythburgh.[48] There seems little doubt that in Blything we are looking at an ancient *regio*; a territory that has all the characteristics of a 'shire', or subdivision of the early East Anglian kingdom.

The topography of Blything hundred reveals its close proximity to the watershed of the river Blyth; indeed it is, in the strictest sense, the territory

[47] *Liber Eliensis*, p. 18; Warner, 'Blything hundred', pp. 75–81.

[48] *Domesday Book*, Record Commission (London, 1783), ii, fo. 312, fo. 312b; Warner, 'Blything hundred', pp. 68–74. This writer does not accept the views of Rigold concerning the supposed siting of the see of Dunwich at Felixstowe: S. E. Rigold, 'The supposed see of Dunwich', *Journal of the British Archaeological Association*, 3rd ser., 24 (1961), pp. 55–9; Rigold, 'Further evidence about the site of "Dommoc"', *Journal of the British Archaeological Association*, 3rd ser., 37 (1974), pp. 97–102; D. Whitelock, 'The pre-Viking age Church in East Anglia', in P. Clemoes (ed.), *Anglo-Saxon England*, vol; 1 (Cambridge, 1972), pp. 1–22.

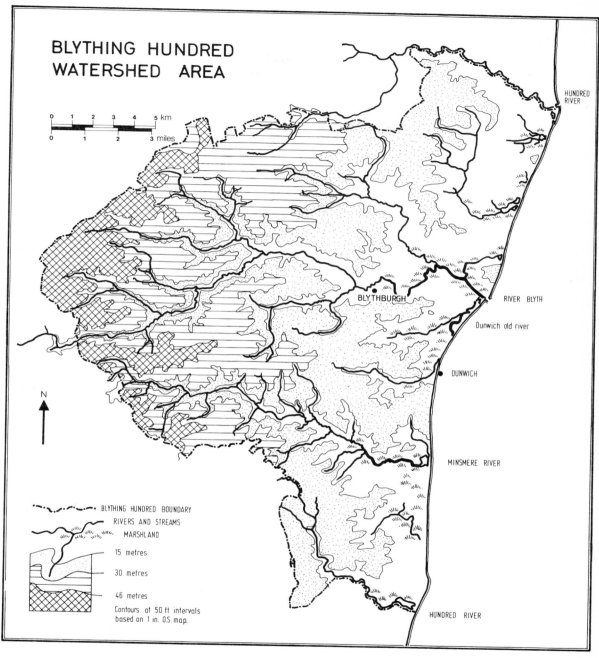

BLYTHING HUNDRED WATERSHED AREA

0 1 2 3 4 5 km
0 1 2 3 miles

N

BLYTHBURGH

DUNWICH

HUNDRED RIVER

RIVER BLYTH

Dunwich old river

MINSMERE RIVER

HUNDRED RIVER

BLYTHING HUNDRED BOUNDARY
RIVERS AND STREAMS
MARSHLAND

15 metres

30 metres

46 metres

Contours at 50 ft intervals
based on 1 in. O.S. map.

FIGURE I.4 *Blything hundred watershed area*

of the people of the river valley (figure 1.4), having a comparable social cohesion perhaps to that of a traditional English county or shire. While Blything happens to be a striking example, it is by no means unusual for ancient 'shires' of this type to coincide with watersheds; similar territorial units have been recognized as far apart as the lathes of Kent, parts of Mercia, Northumbria and southern Scotland, where they are seen as evidence for a primitive 'agrarian and political' lordship underlying later administrative structures.[49] Although minor disruptions to the Blything watershed boundary are evident, they can all be accounted for in later documentation, such as the appearance of Rumburgh Priory on the northern boundary in 1065, which eventually led to the formation of Rumburgh parish sometime after the Norman Conquest. It seems that in Blything hundred we have not only a subdivision of the early East Anglian kingdom, which happened to survive more or less intact down to modern times, but also a territory in essence similar in size and function to the five and a half hundreds of Wicklaw, except that whereas Blything hundred survives as a single large administrative unit, Wicklaw was divided up at an early date into small fragmented hundredal units.

In order to understand the curious pattern of smaller hundreds in Wicklaw, we must first look at the subdivision of Blything hundred into letes, for it will soon become clear that the smaller hundreds in Wicklaw are in fact letes upgraded into hundreds, an administrative decision made by the monastery at Ely sometime before AD 970. In other words, to understand the full complexity of the hundredal pattern within the county, we must look at the lower-order boundaries of lete and vill.

Letes and *Ville Integre*

East Anglia is distinctive in the subdivision of its hundreds into letes, or what were later known as *ville integre*. Round, obsessed by the idea of the Domesday *ora*, sought a Danish origin for letes.[50] Likewise Homans, inspired by Myres's interpretation of Frisian place-names, considered the lete to be of Danish origin and pointed to similar administrative units, as he saw them, in ancient Friesland.[51] Although there has been a controversial reassessment of the impact of Scandinavian settlement upon England as a

---

[49] G. W. S. Barrow, *The Kingdom of the Scots* (Edinburgh, 1975), pp. 8, 11; F. W. Maitland, *Domesday Book and Beyond: Three Essays in the Early History of England* (Cambridge, 1897), pp. 266–7, 410; C. S. Taylor, 'The origin of the Mercian shires', in H. P. R. Finberg (ed.), *Gloucestershire Studies* (Leicester, 1957), pp. 58–9.

[50] J. H. Round, 'The Domesday ora', *English Historical Review*, 23 (1908), pp. 283–5.

[51] Homans, 'The Frisians in East Anglia'; R. G. Collingwood and J. N. L. Myres, *Roman Britain and the English Settlements* (Oxford, 1945), pp. 340–1.

whole, supported in part by Whitelock's argument for a rapid return to Christianity in the eastern Danelaw, this reassessment has not been resolved at a local level.[52] The Danish origin of letes must therefore remain suspect.

It is a characteristic of letes that they do not form homogeneous units, but consist of several vills scattered about the hundred. The reason for this relates to their administrative function: the collection of geld imposed as a fixed sum, usually 20s, on the hundred. Vills were thus grouped within the hundred into approximately equal clusters of twos and threes and the tax burden was divided between them. Superficially, letes appear to be purely administrative structures, in origin serving a fiscal function.[53] However, the system of letes in Norfolk and Suffolk is very similar to the grouping of vills in Cambridgeshire evident in the *Domesday Book* and the *Inquisitio Comitatus Cantabrigiensis*, which Hart related to the early Anglo-Saxon system of hidation.[54] It is possible therefore that some letes may be very much earlier than their later function might suggest.

Letes are illusive in *Little Domesday Book*, because, geld, where given is apportioned by vill, usually following an entry for the main manor; sometimes geld appears at the end of a series of minor entries. Letes are not mentioned in association with geld, but only with hundreds. Thus the Norfolk hundreds of Clacklose and Greenhow contained fourteen letes and ten letes respectively.[55] Never are letes listed with their constituent vills; their composition clearly lay outside the brief of the Domesday commissioners. However, the *Kalendar of Abbot Samson*, a twelfth-century document, lists the letes or *ville integre* of the eight and a half hundreds of Thingoe in West Suffolk, where at Cosford half-hundred: 'every lete gives thirteen shillings and sixpence and divides it within itself'.[56] Using the Thingoe model, Douglas suggested that it was normal for some hundreds to be divided into twelve letes, each parcelling out its burden of geld among its constituent vills in an equitable manner, though not always in exactly equal portions.[57]

[52] N. P. Brooks, 'England in the ninth century: the crucible of defeat', *Transactions of the Royal Historical Society*, 5th ser., 29 (1979), pp. 1–20; P. H. Sawyer, 'The density of Danish settlement in England', *University of Birmingham Historical Journal*, 6 (1958), pp. 1–17; D. Whitelock, 'The conversion of the eastern Danelaw', pp. 159–76.

[53] The letes discussed in this chapter should not be confused with 'leets', which served a judicial function as petty moot-courts, often under the aegis of later memorial courts.

[54] C. Hart, *Early Charters*, p. 14; J. Campbell, 'The first Christian kings', in J. Campbell (ed.), *The Anglo-Saxons* (London, 1982), pp. 59–61; W. Davis and H. Vierck, 'The contexts of tribal hidage: social aggregates and settlement patterns', *Frühmittelalterliche Studien*, 8 (1974), pp. 223–93.

[55] B. Dodwell, 'The making of the Domesday survey in Norfolk: the hundred and a half of Clacklose', *English Historical Review*, 84 (1969), pp. 78–83; Rev. C. Johnson, 'Introduction to the Norfolk Domesday', in *The Victoria History of the County of Norfolk*, vol. 2, edited by W. Page (London, 1906), pp. 5–6.

[56] Davis (ed.), *Kalendar of Abbot Samson*, pp. 60–1.

[57] D. C. Douglas, *The Social Structure of Medieval East Anglia*, Oxford Studies in Legal and Social History, 9 (Oxford, 1927), pp. 55–6; and also 'Fragments of an Anglo-Saxon survey of Bury St Edmunds',

The fact is that a large number of vills in the Domesday survey of Suffolk and Norfolk are given no geld assessment and when they are, there is little evidence for equality. When Round and Douglas were writing, geld was thought to be one of the primary functions of the great survey of 1086; now scholars see tenural relationships as equally, if not more important, the references to geld being perhaps the residue of earlier pre-Conquest surveys.[58] With so many geld assessments missing, it is unlikely that a reliable conclusion based on numerical evidence in *Domesday Book* can be reached. Inevitably the contrived reconstruction of letes by early writers, outside the area of the Thingoe hundreds, must be discarded.[59]

In Blything hundred, there are four fourteenth-century lists of vills (table 1.1), the order and grouping of which, although dependent to a degree on medieval plagiarism, almost certainly relate to an ancient system of letes. The order of vills in these later lists does not relate to the sequential order of vills under tenants-in-chief as given in *Domesday Book*, where on the whole irregularity is the norm, although there is some evidence for a sequence of vills under one or two tenants-in-chief.[60] The later lists of vills

TABLE 1.1 *Four lists of vills*

Document	Date	Source
1 *Ville Integre*	14th century	BM Add. MS 34560 (Sibton Abbey Estates)
2 *Nomina Villarum*	1316	*PSIA*, XI, p. 173
3 Lay Subsidies	1327 & 1334	*SRS*, IX, ii, pp. 60–77 and Glasscock[a]
4 Ipswich DB	15th-century copy of 14th-century document	*PSIA*, VI, p. 185

[a] R. E. Glasscock (ed.), *The Lay Subsidy of 1334*, British Academy Records of Social and Economic History, new ser. 2 (1975), pp. 288–9.

English Historical Review, 43 (1928), p. 376: he suggested that the late 'bears a striking resemblance in size and organisation to the small Danish Hundreds' but he made no attempt to explain the fragmented arrangement of many letes.

[58] S. P. J. Harvey, 'Domesday Book and its predecessors', *English Historical Review*, 86 (1971), pp. 753-73.

[59] There was, according to Round, the single 'ora' or 20d unit group, a unit of an 'ora and a half or 30d, a third group of $17\frac{1}{2}d$ and $34\frac{1}{2}d$, which he saw as a 'double *ora*' or 40d unit group, and a fourth unit of $13\frac{1}{2}d$ or 27d, which he took to be 'a reduced *ora* and a half'. These ideas were expressed in Lees, 'Introduction to the Suffolk Domesday', p. 362, citing Round, pp. 361–2, and Round, *Feudal England: Historical Studies on the 11th and 12th Centuries* (London, 1909), p. 102. Such figures should be approached with healthy scepticism.

[60] For example, Rapton, Sibton and Stickingland tend to follow Darsham under the holdings of Robert Malet and Robert Malet's mother.

can, however, be compared with the fragmentary geld assessments given in *Domesday Book* and a tentative reconstruction of letes within Blything hundred can be made (table 1.2). However, the Domesday survey fails to give a geld assessment for twenty-seven of the fifty-six vills mentioned in Blything and at least eight of these were nothing more than hamlets of larger places already assessed for geld.[61] A number of these minor vills do not appear on later lists, so any reconstruction of letes based on later groups of vills in Blything hundred is necessarily tentative. Figure 1.5 presents the pattern of *ville integre* as they were in the fourteenth century; the map is based upon nineteenth-century parish boundaries and, although it inevitably gives a false impression of precision, it serves to illustrate the fragmented character of some letes.

The grouping of vills in later documents (table 1.2) indicates that Blything hundred once had twenty-four or twenty-five letes; perhaps it was originally a double hundred, if the twelve-lete hundreds of West Suffolk are regarded as the norm. Some of the larger tenants-in-chief have two Domesday lists for their Blything hundred vills, again suggesting that it was in origin a double hundred.[62] A similar pattern has been noted in Essex and Cambridgeshire and commented upon by Hart.[63] However, where two Blything hundred lists appear under one tenant-in-chief, some vills appear in both lists, but with different entries, a factor that would seem to discredit the double-hundred theory.[64]

There are certain similarities between the geld assessments for Blything hundred and those for Cosford half-hundred. In Blything, there were nine vills with a geld of $7\frac{1}{2}d$ and one *ville integre* with a Domesday geld amounting to $7\frac{1}{2}d$; in Cosford, there are two assessments of $7\frac{1}{2}d$ and four or possibly five letes totalling $15d$. In Blything hundred, the vills of Sibton, Walpole and Cookley, which comprise a single *ville integre*, are each assessed at $7\frac{1}{2}d$; the very large assessment for Leiston of $3s$ $1\frac{1}{2}d$ can only be explained as five units of $7\frac{1}{2}d$. Round observed a similar pattern of $7\frac{1}{2}d$ and $15d$ units in Bishop's, Carlford, Stow and Risbridge hundreds.[65] Clearly the lete pattern within Blything hundred fits into a wider pattern of letes within the county.

The disjointed geographical pattern of some letes or *ville integre* is clearly seen in figure 1.5. Most striking are Benacre, Bulcamp and Brege, also

---

[61] Places with a geld assessment in *Domesday Book*, which do not appear in later lists of vills: Stickingland (in Yoxford parish), $7\frac{1}{2}d$ geld; *Brincas* (probably Breggestreet in Westleton), $1\frac{3}{4}d$ geld; Wangford (once probably a daughter parish of Reydon), $7d$ geld.

[62] Hundredal order is a highly contentious issue: see Hart, *The Hidation of Cambridgeshire*, p. 5, fn. 2. The clash of views on this subject between Hart and Glabraith: V. H. Galbraith, *The Making of Domesday Book* (Oxford, 1961), is irrelevant to the early boundaries discussed in this chapter.

[63] Hart, *The Hidation of Cambridgeshire*, p. 15.

[64] For example, Middleton appears under both Blything hundred lists for Count Alan, similarly Rapton appears under both lists for Robert Malet's other.

[65] Lees, 'Introduction to the Suffolk Domesday', p. 362, citing Round.

TABLE 1.2 Ville integre *in Blything hundred*

Domesday Book	Groups of vills	Sources (Table 1.1)	lete
$7\frac{1}{2}$d	Huntingfield	2, 3	1
$7\frac{1}{2}$d	(Linstead)		
3s $1\frac{1}{2}$d	Leiston	1	2
	Sizewell (not in *DB*)	1	
	Theberton	1	3
	Thorpe	1	4
	Aldringham	1	
	Knodishall	1	5
	Buxlow (not in *DB*)	1	
$7\frac{1}{2}$d	Middleton	1	6
	Fordley	1	
$7\frac{1}{2}$d $+$ $7\frac{1}{2}$d	Westleton	1, 2	7
	(2 geld assessments in *DB*)		
$7\frac{1}{2}$d	Sibton		
$7\frac{1}{2}$d	Walpole	all documents	8
$7\frac{1}{2}$d	Cookley		
$3\frac{3}{4}$d	Bramfield		
	Peasenhall	all documents	9
2d	Mells		
3d	Ubbeston	all documents	10
$4\frac{1}{2}$d	Heveningham		
$5\frac{1}{2}+7\frac{1}{2}$d	Chediston	1, 2, 4	11
	(2 geld assessments in *DB*)		
$3\frac{1}{2}$d	Blyford (not listed in 3)	1, 2, 4	12
	Wissett		
	Spexhall (not in *DB*)	all documents	13
	Holton		
	Rumburgh (in Elmham in *DB*)		
	Westhall (not in *DB*)		
$1\frac{3}{4}$d	Sotherton	1, 2	14
	Henham		
6d	Uggeshall	all documents	15
4d	Frostenden		
	Henstead	1, 2	16
	Cove		
	Benacre		
$1\frac{1}{4}$d	Bulcamp	all documents	17
$1\frac{3}{4}$d	Brege		
$6\frac{1}{2}$d	Reydon	1, 2	
(7d)	Wangford (not listed)		18

TABLE 1.2 (*cont.*)

Domesday Book	Groups of vills	Sources (*Table 1.1*)	lete
2½d	Southwold	1, 2	
6d	Easton	1, 2	
	Northales (Covehithe)	all documents	19
	Brampton		
	Stoven	all documents	20
7½d	Thoringen		
	Wenhaston	all documents	21
	Darsham	2	22
3d	Yoxford	2	
(7½d)	(Stickingland)		
7½d	Halesworth	1, 2	23
3½d	Cratfield	1, 2	
	Wrentham	1, 2	24
(Royal demesne)	Blythburgh (with Walberswick)		25

The *ville integre* are based on the order and grouping of vills as they appear in the documents listed in table 1.1, combined with the geld assessment from the *Domesday Book*, where given.

Halesworth with Cratfield, and Chediston with Blyford. Not only do they have a disjointed pattern with detached portions, but they are also similar in size and form to the hundreds of Wicklaw; a comparison can be made in figure 1.1 with the hundred of Loes and Parham half-hundred. Some letes or *ville integre* have a long extended appearance, such as Sibton, Walpole and Cookley in Blything hundred, similar to Wilford hundred in Wicklaw. One can only conclude from this that the pattern of hundreds in Wicklaw may be derived in part from an ancient pattern of letes, a pattern that was already established before the hundreds were first recorded in King Edgar's charter of AD 970. But if Wicklaw was indeed part of the original endowment of Ely, as established by Etheldreda in AD 673, is it possible that these anomalous hundreds represent a much earlier cadastre, or system of territorial organization, upon which tax or tribute might be levied? The place-name evidence from Wilford hundred would seem to suggest that at least one of these hundreds had a pre-Christian meeting-place and probably related to an early Anglo-Saxon system of administration. In other words, the origins of the hundredal pattern of Wicklaw and the pattern of letes from which it was in turn derived must be sought in the formative years of early Anglo-Saxon settlement.

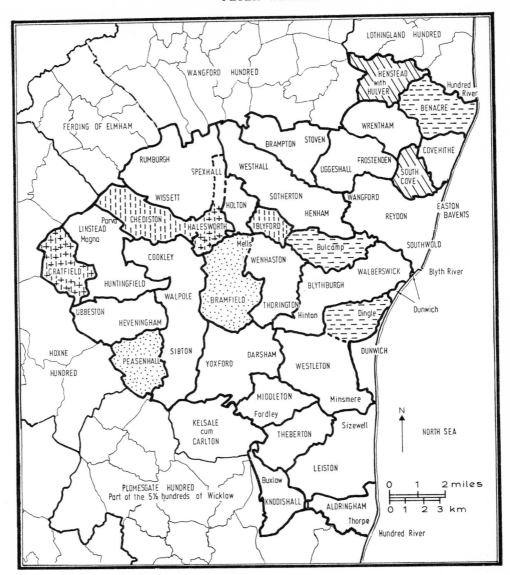

FIGURE 1.5 Ville integre *in*
Blything hundred

Discussion

We know that ecclesiastical authorities were making use of hundredal sub-divisions in the post-Conquest period and that Ely was itself later involved in upgrading the Trelling of Claydon into Thredling hundred; we can be reasonably sure that at an early date Ely was benefiting by upgrading letes into hundreds in the Wicklaw territory. This conclusion, however, does not answer the central question as to why there are such differences between the two very similar geographic areas of Blything hundred and Wicklaw, for it is clear that differences in boundary structure are but one aspect of a series of related problems. The differences and similarities can be spelled out in tabular form (see table 1.3), and although this may disguise the complexity of some of the evidence, it may also serve to clarify the picture.

TABLE 1.3 *Similarities and differences between Blything and Wicklaw*

	Blything hundred	Wicklaw
Similarities		
Regio (royal estate)	Blythburgh	Rendlesham
Royal burials	King Anna	Sutton Hoo
Watershed territories	River Blyth	River Deben
Both areas have good archaeological evidence for concentrations of prehistoric and Roman populations within their watershed territories.		
Differences		
Pagan cemeteries	none	many
Late Roman hoards	none	six
Number of hundreds	one	five and a half
Roman shore-forts	none (?)	one (Walton)
Latin loan-words	one (Bulcamp)	four

In Blything hundred, the comparative lack of archaeological material may be nothing more than negative evidence, but when seen beside the wealth of late Roman and Anglo-Saxon material from Wicklaw, the contrast is indeed surprising. Again, it may be argued that coastal erosion has caused the loss of a possible shore-fort at Dunwich in the same way that the fort at Walton is now under the sea. But there are no late Roman coin series from Dunwich comparable with the large numbers of fourth-century coins and other finds from Walton and Felixstowe.

The Theodosian and Honorian hoards from Wicklaw could relate to the departure of Roman troops from the shore-fort at Walton in the early fifth century; the hoard-buriers clearly intended to return. The hoards speak for discontinuity within the Roman population, at least within a certain section of society. The Latin loan-words in Wicklaw place-names, on the other hand, argue for a degree of continuity between indigenous Latin word-users and the first Anglo-Saxon settlers. It is logical to conclude that these first settlers, who were eventually to take control as an aristocratic military elite by the late sixth century, filled a gap in the indigenous society left by the departing Romans. However, there is insufficient cemetery evidence from the Wicklaw area to suggest large numbers of early fifth-century settlers, so perhaps there was a significant gap in time between the departure of hoard-burying Romans and the arrival of the first Anglo-Saxon settlers, but not such a gap that Latin loan-words could not be incorporated into local Anglo-Saxon place-names.

Blything, on the other hand, may have continued with a declining indigenous population, only to be taken over as a royal estate and absorbed into the East Anglian kingdom before the early seventh century at a time when Latin elements in the local language were largely forgotten. Wicklaw was a focus for the early pagan kings of the Wuffinga dynasty, but Blything was to replace it as a focus for the early Christian kings of the same dynasty – why? Was it a coincidence that Bishop Felix chose Dunwich as his base for the first East Anglian see? Perhaps Dunwich and the *regio* of Blythburgh were in some way free of pagan associations and therefore acceptable to a new continental style of Christian monarchy. The gradual phasing out of pagan Anglo-Saxon cemeteries and the use of Christian burial grounds elsewhere was not in any sense a prerogative, it was widespread through-out Anglo-Saxon England; indeed it is seen as one of the most formative developments in the history of English settlement. It is possible, however, that in moving away from traditional burial places to new Christian sites, the royal household set an example which was then followed by succeeding generations of lesser folk.

It is plausible that the differences between these two areas, particularly the differences in administrative boundaries, reflect two fundamentally different social structures with different settlement histories. Blything was an area relatively unaffected by early Anglo-Saxon settlement; Wicklaw was an area profoundly affected and ultimately dominated by Anglo-Saxon settlers.

If Hart is correct in linking *ville integre* to an ancient system of hidation, if the Wicklaw hundreds are in fact letes or *ville integre* upgraded into hundreds at an early date, we may see in Wicklaw the fossilization of an ancient administrative cadastre, adapted and modified to serve the needs of the monastery at Ely, but still preserving a palimpsest of pre-Christian boundaries and meeting-places. Over East Anglia as a whole, the patchy nature of the early Anglo-Saxon cemetery evidence has given archaeo-logists food for thought. It would seem from the study of boundaries and settlement in East Suffolk that each area must be studied on its individual merits and its settlement history worked out accordingly. No doubt differ-ent stories will emerge elsewhere, but in the early Anglo-Saxon period we are not dealing with the history of a single unified nation, but with the histories of many petty states, kingdoms, sub-kingdoms and provinces; until we understand the histories of these separate parts, the history of the whole is bound to remain more or less obscure.

2

Minster Churches in the Landscape

JOHN BLAIR

Introduction

Recent research has emphasized both the original and the continuing importance of the regional mother churches known by the tenth century as the 'old minsters'. Usually royal foundations, and often sited at important central places, they were staffed by teams of priests who ministered to the scattered rural populations. Even in the late Anglo-Saxon and Norman periods they remained significant as religious communities, as objects of noble patronage, and as influences on the developing parochial system.[1]

Great advances are also being made in understanding the archaeological and topographical contexts of Anglo-Saxon churches of all kinds. But such studies rarely emphasize the essential distinctness of the minsters as 'central places'. This chapter argues that they were the main foci of ecclesiastical organization and pastoral care, as well as important centres for economic growth, for most of the Christian Anglo-Saxon period.[2] Four main hypotheses are offered. First, that in the seventh and eighth centuries most institutions to which the word *monasterium* was applied had their place in a coherent pastoral system, with territorial *parochiae* and responsibility for supporting a ministry within them. Secondly, that early minsters usually lay at some distance from their counterpart royal *villae*, often in Roman enclosures with the *villae* outside on open ground. Thirdly, that minsters are more important than royal *villae* in the origins of small towns,

For comments on an earlier draft of this paper I am very grateful to Dr Brian Golding, Dr R. K. Morris, Dr Gervase Rosser, Dr Julia Smith, Dr Alan Thacker and Mr Humphrey Woods.

[1] See J. Blair, 'Secular minster churches in Domesday Book', in P. H. Sawyer (ed.), *Domesday Book: A Reassessment* (London, 1985), pp. 104–42, and earlier works cited ibid., pp. 104–5, n. 2; M. J. Franklin, 'The identification of minsters in the Midlands', in R. A. Brown (ed.), *Anglo-Norman Studies*, vol. VII (Woodbridge, 1985), pp. 69–88; essays in J. Blair (ed.), *Minsters and Parish Churches: The Local Church in Transition 950–1200*, Oxford University Committee for Archaeology, Monograph 17 (1988).

[2] Several of the themes are also discussed by R. K. Morris, *The Church in British Archaeology*, Council for British Archaeology Research Report 47 (London, 1983). My approach is often different from this book's, but my debt to it will be obvious.

and that such 'minster towns' often show a distinctive topographical development. Fourthly, that centralized control was compatible with decentralized worship: the *parochiae* assimilated a class of heterogeneous and often older cult sites, controlled and served by the minster clergy, where baptism and burial sometimes continued to be practised through the seventh, eighth and ninth centuries.

The Making of a System

Laws and other sources from the mid-tenth century onwards show a system of minster parishes in decline. The view is now widely held that this system was as ancient as the minsters themselves, and that the residual rights of mother churches in the post-Conquest period often reflect the extent of mid-Saxon *parochiae*.[3] The strongest argument against this view is from silence: no seventh- or eighth-century English source refers explicitly to a network of *parochiae* controlled from monasteries. To this it may be answered that the most familiar areas of life are often the most liable to be taken for granted. Corporate ministries such as are proposed for England were the normal parochial system of much of early medieval Europe. In the Carolingian world the transition, at least in theory, to local parishes can be traced from around AD 800;[4] in England it seems that minster parishes were still being developed and remodelled in the early tenth century in a context of existing mother-church rights.[5]

The most intractable problem is that of terminology and personnel. In Anglo-Saxon England, use of the word *monasterium* ranged from monasteries in the strict sense, observing a version of the Benedictine rule, through mixed communities ruled by royal abbesses, to groups of secular clerks pure and simple. Only the 'true', 'respectable' houses have left records of their inmates' lives, and these records are concerned with devotion and learning. Not unnaturally, many commentators have accepted this preoccupation, and have concluded that such monasteries were remote from pastoral cares. Thus in a recent paper Mr Cambridge argues that 'there is an important functional difference in principle between a church whose *raison d'être* is to provide for the pastoral needs of a lay population ... and one whose prime purpose is to accommodate the liturgical requirements of a community which has come into being as a result of a desire to

---

[3] These themes are central to many of the papers in Blair, *Minsters and Parish Churches*.

[4] Cf. S. Reynolds, *Kingdoms and Communities in Western Europe 900–1300* (Oxford, 1984), pp. 81–2.

[5] Thus M. J. Franklin, 'Minsters and parishes: Northamptonshire studies' (unpublished Ph.D. thesis, University of Cambridge, 1982), argues that the re-conquest of the Danelaw led to the creation of new parochial minsters financed from tithe, whereas older minsters tended to retain the church-scot.

live according to a monastic rule'.[6] He seeks to demonstrate that in County Durham 'true' monasteries and their dependencies, with stone buildings and sculpture, can be clearly distinguished from 'pastoral' minsters, which have left no material trace. But the distribution of these sites is really not a very convincing argument against their pastoral character. While accepting both the links between early monasteries and daughter houses, and the presence of minsters of other kinds, it is perhaps more convincing to see the latter as ninth- or tenth-century foundations, filling in a pattern of large *parochiae* served from the sites with early remains.[7]

Even if monks cared as little for supporting parochial work as they did for writing about it, they were beholden to founders, patrons and bishops who may well have had different ideas. In fact there are clear, if rare, indications that even strict monasteries and nunneries maintained priests to serve the surrounding countryside. The insistence of Theodore's *Penitential* (AD 668×91) that *presbiterum ad ministeria aecclesiae* must be left on the old site of a monastery that has moved away is surely meant to safeguard existing parochial arrangements.[8] The foundation charter of AD 675×92 for Breedon-on-the-Hill (admittedly a dubious text) requires the monks 'to appoint a priest of good repute to minister baptism and teaching to the people assigned to him'.[9] Mr Godfrey's paper of 1976 gives other examples, concluding that 'it is difficult to see how any English religious house in the seventh and eighth centuries, Celtic or otherwise, could have divorced itself wholly from the missionary and pastoral side of the Church's work'.[10] Perhaps the strongest evidence that the early monasteries had *parochiae* is the simple fact that such a high proportion of them emerge as the foci of large, multi-vill parishes in the eleventh and twelfth centuries. Whether his minster consisted of monks who maintained priests, or of priests who

---

[6] E. Cambridge, 'The early Church in County Durham: a reassessment', *Journal of the British Archaeological Association*, 137 (1984), pp. 65–85. Although I disagree with Mr Cambridge's views on parochial organization, I am indebted to this paper for its demonstration of links between mother and daughter houses.

[7] Cambridge, ibid., figures 2 and 4. It seems to me that figure 2 shows insufficient sites for analysis of their distributions to be statistically valid. They are not incompatible with a series of big *parochiae* running west from the coast into the uplands, later subdivided to be served by the churches shown in figure 4. For monks and pastoral work in Europe, see G. Constable, 'Monasteries, rural churches and the *cura animarum* in the Early Middle Ages', *Settimane de Studio del Centro Italiano di Studi sull'Alto Medioevo* 28(1) (Spoleto, 1982), pp. 349–89. See also the revealing comments by R. Sharpe, 'Some problems concerning the organisation of the church in early medieval Ireland', *Peritia*, 3 (1984), pp. 260–1, on earlier views: 'Altogether, the terminology associated with monasticism was interpreted too narrowly: an eighth-century *monasterium* might have had far more non-monks than monks'.

[8] A. W. Haddan and W. Stubbs (eds), *Councils and Ecclesiastical Documents*, 3 vols (Oxford, 1869–71), vol. III, p. 195.

[9] P. H. Sawyer, *Anglo-Saxon Charters: An Annotated List and Bibliography* (London, 1968), S. 1803; W. de Gray Birch, *Cartularium Saxonicum* (London, 1885–99), B. 841.

[10] J. Godfrey, 'The place of the double monastery in the Anglo-Saxon minster system', in G. Bonner (ed.), *Famulus Christi* (London, 1976), pp. 346–7.

served the countryside themselves, no patron can have been blind to the pastoral implications of his patronage.

Hence the evident concern of seventh-century kings not simply to endow the Church, but to found, as quickly as possible, a network of minsters spreading across their kingdoms.[11] In AD 654, King Osuiu of Northumbria vowed before battle to found twelve small *monasteria*, six in Bernicia and six in Deira, each endowed with ten hides.[12] In Wessex, Dr Hase's work suggests an equally deliberate programme of minster-building by the successive kings Cædwalla and Ine: the Southampton Water minsters of Eling, Southampton, Bishop's Waltham, Titchfield (plate IV) and Romsey were all founded in the late seventh or early eighth century on important royal estates.[13] The ramifying patronage of the Mercian royal house and its dependants between the 660s and the 680s suggests especially clearly the building of a system. To take only some obvious examples: King Wulfhere's sisters Eadburh, Cyneburh and Cyneswith were all reputedly the first abbesses of double houses, while hagiographies refer to a fourth sister, Wilburh, as mother of St Osyth and wife of the sub-king Frithuwold who endowed Chertsey minster.[14] Mildburh and Mildrith, daughters of the Mercian sub-king Merewalh of the Magonsæte, were heads of minsters at Much Wenlock and Minster-in-Thanet: thus this family's patronage operated in the context of both Mercian and Kentish lordship.[15] Sometimes a geographical rationale is evident: St Osyth's minster at Aylesbury was the next along Akeman Street from her aunt St Eadburh's at Bicester.

The pastoral dimension makes it easier to understand this frenetic minster-building within a tangled web of alliances, this pensioning-off of surplus daughters to be the first abbesses and eventual saints of their houses. In planning the locations of minsters, kings would have been advised by bishops with views on the broad development of the Church (such as Eorcenwald of London, whose influence can be seen in several endowment charters[16]), not to mention Archbishop Theodore himself.

---

[11] For an overview of the political context, see Morris, *Church in British Archaeology*, pp. 46–8.

[12] Bede, *Ecclesiastical History* in *Venerabilis Baedae Opera Historica*, edited by C. Plummer, 2 vols (Oxford, 1896), vol. I, pp. 177–8.

[13] P. H. Hase, 'The mother churches of Hampshire', in Blair, *Minsters and Parish Churches*, pp. 45–8.

[14] C. Hohler, 'St Osyth and Aylesbury', *Records of Buckinghamshire*, 18 (1966–70), pp. 61–72; see also fn. 31 below.

[15] For Mildrith and the Kentish minsters, see D. W. Rollason, *The Mildrith Legend* (Leicester, 1982); S. E. Rigold, 'The "double minsters" of Kent and their analogies', *Journal of the British Archaeological Association*, 3rd ser., 31 (1968), pp. 27–37; K. P. Witney, 'The Kentish royal saints', *Archaeologia Cantiana*, 101 (1984), pp. 10–22 (esp. pedigree p. 22, illustrating royal dominance of the Kentish minsters). The oft-repeated statement that Mildgyth, a third daughter of Merewalh, was a nun at Eastry seems to be erroneous.

[16] P. Wormald, *Bede and the Conversion of England: The Charter Evidence*, Jarrow Lecture (Jarrow, 1984), pp. 9–11.

PLATE IV: *West front of Titchfield minster church, Hampshire.*
© John Blair.

There are signs here of a policy: not merely to recruit more monks and nuns, but to create a framework for future evangelization.

Foundation of minsters continued into the eighth century, but a fast-developing society brought its own problems. The first minsters had been 'public' in the sense that kings had normally founded them. But, as Bede notoriously tells us, by his day men 'totally ignorant of the monastic life . . . give money to kings, and under the pretext of founding monasteries buy lands on which they may more freely devote themselves to lust, and in addition cause them to be ascribed to them in hereditary right by royal edicts'.[17] Bede's censure of the lay founders' motives was fair enough, of course, by his own standards: in Mr Wormald's recent phrase, 'the profusion of monasteries in Bede's time . . . was not only a response to the impact of a new faith, but also a way in which families enlarged their resources at the expense of kings, and at the price of turning their younger sons and withered daughters into churchmen and churchwomen'.[18] On the other

---

[17] Bede, *Venerabilis Baedae Opera Historica*, I, pp. 414–16.
[18] Wormald, *Bede and the Conversion of England*, pp. 19–23.

hand, to judge the whole range of communities by the standard of Jarrow may be rather less than fair. Probably all or most of the 'false monasteries' had their place in the framework of pastoral minsters; *parochiae* can, for instance, be traced for such firmly 'proprietary' West Midland foundations as Fladbury, Bredon, Withington and Bibury.[19] Wider lay *dominium* was an inevitable, indeed necessary, consequence of a more complex aristocratic society. The new aldermannic families of the eighth and ninth centuries founded minsters as naturally as kings had done in the seventh; indeed, further development of the *parochiae* positively required such patronage.[20] The system changed with the times, but its basic character was still unthreatened.

The Local Context of the Early Royal Minsters

Most work on minsters has emphasized their proximity to centres of royal power, the correspondence of their *parochiae* to the territories those centres controlled, and the likeness of early church dues to royal taxation systems.[21] From this it is a natural conclusion that king's *tūn* and minster church were normally juxtaposed; and that the numerous minsters in Roman towns or forts reflect a prior re-use of the stronghold as a royal centre to which the church was then attached. Thus Mr Biddle argues that the palace at Winchester, which stood immediately west of Old Minster in the tenth century, was the earlier focus: it 'would explain the king's foundation of a church in AD 648 as the provision of a *hof-* or *pfalzkapelle*'.[22] Dr Haslam has suggested that many southern English towns developed around *villae regales* with adjacent minster churches, palace and minster thus forming one nucleus at the core of the town.[23]

Such arrangements may indeed have been common; but it is only an assumption that they were general, and one which becomes self-fulfilling. The church site is often known, but the palace beside it is rarely more than

---

[19] For these minsters, see C. Dyer, *Lords and Peasants in a Changing Society* (Cambridge, 1980), pp. 12–15; D. Hooke, *The Anglo-Saxon Landscape: The Kingdom of the Hwicce* (Manchester, 1985); C. J. Bond, 'Church and parish in Norman Worcestershire', in Blair, *Minsters and Parish Churches*. For Bibury *parochia*, see introduction to Blair, *Minsters and Parish Churches*.

[20] Cf. P. Wormald, 'The age of Offa and Alcuin', in J. Campbell (ed.), *The Anglo-Saxons* (London, 1982), pp. 123–4.

[21] See M. Deanesly, 'Early English and Gallic minsters', *Transactions of the Royal Historical Society*, 4th ser., 23 (1941), pp. 25 ff., and papers in Blair, *Minsters and Parish Churches*, especially those of P. H. Hase, 'The mother churches of Hampshire', and J. Croom, 'The break-up of the minster *parochiae* of south-eastern Shropshire'. Minster dues are also discussed by Franklin, 'Identification of minsters', pp. 69–73.

[22] M. Biddle, 'Winchester: the development of an early capital', in H. Jankuhn, W. Schlesinger and H. Steiner (eds), *Vor- und Frühformen der europäischen Städt im Mittelalter*, pt 1 (Göttingen, 1973), p. 239.

[23] J. Haslam, 'The towns of Wiltshire', in J. Haslam (ed.), *Anglo-Saxon Towns in Southern England* (Chichester, 1984), pp. xiv–xvi, 135–40.

inference or assumption. One case known from excavation is Cheddar (Somerset), where both minster and palace existed by the ninth century; they formed separate nuclei 200 metres apart beside the two main roads of the town, with the church adjoining a Roman villa site.[24] Northampton (see figure 2.2), where a sequence of grand eighth- and ninth-century halls lay immediately east of St Peter's minster church, has been claimed as another.[25] But there is no firm proof that this was royal. The position of the hall, between two early churches on a west–east axis, recalls important monastic sites with aligned groups of churches: we are in no position to say that the domestic quarters in pre-Viking minsters may not have been like this.

It is in fact arguable that a pattern slightly different from the palace/church group was at least as common: the minster set apart from the palace, and often later forming an urban nucleus. St Peter's minster at Gloucester (founded in AD 679–81) lay in a corner of the Roman town, but the royal centre was at Kingsholm, just over half a mile to the north.[26] At Chesterfield (Derbyshire) (figure 2.1), the minster church stood in a small Roman fort on Ryknield Street, whereas the Domesday manorial centre was at Newbold, on higher ground $1\frac{1}{2}$ miles to the north-west.[27] At Leighton Buzzard (Bedfordshire) (figure 2.2), the church was in the town, but the Norman and probably late Anglo-Saxon royal manor was at Grovebury, a similar distance to the south.[28]

An intriguing case is Aylesbury (Buckinghamshire), where excavation has now shown that the town and St Osyth's church are within an Iron Age hillfort ditch re-cut in about the seventh century.[29] According to Osyth's twelfth-century *vita*, she was born in her father Frithuwold's palace at Quarrendon, on a site still known to the locals.[30] Late though this evidence

[24] P. Rahtz, *The Saxon and Medieval Palaces at Cheddar*, British Archaeological Reports, British series, 65 (Oxford, 1979), p. 33. Cheddar minster is mentioned in King Alfred's will.

[25] J. H. Williams, M. Shaw and V. Denham, *The Middle Saxon Palaces at Northampton* (Northampton, 1985).

[26] C. Heighway and R. Bryant, 'A reconstruction of the 10th century church of St Oswald, Gloucester', in L. A. S. Butler and R. K. Morris (eds), *The Anglo-Saxon Church: Papers in Honour of Dr H. M. Taylor*, Council for British Archaeology Research Report 60 (London, 1986), pp. 188–9. Dr A. G. Rosser points out to me that Westminster and London may illustrate the same phenomenon in reverse: the minster outside the city, and Offa's palace traditionally at Aldermanbury in the Roman fort. But in this case, of course, St Paul's Cathedral already existed within the Roman walls.

[27] P. Riden and J. Blair on the origin of Chesterfield (*Derbyshire Archaeological Journal*, forthcoming). In *Domesday Book* the royal manor of Chesterfield is called Newbold: F. M. Stenton, 'Text of the Derbyshire Domesday', in *The Victoria History of the County of Derby*, vol. 1, edited by W. Page (London, 1905), p. 329.

[28] Excavations by Mrs E. Baker have located the early twelfth-century royal buildings and traces (though inconclusive ones) of earlier occupation: see D. Hall (ed.), *Council for British Archaeology Group 9 Newsletter*, 12 (1982), pp. 7–9.

[29] P. A. Yeoman, 'Excavations at the prebendal court, Aylesbury, 1981', in A. Pike (ed.), *South Midlands Archaeology*, 16 (1986), pp. 37–8.

[30] Hohler, 'St Osyth and Aylesbury', p. 66.

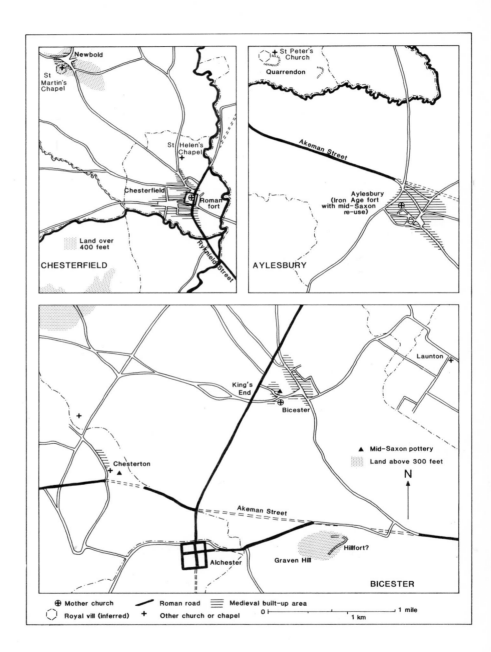

FIGURE 2.1 *Towns, minster churches and royal vills: Chesterfield, Aylesbury and Bicester*

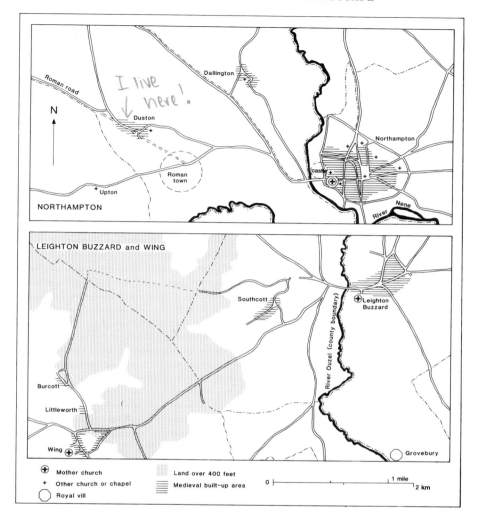

FIGURE 2.2 *Towns, minster churches and royal vills: Northampton and Leighton Buzzard*

is, the relationship between Quarrendon and Aylesbury (figure 2.1) is strikingly similar to the other cases just mentioned. And by a strange chance, a more reliable source records another of Frithuwold's palaces. His Chertsey charter of AD 672–4 defines the east boundary of the estate in which that minster lay as the *antiqua fossa ... id est Fullingadic*, and later gives its place-date as *iuxta villam Friðeuuoldi iuxta supradictam fossatum Fullingadic*.[31] The ditch can be identified as a linear boundary running

---

[31] Sawyer, *Anglo-Saxon Charters*, S. 1165; Birch, *Cartularium Saxonicum*, B. 34. The context and topography of the Chertsey charter are discussed by J. Blair, 'Frithuwold's kingdom and the origins of Surrey', in S. Bassett (ed.), *The Origins of Anglo-Saxon Kingdoms* (Leicester, forthcoming).

south from the Thames some two miles east of Chertsey minster, suggesting a distance between Frithuwold's vill and the minster comparable to that between Quarrendon and Aylesbury.

These cases suggest a context for a more important event: the foundation of the see of Dorchester-on-Thames in AD 635. Bede says that King Cynegils 'gave' to the bishop Birinus 'the *civitas* called Dorcic to make his episcopal seat there'.[32] Clearly if Cynegils gave Dorchester away he can scarcely have lived there himself: possibly his palace was at the later royal vill of Benson, four miles away.[33] Bede's phrase expresses one of the most regularly occurring patterns: the Roman enclosure handed over for ecclesiastical use, the royal vill on open ground outside it. Furthermore, the word *civitas* implies some awareness of the Roman past: it mattered that Dorchester was a *ceaster* rather than a *burh*.[34]

To summarize the argument so far: early royal minsters were often set within their own precinct enclosures, a little way apart from the companion royal vill. The precinct might be a Roman town or fort, an ancient enclosure of some other kind (plate V), or a new site. The reasons for so frequent a choice of Roman sites, which need not have been existing centres of government, must go beyond the purely practical. Without denying the influence in specific cases of surviving Roman cults, it still seems best to invoke a general sense of historical and even architectural fittingness. The continental missionaries could recognize a Roman town, and knew that it was the right and proper place for a great church; if surviving public buildings enhanced the dignity of the site, so much the better. At York, the legionary headquarters building stood until the ninth century, a grand setting for whatever church King Edwin built within or beside it.[35] Recent excavations suggest something similar in kind, if lesser in scale, at St Mildburh's minster of Much Wenlock (Shropshire) (plate VI). Occupation layers outside the walls of a large Roman building, perhaps the courtyard of a villa, have produced radio-carbon dates in the late seventh century; later deposits contained burials of the tenth to eleventh centuries, at which date the Roman walls were still standing. The late eleventh-century church overlay the Roman walls, but was aligned squarely on them, suggesting that

[32] Bede, *Venerabilis Baedae Opera Historica*, I, p. 139. The exact site of Birinus's church is unknown, but the eleventh-century church may lie just *outside* the Roman ramparts: see N. Doggett, 'The Anglo-Saxon see and cathedral of Dorchester-on-Thames', *Oxoniensia*, 51 (1986).

[33] Benson occurs as a royal vill in AD '571', 779 and 887: P. H. Sawyer, 'The royal *tūn* in pre-Conquest England', in P. Wormald (ed.), *Ideal and Reality in Frankish and Anglo-Saxon Society* (Oxford, 1983), p. 291. It has produced substantial Anglo-Saxon settlement evidence: C. J. Bond, 'Medieval Oxfordshire villages and their topography: a preliminary discussion', in D. Hooke (ed.), *Medieval Villages: A Review of Current Work*, Oxford University Committee for Archaeology, Monograph No. 5 (Oxford, 1985), pp. 107–9.

[34] Cf. J. Campbell, 'Bede's words for places', in P. H. Sawyer (ed.), *Names, Words and Graves: Early Medieval Settlement* (Leeds, 1979), pp. 34–42.

[35] Campbell, *The Anglo-Saxons*, p. 39. For a general survey of churches in Roman towns and forts, see Morris, *Church in British Archaeology*, pp. 40–5.

PLATE V: *Hanbury, Worcester. The church stands on the site of the Anglo-Saxon minster which was established here by the eighth century within the ramparts of an Iron Age hillfort.* © Geoff Dowling.

PLATE VI: *The abbey ruins,*
Much Wenlock, Shropshire.
© Della Hooke.

the Anglo-Saxon church had also been symmetrically placed.[36] This formal adoption of a Roman building to house a minster community is worlds away from the mere digging of fifth-century burials into villa ruins, or the building of an eleventh-century church on a convenient villa platform. It implies, as they do not, a valuing of the Roman structure for its own sake.

With other types of minster location, reasons for the choice are rarely evident. The possibility of Celtic *llan*-type sites, perhaps given away by circular or concentric layouts, deserves more investigation than it has yet received, except in western Britain.[37] Where the minster is near, but not inside, a Roman town, it may often perpetuate a tomb-cult in a Roman

[36] H. Woods, 'Excavations at Wenlock Priory, 1981–6', *Journal of the British Archaeological Association*, 140 (1987), pp. 36–75.

[37] For the form that such sites might take, see C. Thomas, *The Early Christian Archaeology of North Britain* (London, 1971), ch. 3. Some likely sites in Cheshire are discussed by A. T. Thacker in *The Victoria History of the County of Cheshire*, vol. 1, edited by B. E. Harris (London, 1987), pp. 239–40, 273. Cf. H. R. Loyn, 'The conversion of the English to Christianity: some comments on the Celtic contribution', in R. R. Davies, R. A. Griffiths, I. G. Jones and K. O. Morgan (eds), *Welsh Society and Nationhood* (Cardiff, 1984), pp. 5–18.

suburban cemetery, the *locus classicus* for which is of course St Albans.[38] Some churches thus sited, as at Ilchester, Colchester and Gloucester, have been found to overlie Roman cemeteries.[39]

Bicester and Northampton (figures 2.1 and 2.2), two medieval towns centred on minsters just outside Roman towns, illustrate a phenomenon of some significance for the Anglo-Saxon landscape and economy: the diversion of roads away from the Roman site to the new minster centre. At Northampton, the roads from all directions lead to the market-place beside the mid-Saxon church complex, leaving isolated the Roman town at Duston.[40] At Bicester, the line of Akeman Street past the site of Alchester is abandoned in favour of a road which deflects northwards to the minster and the medieval town. It can scarcely be coincidence that Bicester ('*ceaster* of the warriors' or 'Beorna's *ceaster*'), one of the rare cases of a non-Roman place with a *ceaster* name, thus replaces the deserted Alchester, almost as though the minster carried with it the attributes of *Romanitas* from the old site to the new. To complete the picture, a village just outside Alchester is called Chesterton ('the *tūn* by the *ceaster*'): like the area around the church it has produced mid-Saxon pottery, and seems a good candidate for an early secular centre.[41]

These cases and many others show a recurring pattern: if a town develops in the neighbourhood of a minster and royal vill, its focus is more usually the church than the palace. Roman towns usually re-emerged as medieval towns when they contained minsters, rarely when they did not: if St Eadburh's minster had been built at Alchester instead of just outside it, the present market town would probably be there and not at Bicester. Obviously not all former minsters are now urban, but a very high proportion of the 'organic' Anglo-Saxon towns seem to have grown around minsters. It is also most striking how many *burh* towns on non-Roman sites, as at Hereford, Wareham and Oxford, were sited to contain pre-existing minsters. The developing Anglo-Saxon road system funnelled traffic to the larger minsters, and markets were established at their gates. It must have been with such places in mind that the late ninth-century translator of Bede rendered his *per urbana loca* as *þurh mynsterstowe*.[42]

Why did kings, who must have given these 'minster markets' their rights and immunities, not found them instead at their own nearby *villae*, where

[38] M. Biddle, 'Archaeology, architecture and the cult of saints in Anglo-Saxon England', in Butler and Morris, *The Anglo-Saxon Church*, pp. 13–16.

[39] Morris, *Church in British Archaeology*, p. 26.

[40] Williams, Shaw and Denham, *Middle Saxon Palaces*, pp. 37–8.

[41] J. Blair in *Medieval Archaeology*, 28 (1984), pp. 235–6.

[42] J. Campbell, 'The Church in Anglo-Saxon towns', in D. Baker (ed.), *The Church in Town and Countryside. Studies in Church History*, 16 (1979), p. 121. Dr A. T. Thacker points out that St Peter's in the Roman fortress at Chester, reputedly a minster before Æthelflæd moved the mother church to St Werburh's, stood by the medieval market and was known by the twelfth century as St Peter's *de foro*.

taxes and tolls were collected? The pattern suggests an organic growth of commercial activity in response to the economic stimulus which the minsters provided. The biggest and most complex settled communities, they attracted all classes of society.[43] For the great, they were the shrines of the saints, the meeting-places of church councils, and often the scene of solemn judicial acts: thus at Northampton all ordeals were conducted in St Peter's minster.[44] For the ordinary, they provided employment and a regular market: monks, nuns and minster-priests had the lay nobility's high standard of living without their migratory life-style. For the poor and disreputable, they afforded alms distributed at anniversaries and funerals, and sanctuary from the law. Dr Dyer has lately emphasized the role of the poorest classes, the occupants of suburban cots, in the economy of Domesday towns:[45] they may already have been important two centuries earlier.

The topography of 'monastic towns' has been more studied in the Celtic world and on the Continent than in England. The 'ideal' Celtic monastery, with concentric circles of increasing holiness, is realized in numerous Irish sites; sometimes, as at Armagh, towns have developed between the central and outer enclosures.[46] A useful parallel is M. Fournier's study of Auvergne, where towns such as Moissat and Brioude grew during the tenth and eleventh centuries like successive tree-rings around their monastic nuclei.[47] If distinctive 'minster towns' occur in England, they may be expected to show three stages of development: first, the precinct itself, whether rectilinear (especially if based on Roman alignments), concentric (especially if of Celtic origin), or curvilinear; secondly, organic late Anglo-Saxon growth around the perimeter or along an approach-road, perhaps including a market-place; and thirdly, twelfth- or thirteenth-century burgage-plots peripheral to the earlier core.

These features are illustrated by the towns already discussed (see figures 2.1 and 2.2), and by those shown to a larger scale in figure 2.3. At Chester-

---

[43] Cf. Campbell, 'The Church in Anglo-Saxon towns'; A. Everitt, 'The Banburys of England', *Urban History Yearbook 1974* (Leicester, 1974), pp. 28–38. For a good French parallel see G. Fournier, 'Rural churches and rural communities in early medieval Auvergne', in F. L. Cheyette (ed.), *Lordship and Community in Medieval Europe: Selected Readings* (New York, 1968), pp. 327–8.

[44] Franklin, 'Minsters and parishes', pp. 80–2.

[45] C Dyer, 'Towns and cottages in eleventh-century England', in H. Mayr-Harting and R. I. Moore (eds), *Studies in Medieval History presented to R. H. C. Davis* (London, 1985), pp. 91–106.

[46] E. R. Norman and J. K. St Joseph, *The Early Development of Irish Society: the Evidence of Aerial Photography* (Cambridge, 1969), ch. 5. Cf. Sharpe, 'The church in early medieval Ireland', pp. 260–2, 267: 'the churches were centres of population and wealth, including the treasures of kings in some cases. They were the towns of pre-Viking Ireland.' For an argument for comparable Welsh sites see L. A. S. Butler, 'The monastic city in Wales: myth or reality?', *Bulletin of the Board of Celtic Studies*, 28(3) (1979), pp. 458–67. A Scottish parallel is St Andrew's, though here proto-urban growth around the early ecclesiastical nucleus was obliterated by a grand replanning of *c* AD 1150: N. P. Brooks and G. Whittington, 'Planning and growth in the medieval Scottish burgh: the example of St Andrew's', *Transactions of the Institute of British Geographers*, new ser., 2(2) (1977), pp. 278–95.

[47] Fournier, 'Early medieval Auvergne', pp. 328–35.

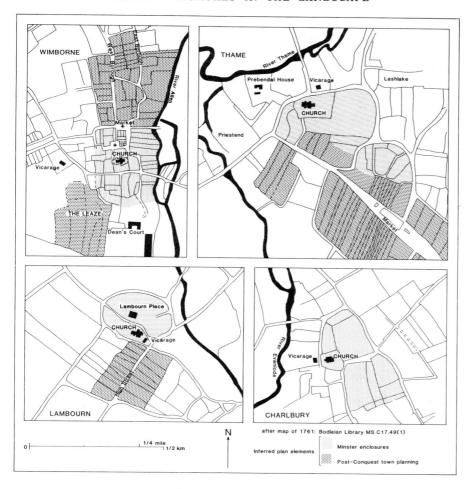

FIGURE 2.3 *Four 'minster towns': Wimborne, Thame, Lambourn and Charlbury.*

field, the first tenements (which, significantly, were nearly all held of the rectory manor in the later Middle Ages) spread along Ryknield Street in both directions; a space outside the north gate of the Roman fort was later known as the 'old' or 'weekday' market.[48] At Wimborne (Dorset), a ninth-century source mentions a double monastery with 'high and stout walls' separating the male and female communities, and the town plan gives a strong suggestion of a concentric precinct; tenements fill the outer circle, and a market-place with a *capella ante portas* lies at its north entrance.[49] Thame and Charlbury, both in Oxfordshire, suggest paired enclosures in figure-of-eight formation. Lambourn (Berkshire) illustrates the simplest and commonest pattern: a single sub-oval enclosure including the churchyard.

[48] Riden and Blair (forthcoming).
[49] J. Blair, 'Wimborne Minster', *Archaeological Journal*, 140 (1983), pp. 37–8.

At Bicester and Leighton Buzzard, the main roads funnel into a triangular market-place pointing towards the presumed precinct entrance, recalling the plan of Abingdon, where *Domesday Book* specifically mentions ten *mercatores ante portam ecclesiae manentes*.[50] Most of the towns have post-Conquest extensions with their distinctive burgage-plots, grouped at Chesterfield around a new and much larger market-place west of the old town, and at Thame along a cigar-shaped market street which cuts across the old curvilinear boundaries.

These topographical conjectures are presented without apology, for archaeologists have yet to provide a firmer basis. So far, not one such site has received systematic investigation of its boundaries and internal layout. One major research excavation would scarcely be extravagant; on a smaller scale, strategic sectioning to test whether curvilinear road patterns really do reflect precinct boundaries might accomplish much. The work of the last thirty years has turned Anglo-Saxon planned towns from inference into solid fact; it remains to be seen whether the same can be done for the much larger number of 'minster towns'.

The Minsters in their Communities: Baptism and Burial

In post-Conquest sources, ex-minsters are best identified from traces of the rights they had once exercised in their *parochiae*. Some rights were ancient, notably the fixed renders of grain called church-scot.[51] Others were less so, or at least represent a formalization of what were once matters of mere piety or custom. Tithe payment was always enjoined, but is first mentioned as obligatory in the 920s: partly it suggests a wish to tap an expanding economy more effectively, partly the response of institutions under threat.[52] From the eleventh century the rights to control baptism, and far more to claim corpses for burial, were closely guarded attributes of mother-church status. The perspective of seventh- and eighth-century minster-priests may have been different, however. Baptising infants and converts, and burying the dead, were part of their duties: there was no need for a jealous centralization of functions which there were as yet no rivals to contest.

Alongside the new, politically-determined geography of minsters must be remembered St Gregory's instruction to cleanse heathen shrines and use them as churches. The two are hard to reconcile, unless we postulate a

[50] Rev. F. W. Ragg, 'Translation of the Berkshire Domesday', in *The Victoria History of the County of Berkshire*, vol. 1, edited by P. H. Ditchfield and W. Page (London, 1906), p. 337.

[51] Experience suggests that church-scot is one of the strongest relict traces of early minster status. It is first mentioned in the *Laws of Ine*, though since the extant text is late ninth century this is not firm evidence that church-scot was imposed from the earliest stages.

[52] Blair, 'Secular minster churches', p. 119; Franklin, 'Identification of minsters', p. 70.

class of subordinate, but older, cult sites incorporated into the new system like fossils during the Conversion period. Holy wells and graveyards were the raw materials with which the first missionaries worked: the English Church's natural meeting-places with Romano-Celtic Christianity on the one hand and Anglo-Saxon paganism on the other. Even when they were not themselves refounded as minsters, such sites could be assimilated as subordinate elements into the new *parochiae*. Controlled from the centre, and not subject to separatist private interests, they rarely developed later into parish churches.

In much of Europe, it was the essence of regional mother churches that they were baptismal churches, a fact reflecting the centralized character of the Roman baptismal rite.[53] This applies most obviously to the Italian *pievi*, while in Auvergne M. Fournier uses dedications of town churches to St John Baptist as the normal means of identifying fifth- and sixth-century parish centres.[54] In England, by contrast, the primacy of baptismal churches was rarely emphasized: it is symptomatic that the thirty-four seventh-century dedications known from contemporary sources do not include a single case of St John Baptist.[55] The minsters did of course control baptism, but not necessarily to the extent of centralizing it on their own premises: thus in the eleventh and twelfth centuries the mother churches of Kent, and of Leominster in Herefordshire, received payments for distributing chrism among their daughter churches.[56] The one certain case of a baptismal church forming part of a great complex is at Canterbury, where Archbishop Cuthbert (AD 740–60) built the church of St John Baptist immediately east of Christ Church.[57] In fact the Canterbury churches suggest a dualism that defers to Roman practice, if not actually perpetuating a Roman arrangement: St Augustine's outside the walls amid Roman cemeteries, where the kings and archbishops were buried, and Christ Church in the city where baptisms were performed.[58]

But early baptisteries can be found away from the great churches. The late fourth-century church at St Paul-in-the-Bail, Lincoln, was built in the middle of the forum, with its east end pointing towards a stone well.[59] The church site survived as a sixth-century graveyard and seventh-century mortuary chapel, while the well remained exposed into the tenth century: a relationship which suggests continuing baptismal functions. Holy wells beside chapels can be found throughout England, and some cases suggest

[53] Morris, *Church in British Archaeology*, p. 66; cf. Reynolds, *Kingdoms and Communities*, pp. 81–4.

[54] Fournier, 'Early medieval Auvergne', p. 316.

[55] Morris, *Church in British Archaeology*, table pp. 35–8; cf. p. 66.

[56] T. Tatton-Brown, 'The Church in Canterbury diocese in the eleventh century', and B. Kemp, 'Some aspects of the *parochia* of Leominster', in Blair, *Minsters and Parish Churches*, pp. 84, 105.

[57] N. Brooks, *The Early History of the Church of Canterbury* (Leicester, 1984), p. 51.

[58] cf. Ibid., p. 36.

[59] P. Stafford, *The East Midlands in the Early Middle Ages* (Leicester, 1985), p. 88.

early origins.[60] Thus a little chapel of Chertsey Abbey at Bisley in Surrey, dedicated to St John Baptist, is near a holy well where baptisms were still being performed in the eighteenth century; charter-bounds of AD 956 that pass the site include an *eceles hamme*, a plausible candidate for an *eccles* place-name.[61] Such cases suggest an unbroken tradition of decentralized baptism.

The clearest dichotomy between seventh- and tenth-century practice is with burial.[62] In contrast to the Church of the central Middle Ages, 'the early Church showed itself surprisingly indifferent to where Christians were laid to rest'.[63] Since burial in holy places was always prized by high-status laymen,[64] it is no surprise to find large early graveyards around minsters, as with the eighth-century burials near the enclosure boundary at Brixworth, or graves packed close around shrines, as at Winchester (plate VII).[65] But at this date it may be more a matter of privilege than of compulsion: there is no written evidence for anything resembling the monopolistic minster graveyards of the tenth, eleventh and twelfth centuries. For the ordinary population, there is a gap to be filled between their abandonment of 'final-phase' pagan cemeteries during *c.* AD 650–750, and the age when minster and manorial graveyards contested for their corpses.[66]

Here archaeologists have pointed, doubtless rightly, to the frequent cases of parish graveyards adjacent to pagan cemeteries. In fact some of these surround churches that were probably minsters;[67] nevertheless, many do not, and it may eventually prove that a larger number of 'successor' graveyards have no associated buildings, or are associated with chapels that never become parish churches. Such cemeteries must be the subject of the passage in Theodore's *Penitential* (AD 668×91) dealing with wooden *ecclesiae* with consecrated altars on sites where either Christians or pagans are buried.[68] To quote D. Bullough, it 'apparently envisages a modest equivalent of the old Roman "cemeterial basilicas", not intended for regular liturgical worship, in cemeteries whose development began in the pagan period and remained unconsecrated'; such oratories are 'apparently not

---

[60] Morris, *Church in British Archaeology*, p. 67.

[61] Blair, *Early Medieval Surrey*, ch. 5; the charter is S. 621, B. 955.

[62] This section is indebted to Morris, *Church in British Archaeology*, pp. 49–62, and to D. Bullough, 'Burial, community and belief in the early medieval West', in P. Wormald (ed.), *Ideal and Reality in Frankish and Anglo-Saxon Society*, pp. 177–201.

[63] Bullough, 'Burial, community and belief', p. 186; Morris, *Church in British Archaeology*, p. 50.

[64] Cf. the story of Hildmer and St Cuthbert: B. Colgrave (ed.), *Two Lives of St Cuthbert* (Cambridge, 1940), p. 205.

[65] P. Everson, 'Excavations in the vicarage garden at Brixworth, 1972', *Journal of the British Archaeological Association*, 130 (1977), pp. 55ff.; Biddle, 'Archaeology, architecture and the cult of saints', pp. 22–5.

[66] Morris, *Church in British Archaeology*, pp. 51–8.

[67] Ibid., pp. 59–62; Bullough, 'Burial, community and belief', p. 198.

[68] Haddan and Stubbs, *Councils and Ecclesiastical Documents*, vol. III, pp. 190–1.

PLATE VII: *The debris from a minster graveyard: fragments of Anglo-Saxon crosses and gravestones built into the later church at Bakewell, Derbyshire.* © John Blair.

uncommon in parts of Francia ... although interestingly they only rarely develop later into "parish" churches'.[69]

Bampton in Oxfordshire suggests an English parallel in the context of a minster *parochia*.[70] A community of priests there is mentioned in the 950s, presumably based at the present parish church, which contains remnants of a pre-Conquest nave. In the fourteenth century it still controlled a large *parochia* (figure 2.4) containing several settlements and daughter churches; all corpses went to the mother-church graveyard, as is explicitly ordered in the case of one chapelry at the beginning of the twelfth century. Thus Bampton seems a classic instance of a centralized minster cemetery.

On the east side of the *parochia*, in the Windrush valley, was a group of pagan Anglo-Saxon cemeteries, including rich early seventh-century burials

[69] Bullough, 'Burial, community and belief', pp. 189, 197.
[70] Bampton minster research project, in progress: for summaries to date, see J. Blair, 'St Beornwald of Bampton', *Oxoniensia*, 49 (1984), pp. 47–55; J. Blair, 'Parish versus village', *Oxfordshire Local History*, 2(2) (1985), pp. 34–47; J. Blair, 'The Bampton minster research project', in A. Pike (ed.), *South Midlands Archaeology*, 16 (1986), pp. 87–91.

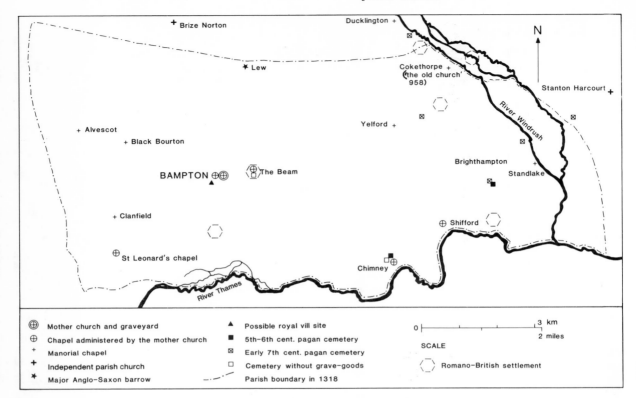

Legend:

⊕ Mother church and graveyard
⊕ Chapel administered by the mother church
+ Manorial chapel
✛ Independent parish church
✴ Major Anglo-Saxon barrow
▲ Possible royal vill site
■ 5th–6th cent. pagan cemetery
⊠ Early 7th cent. pagan cemetery
☐ Cemetery without grave-goods
⬡ Romano-British settlement
—·—· Parish boundary in 1318

SCALE
0 — 3 km
0 — 2 miles

FIGURE 2.4 *Bampton minster parish, showing pagan and Christian Anglo-Saxon burial sites*
Source: Bampton Research Project

at Brighthampton, Ducklington, Standlake and Yelford.[71] Two other cemeteries, however, have been found nearer the later mother church – one beside the Thames at Chimney and one at a site called the Beam by Bampton itself; there were no grave-goods at either site, except for a 'Saxon knife' from Chimney and a pin of *c.* AD 700 with one of the Beam burials.[72] The Chimney cemetery had evidently succeeded an earlier one, which produced 'swords and armour'. Adjoining both sites were chapels which, unlike most of the other churches in the *parochia*, were on land belonging to the mother church and entirely controlled by it. At Shifford, a little further along the Thames, there was a chapel of comparable status, which was still served as late as the fourteenth century by a curate sent out from Bampton.[73] A fourth chapel at Cokethorpe, between the old cemeteries at Yelford and Ducklington, is called the 'old church' in charter-bounds of AD 958.[74] All these are candidates for cemetery chapels marking dispersed

[71] A. Meaney, *A Gazetteer of Early Anglo-Saxon Burial Sites* (London, 1964), pp. 203–4, 208, 212–14.

[72] Ibid., p. 206 for Chimney; notes in Oxfordshire County Museum Sites and Monuments Record for the Beam.

[73] *The Eynsham Cartulary*, edited by H. E. Salter, 2 vols (Oxford, 1908), II, p. 6.

[74] Sawyer, *Anglo-Saxon Charters*, S. 678; Birch, *Cartularium Saxonicum*, B. 1036.

'first-generation' Christian sites, assimilated into the *parochia* and in most cases maintained from the central church.

The relationship between the parish church and the Beam chapel (figure 2.5) is intriguing. Since the name Bampton means '*tūn* by the *bēam*', the Beam was evidently the earlier or more important site. The cemetery overlay an Iron Age and Roman settlement, and the chapel bore the potentially early dedication to St Andrew.[75] Although half a mile apart, the church and chapel are on nearly the same alignment, conforming to a rectilinear and clearly ancient pattern of boundaries. West of the church another chapel stood by the twelfth century, and further west still was a holy well.[76] The duality of Bampton and the Beam even suggests something like a miniature Canterbury, with the parish church (dedicated to St John Baptist by the thirteenth century[77]) originating as a baptismal church, and St Andrew's as a cemetery church. If so, the main cemetery around St John's must have been a later development.

The view that most churches which existed because of links to the Celtic or pagan past were subject to minsters from the outset is strengthened by the frequency with which they were subordinate later. St Paul's at Lincoln was not a mother church; in Kent, the Roman buildings re-used as churches at Lydd, Stone-by-Faversham and St John's, Lullingstone, were daughters of Lympne, Teynham and Eynsford minsters respectively.[78] The best excavated analogue for the cemetery churches envisaged by Theodore's *Penitential* is the wooden building at Yeavering with its graveyard and pagan cult focus, and this failed to survive even as a chapel.

Thus the early coherence of the *parochiae* did not preclude dispersed cult sites within them. It mattered little that rural Christians were baptized at outlying wells, or buried where their ancestors had been buried: all were parishioners of the mother church, and the only possible beneficiaries of their ecclesiastical dues were its priests. By the late tenth century, arrangements were more centralized and legalistic: a legalism which shows insecurity in a world that was starting to turn against the minsters.

Conclusion: The Minsters in a Changing World

A recent trend of research has been to identify major changes in rural economy and exploitation towards the end of the first millennium AD.

---

[75] Exeter Cathedral Library, MS 2931.

[76] The house called the Deanery immediately west of the church contains remains of an early twelfth-century two-storey range aligned west-east; an early fourteenth-century survey mentions a *capella cum bassa camera*.

[77] *Calendar of Entries in the Papal Registers Relating to Great Britain and Ireland: Papal Letters I. AD 1198–1304*, edited by W. H. Bliss (London, 1893), p. 544.

[78] Lists edited by T. Tatton-Brown, 'The Church in Canterbury diocese in the 11th century', in Blair, *Minsters and Parish Churches*, pp. 114–17.

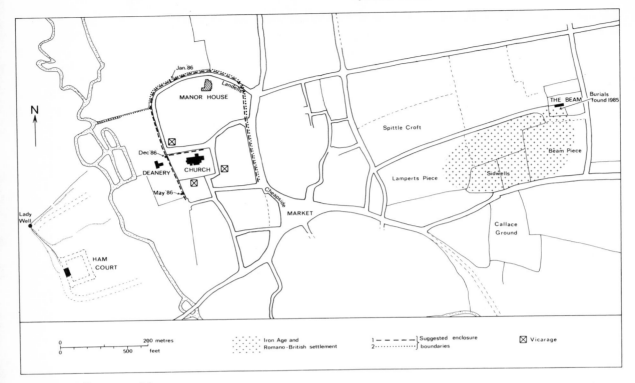

FIGURE 2.5   *Bampton and the Beam: early sites shown in relation to the post-medieval town plan*
Source: Bampton Research Project

Briefly, it seems that the complex, multi-vill estates and territories broke up into internally-focused, 'cellular' manors, a shift which went hand-in-hand with intensified management of resources and nucleation of settlement. With local manors came local lords: a broad class of minor thegns whose needs can scarcely have failed to influence the emerging village communities.[79] The details and chronology are still controversial (as other chapters in this volume demonstrate), but a consensus may be emerging that the critical period was between the late ninth and eleventh centuries.

It is thus arguable that, in so far as lesser churches were founded by local thegns for local manors, a social context for them existed by the 950s as it had not a century earlier. The evidence, such as it is, for manorial church origins supports this view.[80] The chapels on early cult sites described above were in no sense 'proprietary': rather, they were founded or assimilated by the minsters and wholly subordinate to them. Apparent references to thegnly churches and single, locally-based priests in English sources before the tenth century are rare and equivocal: some may actually be describing minsters, whereas others are taken verbatim from Frankish legislation and

[79]   This view of the economic context is presented more fully in the introduction to Blair, *Minsters and Parish Churches*, pp. 7–9.

[80]   This section summarizes the arguments in J. Blair, 'Local churches in Domesday Book and before', in J. C. Holt (ed.), *Domesday Studies* (London, 1987), pp. 265–78.

are not necessarily applicable to England. Excavation of ordinary rural churches is producing a rapidly-growing number of stone or timber phases of the tenth or eleventh century, but strikingly few of the eighth or ninth. The signs are, in short, that small private churches were still rare in AD 900, whereas by AD 1000 a church was something that any prosperous *ceorl* aspiring to thegnhood might be expected to have.

This change threatened the minsters. However chequered their individual fates, their collegiate structure and large *parochiae* had been essentially well suited to the old pattern of scattered settlements and centralized lordship. But now the new country gentry desired their own churches, and the new villages were better served by resident priests. From their old position of central and unquestioned importance, the minsters started to become anachronisms founded on entrenched rights.

The transition of obedience and loyalties spanned more than two centuries, and there are many signs of an intermediate stage.[81] Early private churches may not have inconvenienced the minsters until the stage came when their lords claimed parochial independence; indeed, it is clear that at least some manorial churches were founded in consultation with the minster clergy and served by minster priests. Dr Rosser writes of the federation of Devon village gilds in *c*. AD 1100 that it 'may indicate a transition period of ambivalent loyalties, divided between the old minster and the nascent parish'.[82] None the less, the main trend is clear. From the 950s onwards, lay wills, which previously mention only the minsters, contain increasingly frequent bequests to local priests and churches.[83] More and more were manorial churches endowed with their own lands; more and more were they served by resident priests, who were members of village communities and owed their first loyalties to their lords and neighbours; more and more was patronage directed to providing permanent stone churches, and carved tombstones in the churchyards around them.[84] Burial at the minster had once been an honour; now it started to become a nuisance. This is the context of the tenth- and eleventh-century laws enforcing mother-church rights, enjoining payment of minster tithes, safeguarding the minster's soul-scot when a corpse is buried outside its *rihtscriftscire*.[85]

This chapter has suggested ways in which the minsters themselves influenced the development of the Anglo-Saxon landscape. In a more general sense, however, their fortunes mirror its critical transformation: from

---

[81] This transition is discussed more fully by J. Blair in the introduction to Blair, *Minsters and Parish Churches*.

[82] A. G. Rosser, 'The Anglo-Saxon gilds', in Blair, *Minsters and Parish Churches*, p. 31.

[83] Blair, 'Local churches', pp. 269–71.

[84] Cf. Stafford, *East Midlands in the Early Middle Ages*, pp. 173–5.

[85] V Æthelred 12: 1: *The Laws of the Kings of England from Edmund to Henry I*, edited and translated by A. J. Robertson (Cambridge, 1925), pp. 82–3.

scattered to nucleated settlement, and from 'extensive' to 'localized' systems of land management and jurisdiction. Through the twelfth century, and sometimes much later, minsters still stood apart from the mass of ordinary churches. Their parishes, if much reduced, remained different in kind, and their residual mother-church rights had a powerful influence on the later medieval parochial system.[86] But by AD 1100 it was with the village churches, soon to become parish churches, that the future lay: the minsters remained, but as relics of a former age.

Addendum

Since going to press, an important paper by Susan M. Pearce, 'The early church in the landscape: the evidence for north Devon', has appeared in the *Archaeological Journal*, 142 (1985). This argues that British minsters endowed by sixth-century landlords coexisted with scattered graveyards, also of mid-sixth-century origin, which served local settlements. At St Nectan's, Hartland, which survived through the Middle Ages as a minster with a typical English *parochia*, at least two of its eight outlying chapels may have begun as early British cemeteries. For the whole north Devon area it is argued that 'the necessary priestly services at the graveyards must have been supplied by the monasteries, and so a scheme of three loosely defined areas emerges, centred upon St Nectan's, St Brannoc's and St Stephen's, together, probably, with a fourth centred upon Exeter'. For minster endowment within an existing territorial context, and for relationships between centralized religious communities and devolved burial and cult sites, this view of the British south-west in the sixth century has clear parallels with the present discussion of Anglo-Saxon organization in the seventh and eighth centuries.

---

[86] Blair, 'Secular minster churches', pp. 138–42.

3

Towards a Chronology for English Place-Names

MARGARET GELLING

The treatment of place-name evidence in a number of prestigious books published this year has caused me to feel that there is an urgent need for a statement about the nature of this evidence and its true potential as historical material.[1]

The three major characteristics of place-name evidence are abundance, ubiquity and internal consistency. As regards abundance and evenness of distribution, there is an obvious contrast with documentary sources and with archaeology; but the advantages place-names enjoy in these respects could be offset, or even nullified, if they were also characterized by an unacceptable level of unreliability. So the third characteristic, internal consistency, requires constant emphasis. The failure to appreciate this is still leading distinguished historians into embarrassingly elementary mistakes.

This internal consistency is manifested in a number of ways. It shows itself in the regularity of the relationship between details of topography and the words used in place-names for landscape features. I endeavoured to establish this in my book *Place-Names in the Landscape*,[2] and it is disappointing

---

[1] Three books may be instanced: J. N. L. Myres, *The English Settlements* (Cambridge, 1986); P. Coones and J. Patten, *The Penguin Guide to the Landscape of England and Wales* (Harmondsworth, 1986); and O. Rackham, *The History of the Countryside* (London, 1986). Dr Myres's chapter-headings on p. viii are eloquent testimony to his attitude:

Place-name evidence
  Unsatisfactory nature as historical material
  Confusing effects of oral transmission in illiterate societies
  Lateness of most written forms
  Mistakes due to linguistic ignorance of scribes
    . . .
Enduring complexities of place-name study

The *Penguin-Guide* contains two dismissive sentences: 'The same can be said of place-names, the analysis and derivation of which is a potentially valuable but extremely hazardous operation. Even the experts rarely agree, and the pitfalls are so numerous that the validity of the whole exercise might well be called in question by the layman as a far-fetched linguistic indulgence.' Oliver Rackham's treatment is surprisingly poor throughout his book.

[2] M. Gelling, *Place-Names in the Landscape* (London, 1984).

to note that I have totally failed to influence Oliver Rackham; perhaps his work was too far advanced in 1984. There is consistency also between the settlement-terms used in place-names and the types of institution to which they refer. There has not yet been a large-scale study of this aspect of the subject, but recent work on some words such as *wīc*, *cot* and *stōw* indicates the potential of it.[3] Like the words for valleys and hills, the place-name-forming terms for farms and villages are not synonyms, and the choice of term for use in each name owes nothing to chance.

There is consistency in the treatment in Old English place-names of elements from other languages. It is of vital importance for the historian to appreciate that British names adopted by Old English speakers were subject to clearly defined developments of pronunciation, and that these developments are clearly and consistently manifested in the manner in which the names are written down in Old English and Middle English documents. Generations of place-name scholars have striven to explain these two vital points to historians and archaeologists, but three of Dr Myres's chapter headings (quoted in fn. 1) demonstrate total incomprehension of them. I want to make another attempt at explanation, using Dr Myres's mistakes of 1986 as my examples.

Let us take first the name *Badon*, which may be deduced from Gildas's Latinized name *Mons Badonicus*, the site of the famous victory over the Saxons, which he tells us occurred in the year of his birth.[4] In order to judge how this name would appear if it were taken into Old English speech, we can look up the vowels and the consonants in Professor Kenneth Jackson's book *Language and History in Early Britain*.[5] The first vowel of *Badon* has to be ă, because otherwise (p. 287) as a long vowel it would have become ō in Primitive Welsh (PrW). On pp. 271–2, Professor Jackson tells us that PrW short *a* when followed by a back vowel in the next syllable became Old English (OE) short *a*. He instances the river-name Avon, recorded in OE as *Aven*, which is from PrW *Aƀon*, an exact parallel to *Badon* as regards its vowels, though in the modern name the first vowel has been lengthened.

---

[3] For the earliest use of *wīc*, in the compound *wīchām* ('village associated with a Romano-British *vicus*'), see M. Gelling, 'English place-names derived from the compound *wicham*', *Medieval Archaeology*, 11 (1967), pp. 87–104. For a later use to mean 'trading centre' see A. Vince, 'The Aldwych', *Current Archaeology*, 93 (August 1984), pp. 310–12, and M. Biddle, 'London on the Strand', *Popular Archaeology*, 6(1) (July 1984), pp. 23–7. The use of *cot* for settlements with a special relationship to boroughs is argued in C. Dyer, 'Towns and cottages in eleventh-century England', in H. Mayr-Harting and R. I. Moore (eds), *Studies in Medieval History presented to R. H. C. Davis* (London, 1985), pp. 91–106. The specialized uses of *stōw* are discussed in M. Gelling, 'Some meanings of stōw', in S. Pearce (ed.), *The Early Church in Western Britain and Ireland*, British Archaeological Reports, British series, 102 (Oxford, 1982), pp. 187–96.

[4] *Gildas, The Ruin of Britain and Other Works*, Arthurian Sources, vol. 7, edited and translated by M. Winterbottom (London and Chichester, 1978).

[5] K. Jackson, *Language and History in Early Britain. A Chronological Survey of the Brittonic Languages, First to Twelfth Century AD* (Edinburgh, 1953).

So PrW *Badon* would have become OE *Badon*, perhaps later *Baden*. If the site were a hillfort, and if the Anglo-Saxons added *byrig*, dative of *burh* 'fort', it would become Badbury, and the only suggestion we can offer for identification is that it might be one of several Badburys. Professor Jackson observes (p. 199) that 'Badbury Hill above the Vale of White Horse and Badbury near Swindon are possible candidates', and there is nothing more that can usefully be said. But archaeologists and historians keep trying. Professor Leslie Alcock suggested Bath,[6] which is ruled out partly by common sense and partly by our evidence that PrW *d* did not become English *th*. Now, in 1986, Dr Myres has published another suggestion. On pp. 159–60, he postulates the survival of *Badon* in the modern name Baydon, a place three miles south-east of Badbury near Swindon. In a footnote he says 'Early forms of Baydon do nothing to support Ekwall's derivation from OE *beg-dun*, "berry hill".'

In fact, the Middle English (ME) spellings for Baydon point inescapably to an OE *begdūn*. The vast majority of them have *Bei-* or *Bey-*. Why would a Primitive Welsh/Old English short *a* be spelt *ei* or *ey* in Middle English? We can demonstrate that *ei/ey* is the regular ME spelling for OE *ĕg*. We have place-names recorded in Old English spellings that contain the words *ēg*, 'island', *hēg*, 'hay', *weg*, 'way', and for these names there are many Middle English spellings with -*ei*- and -*ey*-.[7]

Another unsatisfactory identification is that of Nennius's battle-site called *Gwoloph* with Wallop in Hampshire, which Myres comments favourably upon in n. 1 on p. 164, and which appears, together with Baydon, on his map 3.[8] He says 'Ekwall suggests a Germanic origin for the name Wallop, but as it does not appear in any written form earlier than Domesday Book, this is clearly no more than an implausible guess'. I do not know how a ninth-century Welsh name *Gwoloph* would appear in Middle English, but Domesday *Wallope* does not look right. The identification probably owes something to the unconscious projection backwards of the pronunciation *Wollop*, of which there is no indication in the spellings till *c.* 1270. The name is *Walhope* in 1230. There are two other examples of this place-name, one in Gloucestershire and one in Shropshire. It is surely an OE compound, with *hop* ('secluded place') as its final element.

Underlying Dr Myres's remark about Wallop not appearing in any written form earlier than *Domesday Book*, and clearly emerging in his chapter headings (particularly 'Confusing effects of oral transmission in illiterate societies' and 'Lateness of most written forms'), there is either a

---

[6] L. Alcock, *Arthur's Britain* (London, 1971), pp. 69–71.

[7] Eye, Northamptonshire, is *Ege* AD 970, 972, *Eya* 1199. Heyford, Oxfordshire, is *Hegford* AD 995, *Haiforde* 1086, *Heyford* 1242. Broadway, Worcestershire, is *Bradanwege* AD 972, *Bradeweia* 1086.

[8] *Nennius, British History and the Welsh Annals*, Arthurian Sources, vol. 8, edited and translated by J. Morris (London and Chichester, 1980), pp. 39, 80.

failure to understand, or a refusal to accept, the basis of English place-name study. This basis is the belief that Middle English spellings faithfully reflect Middle English pronunciation, and that oral transmission of place-names is an outstandingly reliable process. A substantial number of our place-names are recorded in Old English sources, and by observing the spelling of those names in Middle English documents we have built up a great body of evidence, which enables us to project back from Middle English spellings to the probable Old English forms of names which are first recorded in *Domesday Book* or later. Myres's footnote on Wallop could be taken as imply-ing that for all names not recorded earlier than 1086 place-name scholars can offer nothing but implausible guesses. This really is an outrageous suggestion.

As regards oral transmission, it is commonplace for names to be recorded in the boundaries of Anglo-Saxon charters and then not to appear again until the nineteenth century, when they were written down in an excellent state of preservation in tithe awards. Sometimes, without even that documentation, they are recovered in their modern forms from the speech of people living in the area today. Myres's remark about 'illiterate societies' is particularly unfortunate. Illiteracy is, of course, particularly conducive to accurate oral transmission.

These observations are a necessary preface to my main theme, which is the potential of place-name evidence as a guide to the events of the fifth and sixth centuries, and as a useful tool in the study of settlement history. Place-names should not be used at all for such purposes unless certain principles are accepted. These principles are:

1 That speakers of Old English adopted place-names from speakers of Primitive Welsh with precise reproduction of the pronunciation when the necessary sounds were available in their own tongue; but when the exact sound was not available, the nearest Old English one was substituted. We have good evidence about the process of sound-substitution, and this is set out clearly in Professor Kenneth Jackson's *Language and History in Early Britain*.

2 'Popular etymology', an instance of which would be the replacement of British words by Old English words of similar sound, but different meaning, is extremely rare among the names for which we have evidence. This applies to British names adopted by Anglo-Saxons, Old English names when they ceased to be meaningful in later English, and English names when used by Norman French speakers. This being so, it is not permissible to equate a British name with an English name by presuming popular etymology, unless there is a very strong third factor supporting the equation. If it is certainly established that a Romano-British settlement was in the immediate vicinity of an existing settlement with a very similar name,

the assumption is not unscholarly. Speen is the clearest instance.[9] Brougham, Westmorland, which may be *Brocavum*, is a more doubtful possibility. Some popular etymology is involved in the development of York and Gloucester. It is not necessary to assume it in Salisbury, though this is frequently cited as an instance.[10] I don't think Rochester is relevant, as I don't accept the derivation of *Hrof* (in *Hrofesceaster*) from the Romano-British name *Durobrivis*.[11]

These few instances of the exercise of popular etymology by early English speakers are heavily outnumbered by examples of careful transmission of names which must have been meaningless to them. In *Signposts to the Past*, I listed all the instances I could find of recorded Romano-British names which survived later. The score is about thirty-five, of which four are in Wales, so are not relevant. Among names taken over by Anglo-Saxons we have four, at most, which were affected by popular etymology, as against twenty-seven which were not.

3 Oral transmission of place-names during the Anglo-Saxon period can be shown to have been reliable by the use of our extensive documentation. Something has been said about this already, so I will only instance here the Old English renderings of Romano-British toponyms. Jocular references are frequently made to the reduction of names like *Uriconium* and *Mamucion* to single syllables in Wroxeter and Manchester, as if this demonstrated Anglo-Saxon inability to cope with polysyllabic names.[12] But when we have an early Old English spelling, as we have for Lichfield and for Dorchester (Dorset), the whole name is preserved. The shortening that is observed in tenth- and eleventh-century spellings is a later phenomenon, which takes the form of dropping the middle element of a three-element name; this was frequently practised in triple compounds of purely English origin. The forms for Lichfield in the two earliest manuscripts of Bede's *Ecclesiastical History* (*Lyccitfeld*, *Liccitfeld*) show that the first part of the hybrid Welsh/English name was the Primitive Welsh form of the Romano-British *Letocetum*, with both its syllables carefully represented.[13] It is an

[9] *Spinis*, in the *Antonine Itinerary*, must be located near Speen, Berkshire. Latin *spīnis*, 'at the thorn bushes', could not develop by ordinary phonological processes to Old English *spēne*, modern Speen. The Anglo-Saxons appear to have assimilated *spīnis* to an Old English word *spēne*, 'place where there are chips of wood'.

[10] See K. Jackson, 'Some Romano-British place-names', *Journal of Roman Studies*, 38 (1948), p. 58. The Romano-British name was *Sorviodunum*. By the time the English reached the Salisbury district, British *Sorvio-* would have developed into *Serw*, from which the *Searo-* of Old English *Searobyrg* can be derived without insuperable difficulty.

[11] M. Gelling, *Signposts to the Past: Place-Names and the History of England* (London, 1976), p. 56.

[12] A recent example occurs in C. Smith, 'The survival of Romano-British toponymy', *Nomina*, 4 (1980), pp. 32–3: 'the Anglo-Saxons found the compounded and polysyllabic R-B names "too much of a mouthful", and by convention took the first syllable, all that was necessary for identification.'

[13] Bede, *Ecclesiastical History*, in *Venerabilis Baedae Opera Historica*, edited by C. Plummer, 2 vols (Oxford, 1896).

absurd anachronism to impute the modern Englishman's poor linguistic skills to his fifth- and sixth-century forebears.[14]

4 The fourth principle, perhaps the most important, is that there is a very high level of consistency in Old English and Middle English spellings for place-names. I have given some instances of this above, in my discussion of the early forms for Baydon, Wiltshire. I belong to the third generation of scholars who have spent their working lives handling these spellings, and another generation is following mine, without any signs of unease about the validity of the study. We cannot all be making it up. Norman French clerks spell names differently from English clerks, but the differences are systematic, and scholars have identified and listed them.[15] Dr Myres failed to notice these studies when he wrote his paragraph on 'Mistakes due to linguistic ignorance of scribes'.

The principles concerning the accurate representation and transmission by Old English speakers of Primitive Welsh place-names have to be accepted, if the pre-English stratum in the corpus of English place-names is to be used as evidence for coexistence between Welsh and English speakers. This is probably the most important single contribution which place-name studies have made to our perception of the events of the English settlement, but it would be nullified if credence were given to claims that we cannot distinguish British names because the Anglo-Saxons mispronounced them, or transformed them into apparent English names by the process of popular etymology.

The corpus of pre-English material preserved in place-names is sufficiently well defined to be useful as historical evidence; also, auxiliary classes of Old English names have been identified, the most important being those that refer to Britons by the words *walh* and *cumbra*, and those that use words borrowed from Latin. This is not, however, a static body of material. New items are still being recognized, and occasionally a name previously considered to be pre-English is shown by the discovery of new spellings to be of later origin. I will cite two instances of this process of revision. In 1980, Dr Richard Coates demonstrated that Leatherhead is a Celtic name meaning 'grey ford'.[16] His paper has the significant title 'Methodological

---

[14] Cf. L. Alcock, *Arthur's Britain*, pp. 194–5: 'It may well be that apparent absence of settlement-names derived from Primitive Welsh is proof only that the Englishman's traditional inability to pronounce a foreign language correctly is a trait of very long standing.'

[15] R. E. Zachrisson, 'The French element', in A. Mawer and F. M. Stenton (eds), *Introduction to the Survey of English Place-Names*, English Place-Name Society, vol. 1 (Cambridge, 1924), pp. 93–114; O. von Feilitzen, *The Pre-Conquest Personal Names of Domesday Book* (Uppsala, 1937), pp. 34–129. (The same principles apply to Domesday spellings of place-names as to the personal names with which Dr von Feilitzen was mainly concerned.)

[16] R. Coates, 'Methodological reflexions on Leatherhead', *English Place-Name Society Journal*, 12 (1980), pp. 70–3.

reflexions on Leatherhead', and his method was to examine philological opinions on the likely development in the post-Roman period of the sounds in the two words *lēto-* and *-rito-*, and to show that the Middle English spellings for Leatherhead conformed to these developments. The other process may be illustrated by Avenbury in Herefordshire. This has naturally been suspected of containing the British river-name *aƀon*, and it is tentatively explained in that way in the *Concise Oxford Dictionary of English Place-Names* on the basis of a *Domesday Book* spelling *Aweneburi* and a 1242 form *Avenebiri*.[17] A fuller collection of spellings is now available, and these justify the *-w-* of the Domesday form and make it clear that there is no question of a river-name Avon in this compound.[18]

Revision of this kind is a constant requirement of place-name studies, as it is for any healthy discipline. Archaeological material is also subject to re-examination, reclassification and modification of dating, and historical manuscripts have their status constantly debated. Place-name scholars are entitled to revise their opinions about individual names without the soundness of the whole discipline being questioned because of it. There is a difference, however, between revision and revisionism, and I acknowledge that many of the disparaging and dismissive remarks in recent publications have been due to the latter process, particularly as applied to names of the Reading, Hastings, Birmingham type. For some scholars in related disciplines, the last straw seems to have been my reconsideration of Mucking. One of my favourite dismissive sentences is by Barry Cunliffe, who said in 1978 'place-name evidence is coarse-grained and still notoriously difficult to interpret with any degree of accuracy'.[19] The note to this reads 'See for example, Margaret Gelling, "The place-names of the Mucking area", *Panorama*, 19 (1975/6), pp. 7–20.' Predictably, this attempt to clarify Mucking upset Dr Myres also. In his book he comments: 'Doubts have recently been raised about the classification of Mucking as an *-ingas* name: since there are no spellings known before the Norman period, the matter must clearly be left open. But one cannot fail to note that the question would never have been raised at all had not the discovery of the very important early settlement and cemeteries at Mucking seemed to threaten the new notion that *-ingas* names were only given to secondary settlements: see Gelling . . .'[20]

This 'new notion' (as Dr Myres calls it) burst upon the world in 1966,

---

[17] E. Ekwall, *The Concise Dictionary of English Place-Names* (Oxford, 1936; 4th edn 1960), p. 19.

[18] In a collection of material made by Mr B. Coplestone-Crow. In the few remaining counties which, like Herefordshire, have no detailed place-name survey, there will be more need for re-classification than in counties for which the medieval material has been assembled.

[19] B. Cunliffe, 'Saxon Sussex: some problems and directions', in P. Brandon (ed.), *The South Saxons* (Chichester, 1978), pp. 221, 248.

[20] Myres, *The English Settlements*, p. 41, n. 1.

when John Dodgson published his famous article in *Medieval Archaeology*.[21] This was a long-overdue critical examination of the hypothesis (which dates back to 1850) that names of the Reading and Hastings type were the first to be bestowed on the settlements of Germanic immigrants. I am not going to rehearse the argument here. I have summarized it, I hope with reasonable clarity, in my book *Signposts to the Past*. One point which I think might have been stated more clearly is that we are not saying that folk-names like *Hæstingas* and *Rēadingas* were not in use among the Anglo-Saxons when they first came to this country. What we are saying is that the likely time for these ancient folk-names to be used as settlement-names is several generations after the first arrival, when settlements had expanded to the boundaries which separated the folk-groups from each other. A particularly clear instance is that of the *Rēadingas* and the *Sunningas* of the middle Thames. We know the extent of these people's territories from later historical evidence, and Reading and Sonning are adjacent settlements on either side of the boundary between them. These names should not be shown as dots on a map, as if they had the same value as pagan cemeteries in the pin-pointing of precise early settlement locations.

The discrepancies in distribution between -*ingas* names and pagan cemeteries were, of course, particularly well known to Dr Myres, and he discussed them in 1935, when reviewing the first edition of the Ordnance Survey's *Map of Britain in the Dark Ages*.[22] He advanced the theory that the absence of these names from some areas where the archaeological evidence was outstandingly rich, in particular the middle Thames, the Cambridge area, Lindsey and the Isle of Wight, could be due to warfare between rival Anglo-Saxon kingdoms in which these regions were devastated, so that villages had to be refounded, and the earliest place-names were forgotten.

There can obviously be no proof that the Oxford/Abingdon/Dorchester area was not once furnished with names of the Reading type, which were forgotten because the settlements they referred to were wiped out in war. But it is a hypothesis built on a hypothesis (since there is no independent proof that -*ingas* names do belong to the earliest settlement period); and it is questionable whether Dark Age power-struggles between kingdoms would involve this sort of devastation. It seems reasonable to consider the alternative possibility that some of the place-names which are actually found in the area go back to the fifth century. At least they should be studied with that possibility in mind, and consideration should be given to whether they are appropriate to the likely conditions of that century.

[21] J. Dodgson, 'The significance of the distribution of English place-names in -*ingas*, -*inga*- in south-east England', *Medieval Archaeology*, 10 (1966), pp. 1–29.

[22] J. N. L. Myres, Review in *Antiquity*, 9 (1935), pp. 455–64; Ordnance Survey, *Britain in the Dark Ages* (Southampton, 1935).

This leads to my next main point, which concerns the types of place-name which some of us now feel to be 'earlier' than the -*ingas* type. But before moving on to that, I should like to consider the charges of failure to agree with each other, and failure to be consistent in their views, which are levelled against 'experts' in place-name studies in this and other respects.

The extract from *The Penguin Guide to the Landscape of England and Wales* quoted in fn. 1 states that 'even the experts rarely agree'.[23] No account, however, is taken of the generation to which these experts belong. John Dodgson disagrees with Ekwall, Stenton and Myres about the significance of -*ingas* place-names;[24] but as there is agreement on the matter between John Dodgson, Kenneth Cameron and myself, this is not evidence for a subject in disarray. There are comparable swings of opinion in related disciplines. What about the date of Stonehenge? Or the origins of open-field agriculture? As far as I know, terms like 'far-fetched indulgence' are not applied to Bronze Age archaeology or to agrarian history on the grounds that present-day opinions on these matters are vastly different from those held fifty years ago.

As regards my critical look at Mucking, and its neighbour Fobbing, in the light of the archaeological discoveries of the 1960s, I would ask our critics to take account of the quantity of place-name material and the circumstances under which it has been studied. Faced with the task of producing a county survey, no scholar can spend too much time on any one name. And some place-name scholars are less critical than others. P. H. Reaney, who produced the Essex survey, was a man of vast industry and learning, but he was not noted for discrimination or judgement.[25] He made little attempt in the Essex volume to distinguish between the two types of Old English name that are represented by Barking and Clavering. Both types occur, though in smaller numbers, in Berkshire, and when I was working on the survey for Berkshire I became acutely aware of the importance of distinguishing them from each other. So when Margaret Jones asked me to review the place-name evidence that is associated with her great archaeological discoveries, I felt able to say that Fobbing (certainly) and Mucking (probably) consist of a noun or personal name followed by the singular place-name-forming suffix -*ing*, rather than the folk-name-forming suffix -*ingas*. I do not think that the argument is particularly obscure. I believe it to be highly desirable that archaeologists should ask place-name specialists

[23] Coones and Patten, *Penguin Guide*, p. 122.

[24] F. M. Stenton, whose best-known works include *Anglo-Saxon England* (Oxford, 1943, 3rd edn 1975), was also co-author of numerous English Place-Name Society county volumes between 1924 and 1952, namely vol. 1: *Introduction to the Survey of English Place-Names*, part I (Cambridge, 1924) and the county volumes of Buckinghamshire, Bedfordshire and Huntingdonshire, Worcestershire, Sussex, Devon, Northamptonshire, Surrey, Warwickshire, Hertfordshire, Wiltshire, Nottinghamshire, Middlesex and Cumberland.

[25] P. H. Reaney, *The Place-Names of Essex*, English Place-Name Society, vol. 12 (Cambridge, 1935).

for an up-to-date assessment of names in the vicinity of newly excavated sites, and I do not think that it should occasion shock/horror reactions when the focusing of attention on an area in these circumstances causes a suggestion to be made which is at variance with statements to be found in the *Oxford Dictionary of English Place-Names* or in the county volumes of the English Place-Name Society.

It is perhaps because the 'dictionary' element in place-name publication arouses false expectations that reactions of extreme irritation occur when new solutions are offered. People expect a definitive answer from a dictionary. But there was no way in which the opinions given in the early volumes of the place-name survey could have been definitive, and it should be remembered that Ekwall's *Oxford Dictionary* of 1960 is the fourth edition of a work first published in 1936, only twelve years after the beginning of the survey. Place-name study can only be scientific when it is based on a vast quantity of material, and the assembly of the material has been taking place over the last fifty years. Here, again, there is a close analogy with archaeology. We are entitled to ask scholars who use place-name books to note the date of publication, and to take it into account in the same way that they would if they were using a book dealing with archaeology or historical geography, or any other relatively young academic discipline. Dr Myres's new book bears the date 1986, but the discussion of place-names contained in it is to a considerable extent a reiteration of views formulated in the 1930s.

Ekwall's *Dictionary* is probably overdue for replacement. It is a very great work of scholarship, but at present it is possibly doing more harm than good. There has been a considerable quantity of new work since 1960, and a book that contains no account of any of this cannot be authoritative. There are also two specific respects in which Ekwall has always been seriously misleading. In dealing with the common formation in which -*ingtūn* is added to a personal name, he regards -*ingtūn* as an abbreviated form of -*ingatūn*, and he regularly interprets names of the Addington and Beddington type as 'settlement of Ædi's/Beadda's people'. This has never been accepted by English scholars. We have clear evidence for the use of -*ing*- as a connective particle in names of this type, and most place-name specialists would render Beddington as 'estate connected with a man named Beadda', which gives this large class of names a very different historical significance.[26] The other fault that permeates the book is Ekwall's uncritical acceptance of dates for spellings from Old English sources, some of which are centuries too early. An unwary user of the *Dictionary* could

---

[26] A dissentient view is held by Dr Gillian Fellows Jensen, who argues that in many of these names *tūn* was suffixed to earlier place-names which were formed by the addition of the place-name-forming suffix -*ing* to a noun or an adjective. An account of the various views taken about -*ingtūn* names, and the relevant bibliographical references, can be found in Gelling, *Signposts to the Past*, pp. 177–80.

conclude that Warwick is first mentioned in AD 723–37, which would be very misleading indeed. The *Dictionary* could probably have been revised, if Oxford University Press had pursued the matter with sufficient firmness; but it did not, and work has now started on a new Cambridge place-name dictionary, which should make it easier for everyone to obtain up-to-date information.

As regards my main theme, that of the chronological layers which can be discerned in place-names, I have so far expressed an opinion about the reliability of our evidence for prolonged contact between Anglo-Saxon immigrants and the people who were in this country before them, about the likely crystallization of the Reading and Hastings type of name, as used for settlements rather than groups of people, at the end of the immigration period, and about the importance of dissociating -*ingtūn* names from this type. I want now to look at current opinions concerning the earliest place-names coined by English speakers.

A landmark in this study was the publication in 1976 of Dr Barrie Cox's analysis of the 224 place-names that are recorded between *c.* AD 670 (when surviving records begin) and *c.* AD 730.[27] Doubt may fairly be expressed as to whether this material can be regarded as representative of the types of names in use in the fifth and sixth centuries. I believe it can, but there is a gap of more than two hundred years between the earliest extensive Anglo-Saxon settlements and the earliest surviving Anglo-Saxon charters, and theoretically many generations of place-names could have been coined, dropped out of use, and been replaced in that time. Between sixty and seventy of the names listed by Dr Cox have no modern equivalent, and there is later evidence which indicates that there continued to be a fairly high level of instability among place-names for some time after Dr Cox's cut-off date of AD 731. This being so, opinions based on these 224 names about the types of name likely to have been coined by Anglo-Saxon settlers between AD 450 and AD 500 can only be conjectures. But the list can be used as firm evidence that some types of place-name were just coming into fashion *c.* AD 730, and that other types were obsolescent at that date.

Any type that is extremely common in the whole corpus of English place-names, but is poorly represented in Dr Cox's material, presumably became fashionable after AD 730; and any type of name that is well represented there, but is not a common type otherwise, may be supposed to have been in use mainly before AD 730.

A particularly interesting feature of this collection of 224 names is the remarkably poor showing made by the two words that are by far the commonest of all English place-name elements: *tūn* and *lēah*. In the whole

[27] B. Cox, 'The place-names of the earliest English records', *English Place-Name Society Journal*, 8 (1976), pp. 12–66.

corpus of English place-names they are so common as to be virtually uncountable, but among names recorded by AD 731 there are only six containing *tūn* and seven containing *lēah*. In an article published in 1974, I advanced the hypothesis that *tūn* and *lēah* belonged to a middle period of Old English name-giving, because in the West Midlands (where they are in general the predominant types) they are scarce in regions likely to have been settled early by English speakers, and also in areas where agricultural exploitation is likely to have begun very late.[28] The results of Dr Cox's analysis have been generally accepted as confirming this suggestion. In the same article, I also suggested that many villages with names in -*tūn* in the West Midlands were likely to be anglicized survivals of Romano-British villages. Their names may have crystallized in the eighth and ninth centuries, but it is difficult to think of the settlements as new foundations of that period. There is, of course, the question (much debated at present) of whether there were any villages before the eighth century. There is also the problem of whether the village-names belonged originally to a central settlement or to the estate managed from it. But, skating over these problems, it seems to me probable that most of the -*tūn* names replaced earlier place-names at a fairly late date in the development of Anglo-Saxon society; and it is a reasonable hypothesis that the types of name that were replaced by *tūn* formations can be discerned in the material collected by Dr Cox.

These 224 names include at least 32 which are wholly pre-English, and at least 28 in which pre-English bases are compounded with Old English elements. This means that pre-English survival is represented in between a third and a quarter of the corpus, a very much higher proportion than is found in the place-names of England at later dates. A few of the place-names are in southern Scotland (Dunbar, Kinneil) or Wales (Bangor), so should not be counted for this purpose, and some allowance should be made for the bias of the sources. Nineteen of the names are recorded also in Romano-British sources, and a few of these, like *Durovernum* and *Verulamium*, may have been known only to learned ecclesiastics. But no matter how the figures are manipulated, the pre-English element in these 224 names remains significantly high, and it could be argued that the replacement of Primitive Welsh toponyms by English ones was still happening in AD 730.

There is a clear preponderance of the type of name which defines a settlement by describing its physical setting over the contrasting type, in which the main component is a term for a settlement. It is in this respect that I believe this collection of 224 names to be pointing to the nature of

---

[28] M. Gelling, 'Some notes on Warwickshire place-names', *Transactions of the Birmingham and Warwickshire Archaeological Society*, 86 (1974), pp. 59–79.

the earliest English settlement-names. I have written about this elsewhere, and I do not want to labour the point here.[29] There are several lines of enquiry which lead to the conclusion that topographical names are on the whole of greater antiquity than habitative names; and at the moment this is probably a matter of agreement among place-name specialists.

Can we be more precise about the types of topographical names likely to date back to the first use of English speech? Obviously, being topographical, they will vary from one region to another; but Dr Cox's analysis suggests that some words were particularly popular before AD 730. The word that features most prominently is *ēg*, 'island', a word for which I had already claimed special status on account of its frequency in north-west Berkshire. There are nineteen names recorded by AD 731 that contain *ēg*. Also well-represented are *burna*, *dūn*, *feld* and *ford*.

Again, some allowance needs to be made for the bias of the sources. The word *ēg* means 'island' (although its characteristic use in place-names is for a subcircular raised area in wet ground), and the predilection of early ecclesiastics for island sites will have increased the number of names containing this word that get mentioned in early records. But the islands on which early monasteries were situated, like Bardney, Bermondsey, Chertsey, Muchelney and Partney, had these names before the monasteries were founded. The word may score unfairly in comparison with terms for sites less likely to attract religious foundations, but it is nevertheless shown to have been a popular place-name-forming term at an early period.

In order to estimate the significance of these statistics, one needs other statistics with which to compare them. It would be very useful to have a collection and analysis of names recorded in the next slice of time, say AD 732–850. One form of comparison that can be made using the material to hand is that between the incidence of words in names recorded before AD 731 and their frequency in the 20,000 names included in Ekwall's *Dictionary*. For *ēg*, this yields significant results. I make the score in Ekwall about 180, which is low. And the word is not common in minor names or field-names, except in Cambridgeshire. If the use of this word in place-name formation had continued at the same sort of frequency after AD 731, it must have been more common than it is. It was probably the obsolescence of *ēg* in the sense 'dry ground in marsh' that caused a number of other words (*dūn*, *hamm*, *halh*, *hop*, Old Norse *holmr*) to be pressed into service to describe this type of settlement-site.

Judged by the same test, *dūn*, *feld* and *ford* appear to have remained more popular than *ēg* as place-name-forming terms. *Dūn* occurs six times in Dr Cox's material, and at least 350 times in Ekwall. For *feld*, the figures

---

[29] See, in particular, Gelling, *Signposts to the Past*, ch. 5, and Gelling, *Place-Names in the Landscape*, introduction.

are 10 and 250; for *ford* they are 9 and 550. *Ford* is probably the most frequently used topographical term in English place-names, apart from *lēah* (which occurs with a totally different order of frequency). I have discussed the possible significance of these words and of these statistics in considerable detail in *Place-Names in the Landscape*, and in the present context I wish only to adumbrate the possibilities of statistical analysis of place-name material. The work will be easier when we can take advantage of mechanical methods. A beginning at computerization will be made with the compilation of the new Cambridge dictionary.

Before leaving the discussion of the corpus of names recorded before AD 731, it is obviously desirable to enquire how the -*ingas* and -*ingahām* types appear in it. There are fourteen -*ingas* names, and twelve in which the genitive of an -*ingas* compound is followed by a place-name generic.[30] This establishes that such names were frequent in the period before AD 730, but it is surely not a large enough number to confirm the claim that this was the predominant type of place-name in the early years of the settlement. Of the fourteen -*ingas* names, nine belong to settlements or estates. The remaining five (Cunningham, Dent, *Feppingum*, *Stoppingas* and Sonning) are cited as names of regions. As far as we know, there never were settlements called *Fepping* or *Stopping*, and the regional name *Sunningas* may not have been used as a settlement-name until after the date of the foundation charter of Chertsey Abbey, in which it is mentioned. There are a few instances of the connective use of -*ing*-, but (and this was the only respect in which the results were disappointing from my point of view) no instance of the place-name-forming suffix -*ing*, as used in Clavering, Essex.

I said earlier that it would be reasonable to look at the place-names that are found in an area where we have archaeological evidence for an early Anglo-Saxon presence, and to consider whether they seem appropriate to the period of the pagan burials and early dwelling sites. As regards the Oxford/Abingdon/Dorchester region, and the area of south central Essex that centres on Mucking, I am satisfied that this criterion is fulfilled. In both areas there is a heavy preponderance, among the major place-names, of topographical over habitative types, and the topographical names form closely-linked thematic groups.

The Berkshire/Oxfordshire group contains a high number of compounds with *ford* and *īeg* (the West Saxon form of *ēg*). Only a few of the fords are major river-crossings, like Oxford and Wallingford. Most (like Frilford, Garford, Hatford and Stanford) refer to crossing-places on tiny streams, which were canalized and used as drainage channels. The names of these tiny brooks are used with surprising frequency as settlement-

---

[30] Dr Cox classifies Dengie, Essex, as an -*inga*- name, but this is, in my opinion, better explained as a compound of the personal name *Dene*, connective -*ing*-, and *ēg*.

names. Balking, Ginge, Lockinge, Wantage, Childrey, Hendred and Hagbourne are in this category. The first four names in that list are formed by the addition of the singular suffix -*ing* to a word describing the stream; I should have liked independent confirmation that this is an early type of name, but this was not provided by the material recorded before AD 731. There is a marked emphasis in this group on the value of dry sites for villages, on the problems of communication between neighbouring villages, and on the importance of the small streams that drain the farmland. It is reasonable to see these as names bestowed by the first English farmers who tackled the area and who perhaps found it swampy after a period of neglect. The more dignified names, like Kingston and Buckland, are obviously of later origin, as is Fyfield ('estate assessed at five hides'), and the Steventon, Milton, Sutton group may date from after the foundation of Abingdon Abbey (from which Sutton, actually the northernmost of the three, is the 'south estate').

Further south in Berkshire, and in the adjacent part of Wiltshire, we can prove that habitative names like Woolstone, Uffington (plate VIII) and Aughton were replacing topographical names like *Æscesbyrig* (plate IX) (*byrig* here being a hillfort) and Collingbourne in the second half of the tenth century. In south Gloucestershire we have evidence for the replacement of Colne, in one of the estates named from that river, by the habitative name Bibury in the mid-eighth century (*byrig* here being 'manor-house').[31]

Topographical names are even more characteristic of south central Essex than they are of north-west Berkshire. Of twenty-five parish-names which surround Mucking, only four could possibly be considered habitative. Six of the topographical names have as generic the word *dūn*, emphasizing the fact that the most desirable sites are raised above the marshes that border the Thames.

During the years that followed the rejection of the theory that -*ingas* compounds denoted the earliest English place-names, some attempts were made to find another clearly defined category to fill the vacancy. In retrospect, this does not appear a profitable exercise. With the publication of Dr Gordon Copley's study, *Archaeology and Place-Names in the Fifth and Sixth Centuries*, we are released from this search, as Dr Copley has demonstrated that no such category exists.[32] He has compiled a comprehensive list of fifth- and sixth-century archaeological sites in Saxon and Jutish areas of settlement, and studied the place-names in a ten-mile radius round each of the fifth-century sites. Here we have, for the first time, a thorough

[31] See Gelling, *Signposts to the Past*, pp. 123–5, 180–3 for details about the origins of these names.
[32] G. Copley, *Archaeology and Place-Names in the Fifth and Sixth Centuries*, British Archaeological Reports, British series, 147 (Oxford, 1986).

73

PLATE VIII: *The village of Uffington in the Vale of the White Horse, now in Oxfordshire.*
© Della Hooke.

investigation of names associated with early Anglo-Saxon archaeology. Dr Copley says in his introduction, 'all in all, the tentative conclusions reached in this study are disappointingly negative', but I find them wonderfully liberating.

It is demonstrated that no place-name type has a significant overall correspondence with early Anglo-Saxon archaeology. The suffix *-ingas* does better than the habitative term *hām*, but both make a poor showing. *Tūn* is prominent. Dr Copley thinks we should give *tūn* greater credence as an early place-name element, but I think its frequent correspondence with early sites may only be a side-effect of a large-scale replacement of early topographical names by *-tūn* compounds. Topographical names in Dr Copley's lists are in general much more frequent than habitative ones, in spite of the numerous *-tūn* names.

Dr Copley does not say this, but it seems to me possible that it is the natural variation in topographical names between different regions that prevents any one type emerging as having a close overall association with early archaeology. I feel that we should look for dominant topographical themes in the place-names of areas with early Anglo-Saxon burials or settlements, and if these emerge, and if they reflect concerns which would be appropriate for the first English-speaking farmers in the area, it is more likely than not that such names were coined at a very early stage in the settlement.

One point that emerges significantly from Dr Copley's study of names in the ten-mile radius of each fifth-century site is that the heterogeneous category which he labels 'pre-English, etc.' is well represented. This category includes all Celtic names and some river-names that are suspected of being pre-Celtic. It also includes names containing Latin loan-words, and those which make specific reference to Welsh people. Dr Copley comments (p. 74) 'if any correlation is to be found between types of place-names and the earliest Saxon settlements, it is in this broad category of place-names'. There is, of course, a vast quantity of fascinating detail in Dr Copley's material, and in his discussion of it; and I hope that the mention here of a few points brought out by the study will encourage people to make their own evaluation of it, and to give it the careful attention which it deserves.

The quotations I have used for target practice in this paper are characterized by a tone of impatience unusual in scholarly utterances which reach the stage of publication. There is a feeling of disappointed expectations, without any consideration of whether the expectations were justified. Perhaps a previous generation of place-name scholars aroused

PLATE IX: *Uffington Camp, the Æscesbyrig of the charters, and the Ridge Way which follows the crest of the north Berkshire Downs.*
© Della Hooke.

these expectations by the magisterial tone of their writings. Perhaps it is due to the setting-out of the material in dictionary form. However that may be, place-name specialists have a right to expect specialists in other aspects of early English history to appreciate the basic principles of the subject, and to keep up with developments in it, in the same way as I try to keep up with developments in archaeology and historical geography.

Place-name evidence is extremely valuable. I disagree strongly with Barry Cunliffe's epithet 'coarse-grained'. Could a coarse medium have preserved the message now seen to be contained in the name Aldwych? Or produced the now commonplace relationship between field-names that refer to ancient remains and the incidence of archaeological discoveries? Place-names have a precision, a subtlety and a depth of meaning which we are only just beginning to perceive. It will be a pity if archaeologists and historical geographers turn away from this source of knowledge because the subject is not static. They should have been more worried about it in the years before 1966 (when John Dodgson launched his 'new notion'). It *was* relatively static for a considerable period before that. It is much healthier now.

4

Towards a Model of Anglo-Scandinavian Rural Settlement in England

TIM UNWIN

10M. In Ættune 10 thegns had each his hall
Domesday Book, fo. 284b

Introduction

The aim of this chapter is to highlight key questions relating to rural settlements, fields and boundaries in England between the fifth and eleventh centuries, and to suggest ways in which changes in these features can be explained. The central problem it addresses concerns the reorganization of settlement that took place between the end of the Roman era and the twelfth century.

Three fundamental propositions underlie the arguments that follow. The first is that it is not possible to separate the study of settlements, fields and boundaries. If we seek to understand any one element in the rural landscape, it is necessary to analyse how it was integrated into the wider agrarian organization of which it was a part. The second proposition is that these surface features of the past were essentially the products of continually changing economic, social, political and ideological structures which underlay them. This implies that explanations for settlement change will never be found from within the artefactual remains of Anglo-Saxon settlements themselves. Rather, we must search for explanation in the structural transformations giving rise to that surface expression of settlement change. The third proposition is that to understand what happened to settlements in England between AD 400 and 1100 we must know in some considerable detail the nature of the settlements and field systems with which the incoming Anglo-Saxons and Scandinavians were familiar in their own countries.

I am particularly grateful to Mats Widgren for his comments on an earlier draft of this paper, to him and Ulf Sporrong for introducing me to the Viking landscapes of Sweden, and to H.-J. Nitz and J. D. H. Harten for introducing me to the Anglo-Saxon landscapes of northern Germany and the Netherlands.

This chapter therefore explores the reasons why changes took place in the organization of settlements in England between AD 400 and 1100. Rather than presenting a formal model as a simplifed description of a past reality, it seeks to move towards such a model through an analysis of a number of possible explanations of empirically observable change. It begins with a broad review of the evidence concerning the shift within England from a dispersed pattern of settlement to a more nucleated one, culminating in a discussion of a series of questions resulting from the author's research in Derbyshire and Nottinghamshire. From this discussion, basic issues concerning settlements, field systems and boundaries are then examined in the light of research in Germany and Scandinavia.

The Emergence of a Nucleated Pattern of Settlement

One starting point for a discussion of the processes by which nucleated villages came into existence in England is Taylor's paper on polyfocal settlement.[1] Here he argues that many nucleated villages once had more than one focus and that in several cases these foci can be traced back to eleventh-century manors. Taylor does not, though, seek to explain this change through recourse to underlying transformations in the economic or social structure.

Working in Northumberland, Durham and Yorkshire, Roberts and Sheppard have also suggested that there is evidence of extensive reorganization of settlements giving rise to regular two-row or green villages during the late eleventh and twelfth centuries.[2] Similar findings have been reported by Faull, and based on the limited archaeological evidence available for Yorkshire, she suggests that 'the picture in Late Anglo-Saxon times was probably one of small dispersed farms dotted over the landscape in each vill, rather than one nucleated settlement per vill'.[3]

Elsewhere in Britain, Hall, working on the field systems and settlements of Saxon Northamptonshire, has argued for a far earlier date for the shift from a dispersed to a nucleated pattern of settlement, suggesting that

---

[1] C. Taylor, 'Polyfocal settlement and the English village', *Medieval Archaeology*, 21 (1977), pp. 189–93.

[2] B. K. Roberts, 'Village plans in County Durham: a preliminary statement', *Medieval Archaeology*, 16 (1972), pp. 33–56; B. K. Roberts, 'Rural settlement in County Durham: forms, pattern and system', in D. Green, C. Haselgrove and M. Spriggs (eds), *Social Organisation and Settlement* (Oxford, 1978), pp. 291–322; B. K. Roberts, *Rural Settlement: An Historical Perspective* (Norwich, 1982); J. A. Sheppard, 'Pre-enclosure field and settlement patterns in an English township, Wheldrake, near York', *Geografiska Annaler*, 48B (1966), pp. 59–77; J. A. Sheppard, 'Medieval village planning in northern England', *Journal of Historical Geography*, 2 (1976), pp. 3–20. See also P. Allerston, 'English village development: findings from the Pickering district of north Yorkshire', *Transactions of the Institute of British Geographers*, 51 (1970), pp. 95–108.

[3] M. L. Faull, 'Roman and Anglo-Saxon settlement patterns in Yorkshire: a computer-generated analysis', *Landscape History*, 5 (1983), p. 29.

between AD 650 and 850 'a landscape consisting of numerous small settlements was rearranged to form fewer large villages'.[4] Linking together agrarian and settlement change, he argues that 'it is likely that the laying out of the open fields was substantially completed during the eighth and ninth centuries, continued pressure leading to their subdivision before the Norman Conquest'.[5]

Other writers have suggested a variety of dates between the seventh and eleventh centuries for a reorganization of settlements and fields. Aston, working in Somerset, has thus argued that nucleated villages developed out of an earlier more dispersed pattern of settlement, and that 'on balance, villages seem to be of possibly late Saxon or, more probably, early medieval date'.[6] Likewise for Oxfordshire, Bond has suggested that 'the large nucleated village . . . can no longer be viewed as the medium by which the first English settlers colonized a sparsely-populated wilderness. It now appears to be the result of a reorganization carried out in the late Saxon, or perhaps even post-Conquest, period, which took place within a pre-existing framework of much older estates'.[7]

In Hampshire, work done at Chalton, and more recently elsewhere in the county, again indicates settlement reorganization in the Saxon period, with Hughes arguing that Cunliffe's model for a mid-Saxon settlement shift from hilltop sites to valley settlements is supported to some extent, 'though with a possible second settlement change taking place between the eighth and eleventh centuries, when a pattern of nucleated villages and small dispersed hamlets or farms was established'.[8]

A final regional example of settlement reorganization is provided by Hooke's work on the West Midlands. Here she argues that 'village nucleation, associated with a form of open field agriculture, seems . . . to have been a relatively early feature of settlement history'.[9] She adds further that 'Pre-Conquest reorganization of both fields and settlement, whether it developed gradually or as a result of deliberate seigneurial control, seems to

---

[4] D. N. Hall, 'Late Saxon topography and early medieval estates', in D. Hooke (ed.), *Medieval Villages: A Review of Current Work*. Oxford University Committee for Archaeology, Monograph No. 5 (Oxford, 1985).

[5] D. N. Hall, 'The origins of open-field agriculture – the archaeological fieldwork evidence', in R. T. Rowley (ed.), *The Origins of Open Field Agriculture* (London, 1981), p. 38. See also H. S. A. Fox, 'Approaches to the adoption of the Midland system', in Rowley (ed.), *Origins of Open Field Agriculture*, pp. 64–111.

[6] M. A. Aston, 'Rural settlement in Somerset: some preliminary thoughts', in Hooke (ed.), *Medieval Villages*, p. 81.

[7] C. J. Bond, 'Medieval Oxfordshire villages and their topography: a preliminary discussion', in Hooke (ed.), *Medieval Villages*, p. 109.

[8] M. Hughes, 'Rural settlement and landscape in late Saxon Hampshire', in M. L. Faull (ed.), *Studies in Late Anglo-Saxon Settlement* (Oxford, 1984), p. 76; B. Cunliffe, 'Saxon and medieval settlement patterns in the region of Chalton, Hampshire', *Medieval Archaeology*, 16 (1972), pp. 1–12.

[9] D. Hooke, 'Village development in the West Midlands', in Hooke (ed.), *Medieval Villages*, p. 134.

have taken place on a larger scale, however, only in areas where there was already a high population density, a large amount of cleared land and powerful leadership'.[10]

On the above evidence, it is apparent that in many parts of England there was a reorganization of settlement and field systems between AD 650 and 1100, and that the precise date of the change varied between different parts of the country. This gives rise to the question of whether or not the differences in date of this settlement reorganization represent differences in response to a common set of problems, or whether they reflect particular local circumstances in different parts of England. Explanations in terms of common solutions can broadly be divided into two categories: demographic and political. Thus, several authors, including Hall and Hooke, have intimated that the reorganization of a dispersed pattern of farms, each with their own infield, into a pattern of nucleated villages associated with a communal field system partly represented a response to an increase in population.[11] If this was so, differences in the date of this reorganization could reflect varying dates of population growth in different parts of England. This alternative, nevertheless, still begs the question as to why some areas had a denser population in the first place, and what then caused the population growth. The second type of common-solution explanation suggests that reorganization was a response to increasing political control by a centralized polity. Such an argument lies behind some of Roberts's and Sheppard's explanations of the reorganization that took place in northern England, and it is also mentioned by Hall in the context of increasing royal and ecclesiastical taxation in the south Midlands.[12]

In contrast to this type of explanation, though, are arguments positing that different series of processes operated in various parts of England during the period in question. In particular, it might be argued that the Anglo-Saxons and Scandinavians each introduced their own cultural influences into the areas where they achieved dominance. Differences in the date of settlement reorganization could thus be caused largely by the differences in cultural background of the populations in question.

Neither of these two broad types of explanation need be exclusive, and in order to investigate their relative importance the ensuing section looks at the evidence concerning fields, boundaries and settlements in Derbyshire and Nottinghamshire, an area influenced in turn by the Romans, the Anglo-Saxons and the Scandinavians, in an attempt to unravel the questions highlighted above.

[10] Ibid.

[11] Hall, 'Origins of open-field agriculture'; Hall, 'Late Saxon topography'; D. Hooke, *The Anglo-Saxon Landscape: The Kingdom of the Hwicce* (Manchester, 1985).

[12] Hall, 'Origins of open-field agriculture'; Roberts, 'Rural settlement'; Sheppard, 'Medieval village planning'.

Nottinghamshire and Derbyshire:
Settlements, Fields and Boundaries

Settlements

The fundamental characteristic of settlements in Derbyshire and Nottinghamshire in the eleventh century was that most townships had a multiplicity of manors within them, and in cases where it is possible to trace the probable locations of the halls associated with each manor, these are often dispersed within the area of the township.[13] At least five main possible processes could have given rise to this situation (figure 4.1):

1 when the township area was laid out it enclosed the lands of several distinct farms or settlement units which already existed at dispersed locations within the area;

2 the township boundary was agreed upon by several immigrant farmers, who then located their farms/settlements at dispersed locations within the area;

3 following population increase, internal colonization took place from an initial single settlement within a township, giving rise to 'daughter' settlements within the township's boundary;

4 partible inheritance led to the subdivision of a township and the creation of separate settlements/farms within it;

5 dispersal of settlement took place from an initial nucleated settlement within each township.

One critical issue that arises in discussing these issues concerns the interpretation of *Domesday Book* entries that mention several manors in a given township. It is thus frequently not known whether each such manor had its own hall, and, if so, where these halls were located. The only real answer to this question would be for a comprehensive archaeological survey of such a township to be undertaken in which dates could be obtained for the origin of each of the halls mentioned. A further problem also arises over the extent to which each hall complex might be considered to be a separate 'settlement', and it is therefore important to clarify precisely what is meant by the term 'settlement'. In the present context, the most pertinent definition for a settlement would appear to be a functional one in which it is asserted that a rural settlement was a group of buildings whose inhabitants cultivated a discrete area of arable land within a clearly delimited territory.

---

[13] P. T. H. Unwin, 'Patterns and hierarchies of rural settlement in Nottinghamshire before 1700' (unpublished Ph.D. thesis, University of Durham, 1979).

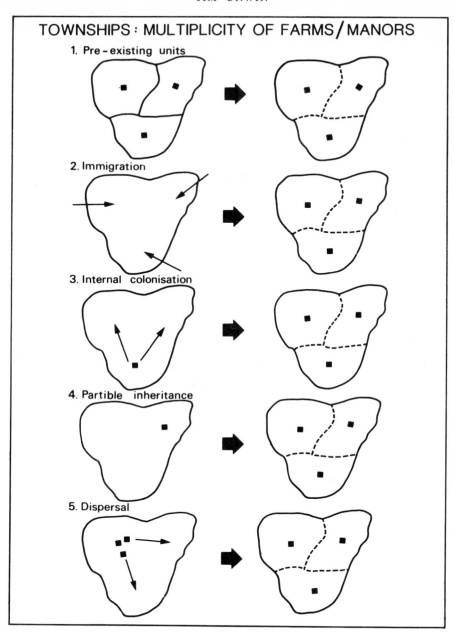

FIGURE 4.1 *Townships:*
multiplicity of farms/manors

With these observations in mind, it is salient to analyse in which parts of the region in question were found the greatest density of townships within which there were several manors. In general, these areas are to be found in the east and south of Nottinghamshire along the Trent valley, and in south-west Derbyshire near the river Dove. Although the dearth of archaeological evidence dating from the Anglo-Saxon and Scandinavian period in these counties makes it difficult to reach any firm conclusions concerning the relative distribution of settlement at different times during this period, when considered together with the place-name evidence it does seem to be the case that the townships with the greatest multiplicity of manors were, in general, in the areas first occupied by the Anglo-Saxons.[14] This suggests either that subsequent subdivision was found most frequently in areas that had been settled for the longest time by Anglo-Saxon and Scandinavian immigrants, or that the earliest Anglo-Saxon settlers tended to create several farms or settlements within each township-sized territory they created.

Boundaries

In a recent major study, Stafford has argued that one of the key elements for understanding the history of the East Midlands is its division into large early estates. Using Jones's multiple-estate model and basing part of her analysis on the work of Bishop, she argues that most of Nottinghamshire and Derbyshire was divided into large estates in which 'townships, settlements and hamlets were organized around the lord's hall and their populations provided tribute and dues'.[15] She goes on to assert that 'the origins of this system lie back beyond the Ango-Saxon period' and that 'between the eighth and eleventh centuries, and especially in the ninth and tenth, these ancient estates underwent a process of fragmentation'.[16] Stafford essentially sees pre-Saxon estates consisting of single village townships surviving to form major territorial units and boundaries in the tenth-century. The multiplicity of manors and the presence of berewicks and sokeland in townships is then seen as a result of the fragmentation of these large estates mainly during the ninth and tenth centuries. Unfortunately Stafford pays negligible attention to the crucial issue of multiplicity of settlement within townships, nor does she consider the origins of the townships themselves.

[14] Trent Valley Archaeological Research Committee, *Gazetteer of Sites in Derbyshire and Nottinghamshire* (Nottingham, 1979); K. Cameron, *Scandinavian Settlement in the Territory of the Five Boroughs: The Place-Name Evidence*, Inaugural lecture, University of Nottingham (1965); K. Cameron, 'Scandinavian settlement in the territory of the Five Boroughs: the place-name evidence, part II, place-names in thorp', *Medieval Scandinavia*, 3 (1970), pp. 35–49; K. Cameron, 'Scandinavian settlement in the territory of the Five Boroughs: the place-name evidence, part III, the Grimston-hybrids', in P. Clemoes and K. Hughes (eds), *England Before the Conquest: Studies in Primary Sources Presented to Dorothy Whitelock* (Cambridge, 1971), pp. 147–63; P. T. H. Unwin, 'The Anglo-Saxon and Scandinavian occupation of Nottinghamshire and Derbyshire', *Journal of the English Place-Name Society*, 14 (1982), pp. 1–31.

[15] P. Stafford, *The East Midlands in the Early Middle Ages* (Leicester, 1985), p. 30; G. R. Jones, 'Multiple estates and early settlement', in P. H. Sawyer (ed.), *Medieval Settlement: Continuity and Change* (London, 1976), pp. 15–40; M. W. Bishop, 'Multiple estates in late Anglo-Saxon Nottinghamshire', *Transactions of the Thoroton Society of Nottinghamshire*, 85 (1982), pp. 37–47.

[16] Stafford, *The East Midlands*, p. 30.

This image of settlement evolution conflicts with the evidence indicating a change from a dispersed pattern of Anglo-Saxon settlement to a more nucleated one during the ninth and tenth centuries. To resolve this issue it is of fundamental importance to date the origins of the townships in the area and to evaluate the evidence for the existence of pre-Saxon estates which are supposed to have continued largely in use until the tenth century. What evidence there is in Nottinghamshire and Derbyshire, in the form of Anglo-Saxon charters, suggests that the boundaries of at least some townships, and thus most probably the townships themselves, were in existence in the mid-tenth century, but it is difficult firmly to prove their existence before this date.[17] A comparison of the distribution of probable Roman fields and the distribution of medieval township boundaries in north-west Nottinghamshire does, however, suggest that in this area at least the township boundaries were not in existence in the Roman period.[18] If the township boundaries of Nottinghamshire are considered, it is interesting to note that it is precisely in the north-west of the county that large and irregular townships are found, in contrast to the rest of the country, where a more 'organized' distribution of townships is apparent. In particular, the township boundaries in the east and south, on either side of the river Trent, can be noted as having a decidedly planned appearance.

If the townships near the Trent and in south-east Nottinghamshire were indeed planned, then four main possible dates would seem possible for their planning:

1. the whole area could have been divided into township-like units in the Roman period;
2. the incoming Anglo-Saxons in the fifth and early sixth centuries could have laid out new township units, based in places on older Roman boundaries;
3. once Anglo-Saxon kingdoms had become firmly established by the seventh and eighth centuries, a series of townships could then have been delimited to 'tidy up' the landscape and provide a basis for taxation and the reorganization of agriculture;
4. the townships could represent the Scandinavian sharing out of Mercia in AD 877.

Of these dates, the second seems to be the most likely. The first founders on the evidence already cited concerning the north-west of the county, and also because there is no clear relationship between the Roman archaeo-

[17] G. T. Davies, 'The Anglo-Saxon boundaries of Sutton and Scrooby, Nottinghamshire', *Transactions of the Thoroton Society of Nottinghamshire*, 87 (1983), pp. 13–22; P. Lyth, 'The Southwell charter of 956: an exploration of its boundaries', *Transactions of the Thoroton Society of Nottinghamshire*, 86 (1982), pp. 49–61.

[18] P. T. H. Unwin, 'Townships and early fields in north Nottinghamshire', *Journal of Historical Geography*, 9 (1983), pp. 341–6.

logical finds in the county and township boundaries. The fourth possible date is also unlikely, because this area was already apparently extensively settled by the Anglo-Saxons by the ninth century, and it is highly probable that by then they would have introduced some form of territorial organization within which to rationalize their agrarian practices. In deciding between the remaining two possibilities, the impression that these boundaries were laid out from the Trent and the other main rivers in the area suggests that, if these were the early lines of access into the area for the Anglo-Saxons, then it may well have been during the early Saxon period that these townships were initially laid out, with each perhaps being the land belonging to a single farm.

The sixth- and seventh-century devastations of population in England nevertheless complicate the issue. If the major population decline noted by Cunliffe began to take place in the fifth century, which Todd considers unlikely, then the early Anglo-Saxons would have been moving into an area that had already encountered a population decline.[19] They could therefore have chosen to have concentrated in the areas near the Trent, which they might have laid out afresh, as suggested above. Nevertheless, if the population remained high during the fifth century, then there might well have been a boundary reorganization following a subsequent demographic crisis.

Whatever the origins of the townships, there is no clear evidence that large estates existed in these counties during the Roman period and survived through to the Saxon era, when they then became subdivided into townships. The onus remains on those who see the remains of estates in the tenth and eleventh centuries to prove that they existed here in the third and fourth centuries. To understand the functional integration between the settlement sites and boundaries already discussed, it is now essential to turn to the agrarian organization of the region.

Fields

The evidence for the existence of Anglo-Saxon and Scandinavian fields in Derbyshire and Nottinghamshire is negligible, and much concerning the nature of the agrarian organization here must be adduced from earlier and later periods. Three features, though, seem to shine through the haze of uncertainty.

The first of these is that the Roman system of agriculture failed to survive through into the late Anglo-Saxon period. This is clearly evidenced by Riley's work on the field systems of south Yorkshire and north

[19] B. Cunliffe, 'Settlement and population in the British Iron Age: some facts, figures and fantasies', in B. Cunliffe and T. R. Rowley (eds), *Lowland Iron Age Communities* (Oxford, 1978); M. Todd, 'Famosa Pestis and Britain in the fifth century', *Britannia*, 8 (1977), pp. 319–25.

Nottinghamshire.[20] It seems logical to argue that settlements and estate boundaries are fundamentally a product of the agrarian economy at any given time. Thus the location of a villa and the boundaries of the Roman estate of which it was the centre would be intimately linked to the type of agriculture and field system in use in the Roman period. If the agrarian economy changed, then there is no reason why the new settlement sites and the associated boundaries of fields and estates should necessarily have remained the same.

The second general observation that can be made is that in much of Derbyshire and Nottinghamshire there is good evidence that at least by the twelfth century a system of agriculture had been developed whereby each township had its own arable fields, and its inhabitants cultivated these with a certain degree of communal agreement. The fundamental feature is that most townships therefore had their own communal field systems regardless of the pattern of settlement within them. From this observation, it is possible to envisage four different scenarios concerning the relationships between fields, settlements and township boundaries (figure 4.2):

1 every township from its creation always had a unified field system, regardless of the subsequent pattern of settlement within it;
2 the unified field system was created at some date from the reorganization of individual small field systems each associated with an individual farm/settlement within the township's boundaries;
3 there had only ever been a single settlement and a single field system within each township;
4 an initial single settlement and field system within each township had at some time become subdivided and then by the twelfth century it had been reunited or regrouped again.

The third broad observation is that if there was a change in agrarian organization between the fourth century and the twelfth century, then this must in some way have been associated with the Anglo-Saxon and Scandinavian immigrants to England during this time period, and that their activities are also likely to have had a significant influence on the patterns of settlements and boundaries in the counties. To relegate their activities to those of mere adapters, as does Stafford, is to swing the balance too far from cataclysm to continuity. To understand the agrarian changes that did take place in England, and their repercussions for settlement, we must move away from a simple view of 'continuity' and begin to understand the rural economy and society of northern Germany and Scandinavia.

---

[20] D. N. Riley, *Early Landscapes from the Air: Studies of Crop Marks in South Yorkshire and North Nottinghamshire* (Sheffield, 1980); Unwin, 'Townships and early fields'.

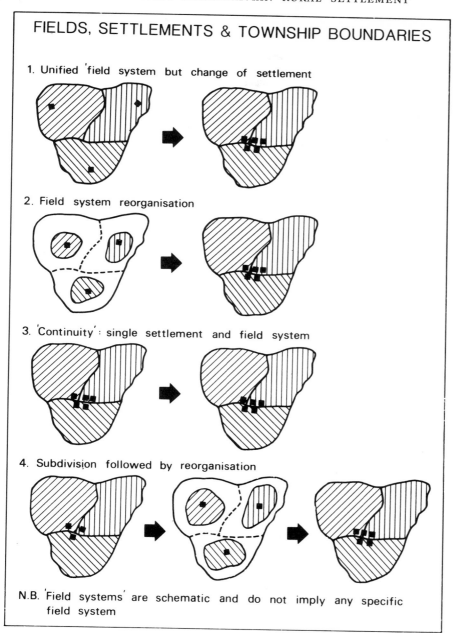

FIGURE 4.2 *Fields, settlements and township boundaries. 'Field systems' are schematic and do not imply any specific field system*

Northern Germany: Fields, Settlements and Boundaries

Although a considerable amount is now known about the economy and society of Ottonian Saxony, very much less is understood concerning the economic structure of northern Germany in the fifth century. Meitzen's suggestion that the original German settlement form was the nucleated village (*Haufendörfer*) with open fields (*Gewannflur*) is no longer accepted. It seems instead that in northern Germany there was a previous form of settlement consisting of 'the small hamlet (*Drubbel*) and the long-strip field pattern (*Langstreifenflur*) on the infield (*Esch*)'.[21] In addition, in the *Marsch* areas along the shores of the North Sea, which were subject to flooding, settlements were established on man-made mounds, known in German as *Wurten* or *Warfen*, and in the Netherlands as *Terpen* (plate X). This system of *Langstreifenflur* on the *Esch* was in turn probably predated by an earlier pattern where the fields were organized into blocks.

What seems likely to have happened in the region north-west of Oldenburg, between the Weser and the Ems, is that in the late Iron Age and Roman era the densest settlement was found in the *Marsch* and *Geest* area. Increased flooding in the coastal areas then led to the relocation of farms here on *Wurten*. However, in the fifth and sixth centuries this was followed by a substantial collapse of the economy and desertion of settlement. It seems likely that the reoccupation of the *Wurten* and the firm establishment of hamlets based on the *Esch* economy took place later, once centralized feudal power had become established. According to Nitz (personal communication), this *Esch* economy with its associated strip fields might well date from as late as the ninth and tenth centuries.

In all probability the 'Anglo-Saxons' who came to Britain during the fifth and sixth centuries were familiar with two types of settlement. On the one hand, there were the small dispersed settlements, many of which will have been no larger than individual farm complexes, each with its own small fields. On the other hand, there were also the varied mound settlements, the *Wurten/Terpen*, some of which were individual in nature and others of which included several farms. One crucial question, though, still remains to be answered. This concerns the social structure underlying both types of settlement, and the extent to which villages consisting of several family groups, or individual family farms, predominated.

The evidence for the introduction of either of these two settlement/field complexes into England is limited. However, three broad conclusions can be drawn. First, the construction of *Wurten/Terpen* was not widespread, although some have recently been reported from eastern Lincolnshire by Hall (personal communication). The second feature to recall is that the Anglo-Saxons would have brought with them a framework both of villages and of individual farmsteads, and it may well be asked how different these were from the Romano-British villages and small farms that they found here. Thirdly, it seems probable that the main Anglo-Saxon settlement of England occurred before the establishment of communal open-field strip

---

[21] A. Mayhew, *Rural Settlement and Farming in Germany* (London, 1973), p. 18.

PLATE X: *Terp village, near Jever, Lower Saxony, northern Germany.*
© Tim Unwin.

farming in north-west Germany. In Hall's work on Northamptonshire, he specifically draws attention to Nitz's observation that planned villages and long strips in Germany seem to be dated to the period AD 775–850.[22] On this evidence, there may well therefore have been a parallel development in England and Germany of a new field and settlement system during the eighth century.

Scandinavian Settlement and Agriculture in the Ninth and Tenth Centuries

The first Scandinavian raids to England, according to the *Anglo-Saxon Chronicle*, took place following the year AD 787, but it was only in the

[22] Hall, 'Late Saxon topography'; H.-J. Nitz, 'Feudal woodland colonization as a strategy of the Carolingian Empire in the conquest of Saxony', in B. K. Roberts and R. E. Glasscock (eds), *Villages, Fields and Frontiers*, British Archaeological Reports, International series, -S185 (Oxford, 1983).

850s that Scandinavians first wintered here and in the 870s that they began to settle and cultivate English soil.[23]

It appears that the settlement and agrarian history of the Jutland peninsula in Denmark represents an extension of the processes already identified in the context of northern Germany. At the time of the Scandinavian raids on Britain, the most common form of settlement in Denmark was probably that of small, 'mobile' villages, associated with numerous dispersed single farmsteads.[24] This would suggest that the process of nucleation, already noted in northern Germany at an earlier period, was also taking place in Jutland, possibly as a result of increasing political centralization at a time of growing population, which gave rise to a reorganization of the agrarian economy and settlement pattern.

It is when attention is paid to Norway and Sweden, however, that a marked contrast is noted. Here, it is evident that even in the ninth century a pattern of dispersed farmsteads predominated in much of the area. For south-west Norway, Myhre has identified three broad phases in the evolution of settlement and agrarian organization:

1 *Pre-Roman Iron Age and early Roman* (500 BC–AD 200). There was a variety of settlement types, with some villages having 15–20 houses, and others being very much smaller; fields were irregular.

2 *Late Roman and Migration period* (AD 200–500). Farms with an infield surrounded by a wall came into use, and there was continuous use of farmhouses for perhaps 200–300 years.

3 *Late Iron Age and early Medieval period* (AD 500–1350). This seems to represent an extension of the previous pattern, with larger walled infields coming into existence and cultivated fields being found on special areas near the farmhouses. The most common settlement type was the self-supporting farm.[25]

On the basis of this archaeological evidence, as well as that of the later sagas, and in particular the *Orkneyinga Saga*, it would seem that during the two centuries of Norwegian settlement in Britain the settlement type with which the immigrants were most familiar in their own country was probably one of individual farms, each with their own independent fields.[26]

A similar pattern is revealed from recent archaeological work in Sweden.

[23] *The Anglo-Saxon Chronicle. Two of the Saxon Chronicles Parallel*, edited by C. Plummer (Oxford, 1892–9), pp. 54–5.

[24] K. Randsborg, *The Viking Age in Denmark: the Formation of a State* (London, 1980); E. Roesdahl, *Viking Age Denmark* (London, 1982).

[25] B. Myhre, 'Agrarian development, settlement history, and social organisation in southwest Norway in the Iron Age', in K. Kristiansen and C. Paludan-Müller (eds), *New Directions in Scandinavian Archaeology* (Copenhagen, 1978).

[26] *The Orkneyinga Saga: The History of the Earls of Orkney*, translated with an introduction by H. Palsson and P. Edwards (Harmondsworth, 1978).

The overwhelming picture from this research is one of dispersed settlements gradually becoming united into a communal system of farming by the end of the Viking period. As Sporrong has argued for the Mälar basin, it is likely that by about the ninth century farming units had been merged into villages, although most of the villages at this time were very small, seldom being larger than two to five farms.[27] The work of Widgren on Östergötland indicates that

stone-wall complexes were established in the first few centuries AD. Settlement then consisted of single farmsteads united by a common stone-wall system to form large complexes (plate XI). The intensively cultivated arable formed a minor part of the enclosed lands ... In the period AD 400 to 700, the agrarian production declined, the stone-wall complexes were split up, and the historically known hamlet territories were shaped.[28]

Widgren, therefore, suggests that settlement reorganization, which he, like Sporrong, argues was caused largely by social change and population growth, took place just before the main Scandinavian migration to England.

These Swedish studies reveal a very specific type of economy prior to about AD 400, in which the inhabitants of individual farmsteads practised a form of agriculture necessitating the construction of walled cattle paths between the farms. Most of the evidence also suggests that by the eighth and ninth centuries this structure had begun to break down, with the reorganization taking place earliest in the most densely settled parts of the country. Nevertheless, many examples of the older settlement and agrarian structure certainly survived through the Viking period, and it seems likely that in peripheral areas the pattern of dispersed farmsteads was probably still common when people from Sweden began to raid and settle in England during the ninth and tenth centuries (plate XII and plate XIII).

Having summarized some of the more important features concerning settlement and agriculture in northern continental Europe, it is now possible to return to the context of Derbyshire and Nottinghamshire to assess the relevance of these observations to processes at work in a particular part of England, before wider generalizations are reached in the conclusion.

---

[27] U. Sporrong, *Mälarbygd: Agrar Bebyggelse ock Odling ur ett Historisk-Geografiskt Persepektiv* (Stockholm, 1985).

[28] M. Widgren, *Settlement and Farming Systems in the Early Iron Age: A Study of Fossil Agrarian Landscapes in Östergötland* (Stockholm, 1983), p. 2.

PLATE XI: *Early Iron Age* (*c.*
AD *300*) *settlement and stone-*
walled cattle tracks at Fläret-
Östergötland, Sweden.
© Tim Unwin.

Anglo-Saxon and Scandinavian Rural Settlement in Derbyshire and Nottinghamshire

The following is proposed as a tentative, and somewhat provocative, description of the processes by which settlements, agriculture and boundaries were changed between the fourth and eleventh centuries in the northern Midlands.

1 Some time during the late fourth or early fifth century it seems that the villa economy and grain-producing estates of the Romano-British population began to disintegrate as part of the wider economic collapse of the late Roman period. This may have been associated with a declining population.

2 During the fifth and early sixth centuries the incoming Anglo-Saxons, who were used to both dispersed farmsteads and also small nucleated villages, settled in the low-lying areas of the Trent valley and south-east Nottinghamshire. The decline in population levels, which had taken place

PLATE XII: *Lingnåre* (*c.* AD *900–1100*), *Viking Age house platform, Uppland, Sweden.* © Tim Unwin.

by the beginning of the seventh century, meant that they were able to settle almost exclusively in areas similar to those from which they had come. Much of the north-west of Nottinghamshire and upland Derbyshire would have remained very sparsely settled. It is highly probable at this time that the Anglo-Saxon population practised a form of agriculture in which each farm had its own independent fields. It also seems possible that the incoming Anglo-Saxons were allocated specific areas of land, particularly on either side of the Trent, and that these areas later became townships. It is possible that initially each allocated area was to be the land of one family farm, or the land for some collective village group, but this is uncertain, as is the precise process by which allocation took place. It is likely that in several instances boundaries of estates that existed in the Roman period were re-used as boundaries during the sixth century, but this does not imply that there was necessarily any continuity in the estate structure.

3 The seventh and eighth centuries were a time of growing population and pressure on the land, which would have necessitated the firmer delineation of boundaries. It seems, though, that the bulk of the population remained in the low-lying areas, which were settled in the early phases of the Anglo-Saxon period. Some small-scale recolonization would, nevertheless, probably also have taken place in the areas of the counties not occupied since the Roman period, and in these areas it seems that firm territorial boundaries may not yet have been established. Towards the end of this period, the growing political power of the Mercian kings probably

PLATE XIII: *Reconstructed Viking Age house at Moesgård museum, south of Århus, Denmark.*
© Tim Unwin.

led to the firm delineation of most township boundaries, and it is possible that large royal estates were established mainly in areas such as Mansfield in Nottinghamshire, and Ashford, Bakewell, Darley and Wirksworth in Derbyshire, which were peripheral to the primary areas of Anglo-Saxon settlement. These probably had little, if any, relationship to Roman precursors. It is possible, too, that during this period some settlement reorganization associated with the introduction of communal strip farming took place. A more likely alternative, however, is that through into the ninth century a process of subdivision occurred within the already defined townships, whereby gradually two or three main farms, each with its own infield, emerged in most townships.

4 The ninth and tenth centuries saw considerable reorganization, following the conflict between Scandinavians and English, and the eventual settlement of people of Scandinavian origin in the region. Considerable debate must range over the exact meaning of the phrase in the *Anglo-Saxon Chronicle* referring to the Scandinavian army in the year AD 877, in which it is stated that 'In the harvest season the army went into Mercia and shared

94

out some of it'.[29] It seems possible that during the late ninth century the Scandinavians literally shared out much of the land among themselves. It is unlikely, though, that it was at this period that new township boundaries were created. The areas of the counties that were only sparsely settled prior to the Scandinavian immigration, such as north-west Nottinghamshire and east and north Derbyshire, also seem to have experienced considerable Scandinavian 'settlement' at this time. On balance, it is likely that the influx of Scandinavian people and ideas may well have retarded the processes whereby nucleated villages and communal farming were being introduced elsewhere in England, and it seems a distinct possibility that the multiplicity of manors per township recorded in eastern and northern England in *Domesday Book* was a direct result of the Scandinavian immigration to the area, which led to the presence there of a number of free, independent 'warrior-farmers'.

5 By the eleventh century, increasing population pressure associated with a growing concentration of both the political and social structure would have provided the framework in which there would have been considerable change in the agrarian structure. It seems likely that prior to the Norman Conquest many townships in the area would have experienced some degree of settlement nucleation and the introduction of communal fields with individual strips within them. Nevertheless, the massive reorganization of the estate and landholding structure in this area consequent on the Norman Conquest of England, notwithstanding Sawyers's reservations on the subject,[30] and also the firm establishment of a feudal mode of production, probably sounded the death knell for the multiplicity of small dispersed settlements, and produced the villages and field system with which we are familiar in the medieval period.

From the above, the following key questions emerge, which need to be answered by future research:

1 Did each farm unit recorded as a manor in *Domesday Book* once have its own separate and distinct fields?
2 When did communal strip farming emerge?
3 How precisely did the precursor of the Norman manor function?
4 When were the township boundaries established? This is related closely to the origin of place-names, because most township names refer to areas rather than to specific settlements. It must therefore be asked whether in townships recorded as having several

---

[29] D. Whitelock, D. C. Douglas and S. I. Tucker (eds), *The Anglo-Saxon Chronicle* (London, 1961), p. 48.
[30] P. H. Sawyer, '1066–1086: a tenurial revolution?', in P. H. Sawyer (ed), *Domesday Book: A Reassessment* (London, 1985), pp. 71–85.

eleventh-century manors within them there was initially only one named settlement, with subdivision occurring later, or whether the unit received its name at a later date, after subdivision had already taken place?

Conclusion

It is now possible to tie together this discussion of settlement nucleation in the form of some general observations upon which models for any particular area in England can be constructed. It seems to be broadly the case that throughout most of northern Europe a generally dispersed pattern of farms, each with its own infield, became transformed into a pattern of villages with arable fields in some form of communal organization during the period AD 400–1200. This seems to have happened in response to changes in the political and social structures of an area at a time of demographic change. Population growth by itself would not guarantee the changes observed, but it can nevertheless be considered as a catalyst providing the circumstances in which particular changes could be introduced.

One important conclusion of this chapter is that the balance of argument has swung too far towards uncritical acceptance of elements of continuity concerning early medieval settlement and agriculture, and the time has come to redress the balance and acknowledge the important influences of the incoming Anglo-Saxons and Scandinavians. It seems clear that when the Anglo-Saxons came to Britain, they did so with a knowledge and experience of both nucleated villages and of dispersed farms. In some areas, large pre-existing estates may have been taken over completely by local kings and lords. Loyn, however, has argued lucidly that Anglo-Saxon settlement in the fifth and sixth centuries was 'overwhelmingly agrarian in nature and concentrated for the most part on the abundant river valleys of south and central Britain'.[31] This concentration is important because the history of precisely where different groups of people settled in Britain will have had important consequences for the later development of settlement and agriculture. Much of the evidence would suggest that the areas settled earliest by the Anglo-Saxons, provided that they were not in turn conquered by later Scandinavian immigrants, would be the most likely to experience early reorganization of their fields and settlements. This would tie in well with Hooke's argument that reorganization probably took place first where there was dense settlement and powerful leadership.[32]

---

[31] H. R. Loyn, *The Governance of Anglo-Saxon England 500–1087* (London, 1984), p. 5.
[32] Hooke, *The Anglo-Saxon Landscape*.

A second, and more controversial, suggestion is that, rather than being early, the development of large estates may in many cases probably have been a feature of the period between the seventh and the ninth centuries. It thus seems to be a distinct possibility that estates similar to those identified by Jones and others as multiple estates were a relatively late feature in the landscape and were a direct response to the emergence of increasingly powerful and centralized Anglo-Saxon kingdoms in the seventh and eighth centuries. Large estates may have been created in areas other than those initially settled by the Anglo-Saxons as a way in which peripheral regions were recolonized after a period of decay following the population decline of the fifth and sixth centuries.

Turning to the areas influenced by Scandinavian settlement, it is possible to argue that a process leading to nucleation was then retarded by the influx of people with a different set of ideas and cultural values. The parts of England with the greatest density of 'classical' nucleated villages are often those of oldest Anglo-Saxon settlement. It seems likely that the Scandinavian immigrants reintroduced an 'earlier' dispersed pattern of settlement and agrarian economy, which in a sense led to its renewed efflorescence. The Scandinavian immigration did two main things to the areas it influenced. First, it probably led to an increase in population, which could in itself have been a factor leading to the reorganization of settlement and the agrarian economy. Secondly, though, it is also possible to argue that because of their cultural background, which probably made them more familiar with individual farms each with its own fields, the Scandinavian immigrants, and particularly those from Sweden and Norway, instead caused a resurgence of an older pattern of dispersed farmsteads. Those who argue against this must explain why, at a regional scale, the multiplicity of manors per township in much of eleventh-century England is generally high in areas of Scandinavian settlement.

Following these arguments, the parts of Britain with the greatest density of early nucleation should be low-lying areas that were settled early by the Anglo-Saxons, but which were not later 'conquered' by the Scandinavians. This would, indeed, broadly appear to be confirmed with reference to the various works cited at the beginning of this chapter. In areas of extensive Scandinavian influence, such as eastern and northern England, the arguments of Roberts and Sheppard may indeed well remain true.[33] Here, a further political and social change may have been necessary finally to introduce a communal system of farming and a more nucleated pattern of settlement. This change was thus brought about by the Norman culmination of the introduction of feudal relations of production into England.

These ideas provide a framework for interpreting the Anglo-Saxon and

---

[33] Roberts, 'Rural settlement'; Sheppard, 'Medieval village planning'.

97

Scandinavian settlement of England. They have been proposed specifically to ask questions of much of the current literature. As a result, three issues stand out forcibly as requiring resolution, and it is to these that future research urgently requires direction. First, detailed archaeological and documentary studies must be undertaken of specific townships that had several manors within them during the eleventh century to identify where and when the different settlement foci were developed. Secondly, those who argue that multiple estates existed in the Roman period and continued in use as the key element of the rural economy throughout the Anglo-Scandinavian period must positively prove this continuity, rather than base their arguments essentially on negative evidence. Finally, we need to know considerably more about the emergence of different types of field system during the Anglo-Saxon and Scandinavian periods in England. Given the density of the subsequent occupancy of the lowlands of England, it seems likely that much of the archaeological evidence for such an analysis may have been destroyed long ago. In order fully to comprehend the processes at work within the English landscape 'before Domesday', we must therefore turn to Germany and Scandinavia to find the images in the minds of the invaders who settled our shores between the fifth and the eleventh centuries.

5

The Late Saxon Countryside: Villages and their Fields

DAVID HALL

This chapter is concerned with some aspects of the Saxon landscape using the results of archaeological field-survey to identify settlement sites and fields. The fields will be analysed for tenurial and spatial structure; although the historical data come from surveys made after the Domesday survey of 1086, it can be shown that much of the information relates to Saxon times.[1]

Archaeological field-survey is made by close examination of large areas (minimum unit a township or parish) in strips of 30-metre width under suitable conditions. Saxon sites can be recognized by the occurrence of characteristic sherds, often accompanied by dark areas of soil with fragments of domestic bone and burnt stone from hearths, etc. Many Saxon remains exist underneath present-day villages and these can only be found during ground disturbance for building or other construction work.

The strip-field systems commonly known as 'medieval fields' are familiar in some parts of the country, surviving as earthwork ridge-and-furrow or marked on estate maps dating from the sixteenth century onwards (plate XIV). Many villages possess neither physical nor documentary record, but the field pattern can be reconstructed from archaeological techniques, since the boundaries of the fields survive as linear soil banks, even under modern arable conditions. The techniques of both these types of fieldwork (i.e. for settlement and for field systems) have been described previously.[2]

---

[1] This chapter continues the series of parish studies presented since 1981. D. N. Hall, 'The origins of open-field agriculture – the archaeological fieldwork evidence', in R. T. Rowley (ed.), *The Origins of Open-Field Agriculture* (London, 1981), pp. 22–38; D. N. Hall, 'Fieldwork and documentary evidence for the layout and organization of early medieval estates in the English Midlands', in K. Biddick (ed.), *Archaeological Approaches to Medieval Europe: Studies in Medieval Culture* (Michigan, 1984), pp. 43–68; D. N. Hall, 'Fieldwork and fieldbooks: studies in early layout', in B. K. Roberts and R. E. Glasscock (eds), *Villages, Fields and Frontiers*, British Archaeological Reports, International series, 185 (Oxford, 1983), pp. 115–31; D. N. Hall, 'Late Saxon topography and early medieval estates', in D. Hooke (ed.), *Medieval Villages: A Review of Current Work*, Oxford University Committee for Archaeology, Monograph No. 5 (Oxford, 1985), pp. 61–9.

[2] D. N. Hall, 'Survey work in eastern England', in S. Macready and F. H. Thompson (eds), *Archaeological Field Survey in Britain and Abroad*, Society of Antiquaries (London, 1985), pp. 25–44; D. N. Hall, *Medieval Fields* (Princes Risborough, 1981).

PLATE XIV: *Ridge and furrow at Grendon, Northamptonshire, SP 8760.*
© David Hall.

Early and Middle Saxon Settlement

It is clear from results obtained over the last twenty-five years that the early Saxons did not arrive to an empty and wild countryside. The Romans had farmed large areas, following on from the Celtic peoples, who were the first to settle on heavy clay soils. There are many hundreds of Iron Age and Roman sites on clayey till in Northamptonshire. However, the major Roman settlements are centred on good-quality agricultural soils along the slopes of major river valleys, especially in the valley of the Nene.[3]

The first waves of Saxon invaders and settlers very much preferred the rich soils of the valleys, and sites are located almost exclusively on river gravels, Northampton sand and limestone. Only two sites are known on clay subsoil and in both cases they are associated with Roman sites. Presumably it was the previous habitation rather than the clay soil that was the attraction.

The distribution pattern is quite unlike that of the later villages, but exactly like that of previous periods. There were many small sites, most of them, in all probability, unpretentious farmsteads. Nearly all the larger

[3] D. N. Hall, 'The countryside of the south-east Midlands and Cambridgeshire', in D. Miles (ed.), *The Romano-British Countryside*, British Archaeological Reports, British series, 103 (Oxford, 1982), pp. 337–50.

Roman sites yield Saxon sherds either from the results of fieldwork or from the excavation of a Roman site. The interpretation would seem to be that the Saxons accepted what they found, continuing occupation of the major Roman villas and farms and also founding small sites of their own *de novo*.

Examples of large Roman sites with significant amounts of Saxon material occur at Clopton, Wollaston, Maidwell and Flore.[4] The last is a large site with much building stone and is probably the villa with a mosaic which gave its name to the village. Figure 5.1 shows Saxon sites in Flore parish, on Roman settlements and at single-period new sites. Figure 5.2 shows the distribution of Saxon sites over the north Welland valley. There are several sites in each parish; a distribution similar to that of the Roman and prehistoric sites is evident. A discussion of the remarkable number of sites around Brixworth has already been published.[5]

The complete Saxon site distribution will take many decades to assemble, because material lying under present-day villages is only discovered by chance. Thus in parishes and townships consisting largely of clay soils, in which the village is sited in the valley of a brook cutting down to better soils, no Saxon sites are found out in the fields because the early settlement was in the same place and is now buried.

The lack of interest shown by the early Saxons in the claylands accounts for the regrowth of scrub and woodland on them. This woodland was often cleared away during the late Saxon and early medieval period, giving rise to place and topographical name-forms indicating its former existence. The occurrence of such names misled nineteenth-century workers into believing that the early Saxons carved settlement sites out of an extensive primeval forest.

Within the sample area, the total number of Saxon sites found away from present vills is eighty-two, while fourteen modern (medieval) villages have Saxon material under them. These figures represent the results of 152 detailed parish surveys. One hundred and eighteen parishes have no Saxon finds, either because of a preponderance of clay or because there are large areas of modern grassland obscuring the surface.

When we come to look at the late Saxon settlement pattern, the arrangement is different. Out in the fields only a single deserted site of tenth- or eleventh-century date has been discovered.[6] All other occupational evidence of this date comes from underneath the present villages or from vills that are now deserted but which survived into the late Middle

---

[4] For Clopton and Flore see this paper figures 5.1 and 5.6 below; Wollaston is published in Biddick, *Archaeological Approaches*, figure 8, p. 61; for Maidwell, see *Council for British Archaeology (CBA) Group 9 Newsletter*, No. 6 (1976), pp. 27–31.

[5] D. N. Hall and P. Martin, 'Brixworth, Northamptonshire – an intensive survey', *Journal of the British Archaeological Association*, 132 (1979), pp. 1–6.

[6] In a field called Hardwick in Oundle, TL0080, 8840.

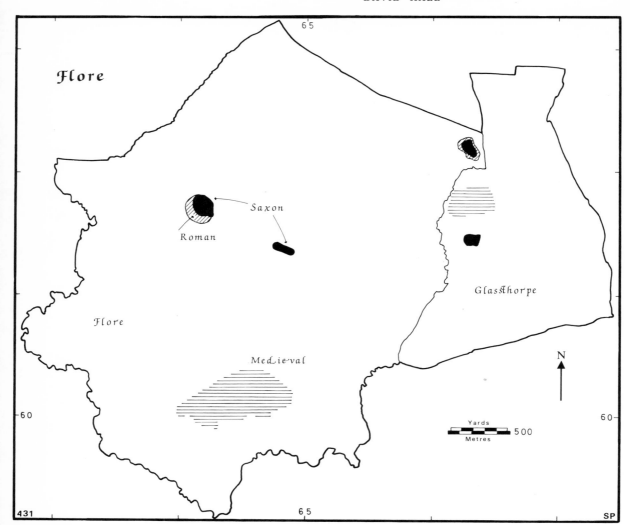

FIGURE 5.1   *Roman and Saxon sites in Flore parish (which includes the deserted township of Glassthorpe)*

Ages. In other words, the Domesday village patterns had been created during the late Saxon period, when the smaller sites were abandoned. Something else had happened too: strip field systems had been laid out. Evidence has been given elsewhere to show that they were initially planned on a large scale, later being divided into smaller groupings called furlongs.[7] On the Yorkshire Wolds and at Holderness, large blocks of land divided into strips up to a kilometre in length survived until eighteenth-century enclosure.[8]

[7] See Hall, 'Origins of open-field agriculture', pp. 31–4.
[8] M. Harvey, 'The origin of planned field systems in Holderness, Yorkshire', in Rowley (ed.), *The Origins of Open-Field Agriculture*, pp. 184–201.

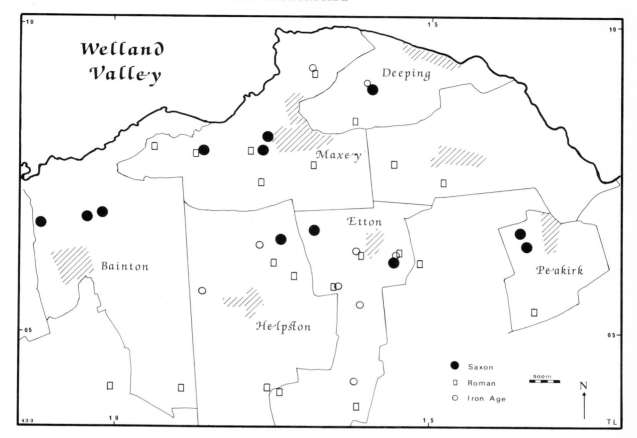

FIGURE 5.2 *Saxon and earlier sites in the Welland valley, north of Peterborough*

The newly created strip fields, which clearly relate to the late Saxon (Domesday) villages, were laid out over the earlier Saxon sites, indicating that the fields are later. The early and middle Saxon sites were not, however, forgotten because in many cases where Saxon pottery can be found the medieval field-name records the settlement name. Table 5.1 lists some examples. Most commonly such places are called 'cotton' from OE *cot*, 'cottage', presumably reflecting their smallness in size.

The archaeological evidence, then, shows that both settlements and fields were reorganized and planned on a remarkably large and surprising scale. The apparent date of earlier settlement abandonment will be given by a closer examination of the pottery collected from the sites. At present the hand-made middle Saxon pottery is believed to have been replaced by wheel-made Saxo-Norman wares in the ninth or early tenth century. Therefore the sites would have been abandoned by about AD 900 at the latest, since wheel-made sherds are not found on them.

TABLE 5.1 *Names of Saxon sites and estates*

Parish	Grid reference	Field name
Brixworth	SP 7375 7025	Shiredalecotes
Courtenhall	SP 7667 5440	Cotton
Hardingstone	SP 7400 5870	Oscott
Harringworth	SP 9325 9814	Bosley
Whiston	SP 8500 6010	Sawcott
Oundle[a]	TL 0080 8840	Hardwick
Higham Ferrers[b]	SP 9810 6715	Buscott
Kislingbury[b]	SP 7020 5715	Hardwick
Thornby[b]	SP 6540 7450	Chilcotes

[a] Late Saxon site.
[b] Saxon estate, settlement unlocated.

Multiple Estates

The grouping of several adjacent settlements, each possessing different resources, into a single 'multiple estate' is an arrangement well known in Celtic regions[9] and also on the Continent.[10] Remnants of such estates can be identified in England by, for instance, the payment of dues by several parish churches to a 'mother church', which had once acted as a minister. The Northamptonshire historian Baker identified such an estate based on the royal manor of Fawsley, which included most of the Fawsley hundred.[11]

Other such groupings can be identified from the Domesday survey. The Saxon thegn Bondi held Earls Barton. This, doubtless, was his *caput* and there is still a notable Saxon church with a motte nearby. The Domesday return states that the villages of Great Doddington, Wilby and Mears Ashby were Bondi's and belonged to Earls Barton. Neighbouring Ecton also belonged to him. Barton is clearly 'the barley or corn-producing estate', and north of it, running on to clay with woodland, is Mears Ashby. The place-name suggests that the village took its name from an ash tree.[12] A survey made in 1577 makes it clear that there was then still a wood to the north. The adjacent furlong names (long stocking, over stocking, short stocking and thornwood) show that the woodland was formerly more

[9] G. R. J. Jones, 'Early customary tenures in Wales and open-field agriculture', in Rowley (ed.), *The Origins of Open-Field Agriculture*, pp. 202–25.

[10] See chapter 12 below.

[11] G. Baker, *The History and Antiquities of the County of Northamptonshire* (London, 1822), vol. 1, pp. 377, 386–7.

[12] J. E. B. Gover, A. Mawer and F. M. Stenton, *The Place-Names of Northamptonshire*, English Place-Name Society, vol. 10 (Cambridge, 1933), p. 137.

extensive.[13] Here, then, is a typical multiple estate with different settlements contributing their specific products. The valley townships of Ecton,
Earls Barton and Doddington would provide fish from the river and hay
from the meadows, which would then be used to graze cattle. The furlong
names show that there was some heath ground at Ecton, which would also
be used for rough grazing and provide furze for kindling.

Figure 5.3 shows the general topography of the estate, with pasture by

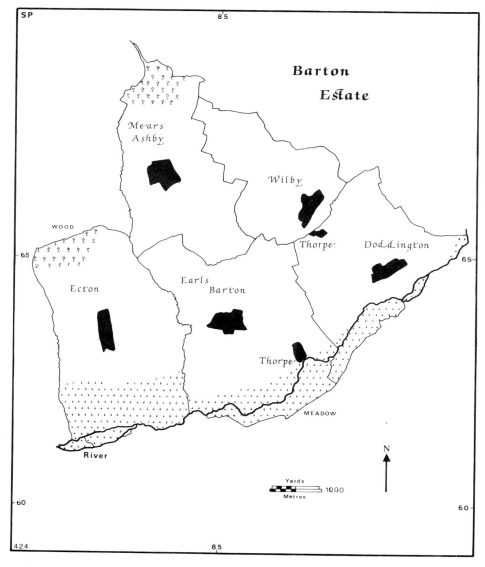

FIGURE 5.3 *Earls Barton
multiple estate and its
component townships and
hamlets*

[13] Worked out from a map made by field survey and a fieldbook of 1577, Northamptonshire Record Office (NRO) ZA 3709.

the river Nene on the south and woodland to the north. The Mears Ashby wood is part of a more extensive area that once linked up small fragments of medieval wood at Badsaddle and Wythemale (in Orlingbury), Hardwick wood and woodland formerly at Walgrave. By Domesday, each village was nucleated and lay more or less in the centre of its arable fields. Barton and Doddington have the extra complication of each having a Scandinavian settlement called Thorpe placed in their township.

The field system of all the parishes within this multiple estate show a marked similarity with a regular repetitive tenurial cycle of landholders. At Mears Ashby there is a cycle of forty tenants, which correspond to the Domesday return of four hides; more comment will be made on this later. Ecton has a fixed order repeating in every 110 strips.[14]

The Higham Ferrers hundred would appear to be another multiple estate. Most of the northern part is stated by the Domesday survey to be appurtenant to Higham, formerly belonging to Countess Gætha, wife of Ralph, nephew of Edward the Confessor. Later records show that the area was divided into four administrative manors, one of which is Raunds.[15] This in itself seems to be a small multiple estate. The manor consisted of Raunds plus the three neighbouring parishes (described as 'hamlets' in a survey of 1591) of Stanwick, Hargrave and Ringstead.[16] Raunds is shown to be the dominant and largest settlement at all times; it intercommoned with Ringstead in the meadows by the river Nene from the earliest detailed record in 1349[17] until enclosure in 1798, and the hamlets were always appurtenant to it administratively until the abolition of copyhold tenure in 1922. At the time of the Domesday survey, the holdings of Raunds in Stanwick and Ringstead were grouped under Raunds without mentioning the hamlets' names. Not until the thirteenth century is it clear that the lands existed. This is true both for the manors of Countess Gætha (William Peverel's in 1086), but also for that part of Raunds and Ringstead that belonged to Burgræd (the Bishop of Coutances in 1086). In neither case is Ringstead mentioned.[18]

Like Earls Barton, there are additional small settlements that are now deserted villages. In the Raunds complex there are three: West Cotton, Mallows Cotton and Mill Cotton. They perhaps owe their existence to the forebears of Burgræd, who held land in what was otherwise very much Gætha's territory.

Figure 5.4 shows the general topography reconstructed from field studies (see below for more detail in the case of Raunds parish). The

[14] See Hall, 'Fieldwork and fieldbooks', pp. 121, 123–5.
[15] *Calendar of Inquisitions Post Mortem Edward I*, iii (London, 1912), no. 423, p. 306.
[16] Public Record Office (PRO), London, DL 42 117 fo. 193.
[17] *Court roll of Raunds*, 23 Edward III, NRO in box X705.
[18] D. N. Hall, R. E. Harding and C. Putt, *A Pictorial History of Raunds* (forthcoming 1987).

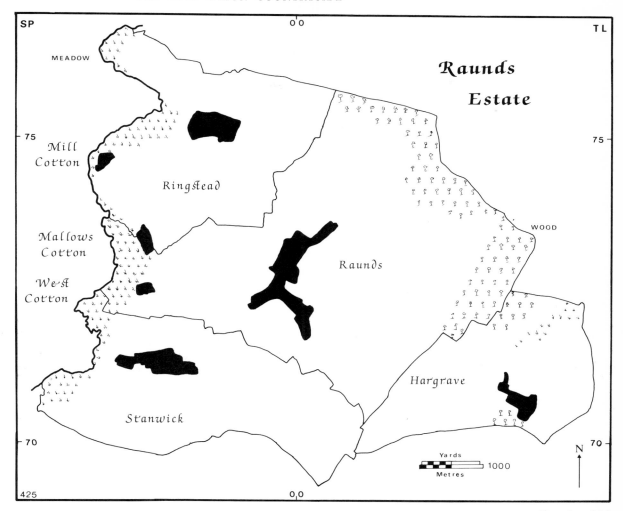

FIGURE 5.4 *Raunds multiple estate with its component townships and hamlets*

riverine townships have the water and meadow resources (Stanwick, Raunds and Ringstead), and Hargrave and the higher ground of Stanwick provided the woodland products. The names of the later medieval fields show where the wooded areas were.

An ancient unity is discernible in Raunds and its hamlets from the township boundaries. As a whole, the combined outer boundary consists of smooth segments following watersheds or brooks, but within, the boundaries of each township have many right-angle irregularities where there are diversions around furlongs. Boundaries of this nature suggest that the townships post-date the fields.

Field Systems and the Landscape

Pre-Enclosure strip fields, surviving in many parts of the country as ridge and furrow, can easily be shown to be of medieval origin. Nineteenth-century workers assumed that they were innovations brought to this country by the Saxons. As mentioned above, this has been shown to be untrue, the overriding of middle Saxon deserted sites by strip fields proving, in general terms, that the new fields must have been laid out after the middle Saxon period.

More detailed analysis is required of specific cases before any statement can be attempted concerning the information that can be discovered about the late Saxon arrangement. On the one hand, it seems improbable that eighteenth-century tenurial data will relate back seven centuries. On the other hand, a communal field system with complex and seasonally variable access rights has every chance of being unchanged because it is difficult to effect any alteration in a conservative agricultural community, especially when legal rights are involved.

It is unlikely that every estate changed from a scattered settlement arrangement to strip fields around one or a few larger nuclei at the same date, or that when such an arrangement did take place, in all cases the whole area available for arable was involved. In many instances there would most likely be rough pasture or woodland remaining, which would be only later incorporated in field systems by assarting. It is therefore unsatisfactory to take a post-medieval field system at its face value and claim it to be 'Saxon' without qualification.

For Northamptonshire, it can be shown that in all those examples so far studied 'medieval' field systems were complete by the end of the thirteenth century at the latest. Changes after then were only matters of various kinds of contraction of arable. As already mentioned, the earliest date expected for a field system is the ninth century. This can only be refined over the years by excavation, when sites with dating material present themselves. Even when they do, caution will be necessary with interpretation. For instance, it is common to find a wholly demesne furlong next to a manor house site, as at Raunds. Here excavations have shown the strips to overlie ninth- to tenth-century occupation.[19] It might be assumed, therefore, that the fields were all set out after that date. However, there was a reorganization of the peasant household plots in Raunds at this time, causing the total area of the village to decrease. The 'vacuum' could have been taken up by the manorial lord as a demesne furlong. In such a case there could have been inward 'expansion' of already existing fields. The archaeological

---

[19] T. Pearson and M. Audouy, personal communication, 1986.

dating of this particular furlong does not therefore necessarily date the whole system.

We are looking, then, for variations in the structure of fields that may tell something about changes taking place from about AD 850 to 1300, and particularly for early ones before 1066. Four case studies will be taken: Kislingbury, Clopton, Raunds and Higham Ferrers.

Kislingbury has no open-field map, but it has a complete parish fieldbook for 1612. Using this and a reconstructed field map, details of the field arrangement can be deduced.[20] The village lies to the north, near the river Nene; the parish has a butterfly shape with an odd 'tail' at the south (shown in figure 5.5). The southern addition appears to have been once a separate

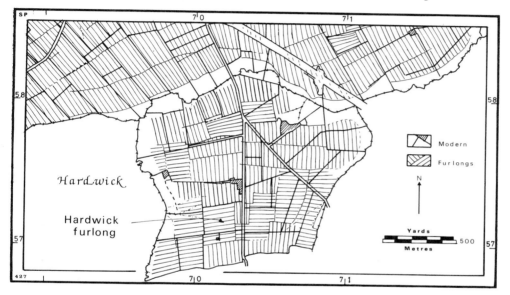

FIGURE 5.5 *Hardwick estate in the southern part of Kislingbury parish*

estate; one of the furlongs is called Hardwick, which is possibly the name of this lost hamlet. Hardwick is shown to have had a separate identity from a thirteenth-century charter, which describes individual strips, although there is no hint that a settlement survived at this date. The strips described are all in the area of the 'tail'. Some of the furlongs have 'wood' names such as *stokkylond*, *westoldefelde* and *eldestobe*.[21] Presumably the sequence of events was some reafforestation after the Roman period, then the foundation of a Saxon settlement, which later became deserted and the land that went with it was absorbed into Kislingbury.

Clopton lies primarily on high boulder clay land, much of which formed part of an extensive Saxon wood called Bruneswold. The reconstructed

[20] NRO MTM 378; see Hall, 'Fieldwork and documentary evidence', pp. 50–1, 62.
[21] NRO, YZ 3637.

furlong pattern (figure 5.6) shows a normal checkerboard area of fields on the west and a part with strange shapes and long strips on the east. This last turns out to be the former woodland according to such names as *sinewold* and *winewic srubbes* recorded in 1255.[22]

The sequence of land use was first the establishment of a cleared Roman countryside dominated by a large villa. The villa was occupied during the early and middle Saxon period, and then the present village and fields were

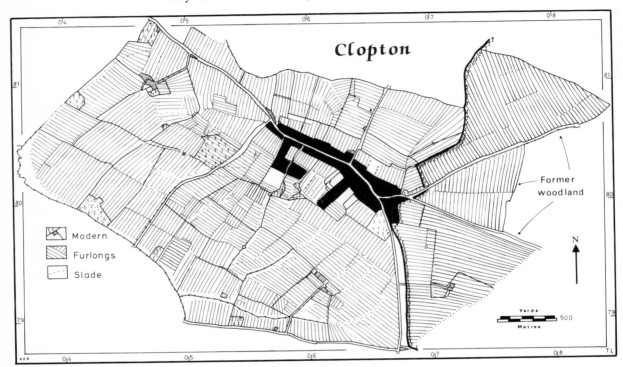

FIGURE 5.6 *Clopton field system showing the area of former woodland*

planned and laid out in a remarkable way. A regular village plan is very unusual in Northamptonshire and only occurs in areas adjacent to former woodland. The new village lay next to the old wooded area, suggesting that the trees were still there, protecting the settlement from cold north-east winds scouring over the high plateau in winter. Subsequently the wood was cleared and added to the open-field arable.

A terrier of the demesne made in 1255 shows that the manorial lands spread throughout the regular fields and the irregular former wooded area.[23] The tithe of this demesne was split into three parts and each was

[22] E. King (ed.), *A Northamptonshire Miscellany*, Northamptonshire Record Society 32 (Northampton, 1983), pp. 48–50.
[23] F. M. Stenton, *Facsimiles of Early Charters*, Northamptonshire Record Society 4 (Northampton, 1930), p. 46.

given to a monastic house, the latest grant being to St Neots Priory in 1182.[24] No distinction is made between the three tithes in the 1255 document, which is part of a detailed enquiry into the descent of land at Clopton since the Conquest. This implies that the demesne as described refers to the state of affairs before the division; had there been wood still surviving at that time, which was later assarted, with the manor taking in some of the new land, then the split demesne would not have been in equal parts. The Domesday survey mentions no wood at Clopton, so the evidence seems to suggest that the irregular fields on the old woodland were already formed by the eleventh century. It is therefore likely that the planned new village sited next to its wood is to be dated to the pre-Conquest, and probably the late Saxon, period.

The early landscape of Raunds can be viewed with the help of surveys made in 1739 to locate lands belonging to the Gloucester Fee, which were the land of Burgræd in 1066.[25] The village structure is complex, with five 'ends' linked together spreading along several small valleys. The main division is between the southern Thorpe End and the North End, in which lies the church. Two manors are identifiable in 1086, both of which are shown from the surveys to lie at the North End, and excavations begun in 1976 showed that the manor of Burgræd had a church in the late Saxon era.[26] In other words, the North End was very much the seigneurial part with the major manors each having a church. Thorpe End is presumably a Danish addition or renamed vill. It is not necessarily much later than the North End, because middle Saxon pottery occurs there.

The division between north and south is reflected in the field systems. There is a road splitting the parish into two parts, each part having an independent three-field system in later centuries, but a two-field system in 1327.[27] The eighteenth-century information can be shown to offer a reliable indication on an earlier situation because a terrier of 1349 shows that the double field-system was in operation then,[28] and a 1356 rental describes some of the demesne parcels of the manor called Burystead (then belonging to the Duke of Lancaster, but formerly to Gætha in 1066),[29] which can be identified as the demesne in 1739.[30]

A plot of the demesne of Burystead manor is given in figure 5.7. It is of the type that spreads throughout the field systems reasonably uniformly.

---

[24] King (ed.), *A Northampton Miscellany*, p. 48.

[25] NRO, ML 124.

[26] A. Boddington and G. Cadman, 'Raunds, an interpretation of the excavations 1977–80', in D. Brown, J. Campbell and S. C. Hawkes (eds), *Anglo-Saxon Studies in Archaeology and History*, 2, British Archaeological Reports, British series, 92 (Oxford, 1981), pp. 103–22.

[27] PRO, C135 6, m27.

[28] See note 17 above.

[29] PRO, DL 29 324/5292.

[30] Hall, Harding and Putt, *Raunds.*

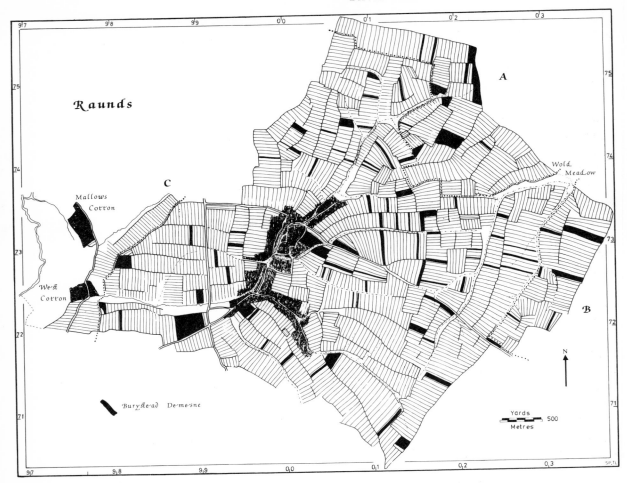

FIGURE 5.7 *Raunds field system and the demesne of Burystead manor*

There is no alignment of demesne forming long strips spreading through several adjacent furlongs, so we have therefore an arrangement with holdings laid out on the existing furlong pattern. Detailed analysis of the holdings in each furlong reveals various elements of substructure. There is an inner region where the demesne lands of both manors lie adjacent. This would seem to be an area opened up (or laid out) at an early date, when there was only one manor, with the split coming later (as with Kislingbury, see below). After the two manors were formed, the demesne lands were laid out separately in the furlongs created by assarting waste land. These assarted areas are characterized by other differences: the tenurial structure consists of larger blocks of groups, whereas the inner area tends to be held in single lands (except for the demesne). To the north, the main area presumed to be assart (figure 5.7A) is hemmed in by furlongs with 'mere' names, which seem to delineate the boundary of the old waste land. A few of the names are assarting ones like 'breach' (newly broken ground) and 'wold' (OE *wald*, 'wood'). To the north-east (figure 5.7B) is another smaller area of different tenurial characteristics and bearing the obvious wood name of 'old' or 'wold' meadow.

To the west of the village (figure 5.7C) is another furlong with abnormal tenurial arrangements. Along with others in neighbouring Ringstead, it forms what was once the field system belonging to the now-deserted villages of Cotton. The boundary of this field system is very clear from the furlong pattern and has been commented on before.[31]

The history of the Raunds manors and field systems appears, then, to indicate first a single manor, the Burystead. By the middle Saxon period this was split into two, and a new site found for one of them (later called Furnells); each had a late Saxon church. The initial field area was laid out in long strips; this is evident from the archaeological data, as shown by six of the furlongs in the north-west, whose strips are aligned in long curves that must represent a primary laying out of a large land block.[32] At a later date, the present furlongs were created by subdivision and the holdings laid out anew within them; assarting completed the open-field pattern.

Higham Ferrers parish has an extension to the west called Buscot. At the time of enclosure in the nineteenth century, the area was split between Higham and the neighbouring parish of Newton Bromswold.[33] No village site can be discovered or is indicated by any document. The first reference to the name is a grant of a few strips of open-field land in the thirteenth century.[34]

Higham Ferrers land can be studied in detail with the help of a fieldbook of 1567.[35] At that time there were three fields, the same as recorded in 1327.[36] The Buscot area is immediately shown to be quite different by the tenurial characteristics. The main open field is split between holdings, so that one owner with a single yardland does not have two adjacent strips. In contrast, Buscot is divided into small blocks of several lands and is held by the lessees of the demesne. In other words, Buscot is not part of the land belonging to the former villeins, but is seigneurial. Buscot is split equally between Higham and Newton. The lands in Newton were enclosed, but the lands of Higham remained open and were added to the three open fields for crop rotation, each Higham field having one-sixth of the total area of Buscot (figure 5.8).

Buscot, then, resembles the lost estate of Hardwick in Kislingbury,

[31] Hall, *Medieval Fields*, p. 29.
[32] Ibid., p. 51.
[33] Newton Bromswold enclosure papers, NRO, box X3474.
[34] British Library (BL) Harl. iii D45.
[35] *Fitzwilliam Misc.*, vol. 47, NRO.
[36] PRO, C135 6, m26.

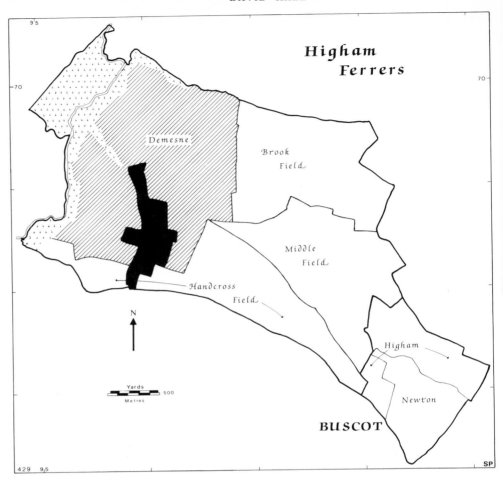

FIGURE 5.8 *Higham Ferrers parish showing the division into demesne, fields and the township of Buscot*

mentioned above, but with the difference that its lands are here shared between two townships. Buscot has always been in the parish of Higham and it is interesting to speculate about its connection with Newton. Could it be that Buscot is an earlier site of Newton, before it moved to the high claylands of its present position and so became a 'new town'? Alternatively, when Buscot became depopulated maybe the inhabitants moved more or less equally to Higham and Newton, its nearest neighbours. After a few generations, the families farming the lands would be considered natives and, by default, Buscot lands would belong to the neighbouring townships.

The date of *floruit* of Buscot is presumably late Saxon. It is not mentioned, or its existence implied, in any estate or taxation document. If it was the former site of Newton, then it is certainly pre-Conquest, because Newton was already in existence by 1066.[37]

[37] *Domesday Book*, ii, Record Commission (London, 1783), fo. 220d.

The Demesne

The seigneurial home farm, the demesne, has already been discussed for Raunds. Higham Ferrers also has an interesting and quite different arrangement. The 1567 fieldbook shows that there is another large area around the town that did not belong to the three 'villein' open fields, and again lay in groups of land in terms of tenancy, most of the owners being lessees of the demesne. The fieldbook does not state that the area is demesne, but this becomes clear from fourteenth-century account rolls, which name the demesne furlongs.[38] The large block around Higham, consisting of about a third of the parish, proves to be the demesne land of this central manor.

In the Domesday survey Higham was assessed at six hides, two of which were in the lord's hands. Therefore the arrangement still visible on the ground in the sixteenth century is the same as that of the late Saxon period. The demesne may possibly represent in some form the continuation of the estate belonging to a large Roman site that partially underlies the town. Wollaston offers another example of a large area of demesne that succeeds a Roman villa.[39]

The demesne of Kislingbury is described in a detailed fourteenth-century terrier. There were two manors in 1086 and in the early twelfth century the tithe of two-thirds of the demesne of both manors was given to the priory of St Andrews, Northampton.[40] From the terrier, it is clear that the demesne of each manor was at all times adjacent to the other. The interpretation is that the two manors were once a single entity, and since they were both in existence in 1066, the single-stage manor was of Saxon origin. The distribution of the demesne throughout the parish shows that the whole area was arable before 1066.

The arrangement of demesne is traditionally claimed to be dispersed throughout blocks of furlongs, as is the case of Clopton and Kislingbury. Higham shows that cases can be found with an intact undispersed demesne. Mears Ashby, already considered as part of the multiple estate of Bondi, is another example. Here, the demesne is consolidated except for one isolated furlong and called 'hall field'. Another case, Watford, will be discussed for other purposes below. It had an undispersed demesne next to the manor house.

---

[38] PRO, DL 29 325/5320.
[39] Hall, 'Fieldwork and documentary evidence', p. 61.
[40] BL, Cotton Vesp. E XVII, fo. 283.

Domesday Assessment and Peasant Holdings

The Domesday survey assesses Northamptonshire in hides and virgates, along with the southern or English counties not in Danelaw. A survey taken in about 1124 gives the hidage of each village and uses two kinds of virgates, large virgates meaning Domesday virgates (a quarter of a hide) and small virgates, which internal evidence in some cases shows are a tenth of a hide. Comparison of some of the later village assessments in yardlands shows that yardlands and small virgates are the same unit, i.e. a standard holding of sixty to one hundred strips (different for every township) dispersed uniformly in the fields and belonging to a toft and croft in the village. Normally yardlands remain unchanged over many centuries.

Domesday assessments and the later small virgates (yardlands) can often be shown to relate, although not always in the ratio of 1 : 10. The remarkable case of Clipston has already been discussed elsewhere.[41] Here the Domesday assessments of all the holdings total 5.25 hides which, at sixteen small virgates to the hide, equates to the eighty-four yardlands which were still found in 1776 on the eve of enclosure. One particular holding of William Peverel, in 1086 assessed at 3.5 hides and one-quarter of a virgate, is stated in 1124 to be 3.5 hides and one small virgate. This information shows that there were sixteen small virgates reckoned to the hide. The Domesday assessors were clearly not taking rough values proportional to the financial value of a holding, but must have found that that the holding was fifty-seven peasant holdings, which they then precisely recorded.

Clipston parish is shown later to be a double township consisting of Clipston and a separate settlement of Nobold, now deserted, each with its own independent field system. The distribution of the four Domesday holdings between the two vills (as proven in details of 1284) show that Nobold must have been in existence by 1066, and that the field and settlement organization not apparent until the thirteenth century is actually late Saxon.

Another numerical analysis with significant results can be made for the adjacent villages of Cold Ashby and Thornby. Within the western 'tail' of the present parish of Thornby is a group of fields bearing the name Chilcots.[42] No settlement is clear on the ground, although there is an earthwork of a fishpond dam straddling a small valley.[43] The vill site is probably concealed under the present farm of Thornby Grange. Chilcotes

---

[41] D. N. Hall, Introduction, in R. W. Erskine and A. Williams (eds), *The Northamptonshire Domesday* (London, forthcoming).

[42] Tithe map, 1840, NRO, map T212.

[43] D. N. Hall and P. W. Martin, *CBA Group 9 Newsletter*, 11 (1981), pp. 36–41.

is mentioned in the Domesday survey as being a holding of one virgate belonging to the Count of Mortain. Other holdings in 1086 are listed on table 5.2. There is another estate belonging to the Count of Mortain of 1.5 hides, following the entry for Cold Ashby, and specifically stated to be in the same vill. In spite of this, the 1.5-hide estate appears to have been in Thornby because a holding of that size is listed in the 1124 survey under Thornby, belonging to the Leicester Fee, the successor of the Count.[44] No such entry for Thornby occurs in the Domesday survey, except that under Cold Ashby. It would seem that the two vills had a close connection, which may account for the confusion.

The total estates in Cold Ashby amount to four hides, which is the same as that given in the 1124 Northamptonshire survey (table 5.2). Most of the

TABLE 5.2 *Early medieval holdings in Cold Ashby and Chilcotes*

	Cold Ashby			Chilcotes		Totals
	Coventry Abbey	Count Mortain	William Peverel	Geoffrey la Guerche	Count Mortain	
1086	$2\frac{1}{2}$	$\frac{1}{2}$ h	$1\frac{1}{2}$ v	$2\frac{1}{2}$ v	1 v	4 h
1124	$2\frac{1}{2}$ h	3 v	1 v	$\frac{1}{2}$ h	—	4 h
1230	38 y	10 y	4 y	8 y	(4 y?)	64 y

h hides
v virgates
y yardlands

Coventry Abbey land went to the monastery of Pipewell, and the whole of Cold Ashby is described in the cartulary of Pipewell, dated about 1230.[45] The total of small virgates was then sixty, split between the estates as shown in table 5.2. These figures seem to be the actual sizes of the holdings and suggest that, as with Clipston, sixteen (small) virgates should be taken to the Domesday hide. The Pipewell estate of thirty-eight should strictly be forty small virgates (or 2.5 hides); the earlier hide assessments seem to be slightly rounded up. In the same way, the Mortain/Leicester estate is stated as ten small virgates, rounded down by 1086 to half a hide (8) and rounded up by the twelfth-century survey as three large virgates (12). It is less easy to see how the Domesday survey made the other two small holdings 1.5 and 2.5 (large) virgates, if they were actually one and two. These are the

[44] J. H. Round, 'The Northamptonshire survey', in *The Victoria History of the County of Northampton*, vol. 1, edited by W. R. Adkins and R. M. Serjeantson (London, 1902), p. 380.
[45] BL, Cott Calig. A xiii, fos. 121–39.

values assigned by the twelfth century and which agree with the 1230 listing. Possibly there could have been some adjustment before 1124.

The total of sixty virgates in 1230 has to be equated with four hides in the two early assessments. Chilcotes is not mentioned in 1124 or 1230, and doubtless had gone out of existence as a vill; its lands too were probably within Thornby parish. Recalling that the 1086 assessment was one virgate, then this should have descended as four small virgates. If this total is added to the Cold Ashby sixty small virgates, then a total of sixty-four is achieved, nicely agreeing with the four-hide rating, at sixteen small virgates to the hide.

Close correspondence between medieval yardland village ratings and the Domesday hidage can be found for many Northamptonshire villages. When studying the individual holdings within a village, the same close relationships are evident. Holdings consisting of fractions of a hide are common, and the above examples show that the reason for this is because they are being precisely assessed at some fixed ratio such as 10, 12, 16 yardlands, etc. to the hide. The assessments are therefore seen to be a fundamental feature of a given vill.

They are so fundamental that in some cases the fiscal assessments affect the structure of the village fields on the ground. Examples have been published where tenurial cycles of thirty-two and nineteen names repeating themselves throughout the field systems represent thirty-two and nineteen yardlands respectively.[46] On the ground, furlongs were made to fit this fiscal assessment, so that at Hardingstone, where there is a cycle of thirty-two lands/yardlands, furlongs have thirty-two or sixty-four, etc. yardlands.

At Wollaston there were about eighty-four yardlands (84 are expected because of the existence of seven Domesday hides and the prevalence in the area of a rating of twelve yardlands to the hide), and furlongs of 490-yard width are common in the fields.[47] This width is what would be expected from eighty-four strips of average width 5.8 yards (a 17.5-foot pole). So, again, there is evidence of the fiscal assessment being reflected in the physical layout of the fields.

Watford has presented problems in the past because of an apparent multiplicity of manors and settlements. Fieldwork and study of a wide range of surviving documents have shown that there is one parish encompassing three separate vills, each with its own independent field system: namely Watford, Murcott (shrunken) and Silsworth (now deserted) (see figure 5.9).

---

[46] D. N. Hall, 'Hardingstone parish survey 1972', *Northamptonshire Archaeology*, 15 (1980), pp. 119–32; Hall, 'Fieldwork and documentary evidence', pp. 52–3.

[47] D. N. Hall, *Wollaston, Portrait of a Village* (Wollaston, 1977), pp. 198, 206–7, where different sources state 89.5 and 86 yardlands respectively. Subsequent work suggests that there were 84.

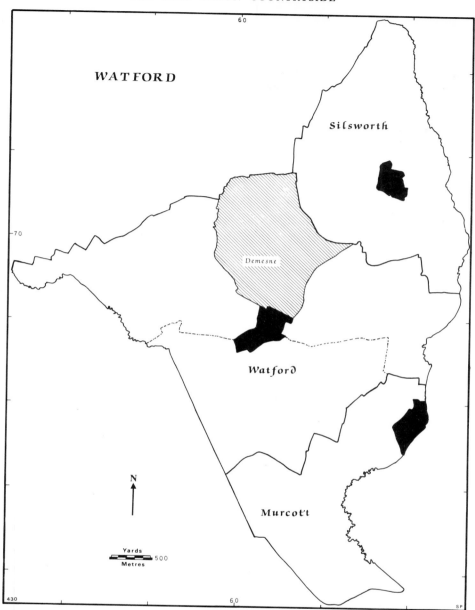

WATFORD

Silsworth

Demesne

Watford

N

Murcott

Yards
500
Metres

The Domesday survey records that Watford was assessed at two hides, but the 1124 survey states that there were four hides.[48] A remarkable survey of 1289, splitting the estate equally between the four daughters of Eustace de Watford, lists all the virgates.[49] Each is stated to be either

FIGURE 5.9 *Watford parish with the townships of Silsworth and Murcott*

[48] Round, 'The Northamptonshire survey', p. 373.
[49] *Calender Close Rolls Edward I, 1272–1279* (London, 1900), pp. 326–31.

demesne, villein or free. The total is ninety-six, which obviously equates with the 1124 four hides at twenty-four yardlands to the hide.

At enclosure in the eighteenth century, only Murcott and half of Watford were still open field; each was rated at twenty-four yardlands. This information leads to an interpretation of the early hidages. Watford was forty-eight yardlands (run as a two-field system) and the hamlets were twenty-four each. The Domesday survey assessed Watford only, missing out the hamlets, but the twelfth-century survey included them.

This numerical identification takes back the recorded history of the hamlets to an earlier date (1124) than hitherto recognized. In all probability they were also in existence in 1066, and again we have small, shrunken and deserted sites, which might easily be mistaken for medieval offshoots of Watford, turning out to be of Saxon origin. In the case of Silsworth, Ipswich-ware pottery (middle Saxon) has been discovered, so the early origin is acceptable. No doubt the survival of an independent small field system is another indication of an early origin.

In contrast to the often irregular and fractional numbers of hides found in eleventh-century manor sizes, the value for the whole village is often a simple round figure, two- and four-hide units being very common. Round pointed this out in 1902 and assumed that it reflected some artificial fiscal assessment.[50] The information given above shows that the hide assessments are fundamental to a vill and are even physically reflected on the ground in the layout of the field systems. This, along with the complexity of the manorial sizes, makes it extremely unlikely that the Normans were responsible either for the manors or the fields that are listed or implied in the great survey. They recorded what they found, and so the Domesday survey is an account of the extraordinary organization of Saxon England quite as much as a Norman fiscal return.

Conclusion

Two techniques have been applied to determine the state of England before the Conquest. Archaeological fieldwork has shown that early and middle Saxon settlement was limited to areas of light soil. There was continued occupation of choice Roman sites and small new settlements were created as well. The settlement pattern was like that of the prehistoric and Roman periods, with small farmsteads scattered over the countryside more closely than present-day villages. Most of these sites were deserted

---

[50] J. H. Round, 'Introduction to the Northamptonshire survey', in *The Victoria County History of the County of Northampton*, vol. 1, pp. 263–4.

before the late Saxon period; there then seems to have been a reorganization of settlement and landscape, with the foundation of the villages recorded in 1086 and subsequently.

The place-name evidence suggests the formation of village-names containing *tūn* compounded with a personal name during the seventh to tenth centuries. This concords well with the archaeological data, both sources suggesting a fairly fundamental reorganization of settlement.[51] That thegns or lords did have the political power to undertake such an operation is paralleled in the seventeenth century with the creation of great houses and their gardens, often involving the movement of a village.

The other technique has been to study in detail the information offered by medieval field systems. Where plans are unavailable, field survey has again been used successfully to reconstruct them. It is then possible to use the data in fieldbooks or other surveys. The information obtainable is of several types. Furlong names afford detail of the topography and former land use, often revealing what was there before, such as marsh, heath or woodland. The distribution of the manorial demesne gives information about the relationships of manors, and analysis of tenurial sequences can reveal the existence of older estates that have been absorbed into a given field system.

These three information types (topographical, demesne and tenurial) may relate to events either before or after the Conquest; in the case of well-documented parishes, it is usually possible to determine which. Here we are interested in the pre-Norman arrangement and it can be seen that nearly all the present villages were in existence. Many of them were probably once part of larger multiple estates. The strip fields were a new creation probably laid out at the same time as the villages. This seems particularly likely in view of the physical layout reflecting the fiscal assessment of the vill. The field names show that in some areas there was still woodland or rough scrub grazing on the edge of the fields, usually on land that was less attractive agriculturally.

This view of the landscape and villages in the late Saxon period suggests that the process of estate fragmentation, well documented during the Middle Ages, had already begun. The place-name evidence and the estates recorded in the Domesday Survey are sufficient to show the former existence of large multiple estates. Detailed studies of the demesnes of vills containing more than one manor in a single settlement indicate that the multiple manors were once a single entity. Field studies are also showing that many small settlements not recorded before the twelfth or thirteenth century were in existence in 1086 and are therefore Saxon and not, as once

[51] D. Hooke, 'Village development in the West Midlands', in Hooke (ed.), *Medieval Villages*, p. 134.

thought, secondary settlements from a major village in the post-Conquest centuries.

As a whole, recent studies have shown that settlement in late Saxon England already existed in an immediately recognizable form. The degree of fiscal and field-system organization was surprisingly complex.

6

Regional Variation in Southern and Central England in the Anglo-Saxon Period and its Relationship to Land Units and Settlement

DELLA HOOKE

Working on the evidence contained in the Domesday survey, Professor Darby and his colleagues have drawn attention to regional variations of land use apparent in much of England soon after the Norman Conquest.[1] This is obviously a state of affairs that owes little to the Normans themselves, although they may have had an important influence upon patterns of landholding and tenurial relationships within estates. The survey reveals a situation which had developed over a very long period of time, but which can most readily be examined in the preceding Anglo-Saxon period when the documentary record first begins to add substantially to that derived from archaeological sources. Some aspects of this pattern may be traced much further back, but the present chapter will examine these regional patterns as they become apparent in selected areas of south-central England in the late Anglo-Saxon period, only a few hundred years before 1086. Nevertheless, the detailed evidence available for this late period has important implications for an understanding of the earlier course of events which produced these patterns.

Areas of Intensive Agriculture

The most prosperous agricultural regions stand out well in 1086, both in concentrations of population, plough teams and ploughlands, and in the location of head manors. Although soil type may have influenced the number of oxen actually required to plough the land, the corroboratory evidence of population figures and ploughlands, whether the latter were fiscal or real land assessments, seems to indicate regions of outstanding

This work is based upon research funded by the Economic and Social Research Council.
[1] H. C. Darby (ed.), *The Domesday Geography of England*, vol. 1–7 (Cambridge, 1952–77).

agricultural prosperity. The whole concept of the Domesday assessment seems to regard the arable potential of an estate as a prime factor in determining manorial revenues. These areas are not necessarily clearly reflected in the pre-Conquest evidence, primarily from charters, for there were other factors that often determined the portrayal of topographical detail in these documents. In north-east Berkshire, for instance, archaeological evidence indicates a concentration of settlement in the upper Thames valley in the late prehistoric, Roman and early Anglo-Saxon periods, indicated by extensive field systems in the earlier period and, later, rich burials and important settlement sites, including two ranges of Anglo-Saxon timbered halls on the south side of the Thames before it loops northwards.[2] This was the most heavily populated area of the county in 1086 and the most intensively cultivated, with large numbers of plough teams operating (figure 6.1).[3] The pre-Conquest boundary clauses of 'Abingdon' and Sunningwell do indeed refer to furrows, headlands and 'acres' to the north of Abingdon, but in the area to the south of the Ock–Thames line, the clauses of Drayton, Milton, Wittenham and Appleford

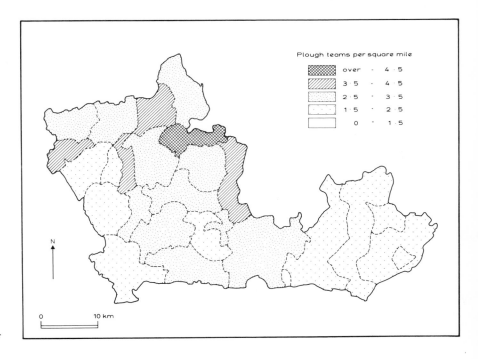

FIGURE 6.1 *Berkshire: Domesday plough-team densities*

[2] D. Benson and D. Miles, *The Upper Thames Valley: An Archaeological Survey of the River Gravels* (Oxford, 1974).
[3] E. M. J. Campbell, 'Berkshire', in H. C. Darby and E. M. J. Campbell (eds), *The Domesday Geography of South-East England* (Cambridge, 1971), pp. 239–86, figure 79.

take more heed of rivers, streams and dykes than of arable features, although a furrow is noted upon the western boundary of Appleford and upon an internal boundary in Wittenham.[4] Here one has to examine the estates themselves to realize the importance of the region (figure 6.2).

On the southern bank, Sutton hundred was focused upon the royal estate of Sutton Courtenay and the estate divisions are of a totally arbitrary nature, as if dividing up a once-compact unit. In a projecting corner of Drayton parish lay one of the probable Anglo-Saxon 'palace' sites, although it was Sutton Courtenay and Steventon that remained royal estates in 1086. A detached portion of Sutton Courtenay, Hulgrove Meadow, also lay between Steventon and Drayton in the early nineteenth century, again suggesting subdivision of a once-larger estate. To the east, Appleford, granted to Deormod c. AD 895, passed out of royal ownership, but remained a chapelry of Sutton Courtenay, as did Sutton Wick in Drayton.[5] One sees here, therefore, the apparently late fragmentation of a former extensive royal estate. The close proximity of rich pagan burials and a second range of timbered halls at Long Wittenham nearby also seem to stress the existence of an early Anglo-Saxon aristocratic element in this region.[6] Roman estates were in evidence to the north of the Ock–Thames line and here a minster was to be established, probably under the sponsorship of the kings of Wessex, and the possibility of continuing British Christianity in this area has not gone unquestioned.[7] By 1086, many of the estates in this region had been acquired by the abbey of Abingdon. It is interesting to note that Barton in Abingdon (OE *beretūn*, 'barley farm', later 'grange, demesne farm') remained the chief administrative centre of the abbey's home manor in 1086, in a locality where Roman estate administration may also have been conducted from a small villa.[8]

Although the agricultural prosperity of the Thames valley region to the south of Abingdon is not clearly reflected in the features noted in the charter boundary clauses, there are other regions in which features denoting arable activity show a marked concentration. These, too, seem at one time to have been areas of intensive cultivation and, for a number of

[4] M. Gelling, *The Place-Names of Berkshire*, part 3, English Place-Name Society, vol. 51 (Cambridge, 1976).

[5] P. H. Sawyer, *Anglo-Saxon Charters: An Annotated List and Bibliography* (London, 1968), S. 355; W. de Gray Birch, *Cartularium Saxonicum*, 3 vols (London, 1885–99), B. 581.

[6] T. Dickinson, 'The Anglo-Saxon burial sites of the Upper Thames region, and their bearing on the history of Wessex, c. AD 400–700' (unpublished D.Phil. thesis, University of Oxford, 1976). Also information from D. Miles, Oxfordshire Archaeological Unit.

[7] F. M. Stenton, *The Early History of the Abbey of Abingdon* (London, 1913); H. T. Lambrick, 'The early history of Abingdon, Berkshire, and its abbey', *Medieval Archaeology*, 12 (1968), pp. 26–34.

[8] D. Miles, 'Abingdon and its region: early Anglo-Saxon settlement evidence', in T. R. Rowley (ed.), *Anglo-Saxon Settlement and Landscape*, British Archaeological Reports 6 (Oxford, 1974), pp. 36–41; P. Morgan (ed.), *Domesday Book, 5, Berkshire* (Chichester, 1979), 7.6; *Domesday Book*, vol. 1, Record Commission (London, 1738), fo. 58c.

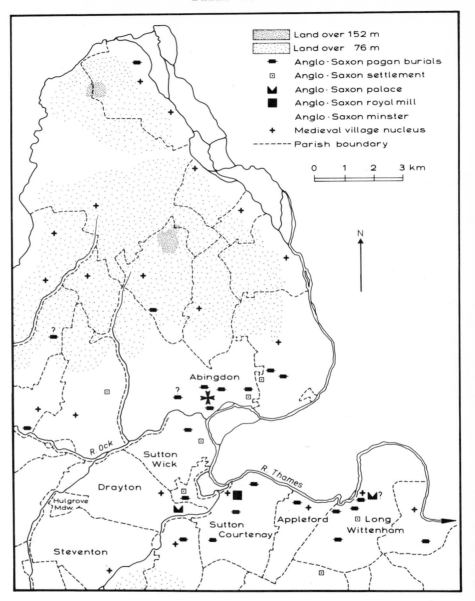

FIGURE 6.2 *The middle Thames valley region of Berkshire: Anglo-Saxon archaeological evidence and parish patterns*

reasons of a historical and environmental nature, more documentary evidence of land use survives for the late Anglo-Saxon period.

By the late Anglo-Saxon period, a pattern of estates had been established in the clay Vale of the White Horse (plate XV), now in Oxfordshire, and in the Wylye valley of Wiltshire, which is not uncommon in riverine areas (figures 6.3 and 6.4). A series of elongated estates ran from the river to the

PLATE XV: *North Berkshire Downs across the Vale of the White Horse; Uffington Camp lies at the highest point.* © Della Hooke.

adjacent chalk uplands, thus including a variety of different kinds of land within each. There is no clear evidence as to when these estates were first demarcated. Evidence of pagan Anglo-Saxon burial on or close to the boundaries has been taken to indicate that the bounds were already established by the seventh century, when boundary burial, often secondary in barrows, seems to have been fashionable, but the evidence is not indisputable.[9] What is clear, however, is that the boundaries often had to negotiate earlier field systems and it is where they are making their way over and around cultivated land that the charter clauses refer to such features as headlands, furrows and 'acres'.

There is ample field and crop-mark evidence to show that a system of roughly rectangular 'Celtic' fields extended over most of the upper chalklands, and in many places such systems are cut through by later estate boundaries (figure 6.5). Moreover, the archaeological evidence suggests

[9] D. Bonney, 'Early Saxon burials and boundaries in Wiltshire', *Wiltshire Archaeological and Natural History Magazine*, 61 (1960), pp. 25–30; A. Goodier, 'The formation of boundaries in Anglo-Saxon England, a statistical study', *Medieval Archaeology*, 28 (1984), pp. 1–21.

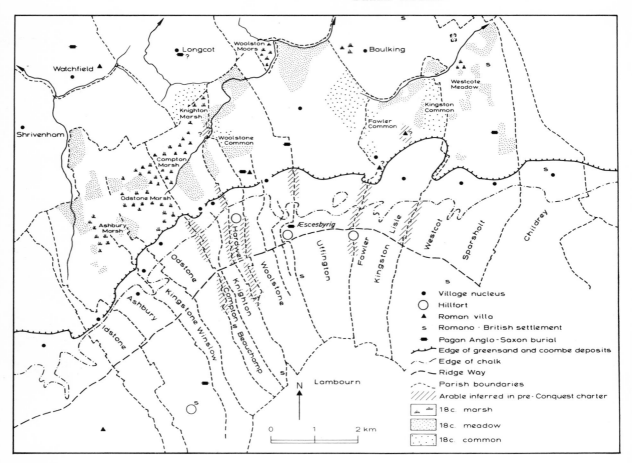

FIGURE 6.3 *The Vale of the White Horse: archaeological evidence and parish patterns*

that the fields were still in use in the fourth century AD, although by that date they may not have been the only type of field system in use. It is most unlikely that they were confined to the higher chalkland, and crop-marks, although much erased by later cultivation, suggest that they extended downwards on to the lower land (figure 6.6). Of some significance, an aerial photograph of Compton Beauchamp, in the Vale of the White Horse ((plate XVI) figure 6.7a) clearly shows a type of field system which may have given rise to many of the stepped features apparent in estate boundaries, features which, from the documentary evidence, seem to be as ancient as the boundaries themselves.[10] The fields shown are larger and squarer than the more widely known 'Celtic' fields and may be of Roman date.

[10] I acknowledge the permission of Berkshire County Council to reproduce this photograph, taken by Clyde Surveys Ltd.

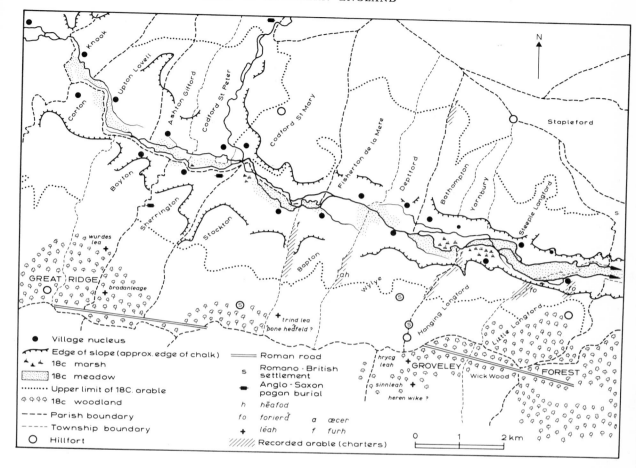

FIGURE 6.4 *The Wylye valley, Wiltshire: archaeological evidence and parish patterns*

The boundary in question is an internal boundary within the present parish, dividing an estate at Hardwell, granted by King Edward to a vassal called *Tata Æthehumflo* (for *Æthe[l]huni filio?*) in AD 903, from the remainder of Compton Beauchamp parish.[11] The bounds in the area can be precisely identified, as Hardwell was a separate unit for tithe redemption in the nineteenth century (plate XVII). Between the Ridge Way and the Icknield Street the boundary runs to *anne gar æcer on an on hæfde . . . þonone andlanges anre fyrh oð hit cymð to anum byge. þanone of þæm byge forð on ane fyrh oð hit cymð to anre forierðe. . . . þon' on Icenhilde weg be tellesburh westan*, thus running to a 'gore acre', a 'head (of a plough strip?)', a 'furrow', a 'bend', another 'furrow' and a feature called a *forierð*, which was either a projecting

<hr />

[11] Sawyer, *Anglo-Saxon Charters*, S. 369; Birch, *Cartularium Saxonicum*, B. 601; printed in Gelling, *Place-Names of Berkshire*, 3, p. 684.

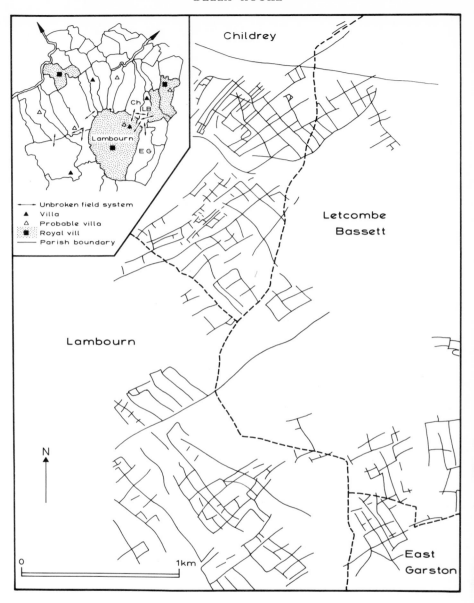

Childrey

Letcombe
Bassett

Lambourn

— Unbroken field system
▲ Villa
△ Probable villa
■ Royal vill
⋯ Parish boundary

N
↑

0   1km

East
Garston

FIGURE 6.5   *North Berkshire:*
early fields and parish
boundaries

piece of ploughland or a headland at the end of plough strips,[12] before
passing to the west of the Iron Age fortification known today as Hardwell
Camp (figure 6.7b). According to the Oxfordshire Sites and Monuments

[12] The first interpretation is offered by Gelling, *Place-Names of Berkshire*, 3, p. 776 but I. H. Adams,
Agrarian Landscape Terms: A Glossary for Historical Geographers (London, 1976), pp. 86–7, notes that a
similar term 'foreacre' was used for a headland in Essex and 'foraker' for an 'area where the strips met
end-to-end' in Kent; *Oxford English Dictionary*, p. 1051, suggests 'headland'.

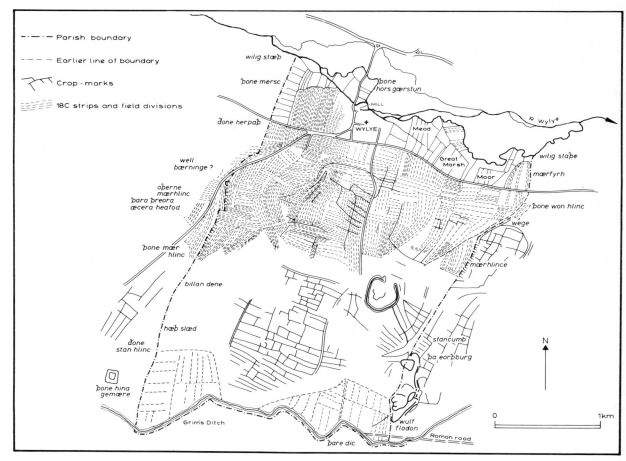

Legend:
— ·· — ·· — Parish boundary
— — — — Earlier line of boundary
Crop-marks
18C strips and field divisions

Map labels: wilig stæþ; þone mersc; þone hors gærstun; MILL; þone herpaþ; WYLYE; Meod; R Wylye; well bærninge?; Great Marsh; wilig staþe; mærfyrh; oþerne mærhlinc; þara þreora æcera heafod; Moor; þone won hlinc; wege; þone mær hlinc; mærhlince; billan dene; stancumb; þa eorþburg; hæþ slæd; þone stan hlinc; þone hina gemære; wulf flodon; Grim's Ditch; Roman road; þare dic; N; 0 1km

FIGURE 6.6 *Wylye, Wiltshire: prehistoric and medieval land use*

Record, the earlier fields are related to a possible drove road, which bears no relationship, in the route it follows, to estate boundaries and is likely, therefore, to pre-date estate demarcation.[13] We may see here the type of field system that influenced the courses of so many estate boundaries in cultivated regions.

There are two points that need further discussion: the size of the estates themselves, and the location of the arable land depicted in the charters. There is evidence that many of the present-day parishes in this area were subdivided by the end of the tenth century.[14] Indeed, the grouping of estates into ecclesiastical parishes was largely an accident of church organization. The charters for the Vale of the White Horse show an eminent thegn, Wulfric, uniting two estates in the tenth century, after

[13] Oxfordshire Sites and Monuments Record, Woodstock, 7527.
[14] Sawyer, *Anglo-Saxon Charters*, S. 856; Birch, *Cartularium Saxonicum*, B. 491; S. 503; B. 796: west Woolstone; S. 575; B. 902: east Woolstone.

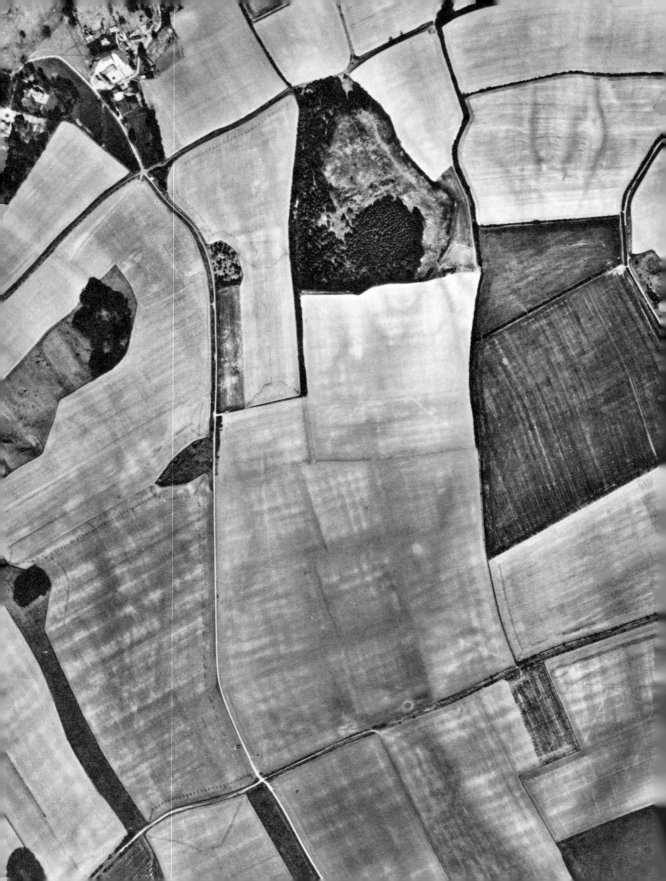

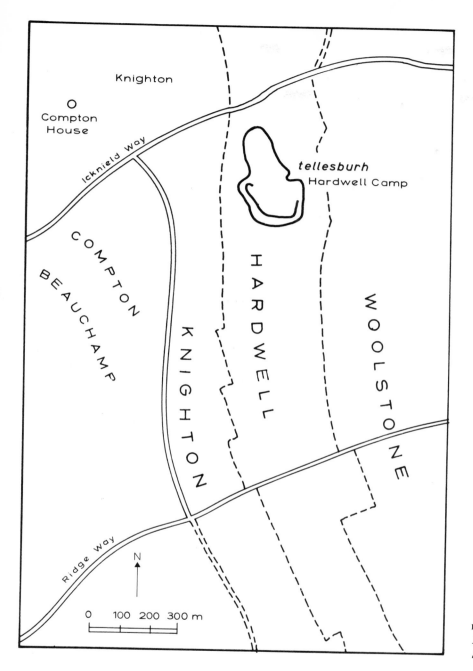

Knighton

O
Compton
House

Icknield Way

COMPTON

BEAUCHAMP

KNIGHTON

HARDWELL

tellesburh
Hardwell Camp

WOOLSTONE

Ridge Way

N

0 100 200 300 m

FIGURE 6.7 *Compton Beauchamp: field systems related to the Hardwell boundary*

PLATE XVII: *The estate of Hardwell: the boundary encloses the two large pasture fields in the centre of the picture.* © Della Hooke.

which the parish and medieval village was known as *Olvricestune*, 'Wulfric's *tūn*', although earlier the estate may have formed only one division of an area referred to as *Æscesbyrig*, 'Ashbury', after the name for the Iron Age hillfort of Uffington Castle (figure 6.3).[15] Usually, however, a manorial centre and related settlement nucleus seem to have developed within each estate unit and can still be identified today. Within the parish of Stockton in the Wylye valley, for instance (see figure 6.4), Stockton village was the medieval nucleus of an estate granted by King Edward to a thegn, Æthelwulf, in AD 901, but the parish also includes the estate of Bapton, which was excluded from the grant.[16] In the Vale of the White Horse, Compton Beauchamp parish includes estates centred upon Compton, Knighton and Hardwell, all separate estates in the tenth century (figure 6.3 and plate XVIII).[17] Today the estate centres are often represented by no more than a single farmstead or hamlet, usually located at the foot of an escarpment in both the Wylye and Ock valleys. Later historical maps indicate further longitudinal division within the estates, for the demesne farm often formed a distinct holding extending from the river to the chalk downs, its lands separate from those of the manorial tenants. The date at which this came into effect has not, however, been established.

[15] Gelling, *Place-Names of Berkshire*, 3, pp. 675–7.
[16] Sawyer, *Anglo-Saxon Charters*, S. 362; Birch, *Cartularium Saxonicum*, B. 595.
[17] Sawyer, *Anglo-Saxon Charters*, S. 369; Birch, *Cartularium Saxonicum*, B. 601; S. 564; B. 908. Cf. D. Bonney, 'Early boundaries and estates in southern England', in P. H. Sawyer (ed.), *Medieval Settlement, Continuity and Change* (London, 1976), pp. 72–82.

PLATE XVIII: *Knighton in Compton Beauchamp, the present village nucleus.*
© Della Hooke.

The location of the early medieval cultivated land is clearly identified by the charter evidence and in the Wylye valley, in particular, there is little doubt that the Anglo-Saxon cultivated zone was precisely that of medieval times, as represented in later historical sources (figure 6.4), and probably cultivated under an open-field system. On the western boundary of Wylye, south of the river (figure 6.6), a stony lynchet (a steep natural slope) and a heathy slade are noted on the downland, but the 'head of the acres' is noted as the boundary runs between the open fields of Bapton and Wylye.[18] The correlation is so precise that on the land beside the river, normally meadowland at all periods, an extension of the arable in medieval times in Hanging Langford seems already present in the tenth century, the Wylye clause noting a 'boundary furrow' to the north of the valley routeway. Some of the *hlinc* features may have described steps formed by ploughing away from a boundary over a period of time and are recorded in this zone on both the eastern and western boundaries of Wylye. At one point, the eastern boundary has been straightened, but the *won hlinc*, 'crooked lynchet', which was still the boundary in the eighteenth century, shows up remarkably well on aerial photographs.[19]

The correlation between Anglo-Saxon and medieval cultivated land is equally apparent in the Vale of the White Horse. The zone extended from about the 100 m contour at the foot of the escarpment up over the brow of

[18] Sawyer, *Anglo-Saxon Charters*, S. 469; Birch, *Cartularium Saxonicum*, B. 757.
[19] Wilts SMR, Trowbridge: County Council Hi-level A.Ps. 1971 Run 14/230050.

the scarp face (figure 6.3).[20] In Kingston Lisle and Uffington, references to agricultural terms cease near the two hillforts of Rams Hill and Uffington Castle, but further to the west the land falls away south-westwards and here the arable land seems to have extended further southwards to reach partway down the dip slope. Once again, the references to arable are explicit, the western boundary of Uffington, for instance, running down to 'the west furrow of the head acre, down over the crosswise furrow' to the north of the Icknield Way, while the western boundary of Compton Beauchamp ran along 'the driven furrow' above the Ridge Way near the Neolithic long barrow of 'Wayland's Smithy'. In general, this zone corresponds closely to that of recorded arable in the eighteenth and nineteenth centuries, but a 1785 map of Uffington and part of Kingston Lisle suggests that much of the high downland was also cultivated at some stage in the medieval period, for strip holdings are indicated which reach to the southern boundary.[21] The charters suggest that this was open, uncultivated land in the late Anglo-Saxon period, as field-names again indicate in the nineteenth century.

There is little information in the charters about the use of such downland, but the cultivated zone had obviously shrunk significantly since late Roman times, when corn-drying ovens were still in operation on the higher downs.[22] Domesday plough-team figures also suggest that the region was one of diminishing cultivation. Although natural or archaeological features form the bulk of the landmarks on the high land, often a feature of lightly settled areas, one of the Uffington charters records a stud fold, implying the rearing of horses, and it is likely that other domestic stock was also pastured here.[23] Sheep-rearing may have been increasing in importance.

There is little indication of woodland regeneration on the north Berkshire downs and only 'a small wood' at Ashbury appears in the Domesday record of the region.[24] On the Groveley Ridge, the watershed between the Wylye and Nadder valleys, on the other hand, woodland is clearly indicated on the highest land, where clay with flint deposits cap the chalk (figure 6.4). The boundary clauses refer to *lēah* features, which were probably areas of woodland, such as *bradanleage*, 'the broad wood', in Sherrington. Here the *wurdes leah*, 'Wurþ's *lēah*', suggests that the

---

[20] D. Hooke, 'Anglo-Saxon estates in the Vale of the White Horse', *Oxoniensia*, 52 (1987, forthcoming).

[21] *A Map of Uffington in the County of Berkshire*, 1785; *A Map of Fawler and Kingston Lisle*, 1785; *A Survey of Lord Craven's Estates*, 1785. Berks RO, Reading, D/EC P12, D/EC P13 and D/EC E13.

[22] For example, Oxon SMR, Ashbury 7905, 9738.

[23] Sawyer, *Anglo-Saxon Charters*, S. 1208; Birch, *Cartularium Saxonicum*, B. 687.

[24] Morgan (ed.), *Domesday Book*, 5, 8,1.

woodland extended further northwards than in the nineteenth century.[25] Earthwork enclosures of probable Iron Age date, however, suggest that the woodland had expanded since prehistoric times. The woodland, too, may have served as summer pasture and an estate of *Wyke* in Baverstock, on the southern edge of the Groveley Forest, seems to have been a herding establishment annexed to the estate of Wylye by the tenth century.[26] By 1086, part at least of the Groveley woodland had been taken in as royal forest.

In the Wylye valley, meadowland existed on the floodplain of the river, but in the Vale of the White Horse this zone was much wider, corresponding to the heavy soils of the Gault clays drained by numerous tributaries of the river Ock, and there were also extensive areas of marsh in the late Anglo-Saxon period. Streams, marshes (OE *mōr*) and areas overgrown with rushes occur frequently as landmarks in this northern zone, but meadows such as 'Bula's mead' and 'the clean meadow' in Uffington can also be identified, frequently corresponding to the meadowland noted on later historical maps. The Domesday survey meticulously notes the acreages of meadow in this zone, with 212 acres in Kingston Lisle and an additional 50 acres in Fawler in that parish, 85 acres in Uffington and 150 acres on one of the Woolstone manors. Indeed, large areas of common meadow and common pasture survived until Enclosure in the eighteenth century. Stock-rearing or dairying in the pre-Conquest period is indicated by a reference to *ðes cincges scypene*, 'the king's cowsheds', in Kingston Lisle near the north-eastern boundary of Fawler, possibly the dairy farm noted in Kingston Lisle in 1086.[27] The grant of Fawler in AD 943 also adds on *an hyrde wic æt bahalacing*, 'a herding establishment at Balking', the estate immediately to the north of Uffington, then associated with one hide of land and twelve acres of meadow. The importance of livestock, especially cattle, in this area in the pre-Conquest period is particularly important, as it is so often masked by the nature of the Domesday record. There was some arable in this northern zone, but this lay mostly at the foot of the escarpment where it bulged northwards.

The main zone of occupation may have moved from the uplands by Roman times, for although native settlements continued to be occupied on the higher downland, villas or substantial farmsteads have been identified in west Woolstone, Kingston Lisle and, possibly, Fawler in the Vale of the White Horse (figure 6.3). They were located near the northern edge of the

---

[25] Sawyer, *Anglo-Saxon Charters*, S. 766; W. Dugdale, *Monasticon Anglicanum*, edited by B. Bandinel, J. Caley, and H. Ellis, vol. 2 (London, 1846), pp. 323–4.

[26] Sawyer, *Anglo-Saxon Charters*, S. 469; Birch, *Cartularium Saxonicum*, B. 77.

[27] Sawyer, *Anglo-Saxon Charters*, S. 713; Birth, *Cartularium Saxonicum*, B. 1121; Morgan (ed.), *Domesday Book*, 5, 1,32.

cultivated zone. It is not inconceivable that the boundaries between their lands may have influenced those of the Anglo-Saxon estates. As yet, however, there is insufficient evidence to argue for direct villa/estate continuity. Indeed, few Roman sites have been identified on the lower land in the Wylye valley, noted so far only in Codford St Mary parish and possibly at Bathampton in Wylye, and further westwards at Norton Bavant. Where one notes a major villa apparently dominating a whole collection of estates, as in the Avon valley of Wiltshire, it seems likely that administrative organization was still largely centralized (figure 6.8).

A shrinkage of the zone under arable, with a recession from the more marginal upland, may have resulted from a number of factors, but is confirmed by the environmental evidence from a number of sites in south-central England.[28] In regions that were no longer under pressure to supply the demands of the Roman occupation and were confronted with a breakdown in the market economy at the end of that period, coupled with a possible decline in population levels, land that was marginal because of environmental reasons would be the first to be abandoned. There are indications, accepted by some, but rejected by others, that the chalklands may have been suffering from a prolonged period of over-exploitation and monoculture, which made them an area of diminishing returns.[29] Occupation, however, is unlikely to have continued at the villas, some of which seem to have lain in ruins when used as sites of pagan Anglo-Saxon burial (as at Woolstone),[30] while that at Fawler was known in the tenth century as 'the holy place',[31] hardly the nomenclature of a thriving settlement. Settlement, however, continued to be concentrated in the most fertile zone and the medieval villages in the Vale of the White Horse are rarely far distant from the Roman centres. The charters also show that agriculture was organized in this zone under some form of open-field arrangement by the tenth century, a factor which may have encouraged the increasing nucleation of settlement.

Estate Demarcation

·The abandonment of the higher land is an important feature, for it permitted the Anglo-Saxon estates to be virtually self-sufficient, probably

[28] P. Waton, 'A palynological study of the impact of Man on the landscape of central southern England, with special reference to the chalklands' (unpublished Ph.D. thesis, University of Southampton, 1983).
[29] P. C. Buckland, 'Cereal production, storage and population: a caveat', in S. Limbrey and J. G. Evans (eds), *The Effect of Man in the Landscape: The Lowland Zone*, Council for British Archaeology Research Report 21 (London, 1978), pp. 43–5.
[30] Oxon SMR, 7316.
[31] D. Hooke, 'Two Christianized sites upon parish boundaries: "Cada's minster", Willersey, Gloucs., and "the holy place", Fawler, Oxon.', *Medieval Archaeology*, 31 (1987, forthcoming).

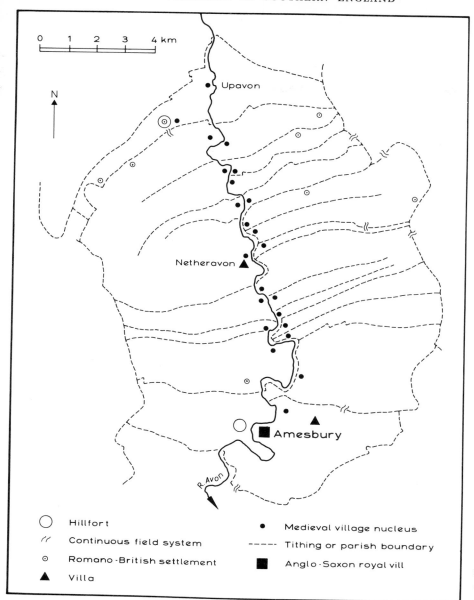

0   1   2   3   4 km

N

Upavon

Netheravon ▲

○

■ Amesbury ▲

R. Avon

○   Hillfort
⌒⌒   Continuous field system
◎   Romano-British settlement
▲   Villa

●   Medieval village nucleus
- - - -   Tithing or parish boundary
■   Anglo-Saxon royal vill

FIGURE 6.8   *Roman settlements and estate boundaries in the Avon valley, Wiltshire*

for the first time, and this may be a pointer towards the date of their consolidation. Boundaries seem to have been drawn up deliberately to include all three types of land within each estate: valley land suitable for cattle; arable on the better-drained soils where they were not too steep; and open downland, particularly suitable for sheep, with, as on the Grovely Ridge, occasional woodland providing additional summer pasture. The estates, therefore, show a close relationship to the nature of the land as it was in the Anglo-Saxon period and not to conditions prevailing earlier, even in late Roman times. Their demarcation may have coincided with the allocation of estates to Anglo-Saxon landholders. This is unlikely to have occurred in the earliest stage of Anglo-Saxon settlement, but seems to represent a later stage, when a hierarchy had become firmly established within Anglo-Saxon society that included a lordly element below the level of the aristocracy. The delineation of the roughly parallel units seems to indicate deliberate planning at some stage and there is some evidence to suggest that the southern side of the Vale of the White Horse, incorporating the scarp face of the north Berkshire Downs, may initially have been appendant to the royal vill of Wantage, just as the eastern part of the Wylye valley in Wiltshire lay within the hinterland of the royal vill of Wilton.

Although these regions seem to have been associated in a special way with royal centres, they also seem to have been areas of diminishing agricultural output, displaying a shrinkage in the amount of land under arable in the early medieval period. Yet the hidage values of the estates in the Vale are surprisingly high in the pre-Conquest period, although they were drastically reduced in 1086. It is not clear whether this reflects the amount of land under cultivation (or considered as potential arable) when hidage values were calculated, and the additional assets of meadowland and livestock, or whether, perhaps, such thegns' estates were highly taxed and failed to benefit from the more beneficial assessments granted to more powerful landowners (including the Church).

As these estates were granted out to thegns and individual landholders, it seems likely that they had to become increasingly self-sufficient. The great build-up of estates, such as those held by the Church, was often still to take place and even on Church estates a system of leasing land to sub-tenants maintained the pressures upon 'manorial' revenue. Under later Norman rule this requirement was probably intensified, as landholders had to provide more and more in the way of military assistance, but even in Anglo-Saxon times taxes were due, the *fyrd* had to be provided for, and the Church was organized more efficiently to draw tithe.

Fragmentation was not universal, and minster and royal estates were often maintained as larger units for a much longer period. The regular subdivisions of the northern slope of the Berkshire Downs are not found, for instance, within the large parish of Lambourn immediately to the south, a royal vill which also possessed a minster church by the late Anglo-Saxon period. Similarly, fragmentation seems to have been late around the royal vill of Wilton, located near the confluence of the Wylye and the Avon. It may have been areas of medium prosperity appendant to, but not immediately adjacent to, royal territory that were allocated in the above manner.

Estates also seem to be clearly related to the existing village nuclei. No date can at present be stated for the foundation of these settlements, but current research suggests that nucleation was a feature of the middle and later, rather than the early, Anglo-Saxon period. While most parishes included a number of estate-related settlement centres, located near the foot of the chalk scarp, the large nucleated villages of Uffington in the Vale is situated much further to the north and may be of somewhat later, perhaps post-Conquest, foundation. The Woolstone estates, not united until the tenth century, also contain a single nucleated settlement near the internal boundary.

'Intermediate' Regions

The move towards individual, more self-sufficient, estates was not, however, absent from more wooded regions, although it may have occurred later. Boundaries also seem to have been less static in the more densely wooded regions, frequently leading to problems of charter 'solution'. Nevertheless, in what may be termed 'intermediate' zones, a pattern of estate fragmentation can readily be identified by the late Anglo-Saxon period, although in regions of poor resource potential the smaller townships often seem to have remained part of a larger ecclesiastical parish in medieval times. Such regions in which woodland was plentiful in the pre-Conquest period can be clearly identified from charter evidence in many parts of south-central England.

In west-central Berkshire, the estates appear to fan out from a core area centred upon the confluence of the rivers Kennet and Lambourn (figure 6.9a and plate XIX). In Roman times, there were two small semi-urban centres in this riverine zone: *Spinis*, which has been tentatively located upon the watershed between the two rivers, although Roman 'finds' have been undoubtedly clustered most thickly near to the actual confluence itself, and Thatcham, a little further to the east. Romano-British settlement nuclei, which may perhaps be termed villages, also lay between the two centres. A number of villas were located to the north of the Lambourn, together with several other buildings, but surface scatters of pottery suggest that settlement was, if not intensive, found throughout the region. Few pagan Anglo-Saxon burial sites have been identified within this area, although a cemetery at East Shefford, of mid-fifth to late sixth-century date,[32] may indicate penetration along the Roman road that ran north-westwards from Spinis towards central Wiltshire, and an undated burial to the east of Spinis may also date from the Anglo-Saxon period.[33] Thatcham

---

[32] Dickinson, 'Anglo-Saxon burial sites', no. 60.
[33] A. Meaney, *A Gazetteer of Anglo-Saxon Burial Sites* (London, 1964), pp. 51–2.

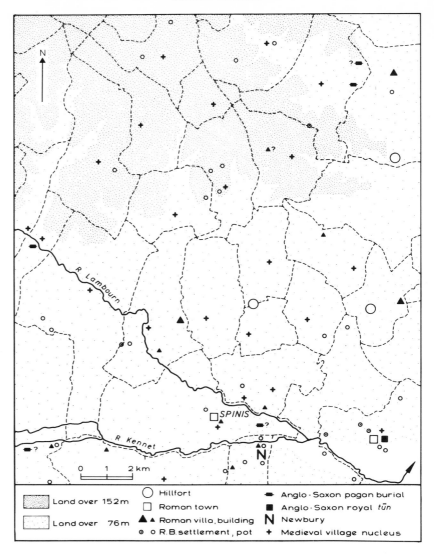

FIGURE 6.9a *Central
Berkshire: the archaeological
evidence*

remained a royal estate at the time of the Norman Conquest, but a new
urban centre was to be created in late Anglo-Saxon times at the Lambourn–
Kennet confluence: Newbury, 'the new *burh*', founded upon the estate of
Ulvertone. Routeways were to focus upon this centre and the charters refer
to a *herpaδ* or *strēt* route running north–south to Newbury from the royal
vill of Wantage, terms which indicate a major highway.

Arable land is not greatly in evidence in the charters of the region.
Although the Kennet valley was a major thoroughfare, the southern part of
the region is composed largely of Eocene beds, which often give rise to soils

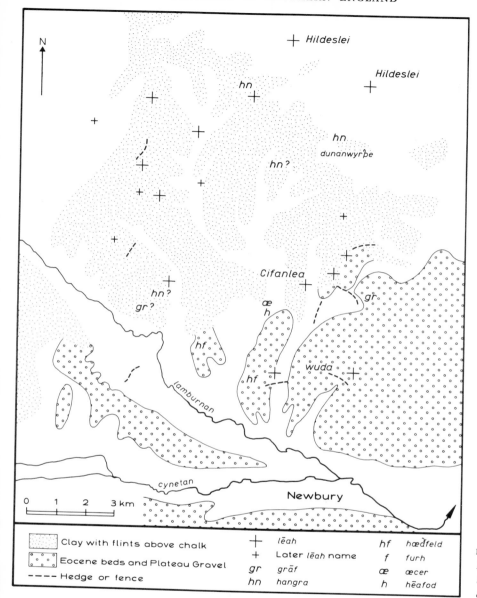

N

+ Hildeslei

Hildeslei

hn

hn
dunanwyrþe

hn?

Cifanlea

hn?
gr?

œ
h

hf

gr

hf

wuda

lamburnan

cynetan

Newbury

0   1   2   3 km

Clay with flints above chalk	+	lēah	hf	hœdfeld
Eocene beds and Plateau Gravel	+	Later lēah name	f	furh
Hedge or fence	gr	grāf	œ	œcer
	hn	hangra	h	hēafod

FIGURE 6.9b *Central Berkshire: pre-Conquest land use, the charter and place-name evidence*

of poor quality, readily degraded by continuous agriculture, while the chalk to the north carries a surface deposit of clay with flints, which produces rather intractable soils. Domesday records indicate a region of only moderate arable activity, with plough teams numbering only 2.5–3.5 per square mile. The charters note arable land near a boundary on only one occasion – on the stepped boundary that separated the two estates of

143

DELLA HOOKE

Winterbourne and Chieveley, near the major *strǣt* route. Here the charters record a furlong, six acres and headlands where the South Field of Chieveley lay in medieval times.[34] Although *feld* has been interpreted by Gelling as originally meaning open pasture land,[35] it is of interest to note that *þone hæðfeld* in Boxford lay near a former villa site and may have been former arable that had reverted to heathland. A *lytlan hæpfeld* is also noted upon the boundary of Chieveley and Donnington, and pollen analysis at a nearby site on Snelsmore Common has indicated intermittent cereal cultivation,[36] perhaps suggesting that the 'heath-fields' were cultivated from time to time. This may indicate a practice of infield and outfield farming not readily recognized from the surviving documentary evidence.

Woodland, however, seems to have been plentiful in this region in Anglo-Saxon times. What were probably isolated patches of woodland are indicated by references to groves and hangers, the latter small woods clinging to the chalk slopes, noted upon the boundaries of Welford, Oare in

[34] Sawyer, *Anglo-Saxon Charters*, S. 558; Gelling, *Place-Names of Berkshire*, 3, pp. 652–3; J. C. Richards, *The Archaeology of the Berkshire Downs: An Introductory Survey* (Reading, 1978), p. 55, is misleading when he takes OE *hlinc* to mean a 'strip lynchet' and OE *gāra* is only 'a triangular-shaped piece of land', not necessarily arable.

[35] M. Gelling, *Place-Names in the Landscape* (London, 1984), pp. 235–7.

[36] Waton, 'A palynological study'.

PLATE XIX: *Central Berkshire: arable land and woodland (view south from Hoe Benham).* © Della Hooke.

Chieveley and Stanmore in Beedon (figure 6.9b).[37] The *lēah* features may be indicative of more generally wooded countryside and although the term may have denoted a glade, it also seems often to have referred to an actual section of woodland. Thus, on the Eocene deposits, *hnæfleage* and *linleahe*, together with *wuda*, 'wood', occur on the southern Chievely boundary. There is also one reference in the south of the region to the term *(ge)fyrhðe*, 'wooded countryside' – *accangefyrðæ*, 'Acca's wood', upon the boundary of Benham. Further north, on the chalk with its surface covering of clay, *bradan leage*, 'the broad ?wood', lay on the Welford/Boxford boundary, and a second *bradanlea* lay in Oare in Chieveley. Other *lēah* features occur on the higher downland to the north and some, like *lilling lea*, Lilley Copse in Brightwalton, and *stanleage*, 'the stony *lēah*' in the detached section of Farnborough parish, are still represented by pockets of woodland today. Even the late-recorded *lēah* names often lie beside boundaries, as if these were the last areas to be taken into cultivation. The detached portion of Farnborough parish, which lay to the east of Catmore, is described in the charters as an area of woodland, and the *stanlege* appended to a grant of Chilton may have lain in the same area.[38] There is little reference to pasture land in the charters, although a grant of Chieveley in AD 951 is accompanied by *pascua quæ in quodam monte habetur*, which may have lain in Peasemore, and a *stodfald*, 'fold for a stud of horses', is noted in Farnborough parish.[39] *Rammes hrycg* in Beedon may be 'ram's ridge', indicating the pasturing of sheep on the downland. It is only the woodland pasture that is noted indirectly in the Domesday evidence, for pasture for herds of pigs is noted upon the manors of Peasemore, Welford, Winterbourne, Chieveley and Shaw. Woodland was, however, carefully managed and was, in addition, an important source of fuel and timber.

Within the Chieveley region, a number of hedgerows are also noted in the charters, and the term *haga* indicates a type of fence that often seems to have run alongside woodland, possibly connected with the management of game animals. *þæs cinges hagan*, 'the king's fence', ran alongside the *hnæfleage* of Chieveley, another ran eastwards from *wealcottes leahe* near the northern boundary of that parish and a further *haga* ran beside an area which is now wooded in Brightwalton. In the West Midlands, it has been found that the prime purpose of hedgerows was to protect arable land from the depredations of woodland animals, but that fields could also be enclosed for the pasture of domestic stock, whereas the *haga* type of fence was seemingly associated with the management and capture of deer.[40]

[37] Gelling, *Place-Names of Berkshire*, 3, pp. 649–70.
[38] Gelling, *Place-Names of Berkshire*, 3, p. 767.
[39] Sawyer, *Anglo-Saxon Charters*, S. 558; Birch, *Cartularium Saxonicum*, B. 892.
[40] D. Hooke, *Anglo-Saxon Landscapes of the West Midlands: The Charter Evidence*, British Archaeological Reports, British series, 95 (Oxford, 1981), pp. 234–54.

Estate Demarcation

Although these wooded regions were more sparsely populated than the older, once heavily cultivated regions, they were not necessarily less prosperous. Perhaps significantly, the estates that eventually gave rise to the parishes of central Berkshire were not noticeably larger than those of the Vale of the White Horse. Although an estate granted to one thegn, Wulfric, in AD 951 included part of Chieveley and part of Peasemore,[41] many of the estates granted in the tenth-century charters of this region are coincident with the later parishes. Fragmentation is, however, as much a feature here as in other regions – Curridge and Oare in Chieveley were granted separately to lords in AD 953 and 968 respectively.[42] There is some evidence to suggest that some holdings had become particularly subdivided at the eve of the Norman Conquest, for Winterbourne contained four different estates in 1086 and Peasemore three. It is pertinent to ask whether this might also reflect a less nucleated pattern of settlement in these regions, one perhaps more suited to a pastoral economy, and the charters occasionally refer to boundary settlements, apparently farmsteads, like *dunanwyrþe* in Beedon. After the Conquest, there is some indication that estates were being again amalgamated and an effect on settlement is suggested by the Domesday entry for Peasemore, which notes that on two of the estates one thegn replaced two as lord, and in each case a hall stood abandoned.[43]

In central Berkshire, immediate pre-Conquest manorial values recorded in the Domesday survey are almost as high as in the Vale of the White Horse, although in both regions they are well below those of Sutton hundred. Although pollen analysis from the site on Snelsmore Common suggests a high incidence of tree and shrub pollen in the period from AD 360 to 1470, with tree, shrub and *Corylus* (hazel) pollen increasing from 60 per cent to 80 per cent in this period,[44] in 1086 plough teams averaged three per square mile, suggesting a mixed regional economy in which a medium amount of crop cultivation was combined with stock-rearing and woodland management to maintain reasonable estate revenues. There is little, other than the sparse charter evidence and estate revenues, to confirm the role of stock-rearing, but it is clear from the charters that neither arable land nor dense woodland covered the whole area. Indeed, the heavier clay soils of many regions appear to have been able to sustain arable activity throughout medieval times rather better than the lighter, more easily degraded soils, which had borne the brunt of earlier activity.

---

[41] Sawyer, *Anglo-Saxon Charters*, S. 558; Birch, *Cartularium Saxonicum*, B. 892.
[42] Sawyer, *Anglo-Saxon Charters*, S. 560; Birch, *Cartularium Saxonicum*, B. 900; S. 760; B. 1225.
[43] Morgan (ed.), *Domesday Book*, 5, 36,6; 46,6.
[44] Waton, 'A palynological study'.

Regions of Woodland and Heath

It would be naïve, in the light cast by this study, to regard regions of intermittent woodland as necessarily areas of little or stagnant development, although, quite clearly, the landscape differed greatly from such regions as the Wylye valley or the Vale of the White Horse, or from such intensively developed areas as the valley of the upper Thames near Oxford. There *were* relatively empty regions, and the districts that later formed part of the forests of Baydon and Savernake in Wiltshire, to quote but two examples, seem to have been both sparsely populated and in parts heavily wooded in the Anglo-Saxon period.[45] In Berkshire, the eastern extension of the county, which was to form the heart of the Forest of Windsor, seems to have been a similar region, together with the south-western part of the county, which bordered upon Wiltshire and Hampshire (plate XX).

Much of eastern Berkshire was to fall within the medieval Forest of Windsor and already by 1086 the woods of Cookham, Windsor and Winkfield had been taken into the king's forest, although quantities of woodland were still available as swine pasture. Much of the area is underlain by Eocene clay deposits, which produce heavy, grade-3 soils, while a band of Bagshot sands capped with gravels produces soils of poor quality across the southern part of the area (figure 6.10). In 1086, plough-team figures were some of the lowest in the county at below 1.5 per square mile, and manorial values were correspondingly low. The medieval parishes here are unusually large, especially those of Bray, Warfield, Waltham and Easthampstead. Gelling has noted the incidence of *feld* names in this region, possibly relating to open land on the edge of a densely wooded tract, suggesting that the region was not all one of continuous woodland.[46] It has been suggested, however, that Waltham, *weald-hām*, may have been a name applied to an area reserved for royal hunting.[47]

A number of charters have survived for this area – notably a grant of an 11-hide estate at Winkfield and Swinley, a 30-hide estate, which included White Waltham, Waltham St Lawrence and Shottesbrooke, and a late grant of the 8 hides of Waltham St Lawrence.[48] In common with many boundary clauses relating to little-developed areas, the landmarks are scanty and often far apart. Both the Winkfield and Waltham estates seem

[45] D. Hooke, *Pre-Conquest Regional Variation in South-Central England* (in preparation).

[46] Gelling, *Place-Names of Berkshire*, 3, pp 835–6.

[47] R. M. Huggins, 'The significance of the place-name *Wealdhām*', *Medieval Archaeology*, 19 (1975), pp 198–201.

[48] Sawyer, *Anglo-Saxon Charters*, S. 482; Birch, *Cartularium Saxonicum*, B. 778; Gelling, *Place-Names of Berkshire*, 3, p. 641, A(b)V, p 646; S. 461; B. 762; Gelling, *Place-Names of Berkshire*, 3, pp. 635–6, A(a)V, p. 646; S. 915; J. M. Kemble, *Codex Diplomaticus Aevi Saxonici* (London, 1839–48), K. 1303; Gelling, *Place-Names of Berkshire*, 3, p. 636, A(a)II, p. 638.

PLATE XX: *South Berkshire: woodland in the Kennet valley.* © Della Hooke.

to have been granted additional meadowland beside the Thames to the north. Upon the Winkfield bounds several *lēah* features are noted, lying in the southern part of the parish: for example, *imbelea*, 'clearing or wood where bees swarm', and *hylneslea* (meaning obscure). Later *lēah* names in this parish include Swinley, 'swine wood or clearing', indicating swine pasture in the south of the parish, and pasture for pigs is recorded on all these estates in 1086.

The term *haga* occurs most frequently in the charter boundaries of the south of Berkshire and two *haga* features are noted here that appear to have run for long distances along the boundary: *westleas hagan*, 'the fence or enclosure of the west wood or clearing' (a Westley Mill lies some 3 kilometres to the west), and *ceawan hrycges hagan*, 'the fence or enclosure of Chawridge' (a settlement within Winkfield). These *haga* features are likely to have been substantial and were most commonly found in little-developed, often densely wooded regions later known to have been used for hunting or as game reserves.[49] They may indeed have already demarcated parts of the woodland set aside for such purposes. Of interest,

---

[49] Hooke, *Anglo-Saxon Landscapes of the West Midlands*, pp. 234–47.

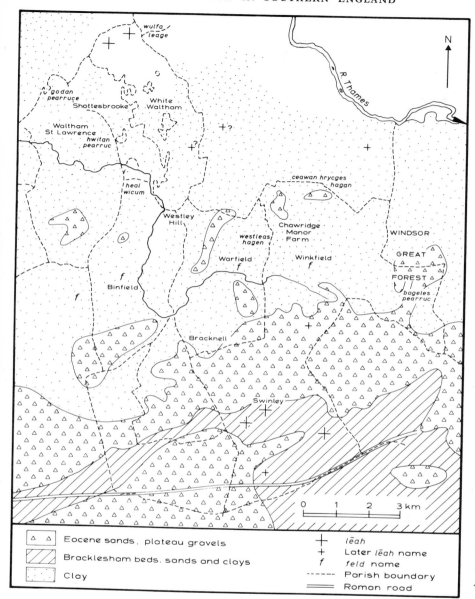

FIGURE 6.10 *East Berkshire: pre-Conquest land use, the charter and place-name evidence*

too, is a reference to *bogeles pearruc*, possibly 'Bægel's enclosure', for *pearroc* may have been a term used for a deliberately enclosed park under private ownership (as in Feckenham, Worcestershire, owned by the king himself). The Domesday survey for the manor of Winkfield, then acquired by Abingdon Abbey, notes that 4 hides of the estate had been taken into the king's forest. Two other *pearroc* enclosures are recorded on the Waltham

149

estate, *godan pearruce*, 'Goda's' or 'good park/paddock', which seems to have lain in the north of Waltham St Lawrence, and *hwitan pearruce*, 'white park/paddock', near the eastern boundary of the estate (probably on the chalkland). In later times, after disafforestation, there were numerous private deer-parks in this area. In Waltham, several other *lēah* features are recorded and include *wulfa leage*, 'wolves' wood or clearing'. In the charter of the 30-hide Waltham estate, a *wīc*, *heal wicum*, may denote a herding establishment, but it may have been the link with woodland pasture that caused the name to survive as that of a wood, *Halewik*, together with another, *Lidlegewik*, recorded *c.* 1060.[50] Hidage assessments in this area are relatively low, possibly reflecting the limited resources of the area.

The south-western part of Berkshire also seems to have been a zone of poor potential. This may have been the heart of the ancient woodland of Barroc, which Peake argued plausibly lay 'on the clay lands between and including Enborne and Hungerford', centred upon Kintbury.[51] This would place it again upon the poorer soils of the Eocene beds to the south of the river Kennet, extending eastwards from Savernake Forest in Wiltshire. In Roman times, there were kilns at Kintbury and Hampstead Marshall utilizing fuel available from the woodland.[52] Again, this was a zone of low plough-team density in 1086 and one of the poorest regions for estate values, although the woods provided pasture for herds of swine. The Kintbury estate had been allotted by King Edward to the warden of the forest and Hungerford was later administered as part of Savernake Forest.[53] As in the area of the later Windsor Forest, parishes were enormous, but in 1086 were divided into numerous lesser holdings, perhaps reflecting the subinfeudation of marginal land. Kintbury parish itself incorporated eight separate holdings, and the small parish of Enborne had four. Apart from the most westerly parishes, the area does not appear to have been retained long as a royal forest.

Conclusions

Estate formation appears to have gone through many stages before the ecclesiastical parishes were consolidated. Land holdings of varying sizes were recognized throughout the Anglo-Saxon period; some areas may have been subdivided at an earlier date than others, presumably by power

[50] Gelling, *The Place-Names of Berkshire*, part 1, English Place-Name Society, vol. 49 (Cambridge, 1982), p. 72; Kemble, *Codex Diplomaticus*, K. 844.

[51] H. J. Peake, *Transactions of Newbury and District Field Club*, 7 (1934–7), pp. 175–80.

[52] Oxon SMR. 1595, 1724; V. G. Swan, *The Pottery Kilns of Roman Britain*, Royal Commission on Historical Monuments, supplementary series, 5 (London, 1984), p. 133.

[53] Morgan (ed.), *Domesday Book*, 5, 31.4.

invested in the rulers of the Anglo-Saxon kingdoms, and estates in wooded regions were often the least stable and most subject to boundary changes. Further fragmentation of holdings proceeded in all regions and was both advanced and irregular at the eve of the Norman Conquest. At the same time, minster *parochiae* were becoming subdivided as churches were established to serve these estates, and the size of the parishes was often influenced by the resources available within a given region. Thus an estate pattern was consolidated that was to survive to the present day and establish the administrative pattern of the rural landscape for the next thousand years.

Both estates and parishes were influenced by the resource potential of the natural environment. The pre-Conquest charters provide a unique source of topographical evidence upon which to base landscape reconstruction, but it is only when these are examined both in the light of earlier archaeological evidence and the later evidence of the Domesday survey that a realistic appraisal of the landscape potential may be made. Changes were certainly taking place in the Anglo-Saxon period that were to influence future medieval land use. The varying regional economies of that period were established and appear to have borne a close relationship to the potential resources of the natural environment. Land use seems, indeed, to have been finely attuned to the natural environment by the later Anglo-Saxon period. Cultural pressures had changed from the overriding demands of a centralized Roman economy to pressure upon the smaller land unit. The system was efficient enough to remain the basis of development well into late medieval times, adapting, but not necessarily altering, as populations waxed and waned and as economic pressures changed. It was capable of maintaining a network of small towns and markets, rather more successfully, some would argue, than during Roman times. While not returning to some early simplistic notions of colonization and consequent change, it is possible that we may have to reconsider the tendency, apparent not so long ago, to refute the importance of the sequence of events ascribed to the Anglo-Saxon period.

7

Settlement Chronology and Regional Landscapes: The Evidence from the Claylands of East Anglia and Essex

TOM WILLIAMSON

Introduction

Archaeologists, geographers and historians studying the development of settlement in lowland Britain have traditionally focused their attention on the 'champion' landscapes of Midland England – those areas which, in the medieval period, were dominated by a settlement pattern of nucleated villages, and by field systems which, while displaying a certain measure of structural variation, were characterized by a wide and relatively equal distribution of holdings across the territory of vills, and by a high degree of co-operative organization and regulated cropping.

Less attention has been paid to areas in which alternative forms of settlement and field system developed. In the south and east of England, and in much of East Anglia, settlement was much more dispersed, and holdings lay in varying proportions of irregular open fields and closes held in severalty. To early topographers like Harrison, or to historians like Homans, these were 'woodland' areas.[1] To Rackham, they are 'ancient countrysides', whose essential framework of boundaries developed by a gradual process of piecemeal accretion and alteration.[2]

Such landscapes are usually explained in chronological terms: that is, they are considered to represent areas in which large-scale clearance and settlement continued late in the Anglo-Saxon and into the post-Conquest period.[3] Yet broad categorizations tend to suppress both the great variety

---

I should like to thank H. J. B. Birks and A. Davison for providing me with details of their unpublished research.

[1] W. Harrison, *The Description of England* (1593), reprinted 1877, edited by F. J. Furnival, *The New Shakespeare Society*, vol. 1; G. C. Homans, *English Villagers of the Thirteenth Century* (Cambridge, Mass., 1941), p. 13.

[2] O. Rackham, *Trees and Woodland in the British Landscape* (London, 1976), p. 17.

[3] B. K. Roberts, *Rural Settlement in Britain* (Folkestone, 1977), pp. 168–9.

that non-Midland landscapes displayed in the medieval period, and also the considerable variations in their earlier development. For while many may owe their pattern of settlement and fields to late colonization, recent research suggests for others a more complicated history. This chapter will consider the development of settlement in one limited sub-region of the south-east: the chalky boulder-clay plateau that constitutes the principal topographic feature of East Anglia and Essex. Discussion will be restricted to the main area of the plateau, excluding the areas of more sandy boulder clays to the west of Norwich. Even this limited area of some 5,500 square kilometres displayed a considerable range of settlement patterns and field systems during the medieval period.

In the south-west – in east Hertfordshire, north Essex and south Suffolk – the clay plateau is extensively dissected by river valleys. Within the deepest of the north-draining valleys the chalk, which everywhere underlies the boulder clay, is exposed. In others, and especially in those draining south, freely-draining fluvio-glacial sands and gravels are found. The soils formed over the chalky boulder clays themselves mainly fall within the Hanslope Association, but within this grouping there are considerable differences between the drier, more calcareous soils of the Stretham series, usually found on the sides of the principal valleys, and those of the Hanslope, Faulkbourne and related series, the seasonally water-logged and often slightly acidic soils that occupy the more level areas of the interfluves.[4] In most parts of the south-western area, the plateau is so extensively dissected that continuous areas of these interfluve soils seldom extend for more than 5 kilometres between areas of lighter clays or other well-drained valley soils (figure 7.1).

Within this area, the medieval settlement pattern included elements of both nucleation and dispersion. Parish churches and larger settlement nucleations were usually located on the floors of, or on the plateau clays adjacent to, the larger valleys. Isolated farms and hamlets of linear or loosely agglomerate form, or clustered around small greens, also favoured such locations. Within these valleys irregular open-field systems existed, most of which gradually disappeared through piecemeal enclosure in the late and post-medieval periods (plate XXI).[5] Only in a few areas – such as the north and west of Essex – did such fields survive until Parliamentary enclosure. Vills usually contained a number of small open fields; Littlebury in Essex, for example, had ten. Farms and hamlets held their land in the fields adjacent to them on the valley slopes, fields which were often

---

[4] Soil Survey of England and Wales, *Soils and their Use in Eastern England* (Harpenden, 1984), pp. 117–22.

[5] F. Hull, 'Agriculture and rural society in Essex, 1560–1640' (unpublished Ph.D. thesis, University of London, 1950); D. Roden, 'Field systems of the Chiltern Hills and their environs', in A. R. H. Baker and R. A. Butlin (eds), *Studies in British Field Systems* (Cambridge, 1973), pp. 338–45, 363–73.

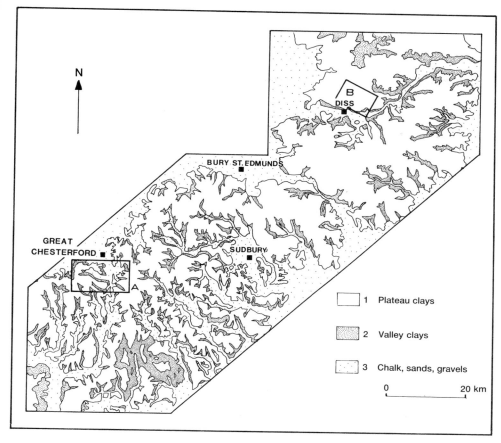

N

BURY ST. EDMUNDS

B
DISS

GREAT
CHESTERFORD

SUDBURY

A

1   Plateau clays

2   Valley clays

3   Chalk, sands, gravels

0   20 km

FIGURE 7.1   *Generalized soil map of the East Anglian boulder-clay plateau, showing principal areas discussed in the text*

associated with particular settlements by name.[6] Away from the principal valleys, settlement consisted of isolated farms and small hamlets, together with some irregular concentrations of farms around substantial greens and commons. Large areas of woodland existed, and had done at the time of the Domesday survey; woods were a more prominent feature of the level interfluves than commons (plate XXII). Some subdivided fields occurred even on the heaviest soils, but such areas were dominated by hedged closes held in severalty. Deer-parks were also, by the thirteenth century, an important component of the landscape, again usually occupying the more level areas of the interfluves.

Towards the north and east, in north Suffolk and south Norfolk, Hanslope Association soils give way to those of the less calcareous Beccles Association. Major valleys containing fluvio-glacial deposits or lighter tills

[6] Roden, 'Field systems of the Chiltern Hills', p. 361; D. Cromarty, *The Fields of Saffron Waldon in 1400* (Chelmsford, 1966), p. 7.

155

become more widely spaced, and the clay plateau itself more gently undulating. In many places, extensive areas of particularly level clays occur.

Progressing north and east, loose clusters of farmsteads around large commons became an increasingly important element in the medieval settlement pattern (plate XXIII and plate XXIV). Sometimes one such common-edge settlement would constitute the main focus of settlement in a vill, with the church isolated, or associated with only a few farmsteads. Churches were again generally associated with the principal valleys, and around the largest valleys – such as that of the Waveney – they were often closely clustered and parishes small. By the time of the Domesday survey, churches could also, however, be found away from major valleys, although they were normally adjacent to pockets of the slightly more amenable Hanslope soils. The degree of field subdivision varied considerably, but in general appears to have been more extensive, and more evenly distributed across soil-types, than in the south-west: irregular open fields could be found even on the heaviest clays. The layout of holdings was highly irregular, and while – at least by the thirteenth century – strips were usually grouped in the vicinity of the tenements from which they were farmed, there was seldom the neat relationship between separate hamlets and fields, mirrored in nomenclature, of the kind often encountered in the south-west of the region. In spite of the extent of level and poorly draining interfluves, the area was not, by the thirteenth century, as well-wooded as the south-west of the region and had less woodland recorded in *Domesday Book*. Those particularly intractable areas that, in the south-west of the

PLATE XXI: *The landscape of north Essex: hedges formed by the early piecemeal enclosure of irregular open fields near Littlebury Green.*
© Brian Horne.

PLATE XXII: *The landscape of north Essex: ancient woodland and hedged fields near Littlebury Green. Some of the boundaries may be of Romano-British origin. Views of hedged scenery such as this have become rare with the impact of agricultural intensification since the last war.*
© Brian Horne.

plateau, were often occupied by woodland were here more likely to be occupied by areas of common land. Commons were a more important component of the landscape in the medieval period than they were by the time the earliest maps were made, for many were enclosed during the sixteenth and seventeenth centuries. Significantly, many bore names suggesting that they had once been wooded. Deer-parks, although common – especially in the area between Halesworth and Stowmarket – were less so than in the south-west of the region.

This is, of course, a considerably over-simplified description of the medieval landscapes of the boulder-clay plateau. In reality, the character of the landscape changed only gradually from south-west to north-east; indeed, some of the more level and continuous interfluve areas of the south-west possessed a landscape more akin to that of the north-east. This description, nevertheless, provides some indication of the range of variation exhibited by what, from a superficial examination, might appear to be a relatively unvarying landscape. Sufficient evidence exists to allow the formulation of only a provisional explanation for the development of these clayland landscapes. The evidence derived from the two principal approaches used here – systematic archaeological field survey and topographical analysis – is, however, sufficient to call into question certain of the assumptions and assertions inherent in the conventional model for

Anglo-Saxon landscape development in 'woodland' regions. First, the evidence suggests that the dispersed settlement pattern characteristic of the region did not, in most areas, exclusively or even predominantly result from the late assarting of extensive forests. The movement of settlement within a landscape already deforested, and often long divided into fields, and the survival of elements of an older, Romano-British pattern of settlement were also of importance, although to varying degrees in different areas. Secondly, it would appear that in many areas the framework of the landscape is of cohesive, rather than aggregate, form. That is, it results not from the slow and piecemeal expansion of cultivation at the expense of forest and waste, but from centuries of piecemeal alterations to landscapes that were originally planned, often on a very large scale, in the Romano-British or prehistoric periods. In most parts of the region, early medieval settlement did not develop within the context of a *tabula rasa*.

At first sight, this might appear an untenable assertion. Pagan cemeteries are (like the few known early or middle Saxon settlement sites) restricted to the lighter soils on the periphery of the region, or in the largest valleys, a

PLATE XXIII: *Common edge settlement in south Norfolk: Langmere Green, Dickleburgh.* © Ben Taylor.

PLATE XXIV: *Common edge settlement in south Norfolk: Upper Street, Billingford.* © Ben Taylor.

distribution confirmed by recent discoveries at Springfield (Essex)[7] and Morningthorpe ((Norfolk).[8] Yet even if this pattern does in large part reflect their original distribution (rather than later patterns of land use: most sites were discovered during gravel extraction), it does not necessarily suggest that clearance and settlement were entirely restricted to a few major valleys. It may reflect the fact that cemeteries were associated with the more important settlements and that these, as to a large extent in the medieval period, were located in such situations. A further complication is that, in the Essex/south Suffolk area, it has been suggested that the paucity of known cemeteries reflects an absence, not of population, but of intrusive Germanic elements in the fifth and sixth centuries, and a measure of continuing Romano-British control; an argument which has been supported, on the positive side, with evidence for the survival of Romano-British

[7] *Medieval Archaeology*, 19 (1975), p. 224.
[8] *Medieval Archaeology*, 27 (1983), p. 176.

159

place-name elements.[9] The difficulties of interpreting received archaeological distributions mean that only systematic field surveys and detailed local landscape studies can provide the kind of data from which wider generalizations about the development of Anglo-Saxon settlement can be made. Such studies and surveys have been relatively few in number, and there are considerable difficulties involved in their interpretation.

The problems with the archaeological fieldwork evidence for Anglo-Saxon settlement are well known.[10] Early Anglo-Saxon pottery is poor in quality and tends to fragment rapidly on the surface: even when present, it is often difficult to see, and when recovered, it is frequently difficult to distinguish from Iron Age material. Over much of this region, grass-tempered fabrics were in widespread use during much of the early and middle Saxon period, and though these are generally easier to distinguish from Iron Age fabrics, there are grounds for believing that they are particularly prone to disintegration, especially in seasonally waterlogged environments. During the middle Saxon period, Ipswich ware – well-fired, hard, grey pottery turned on a slow wheel, mainly, if not exclusively, produced in Ipswich – was widely distributed within the region, but not evenly. In north-west Essex, for example, it occurs in abundance on the excavated site of Wicken Bonhunt;[11] yet at the broadly contemporary site at Hadstock, only 13 kilometres to the north-east, excavation revealed stratified, but aceramic, levels of middle Saxon occupation. Indeed, with the exception of Wicken Bonhunt, Ipswich ware is rarely found in Essex and, in Rodwell's view, 'an almost aceramic Saxon phase existed in Essex between the demise of plain grass-tempered pottery (probably in the seventh or early eighth centuries) and the appearance of Saxo-Norman wares'.[12] Even in Suffolk and Norfolk its distribution is difficult to predict or understand; its close association with church sites hints at its significance as a high-status artefact or, conceiveably, at some ecclesiastical function. Moreover, only small quantities of Ipswich ware are usually recovered from field-walked sites, and in an abraded condition this material can resemble certain kinds of Romano-British pottery.

[9] P. J. Drury and W. Rodwell, 'Late Iron Age and Roman settlement' in D. G. Buckley (ed.), *Archaeology in Essex to AD 1500*, Council for British Archaeology Research Report 34 (London, 1980), p. 71; W. J. Rodwell, 'Trinovantian towns and their setting: a case study', in W. J. Rodwell and R. T. Rowley (eds), *The Small Towns of Roman Britain*, British Archaeological Reports, British series, 15 (Oxford, 1975), p. 99.

[10] S. J. Shennan, 'Settlement history in east Hampshire', in S. J. Shennan and R. T. Schadla-Hall (eds), *The Archaeology of Hampshire*, Hampshire Field Club and Archaeological Society, Monograph no. 1 (Southampton, 1981), p. 119.

[11] K. Wade, 'A settlement site at Bonhunt Farm, Wicken Bonhunt, Essex', in Buckley (ed.), *Archaeology in Essex to AD 1500*, pp 99–100.

[12] P. J. Drury and W. Rodwell, 'Investigations at Asheldham, Essex: an interim report on the church and historic landscape', *Antiquaries Journal*, 58 (1978), pp. 133–51.

The evidence derived from field survey can, to some extent, be supplemented with that from topographic analysis. Pioneered by Flinders Petrie in the 1870s, but only seriously revived by P. J. Drury and W. Rodwell in the 1970s, this technique has been further elaborated in the work of S. J. Bassett.[13] Essentially, it involves the removal of features depicted on the earliest maps to reveal patterns of cohesive organization of roads and fields and the dating of both these, and of non-organized, aggregate patterns, by examining their stratigraphic relationships with dated elements in the landscape, such as major Roman roads. There are numerous dangers and difficulties involved in this approach, and topographic analysis remains a relatively undeveloped approach to landscape history – and one that many regard with a measure of scepticism. It is therefore vital that at each stage of such analyses, the process of subtraction should be described and quantified; otherwise there is the danger that quite spurious patterns might be generated by the judicious selection of features, of the kind frequently encountered in the publications of the archaeological 'fringe'.[14] Properly practised, however, topographic analysis has an important contribution to make to our understanding of post-Roman landscape development, because the survival of prehistoric or Romano-British systems of land division in any area suggests that land use – either pastoral or arable – must have continued with little subsequent long-term interruption. In the areas discussed here, such evidence is of particular importance because, with the exception of John Birk's recent and as yet unpublished analysis of pollen cores from Diss Mere in the Waveney valley, no reliable palynological evidence exists for the post-Roman vegetational history of the central East Anglian claylands.

The Dissected South-western Plateau

The general pattern of post-Roman landscape development in the more dissected, south-western areas of the plateau can be illustrated from the results of a programme of systematic fieldwalking carried out by the writer between 1979 and 1982.[15] The area studied comprises a rectangular block

---

[13] W. M. F. Petrie, 'Notes on ancient roads', *Archaeological Journal*, 35 (1878), pp. 169–75; W. Rodwell, 'Relict landscapes in Essex', in H. C. Bowen and P. J. Fowler (eds), *Early Land Allotment in the British Isles*, British Archaeological Reports, British series, 48 (Oxford, 1978), pp. 89–98; Drury and Rodwell, 'Late Iron Age and Roman settlement'; S. J. Bassett, 'Beyond the edge of excavation: the topographical context of Goltho', in H. Mayr-Harting and R. I. Moore (eds), *Studies in Medieval History Presented to R. H. C. Davis* (London, 1985), pp. 21–39.

[14] T. Williamson and L. Bellamy, *Ley Lines in Question* (London, 1983), pp. 148–70.

[15] T. Williamson, 'The Roman countryside: settlement and agriculture in N.W. Essex', *Britannia*, 15 (1984), pp. 225–30; T. Williamson, 'The development of settlement in N.W. Essex: the results of a recent field survey', *Essex Archaeology and History*, 17 (1986).

of 144 square kilometres in the north-west of Essex, lying to the south of the Roman town of Great Chesterford. The clay plateau is here extensively dissected. Chalk is exposed in the valleys of the Cam and its major tributaries, and even where valleys are less deep, the soils of the valley sides are often relatively free-draining, owing to the gradient: continuous areas of more level interfluve clays are seldom wider than 3 kilometres.

A sample of 28 square kilometres of this study area was systematically fieldwalked, 16 square kilometres in transects spaced at 3 metres, and 12 in transects spaced at 15 metres. In the former areas, particular attention was paid to the distribution of stray sherds, on the assumption that the majority of these had been incorporated into the plough-soil through manuring.

Although evidence of Neolithic and Bronze Age activity was recovered from all parts of the area, only during the Iron Age and Roman periods did the landscape become extensively settled. By the end of the Roman period there were around 1.3 settlements per square kilometre. As in the medieval period, settlements – and especially the largest and wealthiest – tended to cluster near to the margins of the lighter soils of the valleys, or on the floors of the valleys themselves. Where the plateau was less dissected, settlements were fewer in number, smaller and apparently poorer. They were also more short-lived – that is, the settlement pattern was more mobile. This pattern does not, however, imply that the more poorly draining interfluves were occupied by extensive tracts of uncleared woodland. Stray sherds derived from manuring occurred throughout the area fieldwalked; indeed, more were recovered from the interfluves than from the major valleys, occurring (as do some settlement sites) within areas cleared of woodland since the eighteenth century, and within fields bearing names indicative of medieval woodland clearance.

Initially, the survey located only two possible sites of early/middle Saxon occupation, one associated with a Romano-British settlement, one unassociated with other occupation debris. The frequent coincidence or near-coincidence of Romano-British and Saxo-Norman pottery scatters, however, suggested that others might be located by a careful and detailed re-examination of such areas. This produced a number of finds of grass-tempered pottery, together with some sherds of possible early Saxon sand-tempered ware and abraded Ipswich ware. Such material was sometimes directly associated with concentrations of Saxo-Norman or Romano-British debris, since it was sometimes found a short distance away from (i.e., within 200 metres of) either (figure 7.2). Those sites that produced the largest quantities of the most convincing material were mainly located beside the most extensive areas of the lighter valley-side soils; as in the Roman period, distinct clusters of farmsteads appear to have existed in such locations. Few of the sites re-examined away from the principal valleys produced such material in sufficient quantities, or in sufficient state of preservation, to

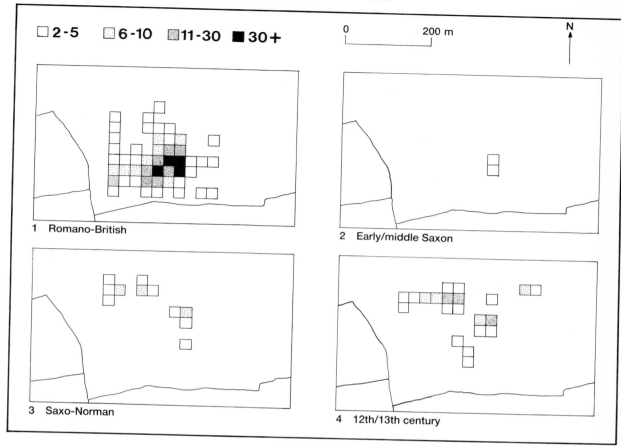

FIGURE 7.2 *Croydons, Elmdon, Essex (T46203615): the development of a small settlement on the margins of light, valley-side clay*

make occupation during the early or middle Saxon period appear likely. This absence of convincing evidence probably indicates that less favourable sites were abandoned in the post-Roman period; but it may in part reflect a continuation of the pattern noted in the Roman period. Early and middle Saxon settlements away from the more extensive areas of lighter soils may have been both poorer, and more mobile, than those more favourably located; the latter feature, in particular, might ensure that they would remain undiscovered by the second, more intensive survey, given its selective nature.

Whatever the fate of settlements away from the major valleys, topographic analysis suggests that the interfluve soils within the area studied did not entirely revert to woodland. In a number of places on the heavier clays there are, on the earliest available maps, traces of small-scale, rectilinear systems of land division, stratigraphically earlier than medieval lanes and disrupted by the expansion of medieval settlements. Although it

is possible that such systems are of early medieval date, they have the
discontinuous appearance characteristic of other, more securely dated
relict field systems, an appearance which appears to result from a
subsequent decline in the intensity of land use in the areas in question. For
despite such survivals, it is clear that there was a considerable contraction
of the area under cultivation in the post-Roman period, especially, but not
exclusively, on the heavier soils. Nevertheless, settlement continued
wherever there were valleys containing sizeable areas of Stretham series or
chalk soils.

Settlement had been re-established in all parts of the area studied by the
end of the Saxon period, and its pattern exhibits a number of similarities
with that of the Roman period. In particular, the farmsteads and hamlets
located away from the major valleys were of lower status than those located
adjacent to them; the former were tenurially dependent on the latter, and
were therefore usually unnamed in the Domesday survey. The area
nevertheless remained less extensively cleared than it had been in the
Roman period; abundant reserves of woodland were recorded in 1086,
amounting in the case of Clavering, for example, to an area sufficient for
800 swine, perhaps 1,000 acres or 20 per cent of the area of the vill. Yet this
abundance of woodland did not mean that, in eleventh-century terms, the
area was sparsely settled. In common with the south-western plateau as a
whole, many parts of which had an equivalent density of recorded
woodland, it had a recorded population and plough-team density
considerably above average for England.

Some of the late Saxon settlements located away from the major valleys
appear to have been isolated farmsteads; others, perhaps, were small
hamlets; a minority were located beside what were, by the time of the
earliest maps, fairly extensive commons. In the post-Conquest period, a
number of new farmsteads appear to have been established at the expense
of woodland; others appeared within areas already cleared of waste and
divided into fields; common-edge settlements expanded; and loose clusters
of farms at the edge of the more extensive areas of lighter valley soils
expanded to produce the 'polyfocal' plan characteristic of the larger
settlement nucleations in the area, a process usually obscured by continuity
of settlement up to the present, but revealed, as at the village of Strethall,
where subsequent contraction has occurred. By the end of the thirteenth
century the area was thus characterized by a dense settlement pattern of
complex and varied origins. The density of settlement is in marked contrast
not only with that at the time of the Domesday survey, but also with that of
the Roman period. To judge from the number and extent of debris scatters,
it is very difficult to accept, for this area at least, estimates of Romano-
British population levels that equate them with those of the late thirteenth-
century.

Evidence of chance finds, field survey, excavation, topographic analysis and environmental studies from elsewhere within the south-western area of the plateau suggests that the local pattern of development outlined above may have a wider relevance, at least where the boulder clays are extensively interdigitated with gravel or chalk. Analyses of river sediments in the valley of the Chelmer by P. Murphy and T. Wilkinson have demonstrated how alluviation increased as arable farming intensified on the claylands from the end of the Bronze Age.[16] Romano-British settlements known from chance finds and fieldwalking cluster noticeably where the soils are relatively free-draining, but they are widespread on the heavier soils.[17] Only where very extensive areas of level interfluve clay occur does evidence of Iron Age and Romano-British penetration appear sparse; such areas were presumably utilized for grazing or managed as woodland. In addition, topographic analysis suggests that enclosed farmland was extensive in the region during the Roman period. Field systems of both cohesive and aggregate form, stratigraphically earlier than Roman roads, survive in a number of major valleys (or rather survived into the first half of this century: agricultural intensification has had a catastrophic effect on the clayland landscape). Examples have been published from around Little Waltham, Braintree and Chelmsford: excavation has demonstrated that elements of the Chelmsford system originated by the middle Iron Age.[18] On the more level clays, there are fewer examples of such superimposition, but organized field systems of Roman date, sometimes laid out parallel with Roman roads, have been suggested in a number of areas.[19]

Excavation has revealed little evidence of destruction on Roman sites occupied at the turn of the fifth century, and some certainly continued to be occupied. The well-known sequence from Rivenhall on the southern edge of the claylands shows the continued occupation of a villa site during the fifth and sixth centuries. The nearby cemetery at Kelvedon in Feering, has revealed late Roman and Anglo-Saxon burials in close association.[20] The survival of systems of land division stratigraphically earlier than Roman roads within the major valleys implies that, in Drury's words, the areas concerned had 'remained in agricultural use (pasture or arable) without substantial interruption from the pre-Roman Iron Age to the present day'.[21] But the evidence for the partial survival of Romano-British landscape

[16] P. Murphy, personal communication.

[17] Drury and Rodwell, 'Late Iron Age and Roman settlement', p. 67.

[18] Ibid., pp. 60-1; P. Drury, 'Braintree: excavation and research 1971-1976', *Essex Archaeology and History*, 8 (1976), p. 121; P. Drury, *Chelmsford Excavation Committee Report 1: Excavations at Little Waltham 1970-1971*, Council for British Archaeology Research Report 26 (London, 1978), pp. 135-6.

[19] Drury and Rodwell, 'Late Iron Age and Roman settlement', p. 135.

[20] Ibid., p. 72.

[21] Drury, *Excavations at Little Waltham*, p. 135.

elements also suggests some continuity of land use on the heavier soils, and in general the extent of dissection in the south-west of the plateau is such that continuous exploitation of such areas, if only for woodland or grazing, would seem inescapable. There can have been few areas in east Hertfordshire, north Essex or south Suffolk where re-expansion of settlement in the middle or later Saxon period occurred within an unutilized wilderness.

The North-eastern Claylands

The development of settlement in the less dissected environments of the north-east of the clay plateau – in north Suffolk and south Norfolk – is less well understood. Field-survey evidence – which comes, in particular, from the work of Peter Warner, Alan Davison and Mike Hardy – suggests that here, too, settlement expanded onto the interfluve clays during the later Iron Age and Romano-British periods.[22] But here, not surprisingly, given the nature of the environment, the density of settlement appears to have been rather less than in the south-west. Romano-British sites were concentrated in the major valleys; away from such locations, they were usually spaced at intervals of between c. 1.5 and c. 2.5 kilometres, depending on the levelness of the clays and the extent of shallow valleys in which pockets of the lighter Hanslope or Stretham series soils are found. The accumulating evidence from field surveys is supported and amplified by recent pollen evidence from Diss Mere, located in the narrow valley of the Waveney, but reflecting the vegetational history of an area of perhaps 10-kilometre radius composed overwhelmingly of Beccles Association soils. This shows that towards the end of the Iron Age there was a sudden episode of massive and extensive clearance.[23]

Topographic analysis suggests that this was often accompanied by, or perhaps soon followed by, the imposition of extensive systems of organized land allotment acorss the interfluve clays.[24] Figure 7.3 depicts two of these systems, laid out across the gently undulating plateau immediately north of the valley of the river Waveney in south Norfolk, an area crossed from north-north-east to south-south-west by the Roman Pye Road (Margary

---

[22] Suffolk Archaeological Unit Sites and Monuments Record; Norfolk Archaeological Unit Sites and Monuments Record and A. Davison, personal communication; P. Warner, 'Blything hundred: a study in the development of settlement AD 400–1400' (unpublished Ph.D. thesis, University of Leicester, 1982); M. J. Hardy and E. A. Martin, 'South Elham St Cross' and 'South Elham St James', in E. Martin, J. Plouviez and H. Feldman, 'Archaeology in Suffolk 1985', *Proceedings of the Suffolk Institute of Archaeology and History*, 36 (1986), pp. 147–50.

[23] J. Birks, personal communication.

[24] T. Williamson, 'Parish boundaries and early fields: continuity and discontinuity', *Journal of Historical Geography*, 12(3) (1986), pp. 241–8.

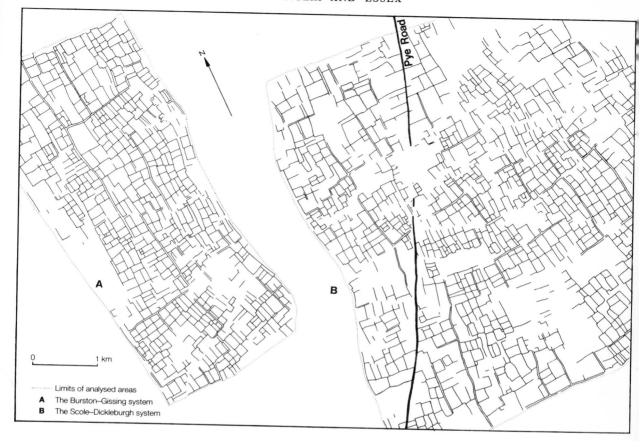

Pye Road

A

B

0   1 km

.... Limits of analysed areas
A   The Burston–Gissing system
B   The Scole–Dickleburgh system

FIGURE 7.3   *Early co-axial field systems in south Norfolk.*
A   The Burston-Gissing system.
B   The Scole-Dickleburgh system

number 3d (Area B, figure 7.1)).[25] Tithe Award maps dating from the 1830s and 1840s exist for the entire area; the field systems have been reconstructed by removing from the areas demarcated the following features:

1 boundaries known to be of seventeenth-, eighteenth- or early nineteenth-century date on the evidence of a number of pre-1840 Enclosure and estate maps for the area;

2 minor boundaries around gardens and farmyards; those demarcating features, such as circular plantations, created for landscaping purposes in the eighteenth century; and minor watercourses (*c.* 42 kilometres, or *c.* 5 per cent of the 1840s boundaries);

3 boundaries that surround medieval or post-medieval encroachments on commons, or assarts from woodland and waste (identified mainly on the basis of field-name evidence); and minor routeways that, on stratigraphic grounds, appear to be of relatively

[25] I. Margary, *Roman Roads in Britain*, vol. 1 (London, 1955), pp. 236–7.

recent origin (total *c.* 35 kilometres, or *c.* 4 per cent of the 1840s boundaries);

4   boundaries that lie perpendicular to or parallel with the Pye Road, and also in its immediate vicinity (on the assumption that these must post-date its construction) (*c.* 30 kilometres or *c.* 4 per cent of the 1840s boundaries).

A further 81 kilometres (*c.* 10 per cent of the 1840s boundaries) have been removed arbitrarily.

The earliest stratum of the landscape revealed within each of the demarcated areas consists of a system of roughly parallel and slightly sinuous lanes and boundaries (plate XXVI): the area between the two systems is occupied by aggregate patterns of fields, or by smaller organized field systems. These are of uncertain date, but the large systems depicted here are apparently of Iron Age, or possibly early Roman, origin. They bear a superficial resemblance to some of the late Saxon 'long-furlong' planned field systems in the Midlands and Yorkshire – a resemblance increased by the fragmentation of many of their constituent fields into strips during the early medieval period. They are, however, considerably larger, and are organized along a single axis of orientation. The Burston–Gissing system, for example, is some 6.5 kilometres from end to end, the Scole–Dickleburgh system extends over some 30 square kilometres. Their overall form is more closely comparable to prehistoric co-axial field systems, especially the larger parallel reave and block systems on Dartmoor, like that around Ripon Tor.[26] The absence of evidence for Bronze Age land use on the clays strongly suggests that the East Anglian systems are not of comparable antiquity: but the Scole–Dickleburgh system – like several others – is stratigraphically earlier than a Roman road, and in general a pre-medieval origin is indicated for these systems by their general relationship to the principal features of the medieval landscape. Their axes are interrupted by greens and commons; and medieval settlements, together with the boundaries of parishes, vills and manors, are imposed on them in an arbitrary and irregular fashion. Moreover, the systems have discontinuities occupied by areas of more irregular fields, suggesting the recolonization of land that had fallen out of cultivation. It is not, of course, claimed that every field boundary or routeway depicted on figure 7.3 is a component of the original system of land division. Centuries of piecemeal alteration, of sub-division and re-amalgamation have preserved the essential orientation of field layout, but less often the original boundaries themselves. In addition, the recolonization of some limited areas that had reverted to woodland or

PLATE XXV: *The landscape of north Essex: an ancient, winding lane near Duddenhoe End, Elmdon.*
© Ben Taylor.

---

[26] A. Flemming, 'The prehistoric landscape of Dartmoor Part 1: South Dartmoor' *Proceedings of the Prehistoric Society*, 44 (1978), pp. 97–124; 'Part 2: North and east Dartmoor', *Proceedings of the Prehistoric Society*, 49 (1983), pp. 195–241.

waste may often have replicated the predominant orientation of field layout.

Not all parts of the north-eastern claylands developed along these lines. Areas in which the interfluve soils are most level and most extensive appear to have experienced less Iron Age penetration and display little evidence of large-scale land allotment. This is especially true of the area to the east and south of Halesworth studied by Peter Warner, where other kinds of relict features appear to survive from the pre-medieval landscape – the curvilinear boundaries of some of the commons.[27] Other areas, however, and most notably that to the north of Halesworth in Suffolk, exhibit large-scale planning of a rather different form. Here a massive and accurately laid out co-axial system survives over an area of some 35 square kilometres.[28] It is in reality two separate systems, laid out on slightly different alignments: the orientation of the eastern system is shared by the Roman Stone Street. The

PLATE XXVI: *Cuttings Lane, Rushall, south Norfolk. Part of a vast network of co-axial boundaries and lanes of probable late Iron Age date. Medieval settlement in south Norfolk and north Suffolk developed within a very ancient framework.*
© Ben Taylor.

[27] P. Warner, 'Origins: the example of green-side settlement in east Suffolk', *Medieval Village Research Group 31st Annual Report*, pp. 42–4.
[28] W. G. Hoskins, *Fieldwork in Local History* (London, 1967); P. Bigmore, 'Suffolk settlement: a study in continuity' (unpublished Ph.D. thesis, University of Leicester, 1973); Warner, 'Blything hundred', pp. 53–4; O. Rackham, *History of the Countryside* (London, 1986), pp. 156–8.

paucity of prehistoric evidence recovered by fieldwalking in the northern part of the system leaves no doubt that the Roman road has not intruded along a pre-existing axis, as suggested by Rackham;[29] rather, the system has been laid out parallel to the road – a relationship shared by similar (though smaller) systems in East Anglia which display an equivalent measure of linear accuracy, most notably that centred on Long Stratton in south Norfolk. A Romano-British origin has been suggested for the system by a number of writers.[30]

Fieldwalking evidence suggests that many of the Romano-British settlements in this north-eastern area were abandoned some time in the late third or early fourth century[31] – an event possibly related to the slight, transient episode of birch/hazel scrub development in the years around AD 300 represented in the Diss Mere pollen sequence. The few known early Anglo-Saxon settlements occur in or near the major valleys, and most middle Saxon sites occupy similar situations (although very seldom the same sites). Yet some middle Saxon settlement sites are known from more remote locations beside the higher reaches of shallow tributary valleys, and it seems clear that in most areas agricultural land use in some form must have continued without major interruption into the medieval period. Survival of relict landscape features and systems of land division suggest at least that intensive grazing of large areas must have continued throughout the post-Roman centuries. The evidence from Diss Mere similarly produced little support for the theory of post-Roman woodland regeneration:[32] stands of woodland and areas of wood-pasture no doubt existed during the Saxon period (as the Domesday entries and the names of commons clearly indicate), but at no time after the late Iron Age did the area carry any very dense tree cover. Grazing on a scale sufficient to prevent large-scale woodland regeneration implies the existence of settlements – if only seasonally occupied ones – within easy reach of the grazed areas, for open- or wood-pasture reverts to woodland within about twenty years, if it is not intensively grazed. It is possible that future field surveys may recover more evidence of early and middle Saxon settlement away from the major valleys.

During the later Saxon period, settlement expanded on the interfluve clays, and by 1086 the area had among the highest densities of recorded population and plough teams in England. Settlement usually took the form of loose concentrations of farmsteads around extensive greens and commons. Such settlement had begun, probably, by the tenth century and

[29] Rackham, *History of the Countryside*, p. 156.
[30] Hoskins, *Fieldwork in Local History*; Bigmore, 'Suffolk settlement'.
[31] Warner, 'Origins: green-side settlement', p. 43.
[32] Birks, personal communication.

was well under way by the time of the Domesday survey;[33] nevertheless, it intensified in subsequent centuries and was sometimes accompanied by a migration of farms away from old sites by the lighter soils of the major river valleys, leading to the isolation or near-isolation of parish churches. This is a phenomenon particularly characteristic of the Norfolk landscape, and especially of the area to the west of Norwich, beyond the area discussed here, as demonstrated by the work of Peter Wade-Martins.[34]

Discussion: A Provisional Model for the Development of Settlement on the East Anglian Boulder Clays

The available evidence thus suggests that the more level, less dissected north-eastern parts of the boulder-clay plateau were more sparsely settled in the Roman period, and experienced a greater contraction of settlement in the late or post-Roman period than the more dissected south-western areas. Paradoxically, by the time of the Domesday survey it was the former areas that carried the greater density of recorded population and plough teams. Such areas also had the highest density of free tenures. I will not discuss here the extent to which these two features may be connected – to what extent, that is, the greater opportunities for the expansion of arable in the north-east of the region preserved, or encouraged the proliferation of, free tenures: or to what extent the high density of such tenures was an independent variable, associated with Danish settlement and raiding. Whatever the connections between these two variables, they together appear to have been responsible for the principal variations already described in the medieval landscape of the boulder-clay plateau.

In the south-west, manorial control appears to have been relatively strong in the later Saxon period: there were comparatively few recorded free or sokemen at the time of the Domesday survey, and by the late twelfth century, at least, many vills were highly manoralized, with large demesne and heavy labour services. It is the strength of manorial organization which probably explains the relatively high density of woodland recorded in the Domesday survey, and the substantial quantities that survived in the area into the modern period. In the north-east, more areas of wood-pasture or woodland continued to have common rights exercised over them; there were fewer areas of woodland under private manorial control. Subject to grazing, such common woodland degenerated to open pasture throughout the early medieval period, creating the extensive commons so characteristic of the area's landscape.

---

[33] Warner, 'Blything hundred', p. 177.

[34] S. Addington, 'Landscape and settlements in south Norfolk', *Norfolk Archaeology*, 35 (1982), pp. 97–139; P. Wade-Martins, 'Village Sites in the Launditch Hundred', *East Anglian Archaeology*, 10 (1980).

In the south-west, numerous small settlements persisted throughout the Saxon period, mainly, but perhaps not exclusively, within or beside the principal valleys. As population expanded, irregular open fields developed around these settlements, presumably through the combined effects of partible inheritance and the need to divide areas converted to arable amongst those who had formerly exploited them for grazing. This led to the pattern apparent in the late and post-medieval periods, of discrete hamlets with holdings clustered in adjacent subdivided fields, fields with which they were often associated by name. In many areas, at least by the twelfth century, some measure of communal organization was imposed across the numerous open fields in a vill, but – even where manors were conterminous with vills, and all tenants were classified as villeins or bordars in the Domesday survey – this never went so far as a redistribution, a regularization, of holdings.[35] Population increase also led to the establishment of new settlements, often in areas of manorial woodland or wood-pasture, more rarely as the result of settlement drift to the edge of commons. The former settlements usually farmed the majority of their land in several fields, the latter were sometimes associated with complex and irregular subdivided field systems.

In the north-east, the development of the landscape took a rather different course, largely because of the greater opportunities for expansion and the nature of tenurial organization. Fewer settlements existed in the early Saxon period, but – perhaps because climatic amelioration increasingly made the claylands suitable for arable agriculture – by the late Saxon period population densities had outstripped those of the south-west. As population pressure built up, in many areas extensive irregular open fields developed around settlements. These were usually more extensive than the hamlet-fields of the south-west of the region, and individual fields were often larger: features which perhaps reflect the greater opportunities for reclamation and expansion in the area, although the prevalence of partible inheritance among the free element of the population, and the early development of an active land market, must also have been important. Yet as population rose, the existing foci of settlement did not simply expand: beginning in the late Saxon period, but increasing in the two centuries following the Conquest, settlement migrated towards surviving areas of common grazing, usually located on the most level areas of the interfluves. In the pre-Conquest period, especially where the interfluves were most extensive, some of these settlements themselves became separate vills. The development of common-edge settlement perhaps reflects the increasing importance of these residual areas of grazing as arable intensified on the clays, but in the post-Conquest period at least it may also reflect the

[35] Cromarty, 'Fields of Saffron Walden', passim.

complexity of manorial organization, the fluidity of the land market, the density of free tenures, and the absence of systems of communal organization, which made such movement both possible and necessary.

Conclusion

This is no more than a provisional model, and one that perhaps raises more questions than it answers. What does seem clear, however, is that there is an underlying pattern and logic to the development of the East Anglian clayland landscapes. The complex environmental and tenurial factors making for landscape variation operated within a framework very different from that which became established in the Midlands – a framework of relatively discrete, rather than thoroughly intermixed, holdings. Yet why did a strongly nucleated pattern of settlement, and regular open-field systems, fail to develop in this region?

In terms of current views, it would seem that the region should have lacked either the demographic pressures which necessitated a reorganization of holdings and settlement, or else the social mechanisms which made such reorganization possible. Yet there seems little reason to believe that, taken as a whole, the East Anglian claylands were a marginal area compared with the Midlands during the crucial period for settlement nucleation – probably the century and a half before 1086. Moreover, if the vital factor in landscape reorganization was the strength of local lordship, then the overall distribution of different forms of tenurial organization ought to have been very different from that which can be reconstructed from the pages of the Domesday survey. For although the north-eastern parts of the region were characterized by a high density of free tenures and by vills subdivided between a number of manors, this was far less true of the south-west, where the proportion of free tenures was usually low, and where – although many vills were tenurially subdivided, and manors varied greatly in size, some embracing single hamlet-settlements, some embracing several – many areas displayed a pattern of tenurial organization little different from that of the central Midlands.

Indeed, looking at lowland England as a whole, neither the densities of population or plough teams recorded in the Domesday survey, nor the variations in patterns of tenurial or social organization that the survey appears to depict, bear much relation to the regional distribution of medieval field systems or settlement patterns. It is, in particular, noteworthy that many eastern parts of the champion Midlands were by the late eleventh century characterized by tenurially subdivided vills and/or by a high density of free tenures. Yet it is possible that the broad regional variations in the landscape of lowland England may, in part, be related to much earlier variations in patterns of territorial and social organization. The nature of such variations may perhaps be sought in such characteristic features of the south-east and East Anglia as the survival of ancient units intermediate between vill and shire – leets, lathes, ferdings, rapes; in the survival of many very large estates at the time of the Domesday survey, beside manors (and often vills) that were much smaller than those common in the Midlands; and in the relative absence of regular hidation assessments imposed on vills based on the five-hide unit. It may also be sought in place-names, for many forms and elements appear to reflect important features of social and tenurial organization, and their distributions – far more than anything we can map from *Domesday Book* or other documentary sources – often appear to correlate with the essential regional variations in the medieval landscape. The clustering of the infamous *-ingas* names in the 'woodland' areas of the south-east is one obvious, but unexamined, example. All these features perhaps hint at a rather different process – or pace – of territorial evolution in the south-eastern areas of England than that which occurred in the Midlands.

8

Countryside and Town: The Animal Resources of Saxon Southampton

JENNIFER BOURDILLON

Towns, Fields and Animals

For any pattern of settlement the needs of provisioning are basic, and provisioning must mean the supply not only of food, but also of materials and power: it is the land, directly or indirectly, that has to provide these resources, and concern for the land and its organization is evident in many chapters of this present volume. The land, however, cannot rightly be understood without the impact of animals for grazing, for the plough and for the all-important manuring, and it may well be that the piles of animal bones which find their last home as urban rubbish can give useful answers about the state of the countryside from which most of them must have been drawn.

The study of animal bone from archaeological excavations is no longer new, but its earlier phases had first to be devoted to a study of the bones themselves, to an interpretation of the animals, and to an examination of the archaeological matrix in which the material was found. For prehistoric times the main economic and social discussion must rely on the results of excavations and all classes of finds may claim a likely relevance; for historic periods, however, such discussion was well under way before the study of animal bones had formed a coherent discipline. It is a step foward, and one of real value, that the inferences from the animal bones should be brought

Work on animal bones from excavations in Southampton has been greatly supported by grants from the Department of the Environment and subsequently from the Historic Buildings and Monuments Commission. In addition, this chapter takes note of a smaller amount of bone from excavations funded by Southampton City Council.

Mark Brisbane of the Southampton Museums Service has given permission for the Southampton animal bone data to be used as the basis of this chapter, and his staff have been generous in their help and discussions over many years.

Jennie Coy, Director of the Faunal Remains Unit in the Department of Archaeology, University of Southampton, has been an active co-worker on the Southampton material and an unfailing source of expertise.

Responsibility for interpretation is entirely my own, but these bodies and these people are most warmly thanked for their help.

177

into discussion beside the latest findings in the traditional disciplines of history, of geography and of archaeology itself.[1]

Animal Bones from Southampton

The particular bone assemblage that forms the foundation of this immediate discussion is the major corpus from Southampton. The bulk of these bones date from the middle Saxon period, and the first report on them was published in 1980, from the excavations from five sites in the present Melbourne Street.[2] At the time there was no large corpus of contemporaneous material in this country with which they could be compared, and it was both inevitable and illuminating that they should be set against bones from the Continent, and in particular from Dorestad and Haithabu, two other trading settlements, or emporia, in that network of north-west Europe of which Saxon Southampton was a part. It was later possible for comparisons to be made with material from medieval Southampton, and this gave the chance to plot changes over time, which have proved to be one of the most exciting things about the study as a whole.[3] More recently, the Southampton animal bones have been studied by various workers, with many different interests and skills: a major programme of sieving has enabled earlier results to be subjected to critical scrutiny, site formation studies have been pioneered on the basis of the bones, and the added subtlety of the recent major programme of excavations in the Six Dials development area has given a far wider range of context types and also secure phasing, which has been of great importance in the interpretation of animal changes. Animal bones have now been studied from a few rural sites in the region and thanks to the kindness of excavators some unpublished material has been made available and has been taken into account in the writing of this chapter.

Detailed presentation of the animal bone data, with full methodological discussion, belongs more to specialist publications. These are to be found in the footnotes to this chapter, and one should stress in particular the forthcoming volume in the Southampton Museums publications series in which the various specialists who have worked on animal bones and on

---

[1] Such integrated discussion was pioneered in this country by P. J. Fowler, 'Farming in the Anglo-Saxon landscape: an archaeologist's review', in P. Clemoes (ed.), *Anglo-Saxon England*, vol. 9 (Cambridge, 1982), pp. 263–80; an important broad assessment from the Continent is K. Randsborg, 'Subsistence and settlement in northern temperate Europe in the first millennium AD', in G. Barker and C. Gamble (eds), *Beyond Domestication in Prehistoric Europe* (London, 1985), pp. 233–65.

[2] J. Bourdillon and J. Coy, 'The animal bones', in P. Holdsworth (ed.), *Excavations at Melbourne Street, Southampton, 1971–76*, Council for British Archaeology Research Report 33 (London, 1980), pp. 79–121.

[3] J. Bourdillon, 'Animal husbandry in the Southampton area, as suggested by the excavated bones', *Proceedings of the Hampshire Field Club and Archaeological Society*, 36 (1980), pp. 181–91.

other environmental topics are presenting their work in a co-ordinated volume and are trying, as far as is possible with the diversity of their material, to consider the same broad environmental questions and to integrate their findings. For the methodological underpinning of this present chapter, the reader is referred to the detailed discussion of the animal bones which is given in that volume.[4]

The Southampton bones stand for a wider area than just the town in which they were found. First, it must be said that the middle Saxon settlement of Hamwic has been shown by excavation to have covered an area of well over 40 hectares, with a coherent layout of planned streets on which a great many structures were aligned. Such a planned urban layout, and with it a stretch of the early boundary ditch, appeared in the major programme of excavations at Six Dials, and these are the more remarkable in that they are at the opposite end of the town, the north-western, from that point on the river Itchen where the natural landing stages must have been. It looks therefore as though right from the start the town was conceived as a major unified entity. The animal bones, however, are not taken unquestioned as coming from urban deposits; although the first expectation would be that these bones should tell a great deal about the condition of the hinterland, the relation of the settlement to its wider environment is one of the questions that has been asked of the bones and not one of the presuppositions to their interpretation.

How far what is put foward from these animal bones may be held to apply to a still wider area is a question that must be left to workers from further afield; it may simply be said that as more work has been published for the Saxon period in this country, it seems that the good assemblage from Hamwic is of more than parochial significance, and that much of the wider countryside may echo these immediate results.

The Animals Established

The first impression has been that the Southampton bones were plentiful. This is established partly by the sheer quantity of their excavated remains: animal bone is the most commonly excavated material from the great numbers of middle Saxon rubbish pits that are closely spread all through the settlement. Bone is also found in wells and ditches and to a lesser extent in the occupation surfaces, on streets, in houses and in yards. Work has been undertaken to show that much bone material has been lost – partly,

---

[4] Various papers by Bourdillon, Colley, Coy, Driver, Hillman, Riddler and Winder in *Environmental Archaeology in Southampton: Bioarchaeological and Related Economic Studies*, Southampton Museums publication series (Southampton, forthcoming).

no doubt, by the known nineteenth-century digging for brickearth in that part of Southampton, when animal bones were found in great numbers and were sold for fertilizer, but also by natural decay, by Saxon disposal elsewhere, by the activities of scavenging animals, or by selection for trade. Whatever the causes, a study of pairing carried out on the lower jaws of sheep suggested that on the most rigorous interpretation at least 95 per cent of these jaws were missing and that this figure might well have risen to some 99 per cent as between the flocks at death and the finds as recovered from the trays.[5] Adding to the impression of plenty is the general style of cuts that were found on the bones, with signs of a bold and slapdash chopping, which did not seem to betoken any need for frugality or care.

These bones are therefore held to represent a considerable resource in animal products and in wealth. The patterns of their cuts and their disposal show that the great bulk of them came from food waste, but they are not to be taken as important solely as the residue from food. Indeed, it may be seen that in the provisioning of middle Saxon Southampton the concern for good, palatable, interesting food was not a top priority. Certainly there was little evidence that food was taken from the wild: although antler (of red deer and very occasionally of roe) was strongly in evidence in the boneworking industry, the finds of the meat bones of venison were minimal, at twelve fragments out of the nearly 50,000 fragments that were identified for the Melbourne Street report. Wild boar has not been certainly established among the Saxon Southampton remains, and apart from the finds in one single rich pit at Melbourne Street, wild birds were also very rare. Fish indeed was eaten, as were oysters; but as far as birds and mammals were concerned, the people of Saxon Southampton were fed overwhelmingly with the results of domestic husbandry, and this husbandry was not specially tailored to the table. Those species that were important solely or mainly for food did not loom large in the finds: at some 15 per cent of the main food mammals by fragment count, pigs were far less common than at Dorestad or at Haithabu, and domestic fowl and geese were more rare at Hamwic than they were to become later on. These three domestic species were raised mainly for food. Otherwise the animals represented were those that served other needs as well, and the patterns of age at their slaughter give good grounds for suggesting that they were valued for the contributions they made in their lifetime as well as for their meat, and for those other products such as horn and hide which would come once and for all after death (table 8.1). Indeed, the meat on the elderly animals might have been tougher than one could readily enjoy, more suited for some form of stewing than for cooking as succulent joints

---

[5] J. Bourdillon, 'The animal bones of Hamwih – some comparisons', in M. Kubasiewicz (ed.), *Archaeozoology*, vol. 1 (Sczeczin, 1979), p. 516.

TABLE 8.1 *Saxon Southampton: ageing by mandibles for cattle, sheep and pig*

(a) Absolute numbers

	Cattle	Sheep	Pig
Stage 1	15	18	6
Stage 1 or 2	—	4	—
Stage 2	42	70	82
Stage 2 or 3	11	5	8
Stage 3	86	87	131
Stage 3 or 4	3	15	5
Stage 4	71	205	115
Stage 4 or 5	7	47	2
Stage 5	136	176	54
Stage 5 or 6	44	33	30
Stage 6	3	7	—
Total	418	667	433

(b) Percentages in broad age-groups

	Cattle	Sheep	Pig
Very young	3.6	3.3	1.4
Juvenile	34.0	26.5	52.2
Younger adult	17.0	30.8	26.6
Older adult	45.4	39.4	19.8
n	418	667	433

Very young:
Stage 1 first molar not yet in wear
Juvenile:
Stage 2 second molar not yet in wear
Stage 3 third molar not yet in wear
Younger adult:
Stage 4 third molar coming into wear
Older adult:
Stage 5 third molar in full wear
Stage 6 third molar in heavy wear

The animal bones are therefore to be seen as indicating a resource that is broader than just food. It is cattle that were the most important animals, with a representation which is good among the main food mammals even by fragment count (some 52 per cent) and which is notably so by weight (75 per cent). The horn cores and the shapes of their lower limb bones suggest the castration of many of the males,[6] and this in turn suggests their

[6] Bourdillon and Coy, 'The animal bones', p. 108.

use for traction, undoubtedly for ploughing in the countryside and very likely also as a source of power in the town. For the balance of the sexes, the likely proportions would seem to be some two cows to each adult ox, with only the occasional bull leaving its bones in the Hamwic pits. The age of the cattle is also impressive, and the use of these animals shows them as a continuing resource, an ongoing source of power over many years. Their sizes, too, were good.

The bones of sheep are also found in good numbers, and for individual animals they are the most numerous species. The castration of many of the males may again be inferred, partly by markings on the horn cores and also by the relative rarity of the known horn cores of rams.[7] In sheep, any widespread castration of males would suggest the running of a wether flock for wool, and since the Hamwic sheep are generally of a good age, this would represent a major animal resource over many years. Comparisons with earlier age profiles for sheep – with the animals from the Roman layers at Clausentum, for example, just across the river Itchen in the eastern part of what is now Southampton – show a major change in management, which would fit with a new and serious emphasis on wool.[8]

Goat bones are quite rare, and are predominantly of horn core. The few postcranial goat bones have been butchered and would represent food waste, but the animals were clearly not reared for the special purpose of being sent to the town for food. There is no evidence of the slaughter of kids for skin, and it seems that the main importance of goats for Hamwic would have lain in the industrial raw material of their horn.

It is clear from the butchery, as from the documents of Christian prohibition, that horses by this time were eaten only rarely, if at all.[9] It does not seem likely that they were used for ploughing, but with the build and general stature of modern New Forest ponies they would have been very suitable for riding and carrying packs. Horses may not have been much in evidence in the town, and although their bones are found from time to time in wells and ditches, they are rarely found with the food waste and the other bone rubbish in the pits. All the animals found have been fully adult and mature, and some of them, from their teeth, would seem to have been very old indeed: each horse would have been available for many years of usage, another continuing resource.

Not only was antler brought in from the wild for working, but many of the domestic animals contributed their bones to the boneworking industry. The foot bones of cattle and horse were especially favoured, and for some

---

[7] Ibid., p. 110.

[8] I. W. Cornwall, 'The animal bones', in M. A. Cotton and P. W. Gathercole (eds), *Excavations at Clausentum, Southampton*, Ministry of Works Archaeological Report no. 2 (London, 1958), pp. 141–2.

[9] For example, W. Levison, *England and the Continent in the Eighth Century*, Ford lecture (Oxford, 1943), p. 101.

purposes the back legbones of sheep; with so plentiful a supply the craftsmen could make a careful selection of the material to suit their particular needs.[10]

The Animals and the Town

Hamwic may be seen as a town on the basis of its size and its archaeology. The results from the animal bones fully reinforce that view. Everything points to a considerable separation of the activities of the town from the normal occupations of the countryside. The bones give no evidence of seasonal differences, and only a little evidence of direct repercussions of animal breeding: there is a dearth of foetal and neonatal material, and there are not the young casualties from the early weeks or months of life that one would expect if most of the animals had been reared nearby. The dearth of bulls, too, suggests a strong measure of selection in the animals that were brought into the town.

The bones can give a further indication of conditions in the settlement. As assessed from its bone waste, the town was quite clean, with most material thrown away in deep pits and without any general build-up of bones on occupation surfaces, either indoors or outside. What is most striking is the broad homogeneity of the disposal of the bone. A particular study was made of bone assemblages from a group of middle Saxon pits and wells in three sites in the area of the present Chapel Road, and the few traces of more interesting living that enlivened the generally dull food, traces either of younger material or of wild species, were found only sporadically and across the various assemblages. Similarly, no one area of the town has yet emerged as having enjoyed a more special diet than the rest: the only pit to give signs of richer living came from a proven industrial complex in the Melbourne Street area and this still remains an enigma.[11] Apart from this, the bone waste was homogeneous, adequate for food, but very dull. One has the impression of an organized artisan community, a contribution which is offered from the faunal assemblages to any general discussion of the life of the town based on the excavated material as a whole.

Similarly homogeneous is the evidence throughout the town of animals that could well have served some industrial purpose. In particular, the sheep remains are scattered widely and in good numbers. It must be acknowledged that they will have ended as food waste and that such use

[10] J. C. Driver, 'Zooarchaeological analysis of raw-material selection by a Saxon artisan', *Journal of Field Archaeology*, 11 (1984), p. 403.

[11] P. Cottrell, 'Sites IV and V', in P. Holdsworth (ed.), *Excavations at Melbourne Street, Southampton*, p. 28.

need not be taken to suggest that their wool had been spread as widely and as regularly as were their bones, but there is no clear location of any single industrial area for cloth.

The Animals and the Region

The providing of these resources for food and for industrial use must have placed a great challenge on the hinterland. One has a sense of considerable integration, of animals that had been reared and used in the countryside coming to end their lives in the town.

One thing that is clear is that the countryside in the area was able to support the range of the needs of the town, and not only the basic needs of feeding, with a very good level of animal husbandry. This has broad implications for settlement studies. Most importantly, it ties in with the question of continuity or change at the departure of the Romans. Although this question has been debated to the point almost of tedium in connection with a great many of the issues of archaeology, the study of animal bones is relatively new for this period and for this country, and its contribution to this question has not yet been brought to the fore.

In the first excavations from Saxon Southampton little stratigraphy was found, nor was much phasing possible from the general distribution of the finds; thus the first report on the Hamwic bones had to deal with the animal bones as one single assemblage in time. When an attempt was made to construct a chronology of a few selected pits on the basis of changing tempering in their pottery,[12] the results were provisionally applied to the bone studies and it seemed that there might have been some increase over time in the abundance of cattle in the town as compared with that of pig, but this could be no more than a hint on the basis of a few pits out of the many hundreds that have been excavated altogether. More recent work is in progress on the basis of the main Six Dials excavations, where careful excavation has revealed stratigraphy and where many of the animal bones may now be confidently phased. This work seems likely to bear out a certain improvement over time in the abundance of cattle and some increase in their size in the main phase of Hamwic's life, but it may already be said with confidence that even in the earliest phases the quality of the animal provisioning was good.

Such a level of husbandry betokens a good degree of organization, not only to have produced such animals in the first place, but also to have supplied them to the town. If there had been a total dislocation of animal

<hr>

[12] J. F. Cherry and R. Hodges, 'The dating of Hamwih: Saxon Southampton reconsidered', *Antiquaries Journal*, 58 (1978), pp. 299–309.

husbandry in the years immediately following the break-up of the Roman Empire in this country, by the time the town was established at Southampton such a break-up had been very well repaired. It must be remembered, too, that the town seems to have been conceived and planned as one broad entity, and did not take shape as a small unit which later waxed much larger with success. The countryside must have been in good heart from the start.

One particular indication of the success of the husbandry comes in the sizes of the animals. When the Melbourne Street report was published few direct comparisons were available, and although it was realized that the animal sizes were good, it was not until later work discovered a marked falling-off in sizes in the post-Conquest town of new Southampton that one was able by contrast to see how impressive the Saxon achievement had been.[13] Essentially and very simply, the history of the main domestic species was marked by a fall-off in sizes in the years following their first domestication, so that cattle, for example, by the time of the later British Iron Age were very small indeed – it was not uncommon to find animals with a shoulder height of a metre or even of less. The Roman Empire was marked by a wider range of animal sizes and with higher mean figures, perhaps through selective breeding, perhaps through changes in the stock: whatever the cause or causes, this improvement was found all through Europe where the Roman influence had spread, and not in the areas beyond – from Britain, Germany, Hungary and Poland, reports have come of such differences between the areas in close contact with the Romans and those beyond the imperial frontier, where animal sizes barely changed.[14]

Sizes are normally measured in shoulder heights and certain factors are commonly accepted, species by species, for the calculation of likely heights for the unimproved varieties, on the basis of length measurements taken on the main recovered bones.[15] In addition, comparisons of width measurements over time have been made possible on the Southampton material by the establishment first of the large corpus of measurements from Hamwic

[13] Bourdillon, 'Animal husbandry in the Southampton area', p. 187.

[14] For Britain, see P. A. Jewell, 'Changes in size and type of cattle from prehistoric to medieval times in Britain', *Zeitschrift für Tierzuchtung und Züchtungsbiologie*, 77(2) (1962), pp. 159–67; and M. Maltby, 'Iron Age Romano-British and Anglo-Saxon animal husbandry: a review of the faunal evidence', in M. Jones and G. Dimbleby (eds), *The Environment of Man: The Iron Age to the Anglo-Saxon Period*, British Archaeological Reports, British series, 87 (Oxford, 1981), pp. 185–90. For the Continent see, for example, M. Teichert, 'Size variation in cattle from Germania Romana and Germania libera', in C. Grigson and J. Clutton-Brock (eds), *Animals and Archaeology 4: Husbandry in Europe*, British Archaeological Reports, International series, –S227 (Oxford, 1984), pp. 93–103. In connection with the problem of changing sizes, my colleague Jennie Coy adds the suggestion of heterosis (hybrid vigour) as an important factor often overlooked in these discussions.

[15] A. von den Driesch and J. Boessneck, 'Kritische Anmerkungen zur Widerristhohen-Berechnung aus Langemassen vor- und fruhgeschichtlicher Tierknochen', *Saugetierkundliche Mitteilungen*, 22(4) (1974), pp. 325–48.

TABLE 8.2 *Shoulder heights (in metres) for cattle, sheep and pig*

	Cattle	Sheep	Pig
Hamwic			
Early phase			
$\bar{x}$	1.142	0.614	
range	0.995–1.335	0.516–0.676	
(*n*)	(19)	(22)	(—)
Main phase			
$\bar{x}$	1.157	0.614	0.730
range	0.999–1.377	0.501–0.730	0.633–0.845
(*n*)	(149)	(333)	(20)
Late phase			
$\bar{x}$	1.120	0.614	
range	1.039–1.197	0.531–0.660	
(*n*)	(10)	(16)	(—)
Southampton new town			
Late Saxon			
$\bar{x}$	1.117	0.588	(0.855)
range	1.032–1.194	0.537–0.652	
(*n*)	(26)	(13)	(1)
12th/13th centuries			
$\bar{x}$	1.092	0.547	
range	0.984–1.170	0.512–0.590	
(*n*)	(12)	(22)	(—)

For cattle: by Fock's factors for the metapodia, and Matolcsi's factors for other bones.

For sheep: by Teichert's factors for prehistoric and protohistoric sheep.

For pig:　by Teichert's factors for pig.

TABLE 8.3 *Bone-width comparisons for cattle, sheep and pig*

	Cattle		Sheep		Pig	
	%	n	%	n	%	n
Hamwic						
Early phase	99.2	111	98.2	135	98.7	64
Main phase	100.0	1,971	100.0	2,891	100.0	989
Late phase	99.4	225	98.9	193	96.7	68
Southampton new town						
Late Saxon	96.0	156	99.4	84	98.0	49
12th/13th centuries	95.6	107	94.5	143	96.4	24

and then of calculations based directly on these (see tables 8.2 and 8.3).[16] What seems clear from this is that the main middle Saxon sizes found at Hamwic, although they were below the best of the Roman sizes, were not so very far below them. A look at other material from the neighbourhood confirms the generally good sizes of the middle Saxon domestic animals and in particular the cattle; and from slightly further afield, from Ramsbury in Wiltshire, Jennie Coy has published measurements that fit the picture well.[17]

This suggests a measure of continuity from the improved stock left in England by the Romans. A system of stop-and-start-again is far less likely: the Saxons came from areas beyond the limits of the former empire, and had they brought their own stock with them to any appreciable extent they could only have brought small animals, animals which would need much improvement to reach their Hamwic sizes. Such efforts at improvement had not been attempted in the Saxon homeland, and on the principle of Occam's razor it would seem far more likely that there was a measure of real continuity in the stock and in the general standard of husbandry in this area of southern Britain.

Further work remains to be done to gain more figures for comparisons, but already one is able to suggest that the inevitable disturbances of invasion and resettlement had not in fact played havoc with the flocks. It seems sure that by the middle Saxon period, which must have been a peaceful time round the properous, open, undefended town of Hamwic, the standard of husbandry was sound.

The sizes may have dropped a little by the end of the life of the settlement, late in the ninth or early in the tenth century: useful evidence has come from the phasing of pits from the excavations at Six Dials and at a recent site (177) in the south-west corner of the town. Nevertheless the abundance of cattle was still impressive and there is no suggestion that the demands of the town had seriously overstretched the countryside. It was in the post-Conquest period that the animal sizes shrank most sharply.

The Likely Mechanisms of Supply

The great mass of bone material has been excavated from the town itself, and one must take care in making inferences on the links of town and country. There are models from the Continent which may first be considered for comparisons. For Dorestad, for example, the archaeological

---

[16] Bourdillon, 'Animal husbandry in the Southampton area', p. 186.
[17] J. Coy, 'The animal bones', in J. Haslam, 'A middle Saxon iron smelting site at Ramsbury, Wiltshire', *Medieval Archaeology*, 24 (1980), p. 47.

evidence drew attention to the existence of structures that could well have been farm buildings, and working both from the archaeology and from the animal bone remains, Dr Wietske Prummel has made detailed calculations which suggest that even at the time of the greatest importance of this Carolingian town it could have been reasonably self-sufficient for food.[18] For Haithabu, by contrast, there has been the suggestion of the provisioning by great farms set up deliberately for this purpose, farms well away from the settlement, with major structures that have been located archaeologically.[19] Their precise relation to the provisioning of Haithabu has not been finally proved, but the pattern of Distribution over the Body of the cattle bones suggests that there was considerable preliminary trimming of the slaughtered animals before the carcasses were brought as food into the town. Further Haithabu studies used other methods to confirm such specialized slaughter.[20]

No such great farms have been located in the hinterland of Hamwic. Negative evidence could not be conclusive, but certainly the pattern of Distribution over the Body differed from that at Haithabu, and all parts of the cattle, trimmings as well as the food waste, were well represented in the town. It would seem that animals reached Hamwic on the hoof. No specialized place of slaughter has been located. When one considers the problems of killing cattle at many different areas within a crowded town, it has to be said that this is strange; but the contrast with Haithabu is clear.

One wonders about the possible provisioning of Hamwic from individual manors (or from multiple estates) direct to their own town property. The dullness and the uniformity make it very unlikely that there was a direct relationship, rural estate to urban household, between productive units in the country and rich consumers in the town. One does not seem to be looking at anything like the mechanics of the Roman villa system as a means of urban provisioning, nor at Maitland's classic analysis of the medieval transfer of rural wealth from their own manorial production to the great town houses of the rich.[21] Professor Whitelock traced back into Anglo-Saxon times some similar pattern of private transfers on the part of distant landowners, but although this may well have taken place in the later Saxon towns, it would seem to be ruled out at Hamwic by the general

[18] W. Prummel, 'Early medieval Dorestad, an archaeological study', *Excavations at Dorestad 2. Berichten van de Rijksdienst voor het Oudheidkundig Bodemonderzoek* (Amersfoort, 1983), pp. 248–58.

[19] S. Hvass, 'The Viking Age settlement at Vorbasse, Central Jutland', *Acta Archaeologica*, 50 (1979), pp. 137–72.

[20] H. Reichstein and M. Tiessen, 'Untersuchungen an Tierknochenfunde 1963–4', *Bericht über die Ausgrabungen in Haithabu*, 7 (Neumunster, 1974), p. 23; F. Johannson, 'Untersuchungen an Skelettresten von Rindern aus Haithabu, Ausgrabung 1966–9', *Bericht über die Ausgrabungen in Haithabu*, 17 (Neumunster, 1982), p. 49.

[21] F. W. Maitland, *Domesday Book and Beyond: Three Essays in the Early History of England* (Cambridge, 1897).

homogeneity of its bone remains.[22] A prevailing uniformity of eating habits seems to be established. In addition, a search has been made for the concentration of any of the minor genetic anomalies that could be peculiar to some particular herd – the location, for example, of a minor malformation of the cattle pelvis that was described in the Melbourne Street report.[23] This seems to be distributed entirely sporadically. Again, the sheep mandibles from Hamwic have a common point of likely weakness where the premolars and molars may impact upon each other and it is only the very occasional jaw which shows such impaction anywhere else. Other flocks from the period – a group from the upper Itchen valley, for example – have been seen to be immediately distinctive, with a strong degree of impaction located further back on the jaw; if animals such as these had been sent regularly to one particular area of Hamwic, they would not have been missed in the study.

The basic dullness of the food would seem to rule out the conspicuous presence of any class of merchants, rising to seize new opportunities rather than springing from some firm manorial base, who might have taken commercial initiatives into their own hands and engaged in foreign trade to their own particular advantage. Again, no positive indication has been found. Even allowing for some levelling out of food remains by joint disposal practices in the pits, there is no suggestion of the presence of any class of people with noticeably greater wealth than all the rest. The absence of high quality of life has been seen in the archaeology and in the general pattern of finds: the wealth that must have been created by Hamwic's crafts and trade was not used to support high standards of living within the town itself.[24] This inference is fully supported by the bone. The bones represent great quantities of meat, but of meat that was far less special in terms of prime ageing than that shown by the good pits of medieval Southampton.

This absence of social stratification at Hamwic seems the more remarkable when one reflects that the whole country at that time is known on historical grounds to have had great social distinctions and divisions. Indeed, the *wergild* and linked payments of compensation, scaled in accordance with the rank of the man on whom death or grievous wrong had been inflicted, were even paralleled in the tenth-century laws of Hywel Dda by a sliding scale of values for dogs to match the social status of their owners.[25] There is no sign of such distinctions in the Hamwic pits, where each and every dog could be a mongrel. The human scale of values gave an upper class of king, fighting men and bishops; there were the different

---

[22] D. Whitelock, *The Beginnings of English Society* (London, 1952), pp. 126–33.
[23] Bourdillon and Coy, 'The animal bones', p. 92.
[24] Holdsworth, *Excavations at Melbourne Street*, p. 133.
[25] Cited by J. Clutton-Brock, 'The animal resources', in D. M. Wilson (ed.), *The Archaeology of Anglo-Saxon England* (London, 1976), p. 385.

levels of status which went with the different types of tenancies of land; and the grim cleft between free man and slave. Against this background, the feeding, the refuse-disposal habits and even the animals of Hamwic are strangely egalitarian.

Yet someone must have given the orders or at least provided the impetus for these animal resources to reach Hamwic. To those reared on Stubbs and his *Select Charters*, the myth of basic Saxon democracy dies hard and one would like to postulate a primitive co-operative of equals in some natural guild;[26] but the first report of any guild comes with the *cnihten* of Canterbury from AD 858, and from their name they sound more like a band of master craftsmen.[27] One would suggest from the bone evidence that those who worked at the industries of Hamwic were the mass of its townspeople, and it is most likely that some external power, at one remove both from the town and from the hinterland, would have set up a centre of industrial production at Hamwic and would have arranged for this to be provisioned from a wider area, when its own immediate resources required to be augmented.

Martin Biddle has pointed out a particular contrast between the complementary urban functions of Hamwic and Winchester in the late seventh to ninth centuries, with Winchester having king, bishop and private estates of high social rank, while Hamwic supplied the industrial and commercial focus.[28] This complementary relationship may seem a little strange, partly from the distance of 18 kilometres between the two places, but more because of the difference in time: Biddle himself acknowledges that Hamwic was a town in the eighth century and that in this, the century of Hamwic's heyday, Winchester was not one. Nevertheless his analysis, in emphasizing the one-sided nature of Hamwic, commercial and industrial only, would tie in well with the thesis that some power external to Hamwic controlled both hinterland and town.

It is known that Hamwic was a royal vill – the term *villa regalis* was used in a charter that was signed by the king in AD 840 at Hamwic (using an alternative, *Hamtun*, version of the name) and had led to the unfulfilled hope that some royal residence might be found there[29] – and it is this which provides the most plausible solution to the problem of its organization and control. One is left with the king as a known force in Wessex. One is left, too, with a large number of craftsmen and artisans provisioned with solid basic food, living close together in quite large numbers and steadily

[26] W. Stubbs, *Select Charters, and Other Illustrations of English Constitutional History from the Earliest Times to the Reign of Edward I* (Oxford, 1870), 9th edition revised by H. W. C. Davis (Oxford, 1921).

[27] H. R. Loyn, *Anglo-Saxon England and the Norman Conquest* (London, 1962), p. 139.

[28] M. Biddle, 'Towns', in D. M. Wilson (ed.), *Archaeology of Anglo-Saxon England*, p. 114.

[29] L. Keen, '*Illa mercimonia que dicitur Hamwih*: a study in early medieval development', *Archaeologia Atlantica*, 1(2) (1975), p. 165–90.

exercising their skills, and with a known wide trading network. What seems most likely is that the king had encouraged the foundation of Hamwic for the sake of production and trade and a widening of contacts overseas.

If Hamwic was planned in layout from the start, rather than growing organically from some early nucleus, it must have been founded with some definite intention. An area of craft concentration was not unknown at about this time, certainly on the Carolingian and even on the Merovingian domain.[30] The pattern of animal provisioning would fit with a craft concentration at Hamwic under the general auspices of the king. One may in some sense consider the totality of royal landed possessions (including, of course, the vill at Hamwic) as component and complementary parts of one complex multiple estate. Still more, there was power exerted and there were dues exacted for the kingdom of Wessex as a whole. Hides, household and ploughlands were customary units both for military service and also for food renders, and herein surely would lie the germ of a latent organization which could be adapted to whatever use was required.[31] Food renders were normally delivered to a royal vill, and some such system of dues being paid to the vill of Hamwic could have provided the basis of the provisioning for the town in the supplies that were needed both for manufacture and for food. The king and his servants could presumably arrange for such diversion, and for such provisioning, without actually living at Hamwic or setting up a major centre of administration there which would leave traces of social differentiation in the ground.

The fruit of such industrial production must surely have been some early form of trade, both regional and overseas, and it is suggested that this reached considerable proportions. In one sense Hamwic's functions would have been as Polanyi described those of a port of trade.[32] Dr Richard Hodges, following a close study of the Hamwic pottery, generally accepted Polanyi's model; but with more detailed awareness of the conditions to which Polanyi's broad generalization might apply, he looked particularly at the role of gift exchange.[33] Broad interpretations from the Continent have also seen the trading network of which Hamwic was a part as primarily a source of contact between the great, the social elite or those in high office in the Church, all of whom would have needs, tastes and social obligations (*générosités nécessaires*) which would enforce an interchange of goods among themselves.[34] What is disputed here on the basis of the very extensive

---

[30] For example, R. Latouche, *Les Origines de l'Économie Occidentale* (Paris, 1956), p. 185.

[31] P. H. Sawyer, 'Introduction: early medieval settlement', in P. H. Sawyer (ed.), *Medieval Settlement: Continuity and Change* (London, 1976), pp. 1–7.

[32] K. Polanyi, 'Ports of trade in early societies', *Journal of Economic History*, 23 (1963), pp. 30–45.

[33] R. Hodges, 'Ports of trade in early medieval Europe', *Norwegian Archaeological Review*, 11(2) (1978), pp. 97–101; also R. Hodges, *Dark Age Economics* (London, 1982), pp. 47–65.

[34] For example, G. Duby, *Guerriers et Paysans, VIIe–XIIe Siècle: Premier Essor de l'Économie Européenne* (Paris, 1973), p. 123.

Hamwic excavations and its massive quantities of bone is the extent of what was traded or exchanged, the bulk of material which was produced for this purpose, the numbers of people likely to have been engaged in the whole operation, the strength of the organization required to arrange or exploit the supporting rural productivity, and the sound and basic quality of the goods that were produced. The justified praise for later commercial initiatives has tended to undervalue the extent of the operations at the time of Hamwic. Hamwic was not just a production centre for a few elitist gifts. In particular, the bone remains give an indication of the importance of wool and cloth and of the manufacture of pins, needles, and of combs, some indeed decorated with traces of refinement but many of them robustly shaped to serve a sound practical use and surely ideal for the various processes involved in the making of cloth.

Why should a king show interest and involvement in something that would seem to be larger and deeper than a network for exchanging the gifts of the great? A king of Wessex at that time could be expected to see the need for international contacts, and a converted Christian king – if one takes the founder as Ine himself – would turn to a focus on the Continent, for the Synod of Whitby a short generation earlier had given insular Christianity a decisive Rome-based shift. The south of England was therefore growing in importance as a natural centre of gravity, and the eighth century was to be the great age of England's outgoing contribution to the Continent.[35] By using the natural advantage of Southampton Water, contact would easily be made with the Christian Frankish kingdom. The chances of bone studies have made Dorestad and Haithabu the focus of our recent contacts, but one must not forget that for the people we are trying to investigate the Continent was nearer at hand. It was to Rouen that St Willibald travelled in the first stage of that journey to Rome that gave the first written reference to the mart at Hamwic;[36] and it is interesting that Hodges' analysis of the imported pot found at Hamwic shows far more sherds with provenance in the area that is now northern France than in Frisia or the Rhineland, both of which were still pagan at the time.[37]

The Wider Setting

Professor Jankuhn, in summarizing and discussing a range of British and continental views on the rise of post-Roman towns in northern Europe, treated with circumspection the trading emporia of the eight and ninth

[35] Levison, *England and the Continent*, passim.
[36] Quoted in Keen, '*Illa mercimonia que dictiur Hamwih*', p. 165.
[37] R. Hodges, 'The pottery', in Holdsworth (ed.), *Excavations at Melbourne Street, Southampton*, pp. 40–58.

centuries: to him these ports were not villages, in that agriculture was not their primary function, but neither would he take most of them as towns on the criteria of population size and density and of sound defence.[38] He saw the chief common denominator in their role as *Handels- und Handwerker-siedlungen*, places of trade and production which might later develop into towns, and for him such development would most likely be accompanied by major works of defence. On such a definition the open undefended Hamwic would rest in limbo, neither town nor village, along with many of its peers.

Alternatively, one could take as a main definition of town life the clear separation of a settled population from primary farming activities, and it is this separation that may be of the greatest significance. Settlement size and density are of importance in relating directly to the weight of the urban demand and inversely to the prospects of meeting such demand through a pattern of rural self-sufficiency; an absence of regular defences, though this may be critical for long survival, is of small importance in the essential relations of demand and supply between town and country. On this definition, Jankuhn's *Handelssiedlungen* may be seen to rank variously, some more urban than others, and Hamwic may emerge far more clearly as a town. It has been shown to have separated clearly from basic agricultural activities, more so than many other places in the network. Compared even with such an important centre as Dorestad, Hamwic is well to the fore as a town.

If the various settlements in the network showed such variation in their supporting rural economies, it is right to look at them separately, and it has first to be faced that while some of the more rural partners emerged as ongoing towns, Hamwic came quite quickly to an end. Had it made a false start in the evolution of post-Roman town life, or may one see something at Hamwic that is of lasting significance for social evolution as a whole?

Hamwic has been seen here as a testimony to the effective richness of its hinterland at a time when such rural prosperity has been in doubt. It is also a testimony to some form of good organization, which has been taken here on inference to be most likely that of the king. Whatever the form of organization, the achievement of such extensive provisioning must have helped to build up sound logistical skills; and if it was indeed the royal power which lay at the root of Hamwic's good supply, then such use of this power must have had some bearing on the coming evolution of the state. Dr John F. Cherry and Dr Richard Hodges, in attempting their chronology of Hamwic on the basis of its pot-types, tried to place the settlement in a wider setting. Cherry, attempting to examine on a world-wide basis the

[38] H. Jankuhn, 'Zusammenfassende schlussbemerkungen', in H. Jankuhn, W. Schlesinger and H. Steuer (eds), *Vor- und Frühformen der europäischen Städt im Mittelalter*, vol. 2 (Göttingen, 1975), pp. 305–22.

germ of early statehood, asked what factors precipitate the change from personal ascendancy to more formalized concepts of power, and saw wars, trade and energy sources as potential triggers of more complex structures of control. Linked with Cherry's broad enquiry, Hodges looked at the transition in Britain from local kinship rule to the independent medieval monarchy and saw the heart of the change in the ninth century (in the context of Viking raids and later Viking invasions), with royal sponsorship of towns and mints causing active market forces to replace the exchange of luxury goods among the great. He linked Hamwic to outmoded simple patterns, small-scale territories and peripatetic kin-based rule, and for him a transition to a new and independent style of monarchy fits well with the settlement's decline.[39]

In the context of Cherry's comments, it may be said that animals were still in middle Saxon times one of the most powerful sources of energy. For Hodges, there is no quarrel over later royal achievement: indeed it is good to see that creative economic development, and not just leadership in the destructive tendencies of war, is stressed in the shaping of the state. One would, however, see this new style of monarchy as in direct line of succession from the old, with Hamwic having played a major part in the shaping of the emerging style.

Save perhaps by default, Hamwic taught no military lessons for the future; but neither was it just an innocent interlude before the state-provoking realities of war. Medieval monarchy, independent indeed of kinship ties, and independent in large measure quite often even of the Church, was never wholly independent of the claims of the common weal. Whatever the actual shortcomings of the noble, nobility was expected to oblige, and some fostering of public good was always linked in theory to the holding of political power.

One may fairly claim the establishment and sustenance of Hamwic as a crucial early exercise in royal concern. It does not matter that peripatetic kings came but rarely to their vill – there would doubtless be the reeve and other officers to control the situation on the ground. What is important is that new initiatives would seem to have been taken in the social and productive use of royal authority. With the Viking threat and with changed conditions, new centres would be needed, trade and market patterns would be altered, the older town would be scrapped; but there was to be no scrapping of the monarchy, which had taken creative economic responsi-

---

[39] Cherry and Hodges, 'The dating of Hamwih'; also J. F. Cherry, 'Generalisation and the archaeology of the state', and R. Hodges, 'State formation and the role of trade in middle Saxon England', both in D. Green, C. Haselgrove and M. Spriggs (eds), *Social Organization and Settlement: Contributions from Anthropology, Archaeology and Geography*, vol. 2, British Archaeological Reports, International series, –S47 (Oxford, 1978), p. 416 and p. 442 respectively; and see Hodges, *Dark Age Economics*, pp. 156–8.

bility and could rise on the strength of good experience to make a positive contribution, and not just a blindly defensive one, in the dangerous years ahead. The great creative value of the network of *burhs* was to be that many of them were capable of turning into economic entities; and the phenomenon of Hamwic with its peaceful pursuits in a well-run rural economy may in this way have had an impact and importance that lasted well beyond its time.

9

Towns as Structures and Functioning Communities through Time: The Development of Central Places from 600 to 1066

DAVID HILL

The recent study of the towns of Anglo-Saxon England has been dogged by a misconception. Since Stenton stated that an Anglo-Saxon town had a wall (it was a *burh*, a fortified place), a mint and a market (port), we have searched for a *definition* that would embrace all towns in all of their states.[1] That we should not be able to define a town is not surprising, for most attempts have fallen down both here and on the Continent because the scholar attempting the definition has tended to be drawn to define, usually in some detail, his own site or sphere of interest. What is needed is a *description*, for that is what Stenton was providing. If we consider the Anglo-Saxon town, it must be carefully considered in context. The context is early medieval Europe; Winchester is unique, as all towns are unique, but it belongs to a European upsurge that encompasses not the one hundred plus sites in this country, but the several thousand sites that are in some way concerned with towns and their development throughout Europe.

The search for a description or a definition may in fact be a waste of time and as a contribution towards it here it would seem sensible to consider two major themes; first, that an early medieval town is a bundle of roles and functions. The Anglo-Saxon town is a function and a population and an event: the functions found in an eleventh-century English town can be found in earlier periods dispersed in many ways; it is the concentration of function, transaction and population that makes the town. Secondly, we should consider the town as a dynamic, living structure. The town develops and grows and changes over time. The eleventh-century town is not like its eighth-century forerunner, neither is the forerunner of the functions of the later town always to be found in an urban context.

[1] F. M. Stenton, *Anglo-Saxon England* (Oxford, 1943; 3rd edn 1971), p. 537.

The Early Centuries

When we consider the English evidence, we must accept that there is a rising tide that leads to urbanization within Europe, and that the English response to that tide may be in the lead or be trailing the activities on the Continent, and that therefore the English situation is an organic part of the European whole. The fact that we have few sites for the early years appearing in the sources, and that even fewer are known archaeologically, should not deter us.

For the late Roman period and into the 'Dark Ages', AD 410–600, a great deal of work has been put into demonstrating elegantly and importantly that the Roman centres were not deserted overnight, but continued to function into the middle of the fifth century. The *Anglo-Saxon Chronicle* reference to Cirencester, Bath and Gloucester as centres of kingdoms in AD 577 simply raises the issue of what was there at that date.[2] The period has yet to emerge from the excavations in any clear way; still less are there 'urban' structures. When John Wacher was dealing with *The Towns of Roman Britain*, he clearly stated the problem of the end of the Roman towns with a chapter 'Town-life or life in towns?'[3] When Bede takes up the story in AD 597 with the arrival of Augustine, other places emerge into the record, but none of them emerge as towns.

It is not the place here for us to rake over the well-known evidence for the period, but to point instead to the fact that England is littered not with towns in these centuries, but with places to which people resorted to carry out various social and economic functions.

Figure 9.1 illustrates the fact that in a pre-urban environment the state may be organized in a system and around centres that are not then reflected in the later towns of that country. In England, the earliest evidence of areas being organized around central places for administration and, perhaps, for defence appears with the written record and the place-names: as, for example, in the origin of such names as Canterbury, 'the *burh* of the men of Kent', the naming of some of the lathes and the origin of some of the other early divisions. Many are group names, of the West Saxon, middle Saxon type; others appear to be set up around more clearly marked central places. It was noted by Stenton that the four central shires of Wessex were organized around four central places: Wiltshire around Wilton, Somerset around Somerton, Hampshire around (South)hampton, and Dorset around Dorchester.[4] This system was in place by AD 722, but

[2] *The Anglo-Saxon Chronicle. Two of the Saxon Chronicles Parallel*, edited by C. Plummer (Oxford, 1892–9), pp. 18–19.

[3] J. Wacher, *The Towns of Roman Britain* (London, 1974).

[4] Stenton, *Anglo-Saxon England*, pp. 336–7.

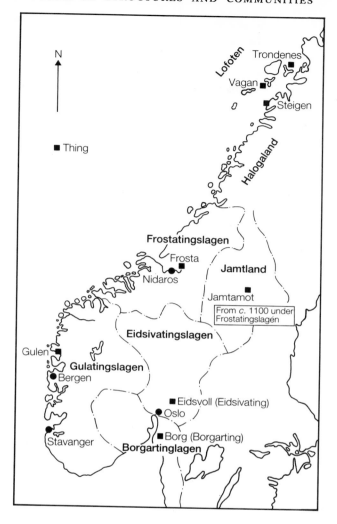

FIGURE 9.1 *Norway* AD *1200. law and things*

there is nothing in the archaeological record to tell us what was happening in physical terms at these sites in the eighth century. Marketing would appear to have been carried out on an *ad hoc* basis in the main, although one would guess after the Scandinavian pattern that a certain amount of trading at moot sites and *witan* meeting-places was taking place. The great *emporia* were appearing in north-western Europe at this time: Quentovic on the Canche estuary in northern France, the so-called Hamwic at Southampton on the southern English coast, Wikj-bij-Duurstede on the Crooked Rhine in Holland, and so on. What is often overlooked is that there seem to be chains of these sites, and it is certain that a series of sites were appearing in Belgium and up the coast. In the British Isles, there was

York, London, Hamwic and Ipswich, but there were also a series of second-rank sites known at the moment mainly from site finds or place-names. Amongst this series, not so much central places as seaports, are those facing onto the Irish Sea: Meols on the Wirral in Cheshire and Luce Sands in the south-west of Scotland. It may be that these sites were nothing more than a seasonal beach market to be equated with Domburg in Holland or Koksijde in Belgium.

The whole of Britain in these centuries was covered with bishoprics, and many turn out to have been in rural places. In fact these rural bishop's seats survive as a feature of Anglo-Saxon England until the Conquest with such sites as Sherborne, Ramsbury and Crediton. Monasteries likewise were to be found both in places that had been urban or were to become so, and also, overwhelmingly, in rural sites.

It should be noted that in Norway the same pattern is detectable: we have seen that the administration of the laws was devolved to non-urban centres; it is also true that the early market system can be traced through a series of place-names – for example, *Kaupangr*, 'a market', as in Hamaricaupangi (present-day Hamar) – the emergence of towns only coming in the eleventh century. This approach is discussed by Della Hooke when dealing with the territorial organization of the West Midlands; in her article, the author adopts a pragmatic approach to central-place theory, but demonstrates convincingly that the concept of central places in the Anglo-Saxon West Midlands can be helpful in discussing a critical period for the reshaping of territories and the places that served various functions.[5]

From Offa to Alfred

It is clear that the great outburst of 'town' construction came in the period from the beginning of the ninth century. In terms of all that we know of town life in the early medieval period, it is in the late eighth century that the range of functions finally converge to make the Anglo-Saxon town.

To return briefly to Stenton's definition, we have mint, wall and market on one site, and in this period we have three such places that we are sure of: York, London, and above all (from the strength of its documents, not its archaeology), Canterbury. The list can be expanded, perhaps doubled, by such sites as Rochester, but the situation there is not so clear-cut. The development of Canterbury is outlined in documentary sources, and already by AD 762 there are small plots and a residence next to the market-

---

[5] D. Hooke, 'Territorial organisation in the Anglo-Saxon West Midlands: central places, central areas', in E. Grant (ed.), *Central Places, Archaeology and History* (Sheffield, 1986), pp. 79–83.

place at the Queen's Gate, and coin evidence exists at this time for a mint.[6] So here, Stenton's three elements exist: in AD 804 there is a grant by Cenwulf, King of Mercia, and Cuthred, King of Kent, to the abbess of Lyminge of 'a small piece of land in the city of Canterbury as a refuge in necessity'; the bounds of this small piece of land include references to a church and to the walls of the city, and we also know of a reeve of the city at this time.[7]

Small plots, 'haws', are actually named in AD 786 and 824, so we may note, therefore, the number of functions that are to be found within the one town of Canterbury by the first half of the ninth century:[8]

Archbishopric (Cathedral)	Administrative centre	Monasteries
Churches	Palace	Market (*port*)
Mint	Fortified centre (*burh*)	Refuge (*fluchtburh*)

One could add that the tenurial heterogeneity so beloved of Ballard can be shown to exist, but the test of a variety of owners really does seem to be essential for urban status.[9] We have the names of various inhabitants and also references to the population as *burgware* and *portweorona* acting in concert as witnesses headed by their reeve. All these references to the life within the town were rehearsed long ago by Tait, but my general point is that in this centre, and in a few others, the range of functions are coming together.[10]

Although in the countryside in general all the functions exist, it is the point of figure 9.2 that all these functions focus in on a single enclosed space. In parallel with these early ninth-century towns there are many rural sites which are single-function sites and are to remain so. The towns are increasingly, however, to be used for many roles; some are added by the crown, others represent goods and services being attracted to the increased marketing opportunities offered by the large numbers attending the town for all sorts of reasons, while, of course, the largest number of transactions in the town will be between the townspeople themselves. An example of the increased use being made of the town is the evidence that appears in laws and charters of the important roles for the town in 'vouching to warranty', 'in the presence of the port-reeve or some other trustworthy man'.[11] This is an attempt to prevent the sale of stolen goods and also to

[6] P. H. Sawyer, *Anglo-Saxon Charters: An Annotated List and Bibliography* (London, 1968), S. 1182; W. de Gray Birch, *Cartularium Saxonicum*, 3 vols (London, 1885–99), B. 192.

[7] Sawyer, *Anglo-Saxon Charters*, S. 160; Birch, *Cartularium Saxonicum*, B. 317.

[8] Sawyer, *Anglo-Saxon Charters*, S. 125 and S. 1621; Birch, *Cartularium Saxonicum*, B. 248 and B. 382.

[9] A. Ballard, *The Domesday Boroughs* (Oxford, 1904).

[10] J. Tait, *The Medieval English Borough: Studies on its Origins and Constitutional History* (Manchester, 1936).

[11] *Liber Eliensis*, edited by E. O. Blake, Camden 3rd ser., 92 (London, 1962), pp. xiv–xv.

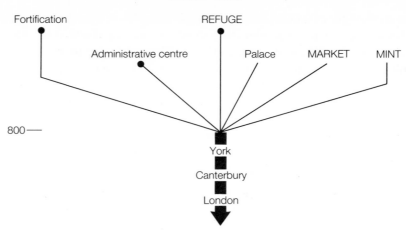

Fortification REFUGE

Administrative centre Palace MARKET MINT

800—

York
Canterbury
London

FIGURE 9.2 *Functions of a*
'central place'

provide witness for land transactions 'with the witness of all the citizens'; this dual role of providing a receipt and acting as a land registry appears more and more frequently through the next, tenth, century.

The setting up of towns and fortresses, the system of '*burhs*', is particularly associated with Alfred the Great, but it should be noted that multi-functional places existed inside his realm before his birth. It is the extension of the system that we should note, an achievement recognized in his lifetime by Asser in his life of Alfred: 'and what of the cities and towns to be rebuilt and of others to be constructed where previously there were none?'[12] The buildings of *burhs*, fortified places, however, did show an important division. It can be clearly demonstrated that in the reigns of Alfred and of his children, Edward the Elder and Æthelflæd, the West Saxons and the Mercians were building a series, a system, of *burhs* that were planned from *their inception* as either towns (that is, multi-functional defended sites) or forts (single-function sites). The key to the division lies in the size: where the sites are more than 16 acres in their original area (and the size reflects the plans of the king for his site), the site was intended as a town and continues on throughout the period and appears in the Domesday survey as a borough (plate XXVII). Where the site was laid out with an area of less than 16 acres, the intention was to have a *fort*, a purely military establishment, and these sites all disappear before the Domesday survey. In fact, figure 9.3 shows this division, first between fort and town, and second, it shows that the new towns of Athelstan reflect different thinking. There is a certain overlap between the two types of *burh*, in that small forts have garrisons and act as refuges for considerable areas, but they do not have a multiple role.[13]

[12] S. Keynes and M. Lapidge, *Alfred the Great: Asser's Life of King Alfred and Other Contemporary Sources* (Harmondsworth, 1983), p. 101.

[13] D. Hill, *An Atlas of Anglo-Saxon England* (Oxford, 1981), pp. 143–4.

PLATE XXVII: *Cricklade, a West Saxon* burh *seen across the water meadows.*
© Della Hooke.

When Edward the Elder completed his campaigns of 'Reconquest' and of consolidation with his final fort at *Cledemutha* (Clwyd, North Wales) in AD 921, he left a network of defensive sites across the whole of England south of the Humber (figure 9.4). These sites had diverse histories, but their main division was that they were either towns or forts. The number is surprising (Hill has a complete mapping of these sites: map 98 and maps 266–34).[14] With the close of these wars, there was a certain redundancy of some sites and the following reign was to reform the system.

The Reform of the Towns under Edward the Elder and Athelstan

Until the reign of Alfred the Great it is possible to consider the development of the *burh*, the town and the *port* as in some way 'organic'. However,

[14] Ibid., pp. 59, 134–42.

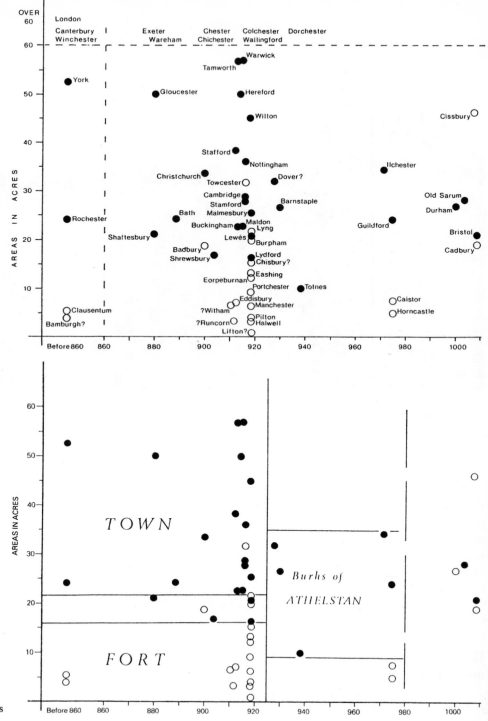

FIGURE 9.3 *Areas of* burhs

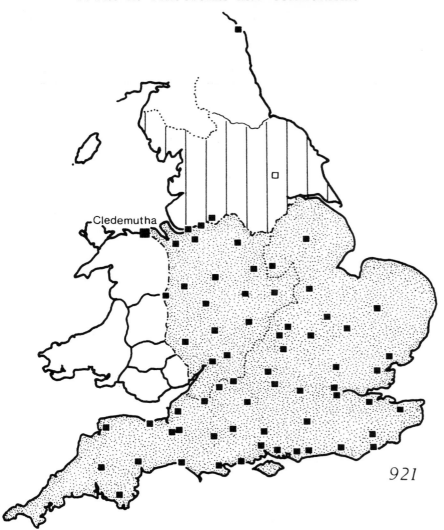

Cledemutha

921

FIGURE 9.4   *The reconquest of the Danelaw* AD *921*

from the accession of Alfred the pattern of urban life and institutions is controlled by the king and there are clearly regal policies directed towards towns. The result of these policies is that England is provided with a network of multi-functional centres which are towns and which fit into Stenton's description and definition as having a wall, a mint and a market. The development can be charted both archaeologically and through the documents.

That the initiative is royal we need not doubt, from the evidence both of Asser and The *Anglo-Saxon Chronicle*; what is instructive is to follow the process in the law codes. The dispersed nature of trade is indicated by the *Laws of Ine*, cap. 25,[15] and that of Alfred, cap. 34 states:

34 Further, with regard to traders, it is decreed: they shall bring before the king's reeve, at a public meeting, the men they are taking with them up into the country, and declare how many of them there are; and they shall take with them [only] such men as they can bring to justice again, at a public meeting. And when they need to have more men with them on their journey, a similar declaration shall always be made to the king's reeve, before the assembled company, as often as need arises.[16]

Although Alfred was at the time involved in spreading his burghal system, no hint appears within the law codes; the whole feeling of this passage is rural, and the central place where the transaction takes place is the 'public meeting'. Edward the Elder's first Law Code shows an increase in the role of the town and a policy that makes the town central to the legal process with regard to trade. Cap. 1 states:

1 And my will is that every man shall have a warrantor [to his transactions] and that no one shall buy [and sell] except in a market town; but he shall have the witness of the 'port-reeve' or of other men of credit, who can be trusted.
§1 And if anyone buys outside a market town, he shall forfeit the sum due for insubordination to the king; but the production of warrantors shall nevertheless be continued, until the point is known at which they can no longer be found.[17]

Now this is an important step forward, for it places the *port*, the market town, in a monopoly position. It also assumes that a network of such towns exists to be used.

Legally, and in its effect on the urban topography of England, the most important legislation is that of Athelstan. Taken with the shiring of central England, the pattern for the rest of the Middle Ages was set down in this half century, from the beginning of the *burh* building programme in *c.* AD 880 to the completion of Athelstan's policies in *c.* AD 940. The shiring of Mercia put a *burh* at the administrative centre of each shire, a fact reflected in the naming, for all the Midland shires have a name-form (name of *burh*)-shire and this link is demonstrated at the outset in Athelstan's first ordinance:

I, King Æthelstan, with the advice of my Archbishop, Wulfhelm, and my other bishops also, *inform the reeve in every borough*, and pray you in the name of God

[15] F. L. Attenborough, *The Laws of the Earliest English Kings* (Cambridge, 1922), pp. 44–5, Ine, cap. 25.
[16] Ibid., pp. 78–9, Alfred, cap. 34.
[17] Ibid., pp. 114–15, I Edward, cap. 1.

and of all His saints, and command you also by my friendship, that in the first place ye render tithes of my own property, both in livestock and in the yearly fruits of the earth, measuring, counting and weighing [them] in accordance with the strictest accuracy. And the bishops shall do the same with their own property, and my *ealdormen* and my reeves likewise.[18]

It can be seen that the channels of command laid down here are to the bishops (for the clergy) and to the reeves of each borough for the laity. It presupposes the shiring of the realm and is, I feel, dating evidence for the origin of the Midland shires.

So Athelstan's Second Code declares (caps 12–14):

12   And we have declared that no one shall buy goods worth more than 20 pence, outside a town; but he shall buy within the town, in the presence of the port-reeve or some other trustworthy man, or again, in the presence of the reeves at a public meeting.

13   And we declare that every fortress shall be repaired by a fortnight after Rogation days.

§1   Secondly: that all trading shall be carried on in a town.

14   Thirdly: [we declare] that there shall be one coinage throughout the king's realm, and no man shall mint money except in a town.

§1   And if a moneyer is found guilty [of issuing base or light coins] the hand shall be cut off with which he committed the crime, and fastened up on the mint. But if he is accused and he wishes to clear himself, then shall he go to the hot iron [ordeal] and redeem the hand with which he is accused of having committed the crime. And if he is proved guilty the same punishment shall be inflicted as we have already declared.

§2   In Canterbury there shall be seven moneyers: four for the king, two for the archbishop, one for the abbot. In Rochester, two for the king, and one for the bishop. In London eight; in Winchester six; in Lewes two; in Hastings one; another in Chichester; two in Southampton; two in Warham; [one in Dorchester]; two in Exeter; two at Shaftesbury, and one in [each of] the other boroughs.[19]

The importance of this legislation cannot be overemphasized: what it does is recognize the need for multi-functional sites, these sites appearing as fortresses, *burhs*, and then, having made sure they are repaired, all trade, *ceaping*, is brought within the site, now called *port*. The link between market and wall having been established, the final link is made with the mint.

[18] Ibid., pp. 122–3, Athelstan.
[19] Ibid., pp. 134–5, II Athelstan, caps 12–14.

Clearly, these linkages are designed to assist in the defence of the realm. The market made money for the traders and the craftsmen, but they could only have their privileges and monopoly if the wall was maintained. Archaeologically, one can see that the new towns of Athelstan were designed to replace the gaps in the network that were covered by mere forts. These single-function sites (Eashing in Surrey, Halwell and Pilton in Devon, for example, replaced by Guildford, Totnes and Barnstaple) disappear and for a period the country has only one type of site, the multi-functional site or town.

The Final Phase of Anglo-Saxon Towns

After AD 973, when the reform of the coinage provides mint names on the coins, we can see the pattern continuing; we need not follow it too closely here, except to say that the impact of the towns on the countryside continued to affect the economy and to lead to its development. The countryside now began to look to 'their' market town as an important part of their lives and the landscape begins to have threads of *portways*, 'market ways', leading to the towns and replacing the *herepaths*, 'army ways' (plate XXVIII). The new towns created in the last century are to be seen as a further development of the network, of which all the important elements were in place. We therefore find limited-function sites arising, such as the emergency *burhs* during the Danish wars of Æthelred II and the secondary market centres, particularly in the south and west.

The Multi-functional Town

It must not be thought that the general pattern of towns completely eradicated the rural central place, not at least within the Anglo-Saxon period. For example, the practice in the late tenth century of crowning kings at Kingston upon Thames, Surrey, ignores the towns, particularly London, Winchester or a great ecclesiastical centre such as Canterbury. Rural centres for bishoprics continued until the Conquest. There appear to have been fairs for trade on the pattern of the long-established fair in France at St Denis, a site to which Anglo-Saxon traders had been drawn for centuries.

With the growth of life in an urban setting, real commerce and activity can be seen to develop. It must be realized that the town was only its own best customer, in the sense that the majority of all transactions within the town would be to other inhabitants in the town. Groups of craftsmen and merchants would act together (or in sequence) on certain materials, or

PLATE XXVIII: Herepað *route approaching Avebury across the Wiltshire downland.*
© Della Hooke.

form chains of interlinked crafts. The citizens of Oxford, for example, improved their communications by arranging for the navigation of the Thames past Abingdon to be improved; the rent was to be paid in fish.[20] An example can be seen *c.* AD 1000 in Winchester, which was an important ecclesiastical centre and a royal seat, with the two facing each other across a piazza in the centre of the town (plate XXIX). Ælfric shows us the stream of pilgrims coming to Winchester and the burial-place of Saint Swithun from across southern England and *The Resting Place of the Saints* shows us other 'central places' for pilgrimage.[21] This document reveals how many of these important churches were either already in towns or attracted town life to themselves by the time of the Domesday survey. The great monastic complexes of Old and New Minster, together with the Nummaminster only a stone's throw away, were the administrative centre for vast estates and also provided services, but upstream along the aqueducts leading water into the minsters was genuine urban Winchester in the tenements revealed

[20] *Chronicon Monasterii de Abingdon*, edited by Rev. J. Stevenson (London, 1858), vol. I, pp. 480–1.
[21] Hill, *Atlas of Anglo-Saxon England*, p. 152.

PLATE XXIX: *Winchester from St Catherine's Hill.*
© Della Hooke.

by Martin Biddle's great excavation of Brooks Street.[22] The chains are clear here because of the charters of the period, which reveal street names. The beef on the hoof came into the town to the markets held in the streets, in the case of cattle in the main street. The king was particularly keen on the town as a mechanism for providing 'vouching for warranty' and had enacted laws to ensure that valuable animals were seen to be sold legally and before witnesses. In the pens, made from hurdles and found in excavation, cattle and sheep were sold (in the case of sheep, the pens and the manure have been found at Gar Street, Winchester), but there were many destinations for the animals, one of the most important being the town. Fleshmonger's Street (later Parchment Street) absorbed and butchered the animals and the practice which survived almost into this century in this country of 'baiting' the animals provided spectacle and 'sport' for the loungers. The hides moved to the next street, 'Tanner Street', where they became leather and provided a wealth of items, including the shields in 'Shieldworker's Street', next again. The labour force themselves were customers for the country people, not only for beef and bread, but for

[22] M. Biddle, 'Excavations at Winchester, 1971. Tenth and final interim report', *Antiquaries Journal*, 55(2) (1975), pp. 304–12.

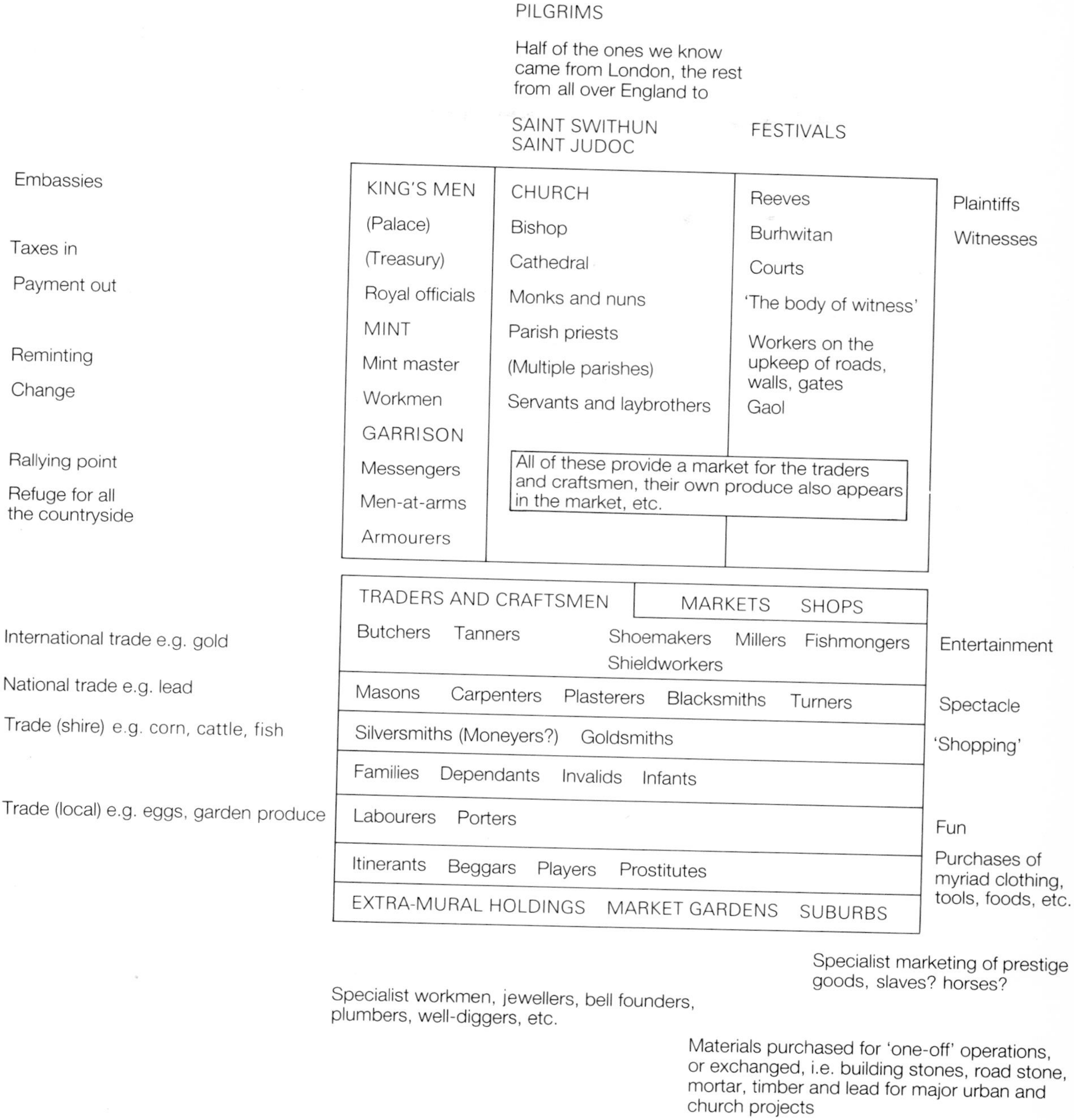

PILGRIMS

Half of the ones we know
came from London, the rest
from all over England to

SAINT SWITHUN   FESTIVALS
SAINT JUDOC

KING'S MEN	CHURCH	Reeves
(Palace)	Bishop	Burhwitan
(Treasury)	Cathedral	Courts
Royal officials	Monks and nuns	'The body of witness'
MINT	Parish priests	Workers on the upkeep of roads, walls, gates
Mint master	(Multiple parishes)	
Workmen	Servants and laybrothers	Gaol
GARRISON		

Embassies — Plaintiffs / Witnesses

Taxes in
Payment out

Reminting
Change

Rallying point
Refuge for all
the countryside

Messengers
Men-at-arms
Armourers

All of these provide a market for the traders
and craftsmen, their own produce also appears
in the market, etc.

TRADERS AND CRAFTSMEN   MARKETS   SHOPS

Butchers   Tanners   Shoemakers   Millers   Fishmongers
                              Shieldworkers

Masons   Carpenters   Plasterers   Blacksmiths   Turners

Silversmiths (Moneyers?)   Goldsmiths

Families   Dependants   Invalids   Infants

Labourers   Porters

Itinerants   Beggars   Players   Prostitutes

EXTRA-MURAL HOLDINGS   MARKET GARDENS   SUBURBS

International trade e.g. gold

National trade e.g. lead

Trade (shire) e.g. corn, cattle, fish

Trade (local) e.g. eggs, garden produce

Entertainment

Spectacle

'Shopping'

Fun

Purchases of
myriad clothing,
tools, foods, etc.

Specialist marketing of prestige
goods, slaves? horses?

Specialist workmen, jewellers, bell founders,
plumbers, well-diggers, etc.

Materials purchased for 'one-off' operations,
or exchanged, i.e. building stones, road stone,
mortar, timber and lead for major urban and
church projects

FIGURE 9.5   *The functions of
eleventh-century Winchester*

the few eggs of the *smereswyf*, 'the butter and egg woman', whose basket of eggs figures in the only miracle performed by Swithun whilst he was alive.

There is also the evidence for a careful survey of Winchester *c.* AD 1057, the fourth city of the realm.[23] The discussion reveals the great range of activities and functions; many others may be guessed at. This masterly picture of the late Anglo-Saxon *burh* can be translated into a simple diagram, which only hints at the complexity of the functions (figure 9.5).

Finally, it has long been a truism of urban archaeology that there is little to distinguish between an early medieval town site and a rural one: all the artefacts and structures are similar. It is only the scale, range and intensity of the activities that makes a particular site appear to be urban rather than rural. It is the contention of this chapter that in real terms there are no functions found in the town of the year AD 1000 that are not found in the countryside two hundred years earlier: the story of the town in these centuries is of the concentration of functions within sites and then, by that 'critical mass', a geometric progression of increased trading and services so that the whole becomes much greater than the sum of its parts.

[margin handwritten note: no new ideas, just concentrated. does success mean innovation?]

[23] F. Barlow (ed.), 'The Winton Domesday', in F. Barlow, O. von Feilitzen and D. J. Keene, *Studies 1: Winchester in the Early Middle Ages: An Edition and Discussion of the Winton Domesday*, edited by M. Biddle, Winchester Studies 1 (Oxford, 1976), pp. 9–10.

10

The Anglo-Saxon Towns of Kent

TIM TATTON-BROWN

Introduction

Some years ago I contributed a chapter on 'The towns of Kent' to a book on *Anglo-Saxon Towns in Southern England*.[1] In this, I looked in turn at each of the ten possible sites in the county that were probably urban centres by the late eleventh century. These places were: Canterbury, Rochester, Sandwich, Fordwich, Dover, Romney, Hythe, Faversham, Milton Regis and Seasalter (figure 10.1). In this chapter, I would like to look in more detail at the major changes that took place in the most important of these places between the seventh and eleventh centuries, and try to show how five of them (Canterbury, Sandwich, Romney, Hythe and Rochester), came to be listed as 'boroughs' in *Domesday Book* (Fordwich and Seasalter are also called *parvus burgus*).[2] Dover, which is only called a *villa*, must also have been a borough. I shall try also to show how the three most important sites (Canterbury, Sandwich and Dover) probably started as open (undefended) trading settlements called *wics* in the late seventh century and then evolved into fortified boroughs or *burhs* in the ninth century as a result of the Viking invasions.

The Earliest 'Towns' in Kent – the *Wics*

When St Augustine landed in Kent in AD 597, there were certainly no places there that could remotely have been called 'urban'. However, Augustine must have learnt in Rome that there had been a series of Roman towns there, and it was in these that he would be expected to build the new cathedral churches of England. He had also probably learnt that London

---

[1] T. Tatton-Brown, 'The towns of Kent', in J. Haslam (ed.), *Anglo-Saxon Towns in Southern England* (Chichester, 1984), pp. 1–36.
[2] *Domesday Book*, Record Commission (London, 1783), fos 1a, 2a, 3a, 4a, 5a, 12b.

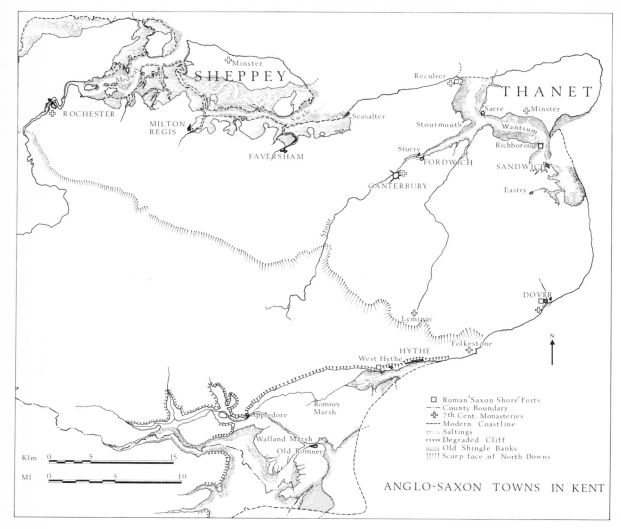

FIGURE 10.1 *Map of eastern Kent showing the positions of the Anglo-Saxon towns and a reconstructed coastline*

was the most important of these towns and would perhaps have been expecting to base himself there. In the event, political considerations meant that Canterbury would be the most important town (*civitas*), with Rochester and London following a few years later; after another pause, the two major Roman towns in the north, York and Lincoln, also received bishops and built cathedral churches. None of these places, however, can be called urban in the first half of the seventh century. Recent excavations in Canterbury have shown that in the later sixth and seventh centuries the area inside the city walls was reoccupied on quite a large scale, with groups of rough timber buildings (mostly *grubenhäuser*) being erected among the

214

ruins of the old Roman masonry buildings, and by the end of the seventh century there was certainly quite a large settlement within the eastern area of the city walls (figure 10.3). Almost all of the buildings and pits associated with this settlement inside the Roman walls have produced only the local very coarse pottery and a very small number of fine objects. A handful of pits (out of a large number of levels and pits excavated in the last decade) have, however, produced *sceattas* and imported Ispwich-type wares of the eighth century. Outside the city walls on the north-east, two small sites, near St Augustine's Abbey and St Martin's church, have recently been excavated and here, by contrast, most of the earliest pits contained Ipswich-type ware.

This area outside the city walls, on the north-east and north of the main road to Sandwich, is famous because it continued both the original Abbey of St Peter and St Paul (founded by St Augustine in *c.* AD 598 and a great centre of learning by the eighth century) and also the church of St Martin, which Bede tells us was used by Æthelberht's queen Bertha (and her 'chaplain', Bishop Liudhard) even before the arrival of St Augustine. Bede also says that St Martin's church was built during the Roman occupation, and it is a distinct possibility that the church may have been part of Æthelberht's *villa regalis* in the late sixth century.[3] (Excavations near the church in 1985 have almost certainly proved that it was not originally a *cella memoria* in a late Roman cemetery.) North-east of St Martin's church and the abbey, there is a large barren sandy area, the later manor of Caldecote. This has been a royal park since 1538 (it is still MOD land today) and lies on the high ground just above the limit of the tidal estuary. East of it is the small manor significantly called Wyke. All of this area has been within the jurisdiction of Canterbury since at least the late Anglo-Saxon period, and in the 1050s the small new borough of Fordwich was cut out of its north-east corner (figure 10.2). Fordwich is first mentioned much earlier than this, however, in a charter of King Hlothhere of AD 675, and it is in the laws of this same king of Kent, Hlothhere, that we first hear of a *wīc-gerēfa* (reeve of the *wīc*)[4]. Fordwich is also mentioned in toll-charters of AD 747 and 761, and there can be no doubt that by the eighth century it was a very important trading centre and that it produced a substantial income from tolls for the Kentish kings.[5] This is backed up by a recent find (with a metal-detector) of two silver pennies of Offa (dated 792–6), which were found just to the south-east of the modern village (Canterbury was at this time the main mint for these new silver pennies of Offa). How large this *wīc* was

[3] Bede, *Ecclesiastical History*, in *Venerabilis Baedae Opera Historica*, edited by C. Plummer, 2 vols (Oxford, 1896), I, 26.
[4] P. H. Sawyer, *Anglo-Saxon Charters: an Annotated List and Bibliography* (London, 1968), S. 7; W. de Gray Birch, *Cartularium Saxonicum*, 3 vols (London, 1885–99), B. 36.
[5] Sawyer, *Anglo-Saxon Charters*, S. 1612, S. 29; Birch, *Cartularium Saxonicum*, B. 173, B. 189.

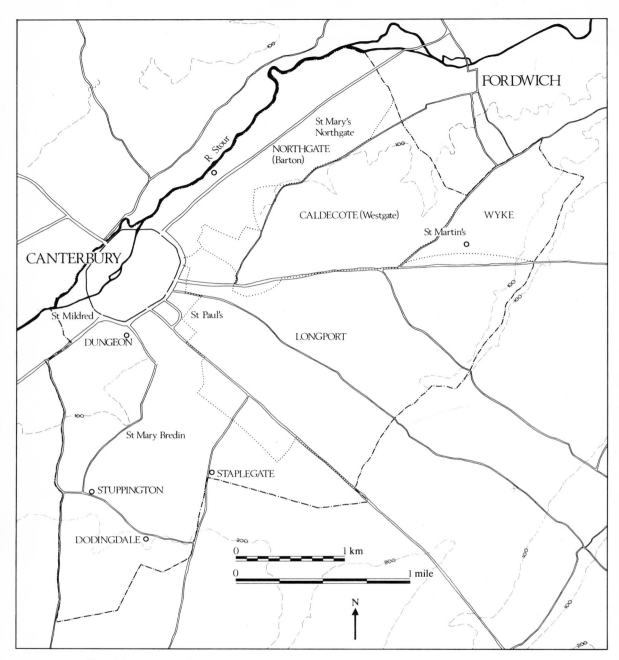

FIGURE 10.2 *Plan of the Canterbury area showing the medieval county borough boundary*

in the eighth century is as yet unknown, but it is quite possible that the trading settlement did occupy much of the area between St Augustine's and the small village which is today called Fordwich (figure 10.2).

This large open area outside the city walls seems to be closely paralleled by the *wīc* at London which has recently been discussed in detail by Martin Biddle and Alan Vince.[6] In London, the *wīc* (called Aldwych – 'old *wīc*' – from the later medieval period) centred on the Strand and perhaps extended between the Roman city walls on the east and St Peter's Abbey at Westminster and the church of St Martin (-in-the-Fields) on the west. The *wīc* at London (*Lundenuuic*) is better documented than all the other *wīcs* and it too must have been founded and controlled by the kings of Kent.

The third most important Kentish *wīc* was Sandwich, at the eastern end of the Wantsum channel (figure 10.4). Here, again, the new trading *wīc* of the seventh century is situated on a virgin site not far from the major Roman port, settlement and the 'Saxon shore' fort at Richborough, and it is quite clear that ease of access to the sea was of primary importance here as well as at all the other trading *wīcs*. It seems likely that by the seventh century the great shingle bank at Stonar had moved south and caused much silting in the Roman harbour area. Richborough is also an isolated site on an 'island', whereas Sandwich had direct access by land to the very important 'royal vill' site at Eastry, only a few miles to the south-west (figure 10.1), as well as to the rich arable area of East Kent.

Sandwich is first mentioned in AD 664–5 in the life of St Wilfrid,[7] and it is this work and other early *Lives of Saints* that first document the travel by sea between the great trading settlements of England and the Continent in the late seventh and early eighth centuries. In England, London, Hamwic and Sandwich are the principal names given, while on the other side of the Channel it is Rouen, Quentovic and Wijk-bij-Duurstede. The traders themselves were presumably Frisians and other people in the Low Countries who had learnt to cope with the large-scale rises in sea level and flooding that had occurred in the post-Roman period. These men may well have been known as *wīc-ings* ('men of the *wīcs*') and when many of these traders (particularly the Scandinavians) became pirates in the ninth century the name was applied to them – 'vikings'.

At Sandwich, no archaeological evidence has yet been found for the later seventh and eighth centuries. This is because the town failed as a port in the sixteenth century and still contains one of the largest collections of surviving timber-framed buildings in England. As well as this, the building-out of quays into the haven in the later medieval period and the continuous

---

[6] M. Biddle, 'London on the Strand', *Popular Archaeology*, 6(1) (1984), pp. 23–7; A. Vince, 'The Aldewych: mid-Saxon London discovered?', *Current Archaeology*, 93 (1984), pp. 310–13..

[7] B. Colgrave (ed.), *The Life of Bishop Wilfred by Eddius Stephanus* (London, 1927), pp. 25, 28.

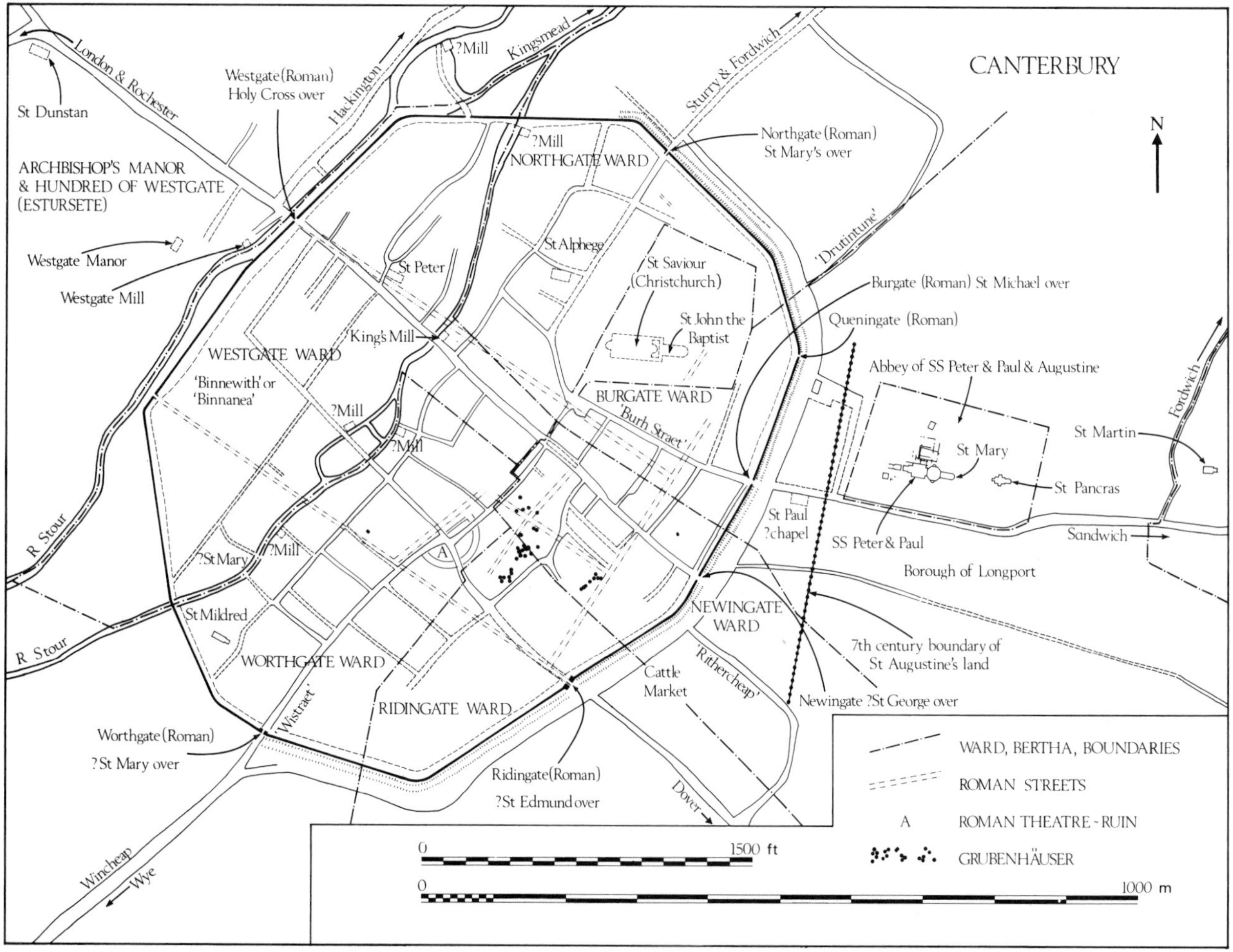

FIGURE 10.3 *Plan of Anglo-Saxon Canterbury*

CANTERBURY

St Dunstan

ARCHBISHOP'S MANOR
& HUNDRED OF WESTGATE
(ESTURSETE)

Westgate Manor

Westgate Mill

London & Rochester

Westgate (Roman)
Holy Cross over

?Mill

Kingsmead

King's Mill

?Mill

WESTGATE WARD

'Binnewith' or
'Binnanea'

St Peter

Northgate (Roman)
St Mary's over

?Mill

NORTHGATE WARD

St Alphege

St Saviour
(Christchurch)

St John the
Baptist

BURGATE WARD

Ruth Street'

?Mill

St Mary's

St Mildred

?Mill

WORTHGATE WARD

Wstraet'

Worthgate (Roman)
?St Mary over

RIDINGATE WARD

Ridingate (Roman)
?St Edmund over

Burgate (Roman) St Michael over

Queningate (Roman)

Abbey of SS Peter & Paul & Augustine

St Paul
?chapel

NEWINGATE
WARD

Rithercheap

Cattle
Market

Dover

Newingate ?St George over

SS Peter & Paul

Borough of Longport

7th century boundary of
St Augustine's land

St Mary

St Martin

St Pancras

Sandwich

Fordwich

R Stour

R Stour

Wincheap

Wye

Dover

1500 ft

0

0   1000 m

WARD, BERTHA, BOUNDARIES

ROMAN STREETS

ROMAN THEATRE - RUIN

GRUBENHÄUSER

N

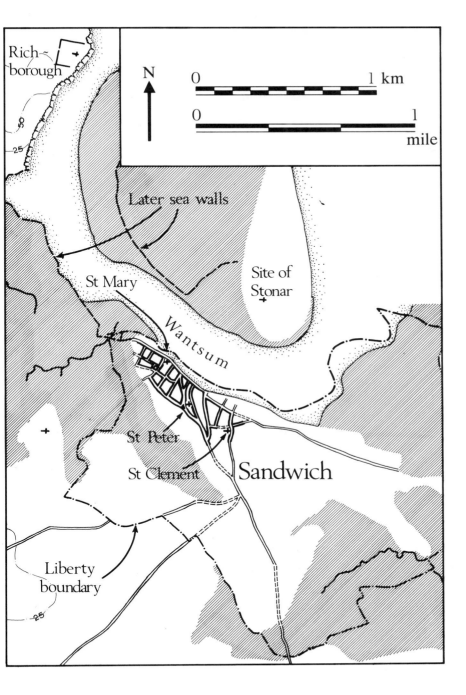

Rich-
borough

50

25

N

0   1 km

0   1
                                mile

Later sea walls

St Mary

Site of
Stonar

Wantsum

St Peter

St Clement

Sandwich

Liberty
boundary

25

FIGURE 10.4   *Plan of Anglo-
Saxon Sandwich. Later
medieval roads, streets and
defences have been omitted.*

rise in sea level has meant that these earliest archaeological levels are deeply buried and largely inaccessible.

One other *wīc* site that is first documented much later on is the area outside Dover, to the south-west. From the early sixteenth century onwards, this area (now the Western Docks) was continuously developed, at enormous expense, as a large new harbour.[8] Before this, the medieval harbour here was called the Wyke or wike, and by the 1490s two wardens (*custodes*) of the Wyke are documented. The geographical position of this site (at the very bottom of figure 10.5) is similar to the other sites mentioned above. It was on the sloping foreshore outside the Roman 'Saxon shore' fort, and protected form the prevailing winds by the Western Heights. To the east, shingle below the castle appears to have moved westwards, causing the Roman harbour at the mouth of the river Dour to become silted up.[9] The Wyke was, therefore, the natural harbour (and roadstead) site for medieval Dover, and the landward side of the beach here is now roughly covered by Snargate Street.

Inside the Roman core of Dover, much evidence for early Anglo-Saxon occupation (including *grubenhäuser*) has been discovered by Brian Philps' recent excavations, and it seems likely that Dover was similar to Canterbury in having a settlement inside the Roman walls as well as a trading centre or *wīc* outside. An early Anglo-Saxon cemetery has also been discovered on Priory Hill, just outside the walled area on the west.[10]

It is possible that other early trading *wīcs* once existed in Kent, and names like Greenwich and Woolwich on the Thames foreshore in north-west Kent may indicate the position of two such sites. One might also expect to find a *wīc* site in the Romney Marsh area, and one place, now called 'The Wicks' on the south side of Dungeness, is indeed first documented in a charter of AD 774,[11] where it is called Bishop's *Wīc*.[12] This was in an area near Lydd belonging to the archbishops of Canterbury, and it is more than likely that this was an early trading centre. By the eleventh century this area was part of the hundred of Langport, and it is possible that the town of Old Romney (see below) is the late Anglo-Saxon successor to Bishop's *Wīc*.

It seems likely, therefore, that in Kent as well as elsewhere on the south and east coasts of England the earliest major settlements of the Anglo-Saxon period that were in any sense 'urban' were these trading *wīcs*.[13] The

---

[8] M. Biddle, 'Dover harbour', in H. M. Colvin (ed.), *The History of the King's Works*, vol. IV (London, 1982), pp. 729–68.

[9] S. Rigold, 'The Roman haven at Dover', *Archaeological Journal*, 136 (1970), p. 81.

[10] A. Meaney, *A Gazatteer of Early Anglo-Saxon Burial Sites* (London, 1964), p. 117.

[11] Sawyer, *Anglo-Saxon Charters*, S. 23; Birch, *Cartularium Saxonicum*, B. 148.

[12] N. P. Brooks, 'Romney Marsh in the early Middle Ages', in R. T. Rowley (ed.), *The Evolution of Marshland Landscapes* (Oxford, 1981), p. 87.

[13] S. Reynolds, *An Introduction to the History of English Medieval Towns* (Oxford, 1977), pp. 34–7.

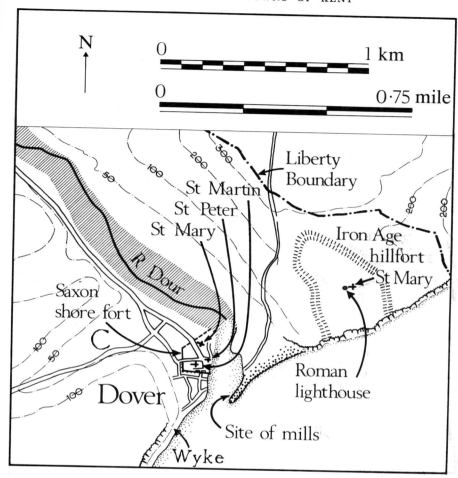

FIGURE 10.5 *Plan of Anglo-Saxon Dover. The Wyke is the area to the south of the Saxon shore fort.*

wīcs must have originated in the seventh century and were in full swing in the eighth century, when many earlier silver pennies (mistakenly called *sceattas*) were being minted in the county (mostly at Canterbury). The arrival of Vikings (or the metamorphosis of the traders into pirates) in the early ninth century changed all this, and when the 'Great Armies' wintered on the islands of Sheppey and Thanet off the north Kent coast in the 850s (see figure 10.1), the *wīcs* had effectively been wiped out.

The Fortified Towns in Kent – the *Burhs*

The second town of Kent has always been Rochester (plate XXX). This is because not only was it the 'capital' of west Kent and the only other late

Roman walled town in the county, but it was also the place where, from AD 604, only the second cathedral in England was situated. Bede calls it *Hrofescaestir*, and describes how King Æthelberht built a church here (dedicated to St Andrew) for the first bishop, Justus.[14] At this time the Roman city walls were clearly in good condition and Bede often refers to Rochester as a *castellum* (for example, in AD 673) (plate XXXI).[15] The evidence from ninth-century charters also suggests that by this time there was substantial occupation outside the walls on the east and it is possible that there was also a trading *wīc* here. One charter of AD 850 even mentions a half-acre plot and a nearby church of St Mary outside the eastern city walls (figure 10.6).[16] Only a few years later, in AD 854, the Vikings were wintering close by on the island of Sheppey, and in AD 885 Rochester is described in the *Anglo-Saxon Chronicle* as the scene of an epic siege by 'the great heathen host'. We are also told that the Vikings 'built another fortification around themselves' and that 'the citizens (of Rochester) defended the city until king Alfred came to their relief with levies', whereupon the Vikings abandoned their encampment and horses and 'went back overseas' in their ships.[17]

[14] Bede, *Venerabilis Baedeae Opera Historica*, II, 3.
[15] Ibid., IV, 5.
[16] Sawyer, *Anglo-Saxon Charters*, S. 299; Birch, *Cartularium Saxonicum*, B. 460.
[17] *The Anglo-Saxon Chronicle. Two of the Saxon Chronicles Parallel*, edited by C. Plummer (Oxford, 1892–9), pp. 66–7, 78–9.

PLATE XXXI: *Rochester: the southern rounded corner of the Roman city walls.*
© Tim Tatton-Brown.

From this time onwards, it is the fortified settlements or *burhs* that are the important places in England and many later Anglo-Saxon urban centres grew out of them. Historians of the period have relied on the very useful compilation of the late ninth or early tenth century called *The Burghal Hidage*.[18] Unfortunately the only part of the kingdom of Wessex that is not included in this document is Kent, and the first list of late Anglo-Saxon *burhs* in Kent is that in *Domesday Book*. To the *Domesday Book* list (Canterbury, Rochester, Sandwich, Romney and Hythe) can be added Dover (a *villa* in the Domesday survey entries), which was clearly a *burh* by 1066. The two *parvi burgi* in *Domesday Book* (Fordwich and Seasalter) are almost certainly late in date (see below) and were not original *burhs* of the ninth or tenth century. To the Domesday evidence for Kent can be added the very important evidence of the mints in the county, which in the later Anglo-Saxon period must have been based in the *burhs*. Canterbury was already minting coins from an early date (*c.* AD 630–40), and Rochester followed with a mint from at least the ninth century. Then came Dover under Athelstan (AD 924–39), 'Limen' (in the Hythe area) under Edgar (AD 959–75), Romney under Æthelred (the 'Unready') (AD 997–1003), and finally Sandwich under Edward the Confessor (AD 1042–66).

In the ninth century, therefore, it seems likely that the only major

---

[18] D. Hill, 'The Burghal Hidage: the establishment of a text', *Medieval Archaeology*, 13 (1969), pp. 84–92.

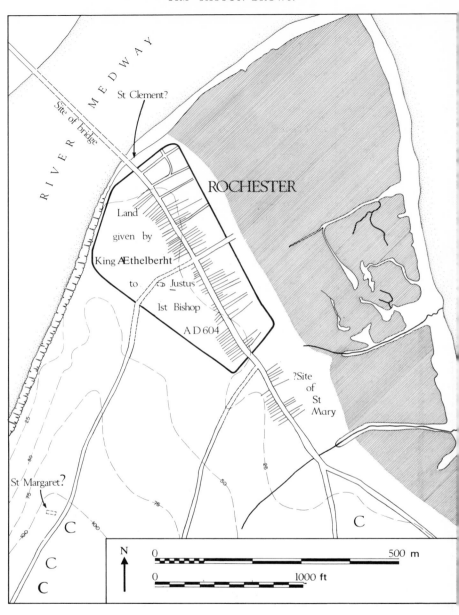

FIGURE 10.6 *Plan of Anglo-Saxon Rochester. C marks the sites of early Anglo-Saxon cemeteries, whereas the later medieval (and ?Anglo-Saxon) market was outside the Roman walls on the north-east.*

fortified *burh* in the county, other than Rochester, was Canterbury, although it is possible that the 'Saxon shore' forts at Reculver, Dover and Richborough (for Sandwich) with their massive Roman walls were once again put into service as forts. It is also just possible that the shore fort at Lympne (Stutfall Castle, as it was later called) was in use again by the tenth century (figure 10.7). The earliest coins minted in the area are inscribed

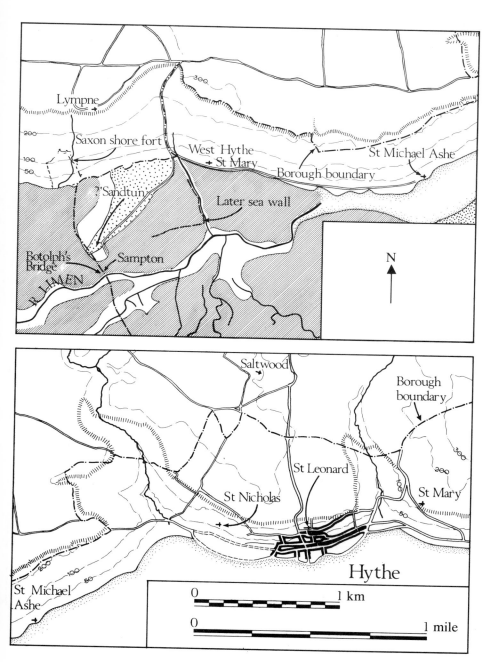

FIGURE 10.7 *Plan of the 'Limen'–Hythe area in the Anglo-Saxon period. The lower map overlaps the upper map on the east.*

'Limen', which was the ancient name of the river that crossed the north side of Romney Marsh and gave its name to the Roman fort *Portus Lemanis*. Just to the south-east of the Roman fort, on a sand and shingle bank, is a place called *Sandtun*, which is mentioned in charters of AD 732 and 833 (plate XXXII).[19] This site may also have been a trading *wīc* in origin, but all the pottery that has been found here is of a tenth- or eleventh-century date, and it seems more likely that this was the earliest 'town' of 'Limen' that was to migrate eastwards during the late Saxon and medieval periods as the longshore drift of shingle from the south-west progressively destroyed the harbours – hence the later names of West Hythe and Hythe (see figure 10.7). During times of trouble the Roman walled area may well have been used, but before the Norman Conquest the whole of this fort had slipped down the cliff and been rendered useless. Its early Norman successor, where a castle for the first archdeacon of Canterbury was built, was on the cliff-top above. This still retains the old name, although it is now spelt Lympne.

At Richborough (the name seems to have changed from *Reptacaestir* in *c.* AD 730 to a *burh* name), the building (or rebuilding) of a chapel (dedicated to St Augustine) within the fort in the later Anglo-Saxon period may also indicate a re-use of this fortified site in time of trouble. It should also be noted that three mid-ninth-century Northumbrian *styca* coins were found here as well as quite a large number of earlier *sceattas* and pennies of King Offa.[20] By the end of the Anglo-Saxon period, however, Sandwich was clearly once again a flourishing town with a large natural harbour. Here, for example, Anlaf's fleet of ninety-three Viking ships was based in AD 994, as well as Æthelred's vast fleet collected to oppose Swein in AD 1009, and it is likely that Sandwich had by this time acquired some sort of defensive bank and ditch. No trace of any defences before the late medieval period, however, have yet been found and it is possible that Richborough was still the only fortified part of the town. In the late Anglo-Saxon period, Sandwich also seems to have expanded to the east and west from its original nucleus, and the parishes and churches of St Mary and St Clement were perhaps created in the early eleventh century (see figure 10.4). It is odd, however, that Sandwich did not acquire its own mint until the mid-eleventh century. This may be related to the new charter granted to Sandwich by Edward the Confessor (when he confirms it as a town belonging to the archbishop and his monks). It is also the time when St Augustine's Abbey first started to build a new trading settlement opposite Sandwich at Stonar (see figure 10.4). By the twelfth century, Stonar was a distinct threat to the town.

[19] Sawyer, *Anglo-Saxon Charters*, S. 23 and S. 270; Birch, *Cartularium Saxonicum*, B. 148 and B. 411.

[20] B. W. Cunliffe (ed.), *Fifth Report of the Excavations of the Roman Fort at Richborough* (London, 1969), pp. 219–28.

PLATE XXXII: *View of Lympne castle from the marshes to the south. The Saxon-shore fort is to the left of the picture and 'Sandtun' lay on the slight rise in the middle distance.*
© Tim Tatton-Brown.

Dover, on the other hand, was minting coins from the time of Athelstan (AD 924–39) and in the tenth century it was certainly an important town. It is probable that this town was situated within the Roman fort walls (see figure 10.5) around the area still known as the Market Place. Also situated here were the churches of St Martin, St Peter and St Mary, the first of which was almost certainly an early Anglo-Saxon minster church. By the early eleventh century, however, a new *burh* appears to have been created on top of the hill where the later medieval castle is now situated. The most striking evidence for this is the great late Saxon church of St Mary (-in-the-castle), which has the Roman lighthouse at its west end (plate XXXIII). The hilltop may already have had an Iron Age hillfort on it and there are at least two references to a pre-Norman Conquest 'castle' here.[21] One of these references also mentions a *burh*, and it is more likely that the hilltop was occupied by a fortified town (hence the great church, the largest pre-Conquest church in Kent) than a 'proto-castle'. With the arrival of the Normans, the hilltop site was turned into a castle and the people as well as

[21] R. A. Brown, *Dover Castle* (London, 1974), pp. 6–7.

PLATE XXXIII: *The early eleventh-century church of St Mary-de-Castro, Dover, from the south-west (the Roman lighthouse is on the left of the picture).*
© Tim Tatton-Brown.

the priests of St Mary's church were sent back down the hill to the 'old' town.

The largest and most important *burh* in Kent was, of course, Canterbury (this name, the '*burh* of the men of Kent', had replaced the old Roman name of *Durovernum*, which was still used by Bede in the early eighth century), and from the ninth century much more of the Roman walled area must have been reoccupied. A whole variety of charters indicate that this occupation was dense (particularly in the charter of AD 868), and it is likely that the street frontage occupation (which still survives) had replaced the irregularly spaced *grubenhäuser* by the ninth century.[22] With the advent of the Vikings at this time (they sacked the city in AD 850 or 851) many of the traders in the *wīc* must have sought shelter within the walls, but ninth- and tenth-century charters still mention the *innan burhwara* and the *utan burhwara* (i.e. 'the people within and without the *burh*'), so some of the population must still have lived and worked outside the walls and only sought shelter in difficult times.[23] Many of the late Saxon markets were in the area immediately beyond the Roman walls on the south and east (see figure 10.3), and certainly before the Norman Conquest the large street markets at Longport and Wincheap had been created. Inside the walls too a new High Street was created, probably in the tenth century, between the Westgate and a 'new gate' (Newingate) on the east, and this must also have had its street market. It is also very likely that almost all the streets of the

[22] Sawyer, *Anglo-Saxon Charters*, S. 1204; Birch, *Cartularium Saxonicum*, B. 519.
[23] N. P. Brooks, *The Early History of the Church of Canterbury* (Leicester, 1984), p. 28.

medieval town were created before the Norman Conquest as well as many of the churches by (or over) the gates, and that the city had already been divided up into wards (or *berthas*, as they were called) based on the gates (plate XXXIV).

In AD 1011 Canterbury suffered a disastrous Danish siege, followed by another sack, and the murder of its Archbishop Ælfheah. This was, however, only a temporary setback and by the Norman Conquest about 450 burgesses are mentioned in *Domesday Book*, suggesting a population of about 6,000, making Canterbury one of the ten largest towns in England.[24] By the eleventh century Canterbury also had a large area around it, which was later to become the County Borough (see figure 10.2). The boundary to this area is first defined in *Domesday Book* as 1 league, 3 perches and 3 feet and it seems likely that this marks the limit to the *territorium* of the Anglo-Saxon *burh*.

In *Domesday Book* three other *burhs* are mentioned. These are Romney, Fordwich and Seasalter; the last two are both called *parvus burgus*. Fordwich has ninety-six dwelling plots (*mansurae terrae*) recorded and it is likely that quite a large new nucleus of population had grown up in the late Anglo-Saxon period around the port for Canterbury. This site, which is 3 miles north-east of the Roman walled city, is at the tidal limit of the Stour, and Edward the Confessor appears to have cut it out of the territory belonging to Canterbury (see figure 10.2) and given much of it to St Augustine's Abbey. At the same time, he was giving (or confirming) the town of Sandwich to the archbishop and his monks at Christ Church. Despite being called a *burh*, Fordwich never had its own defences and the use of the word *burgus* must here have denoted a purely administrative function.

Seasalter is the strangest of all the boroughs recorded in *Domesday Book*. It appeared to have no burgesses (unlike all the other towns), and we are told that it belonged to the archbishop's kitchen and was held from the monks (of Christ Church) by Blize. *Domesday Monachorum* says that *Saesaltre est burgus monachorum et de cibo proprie de coquina eorum*, and eight fisheries are also recorded.[25] It is likely, therefore, that Seasalter was a special centre for the fish trade and possibly also (from its name) for salt-panning. Why it is called a borough, however, is not clear.

Finally, Romney is recorded as a borough with 156 burgesses. I originally suggested that the planned town of New Romney was the late Saxon town, which first had a mint in *c*. AD 997–1003.[26] However, this now seems unlikely and New Romney is probably a new town of the twelfth century,

[24] Ibid., pp. 32–3.
[25] D. C. Douglas (ed.), *The Domesday Monachorum of Christ Church, Canterbury* (London, 1944), p. 90.
[26] T. Tatton-Brown, 'Towns of Kent', pp. 1–36.

which is when the large church of St Nicholas was built and the names 'Old' and 'New' Romney are first documented. The most likely site for the Saxon town is therefore at Old Romney, where today there is only the parish church of St Clement (a dedication usually of the early eleventh century) and a few houses (plate XXXV). No other trace of the town has yet been found and where the important port for ships of AD 1052 (recorded in the *Anglo-Saxon Chronicle*) or the houses of the burgesses were located has yet to be discovered.[27]

PLATE XXXV: *The church of St Clement, Old Romney, once part of a late Saxon* burh.
© Tim Tatton-Brown.

The later Anglo-Saxon towns of Kent, which probably originated in part as defensive strongholds against the Vikings, were also a series of major trading settlements again by the Norman Conquest. All of them, except Canterbury, were situated by the sea (or on a major navigable river close to the sea), and even before the Conquest Dover, Hythe, Romney and Sandwich were doing 'ship-service' for the late Saxon kings. This was the forerunner of the 'Cinque Ports' system (only Hastings was not in Kent) and gave these towns a special relationship with the king as well as great strategic importance. Canterbury and Rochester were the ancient Roman walled towns of Kent (*civitates* in *Domesday Book*) and their importance was as administrative centres both for the two halves of the county and for the seats of the bishoprics. Kent, unlike the rest of the areas controlled by the

PLATE XXXIV: *Canterbury: tenth-century cellar excavated at the Marlowe shopping development site showing the remains of walls constructed of wattle behind posts.*
© Tim Tatton-Brown.

[27] *Anglo-Saxon Chronicle*, p. 179.

kings of Wessex (and later of England), had no large new planned towns of the late ninth or early tenth century.[28] Its towns were concerned with the sea and not the land, and this remained largely the same throughout the rest of the medieval period.

[28] M. Biddle and D. Hill, 'Late Saxon planned towns', *Antiquaries Journal*, 51 (1971), pp. 70–85.

11

The Making of Domesday York

RICHARD HALL

The twenty years that have elapsed between the nine hundredth anniversary of the Battle of Hastings and the celebration of *Domesday Book* have witnessed the greatest progress yet in the archaeological discovery of the England appraised by William's inquisitors. Two decades of survey and excavation, often occasioned by the sweeping away of swathes of historic topography in redevelopment schemes of all sorts, have furnished what in many cases is truly seminal data, and not least in importance has been the information garnered on urban settlements in pre-Norman England. Urban historians, topographers and archaeologists have, of course, for long been attempting to go beyond the seemingly arid tenurial statistics and the nuggets of other information in *Domesday Book* to direct some light into the tracts of town life hidden in its chiaroscuro treatment. In York, the measure of the progress is apparent when comparing the speculations of nineteenth- and twentieth-century antiquarians[1] and even the magisterial cataloguing work of Waterman,[2] perforce presented in a near contextual vacuum, with more recent studies incorporating excavated data.[3]

York represents well the advances made in urban archaeology, and this is entirely fitting for a settlement that was the most substantial single centre accounted for in *Domesday Book*: the 1,418 inhabited dwellings (*mansiones hospitatae*) accounted for in five of its seven shires suggest an overall total of perhaps 1,800 *mansiones*. This size reflected its pedigree as a capital, a status extending back initially to the days when *Eburacum* was the

I am grateful to colleagues at York Archaeological Trust, who have consciously or unconsciously provided the stimulus for much of this discussion, and to the directors and staff of the archaeological organizations referred to in the text, who have provided relevant information. Detailed reports on the York sites will appear in the series *The Archaeology of York*. The text of this article was typed by Stephanie Crosby, and the illustration prepared by Erich Kadow.

[1] G. A. Auden (ed.), *A Handbook to York and District* (London, 1906), passim.
[2] D. M. Waterman, 'Late Saxon, Viking, and early medieval finds from York', *Archaeologia*, 97 (1959), pp. 59–105.
[3] J. Moulden and D. Tweddle, *Anglo-Scandinavian Settlement South-West of the Ouse*, in *The Archaeology of York* 8(1), edited by P. V. Addyman, Council for British Archaeology (London, 1986).

first city of the Roman province of *Britannia Inferior*, resuming in the time when *Eoforwic* was the political, ecclesiastical and commercial focus of the Anglian kingdom of Northumbria, and latterly extending to when *Jorvik* was the nub of a Viking kingdom and an Anglo-Scandinavian earldom.

Domesday Book reflects the political, ecclesiastical and economic facets which Bede, Alcuin, the *Anglo-Saxon Chronicle* and other eighth- to eleventh-century sources mention in relation to York. The two reeves of Earl Harold to whom it refers presumably signal royal interest in the town and its economy; the holdings of the archbishop, including his high court (*curia*), and the houses of the canons are listed; and stalls in the meat market (*in macello*) are noted. Civic or perhaps more wide-ranging jurisdiction is encountered in the four judges whom the king had specially favoured, and the subdivision of the city into shires is another indication of an internal government whose bounds may or may not have been limited by the city ditch into which (*in fossato urb.*) houses were encroaching. Immediately beyond the inhabited area – immediately, since William's creation of the King's pool by damming the river Foss to flood his castle ditches inundated part of it – were the 84 carucates of land that were partly cultivated by the burgesses, and where new mills had been lost to the rising waters.

The making of Domesday York, however, is a topic which should still be approached by the archaeologist with some caution. It is now possible to comment on some very specific aspects of the city's growth, based on the microtopographical investigations occasionally undertaken in controlled archaeological excavation and the more frequent, but less comprehensive and sometimes ambiguous observations made during non-archaeological excavations; but to present an inductively inspired picture of York's entire Anglo-Scandinavian evolution on the basis of excavation of some five or six of the *c.* 1,800 *Domesday Book mansiones* is to place an insupportable strain on the sample of data currently available. In view of the deficiencies of the evidence, it is still more difficult to go beyond the 'what' and 'when' of Anglo-Scandinavian development to the more interesting, but more nebulous 'why' and 'how'.

Naturally, the fabric of York in 1066 reflected not only the more immediate history of the settlement since the Viking take-over two centuries before, but also earlier epochs. York's position on a morainic ridge traversing the lower-lying Vale of York ensured that there was an important land route here from the prehistoric period;[4] the junction of the rivers Ouse and Foss as they intersect with the moraine highlighted the potential of the site for communications and created a defensible tongue of land. There may well have been prehistoric activity or even occupation

---

[4] J. Radley, 'The prehistory of the Vale of York', *Yorkshire Archaeological Journal*, 46 (1974), pp. 10–22.

within the area of the later town, but no traces have yet been recovered, and it was the Roman army which first brought a dense population to York and laid the framework for all subsequent activity. Roman features, which still exert an influence today, must have been equally, if not more prominent in 1066, and clearly at least the north-west and north-east sides of the fortress still delineated part of the defended area north of the river.

South of the Ouse, it is not certain that there were Roman defences to predetermine the later medieval circuit, and the existence of even an Anglo-Scandinavian *enceinte* remains unproven, although likely. A separate walled Roman enclave attached to the north-west side of the fortress is believed to have existed, a possible third intra-mural component of *Eboracum*, and this latter may have been the antecedent of *Earlsburgh*, a name for an area off Marygate noted by the eighteenth-century York historian Francis Drake; the church of St Olaf, associated with Earl Siward of Northumbria (AD 1055), stands here today, perhaps an indication that the earl's residence was adjacent.

Also surviving from the Roman period were some elements of the street plan. Intra-murally, the most obvious are the *via praetoria* and the *via decumana*, represented today by Stonegate and Chapter House Street respectively, and the *via principalis* echoed in Petergate. These served to link opposing gateways. Immediately extra-mural roads such as Gillygate, Lendal/Coney Street, Lord Mayor's Walk and St Andrewgate/Jubbergate/Market Street also follow to varying degrees the lines of Roman thorough-fares either known or surmised. Over the Ouse, the Roman grid plan of the *colonia* is not recognizable, but the Roman approach roads to *Eboracum* continued to channel access to the later settlements on both sides of the river.

Within this framework some individual Roman structures stood for a considerable time after *c.* AD 400, most notably the *principia* at the centre of the fortress, still apparently roofed into the eighth or ninth century.[5] The indirect influence that Roman structure and even the Roman cemeteries had upon Domesday York are discussed below (p. 237).

The influences of Anglo-Saxon *Eoforwic* on Domesday York are generally more difficult to assess (figure 11.1). Indeed, until very recently, the archaeological record of Anglian York amounted to very little, and it was virtually impossible to discuss even the seventh- to ninth-century period in anything but the most speculative terms. Evidence for fifth- and sixth-century activity or occupation by either a relict Romano-British community or incoming Anglo-Saxons is still lacking. The elucidation of this period has seen one advance, however: the flooding of extensive tracts

[5] D. Phillips, 'Excavations at York Minster 1967–73', *Friends of York Minster 46th Annual Report* (1975), p. 24.

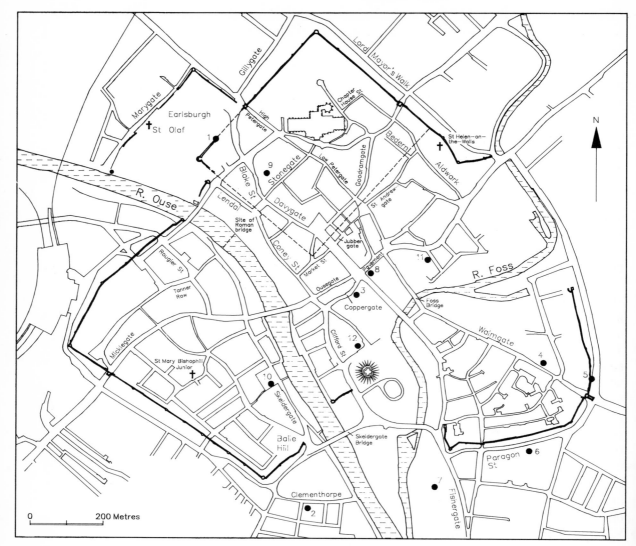

FIGURE 11.1 *York, showing the location of sites referred to in the text*

of the town, a theory proposed on the evidence of observations and old excavations, has not been vindicated in a number of excavations, and now seems rather unlikely.

It is now recognized, however, that there was a seventh- to ninth-century ecclesiastical presence near the site of the medieval Minster, and also that the 'Anglian Tower' (1) and the earliest adjacent refurbishments of the north-west fortress defences could indeed date to the pre-Viking period.[6]

[6] R. A. Hall and B. K. Davison, *Observations of the North-western Fortress Defences Adjacent to the 'Anglian Tower', 1970*, in *The Archaeology of York* 11(2), edited by P. V. Addyman (forthcoming).

And even if the Anglian pottery recovered adjacent to the 'Anglian Tower' is residual within the ramparts, it suggests the probability that there was activity and perhaps settlement at that time in the vicinity. There is a scatter of seventh- to ninth-century material throughout the fortress area, but no coherent evidence for occupation has yet been recognized. Negative evidence does not, of course, necessarily imply that the fortress area was largely unoccupied, and until recently the almost complete absence of mid-Saxon pottery in this area was only part of an all-embracing lack of these wares in York. With their recent recognition at other sites, however, the negative evidence for the fortress assumes greater credibility.

Additionally, the early to mid-Saxon period, rather than the Anglo-Scandinavian era, seems the most likely time for the development of some of the elements in York's medieval street plan that cut across the Roman axes. North of the river, the streets Goodramgate (whose north-eastern sector was re-aligned in the thirteenth century) and Blake Street (whose north-western end was also enclosed then) reflect the disappearance of Roman *insulae* and the establishment of routes diagonally across them to allow passage between adjacent Roman gateways. Whether these routes were created principally for the convenience of communities centred outside the fortress, like the mid-Saxon community recently discovered at The Lawn site to the west of the upper town at Lincoln, where there is an adjacent diagonal street (Chapel Lane) traversing the Roman layout, or whether they were to benefit intra-mural dwellers remains to be seen.

Elsewhere in the Roman occupied area the development of the street plan during the Anglian period remains uncertain, although within the *colonia* the endurance of elements of the Roman plan has been argued at two sites. The cluster of ninth-century artefacts discovered on the approach to the Roman bridge-head opposite the *via praetoria*/Stonegate may suggest the continuing use of a crossing-point there, if not the Roman bridge itself;[7] and in the Bishophill area, Morris has surmised that the original foundation of the church of St Mary Bishophill Junior in the pre-Viking period respected the *insula* pattern there.[8] Otherwise, however, evidence of Anglian activity within the *colonia* is limited to artefacts in either a residual context or with no proper archaeological context whatsoever; no contemporary occupation sites have yet been found there, although to the south of the medieval walled city in the suburb of Clementhorpe (2) a possible church site, perhaps of this time, has been discovered.[9]

[7] Moulden and Tweddle, in *The Archaeology of York*, 8(1), p. 7.
[8] R. K. Morris, 'Alcuin, York and the *alma sophia*', in L. A. S. Butler and R. K. Morris (eds), *The Anglo-Saxon Church*, Council for British Archaeology Research Report 60 (London, 1986), fig. 60.
[9] D. A. Brinklow, 'A pre-Conquest structure at Clementhorpe', in J. Moulden and D. Tweddle, *The Archaeology of York*, 8(1), pp. 57–61.

Occasional finds of Anglian material in later or uncertain contexts also occur around the fortress, the mid to late eighth-century helmet from 16–22 Coppergate (3) being a classic example, but here too occupation levels have not been discovered, and only east of the river Ross have traces of eighth- and ninth-century occupation come to light. Excavation on an extremely limited scale within the medieval walls at 118–26 Walmgate (4), on their line just north of Walmgate Bar (5), and a short distance beyond there at Paragon Street (6), in each case yielded evidence of Anglian activity, within a radius of about 120 m, which was not split by a defensive barrier at this date; excavations in 1986 some 250 m away at Fishergate (7), close to the confluence of the Ouse and Foss, have exposed *c.* 2,500 m² of Anglian occupation with timber buildings, zones of pits, ditches, which may represent property boundaries, and a linear spread of pebbles, which presumably represents a road (plate XXXVI). Fragments of continental pottery and Rhenish lava querns point to the foreign contacts of the settlement, and there is evidence for some industrial activity.

Viewed together, these few investigations seem to have located parts of what must have been at least one focus of *Eoforwic*, although its boundaries have not yet been defined. The position of this settlement outside the Roman fortress and beside a river irresistibly recalls the *Hamwic–Clausentum* or the *Lundenwic–Londinium* relationship, but, like those examples, it is not clear whether this relocation of at least some of the settlement's functions on an unencumbered site was for a physical, legal or some other reason.

At none of the recently recognized sites that lay within *Eoforwic* can it be demonstrated that the Anglian occupation had an influence on Domesday York – either the area excavated in these levels was too small or, as at Fishergate, the establishment of a post-Conquest monastic precinct had vitiated the evidence. It can be said, however, that the artefactual and structural evidence from the Fishergate site does not suggest as intensive activity there during the Anglo-Scandinavian period as before it.

The principal topographical contributions of the Anglian period to the making of Domesday York might be summarized as, first, re-affirming the importance of the central area of the Roman fortress as a focus of activity, although with a change of emphasis from secular to ecclesiastical; second, the retention of parts of the fortress defences and its main streets; and third, perhaps, the introduction of some new routes across the Roman pattern. The greatest influence that *Eoforwic* exerted on later events was in maintaining the site's role as the foremost political, ecclesiastical and economic centre in the north, and thus ensuring that it attracted the attention of the Viking Great Army in AD 866 and became the capital of an independent Scandinavian state which continued, with interruptions, until

PLATE XXXVI: *46–54 Fishergate – view from the east: the Anglian timber-built structure. The scale (50 cm divisions) is located in the centre of the structure parallel to the long sides. The structure respects the linear feature which may be a boundary feature that can be seen running across the photograph just below the centre.* © York Archaeological Trust.

AD 954, when it was incorporated into the new kingdom of England. It was this century that saw the creation of much of Domesday York.

The infrequency with which absolute precision is possible in archaeological dating renders it difficult to assess the immediate impact of the Vikings' capture of York. The best dated evidence comes from the site of 16–22 Coppergate (3), 160 m south-east of the Roman fortress where, after about 450 years of desertion, activity recommenced in the mid-ninth century with the operation of a glass furnace. Whether this was just before or immediately after the Viking take-over is not certain, although some strands of evidence hint at a pre-Viking date.

The 16–22 Coppergate data demonstrate that in the half century *c.* AD 850–900 activity continued on the site, with occupation probably very close by. By *c.* AD 900 elements of the division of the excavated area into the four tenements that were to endure for the next millennium were established, and well-defined buildings start to become apparent in horizons dated *c.* AD 930/5. The establishment of new property divisions in the later ninth or early tenth century is an increasingly well-documented urban phenomenon now known, for example, at Chester, Lincoln, London and Winchester.[10]

These tenement plots at 16–22 Coppergate, presumably each representing one of the *mansiones* of *Domesday Book*, were *c.* 5–5.5 m in width, and in this case ran at least 45 m back down a slope towards the river Foss (plate XXXVII). They seem totally unrelated to the only structures in York for which *Domesday Book* gives dimensions, the '7 very small dwellings containing 50 feet in width' (*VII minutas mansiones continentes L pedes lati*) held by William Percy. Initially, there was a single structure at the head of every tenement, presumably fronting on to a narrower forerunner of the present street Coppergate buried below the central part of the modern road; from *c.* AD 975 the layout that was probably in existence at the Norman Conquest came into being, with supplementary buildings erected almost immediately behind those on the frontage.

These properties were occupied by craftsmen. The products manufactured in each tenement varied through time, and included metalworking in gold, silver, lead-alloy, copper-alloy and iron, notably the sinking of coin dies and perhaps the striking of coins, the making of jewellery in amber and jet, and the lathe-turning of wooden bowls and cups; there was also some evidence for leatherworking, previously discovered in contemporary levels some 70 m away at 6–8 Pavement (8)[11] and for textile production and dyeing.[12] None of these activities, which contributed to the prosperity of

[10] J. P. Mason, *Excavations at Chester, 26–42 Lower Bridge Street 1974–6. The Dark Age and Saxon Periods*, Grosvenor Museum Archaeological Excavation and Survey Report 3 (Chester, 1985), pp. 9ff; D. Perring, *Early Medieval Occupation at Flaxengate, Lincoln. The Archaeology of Lincoln*, IX(1) (London, 1981), pp. 36ff; T. Dyson and J. Schofield, 'Saxon London', in J. Haslam (ed.), *Anglo-Saxon Towns in Southern England* (Chichester, 1984), pp. 285–313; M. Biddle and D. J. Keene, 'General survey and conclusions', in F. Barlow, O. von Feilitzen and D. J. Keene, *Winchester in the Early Middle Ages: An Edition and Discussion of the Winton Domesday*, edited by M. Biddle, Winchester Studies 1 (Oxford, 1976), pp. 449–500.

[11] A. MacGregor, *Anglo-Scandinavian Finds from Lloyds Bank, Pavement, and Other Sites*, in *The Archaeology of York*, 17(3), edited by P. V. Addyman, Council for British Archaeology (London, 1982), p. 136.

[12] A. R. Hall, P. R. Tomlinson, R. A. Hall, G. W. Taylor and P. Walton, 'Dyeplants from Viking York', *Antiquity*, 58 (1984), pp. 58–60.

PLATE XXXVII: *Late tenth-century buildings at 16–22 Coppergate, York, viewed from above, demonstrating the close-set and orderly tenements of this area (scale unit: 50 cm).*
© York Archaeological Trust.

Domesday York, are referred to in *Domesday Book* itself, except for the possible minting; the only professions and trades mentioned or implied in relation to York are military service, the church, the law, administration, meat-marketing, coin-minting, carpentry and milling, as well, perhaps, as whatever 'service' element may be implied by the numerous 'lodgings' referred to.

Also missing from *Domesday Book* is any notice of York's trading role, yet the Coppergate excavations alone have recovered material emanating from the North Cape of Norway in the north to the Red Sea/Gulf of Aden in the south, and from Ireland in the west to Samarkand in the east. While not all these items necessarily point to commercial dealings, some, like the quantity of what are probably Byzantine silks, almost certainly do, and to these international goods must be added the far greater bulk of material brought to the city from within England, and particularly from within Northumbria itself. All of these latter items emphasize York's role in 1086 as a regional market-place of prime importance, a conclusion already suggested by the quantity of coin minted in the city, but now at least partially understood in the more tangible form of a wide range of artefacts.

241

It should be emphasized that a thriving late ninth-, tenth- and early eleventh-century settlement may have existed within the fortress area too; a body of evidence to confirm or refute this has not yet been gathered, thanks to the infrequency of opportunities to excavate here, although there is a corpus of largely unstratified Anglo-Scandinavian material from the area which suggests activity during this period. It is not known whether occupation on the Ousegate/Coppergate/Pavement axis represents the initial burst of Anglo-Scandinavian urban regeneration, which may later have spread westward and may be represented by evidence for tenth-century jewellery-making discovered at 9 Blake Street (9),[13] or whether the Roman crossing-point over the Ouse into the fortress lasted sufficiently long (see p. 237 above) to influence the location of the earliest Anglo-Scandinavian occupation, which then extended quickly beyond the Roman walls.

Within the Roman *colonia* area, where Palliser has suggested that a planned layout may have been instigated at this time under the auspices of the archbishops who held land here, evidence for the laying out of tenements has been clearly seen at only one site, near the riverfront at 58–9 Skeldergate (10).[14] Here the establishment of plot boundaries is dated to the late ninth or earlier tenth century, and once again these initial Anglo-Scandinavian subdivisions of the area remained dominant up to the Norman Conquest and well beyond.[15] Within the Walmgate area, east of the river Foss, there are hints from 118–26 Walmgate (4) that properties were defined there too in the Anglo-Scandinavian period, although the evidence for both date and form is more limited.

It was probably during the Anglo-Scandinavian period, the two centuries before the Norman Conquest, that the outline of York was altered by the enlargement of the defences, and it may have been a desire to get within the shield of these defences that brought occupation and activity back to the fortress area and its surrounds. As noted above, the lines of the north-west and north-east sides of the Roman fortress were maintained in the Anglian and on through the Anglo-Scandinavian periods. There is no evidence, however, that the south-west and south-east lengths of the fortress wall were defended in the Anglo-Scandinavian period – a reconstructed section showing such a defence in Coney Street is speculative,[16] based on undated features that are not necessarily contemporary, which could only be

[13] A. MacGregor, 'Industry and commerce in Anglo-Scandinavian York', in R. A. Hall (ed.), *Viking Age York and the North*, Council for British Archaeology Research Report 27 (London, 1978), p. 42, fig. 24,8.

[14] D. M. Palliser, 'York's west bank: medieval suburb or urban nucleus?', in P. V. Addyman and V. E. Black (eds), *Archaeological Papers from York Presented to M. W. Barley* (York, 1984), pp. 101–8.

[15] S. Donaghey and R. A. Hall, '58–9 Skeldergate', in Moulden and Tweddle, *The Archaeology of York*, 8(1), pp. 48–52.

[16] J. Radley, 'Excavations in the defence of the City of York: an early medieval stone tower and the successive earth ramparts', *Yorkshire Archaeological Journal*, 44 (1972), fig. 14, top left.

recorded quickly in a watching brief at what was then Dorothy Perkins premises, now 8 Coney Street.[17] By the mid-thirteenth century the two southern walls of the fortress had certainly been superseded as a defence, and this redundancy may have taken place before the Norman Conquest. Its precise chronology is not yet known, although the restrictive influence which both lost sides exercised on the street plan and on property and parish boundaries suggests that they may have remained recognizable at least as topographical determinants beyond the Conquest.

The new arrangements involved the extension of the north-east side of the fortress down towards the river Foss, presumably on the line taken by the thirteenth-century wall; a forerunner of another length of medieval wall between Lendal Landing on the Ouse frontage and the upstanding western end of the south-west wall of the fortress may also have been erected at this time. Such a defensive circuit, extending from river to river in the way that the Roman fortress defences of Chester were enlarged at this time, would have protected the settlement against landward attack from the north.[18] Across the Ouse it is likely that defences were raised or augmented at this time against landward attack from the south, but the ramparts here have not been deeply sectioned. Attack up-river may also have been anticipated, but what precautionary measures were taken, if any, is not known.

York's riverine aspect generally receives scant attention in *Domesday Book*, even though the Ouse at least was a more substantial feature than today, being two or three times its present width – the process of encroachment into the margins appears, on the limited archaeological evidence currently available, to have begun at some time after the Norman Conquest. On the Foss, however, there is evidence for stabilization of the foreshore in the Anglo-Scandinavian period. Excavations in 1950–1 at Hungate (11) revealed a Roman waterfront which had been abandoned since the fourth century and covered naturally by a sterile sandy silt. This area was then made usable by covering it in a layer of brushwood 0.6 m thick, pinned to the underlying silt by small posts. Also discovered were alignments of stakes and wattle, running both parallel and at right angles to the presumed course of the river. They were interpreted in the excavation report as each lining one side only of a series of drainage gullies,[19] but this is an inherently unlikely proposition, and although one of them apparently preceded the main raft of brushwood, they are more likely to be further components in the consolidation of the foreshore. They find a good parallel in contemporary developments at the Palace Plain waterfront, Norwich,[20]

[17] H. Ramm, personal communication.
[18] Mason, *Excavations at Chester*, p. 38.
[19] K. M. Richardson, 'Excavations in Hungate, York', *Archaeological Journal*, 116 (1959), pp. 59–60.
[20] B. S. Ayers, 'The growth of a Saxon port', in A. E. Herteig (ed.), *Conference on Waterfront Archaeology in North European Towns*, no. 2 (Bergen, 1985), pp. 50–1.

and perhaps in the discoveries made in 1985 by the Lincoln office of the Trust for Lincolnshire Archaeology, opposite St Benedict's Church, Lincoln, at the former edge of the Brayford Pool. The 'embankment' above the Hungate brushwood raft may, however, be a separate structure, possibly a response to the damming of the Foss by William to flood his castle ditches, a decision which created the King's pool (*stagnu regis*) of *Domesday Book* and caused the loss of the mills, which the pool inundated.

While discussing the river, it is worth noting that the river Ouse was apparently not an administrative divide within Domesday York, since one shire only was recorded in *Domesday Book* as wasted for the twin castles (*vastata in castellis*), which were thrown up on opposite banks of the river. Those who have attempted to use the areas of the two Norman mottes and baileys as an index of the size of a shire now have to reckon with the discovery of an outer bailey beyond Clifford's Tower (12), which increases the enclosed area by a sizeable amount.[21]

Although street names with Old Norse elements such as *gata* (street) continued to be coined into the fourteenth century (and were then revived in the twentieth), there is now some direct and other inferential evidence which indicates that much of the network of the city's streets not inherited and continued from the Roman or Anglian periods had developed during the Anglo-Scandinavian era. This can be deduced in Pavement, Coppergate, Skeldergate and, perhaps, Walmgate; moreover, if Coppergate was in existence by *c.* AD 930/5, if not by AD 900, then it is very likely that the adjoining primary route, via Ousegate to a river crossing on the site of the Ouse Bridge and thence up the sweeping curve of Micklegate, had been established even earlier.

A similar Anglo-Scandinavian evolution is doubtless true for numerous other streets: Aldwark, for example, where the 'lost' church of St Helen-on-the-Walls, pulled down in the mid-sixteenth century, was rediscovered in rescue excavations in 1972 and traced back to an origin in the Anglo-Scandinavian period, when it presumably served a small community hereabouts (plate XXXVIII).[22] Little except the foundations remained of this early church, which was not recorded in *Domesday Book*, however, and for an appreciation of a church building which was probably extant at the time of *Domesday Book* it is necessary to turn to what is now known as St Mary Bishophill Junior, south of the Ouse. This may be the church dedicated to St Mary mentioned in *Domesday Book*, although sculptural fragments indicate that St Mary Bishophill Senior and St Mary Castlegate were also in existence at this time. As discoveries of sculpture at St Mary

---

[21] P. V. Addyman, 'York Archaeological Trust work in 1981', *Annual Report of the Yorkshire Philosophical Society* (1981), p. 51.

[22] J. R. Magilton, *The Church of St Helen-on-the-Walls, Aldwark*, in *The Archaeology of York*, 10(1), edited by P. V. Addyman (London, 1980), p. 18.

Bishophill Junior demonstrate, there was an ecclesiastical centre here from perhaps as early as the ninth century, but the earliest surviving part of the church, the tower, is dated on stylistic grounds to the third quarter of the eleventh century.[23] Stone-by-stone analysis by Buckland has demonstrated *inter alia* that it was constructed throughout with re-used Roman masonry, and this is thus another example of how earlier remains influenced the fabric of Domesday York.[24] It may be that decaying Roman stone structures remained at least partly visible until quite a late date, perhaps even into the twelfth century, as William of Malmesbury may imply.[25]

Wenham's excavation to the north of St Mary Bishophill Junior encountered the skeletal remains of two early tenth-century individuals who, on the basis of associated artefacts, had Scandinavian connections, and this is at present the only instance in York where Scandinavian settlers can be identified with any certainty.[26] In the graveyard surrounding St Helen-on-the-Walls in Aldwark, however, and threatened by the same redevelopment project that necessitated the excavation of that church, were the remains of its parishioners. Some of them made up that population which was the first object of William's curiosity; according to the *Anglo-Saxon Chronicle*'s entry for AD 1085, he discussed with the council at the Christmas-tide Gloucester crown-wearing 'how [the country] was occupied and with what sort of people'.[27]

Almost all of what we might like to know about that population is glossed over in *Domesday Book*, but the careful exhumation and subsequent study of the skeletal remains from the St Helen's cemetery has provided original demographic information on such topics as their life expectancy, health and appearance.[28] Most surprising of all, perhaps, and totally inexplicable, is the contention that around the time of the Domesday survey the average appearance of the people as represented by the skull type was changing.

This conclusion, like so much else that I have referred to, requires further examination and the study of more, carefully excavated data. None

[23] C. Briden and D. Stocker, *The early church of St Mary Bishophill Junior*, in *The Archaeology of York*, 8(2), edited by P. V. Addyman, Council for British Archaeology (London, 1987).

[24] P. C. Buckland, 'The building of stones: petrological analysis', in Briden and Stocker, *The Archaeology of York*, 8(2).

[25] Royal Commission on Historical Monuments, *An Inventory of the Historical Monuments in the City of York*, vol. 4: *Outside the City Walls East of the Ouse* (London, 1975), p. xxviii, citing William of Malmesbury, *Gesta Pontificum*, Prolog iii.

[26] L. P. Wenham and R. A. Hall, 'Excavations to the north of St Mary Bishophill Junior, 1961–3 and 1967', in Briden and Stocker, *The Archaeology of York*, 8(2).

[27] *The Anglo-Saxon Chronicle. Two of the Saxon Chronicles Parallel*, edited by C. Plummer (Oxford, 1892–9), p. 216; translated from *English Historical Documents II, 1042–1189*, edited by D. C. Douglas and G. W. Greenaway (London, 1953; 2nd edn 1981), p. 168).

[28] J. D. Dawes and J. R. Magilton, *The Cemetery of St-Helen-on-the-Walls, Aldwark*, in *The Archaeology of York*, 12(1), edited by P. V. Addyman, Council for British Archaeology (London, 1980).

the less, it demonstrates vividly how archaeology has begun to bring scholars startlingly close to the lives of the Domesday population of York, their predecessors and their achievements. Also required is a research programme to investigate the evolution of settlement dynamics in the city's hinterland throughout this millennium and to trace their relationships with variations in the size and function of York, which at some periods at least must have acted as a powerful stimulus to rural reorganization. Only this integrated approach, casting off the separatist format employed in the presentation of town and countryside in *Domesday Book*, will provide an understanding of the forces that fashioned the Domesday landscape.

PLATE XXXVIII: *The earliest church at St Helen-on-the-Walls, Aldwark, York, subsequently extended by the addition of a chancel, looking west. The church was founded in the Anglo-Scandinavian period, and is an index of the neighbourhood's re-settlement at this time (scale unit: 50 cm).*
© York Archaeological Trust.

12

Settlement Structures and Settlement Systems of the Frankish Central State in Carolingian and Ottonian Times

HANS-JÜRGEN NITZ

Although the high medieval centuries, the twelfth and thirteenth, saw the most extensive progress of settlement planning in Central Europe, including the planning of villages and towns, the preceding early medieval period was also important. It was in these centuries, the seventh to the tenth, that settlement planning in feudal Europe was developed for the first time. Within feudal society it seems to have been under the institutions of the Frankish state that colonization was initiated. Villages and fields of a regular layout and a systematic spatial organization of functional settlement systems around royal centres were created. The village models were soon copied by the church and the high-ranking nobility.

For a better understanding of the circumstances under which settlement planning was developed, a short introduction into the history of the political structure of the Frankish empire will be helpful.

Evolution and Structure of the Frankish Empire

From their home region along the lower Rhine, the Salfranken under the royal dynasty of the Merovingians expanded to the west and the south during the fourth and fifth centuries. They took over the rich manors of the Romans and their effective administration, already known to the Franks from their military service as mercenaries of the Roman Empire. This gave them the economic and administrative basis for further expansion and the creation of a kind of central state, or at least of some basic elements of it. During the sixth century the Franks subdued several Teutonic tribes – the Alamanni in the south, the Thuringians in the east, the Bavarians in the south-east and the Burgundians in the south-west. The core region of this vast empire lay in the west – in France and Belgium – with the upper Rhine valley as a consolidated Frankish settled frontier zone beyond which lay the territories of the subdued tribes, the Alamanni, Thuringians and Bavarians. These were given the status of loosely controlled dukedoms, leaving their social structure more or less intact. The royal control over them seems to have been based on loyalty ties with the dukes and the nobility and these were often unreliable.

Such was the political pattern of the sixth and seventh centuries, at the end of which the strength of the Merovingian dynasty began to weaken. Since AD 687, the actual power had lain in the hands of the *maior domus* (mayor of the house) of the Carolingian family, which in AD 751 took over the legal position of the royal dynasty. They reorganized the empire, imposing a new subjugation on the eastern dukedoms which, in the period of Merovingian weakness, had developed again into almost independent 'tribal principalities'. Although many of the subdued non-Frankish nobility quickly changed sides and co-operated with the royal administration, there remained, for some time, the continued danger of insurgence, instances of which are reported from Alamannia and later from Saxony. It was therefore necessary to organize an effective military control and administration based on the creation, by confiscation, of royal core regions in these subdued territories. For this purpose the Carolingians furthered the creation of a special nobility group with very close connections to the king: historians have termed such nobles *Reichsadel* (literally 'imperial nobility'). As a ministerial elite they served the king as regional administrators, as counts and margraves, organizing the royal core regions and royal focal settlements in all parts of the empire, especially in the subdued eastern dukedoms. A network of royal demesnes was created or re-established, with *palatia* (palaces) for the king and his royal followers. He or his deputies visited these centres when touring the empire. Such a royal complex included royal castles, royal *villas* or *curtes* with large manorial home farms and peasant villages of free and unfree bondsmen. The imperial nobility not only received royal property as fiefs, but were permitted to establish their private manors nearby, frequently holding property in the same villages as the king.

One of the most important activities of the Carolingian mayors of the house and kings seems to have been the establishment of military settlement complexes with a network of castles connected with demesnes serving as regional centres for groups of villages settled with farmer–soldiers. In his narrative history of the Saxon kings of Germany (tenth century), the monk Widukind of Corvey refers to them as *agrarii milites*.[1]

---

[1] *Widukindi monachi Corbeiensis rerum gestarum Saxonicarum libri tres*, 5th edn, edited by H.-E. Lohmann and P. Hirsch. Scriptores rerum Germanicarum 60 (Hanover, 1935), vol. I, 35, p. 48. For the present state of discussion on the problem of the *agrarii milites*, see J. Fleckenstein, 'Zum Problem der Agrarii Milites bei Widukind von Corvey', in *Beiträge zur niedersächsischen Landesgeschichte* (Festschrift H. Patze), Veröffentlichungen der historischen Kommission für Niedersachsen und Bremen, Sonderband (Hildesheim, 1984), pp. 26–41.

They were given the favourable status of *liberi homines* or *ingenui* (free men), although they were, with their farms, bonded to the king as their lord. This institution seems to have been developed even earlier, under the late Merovingian kings, but only under the Carolingians was it systematically expanded, especially in border regions to the east, which formed a chain of marches. The *agrarii milites* were also established in regions of internal friction and insurgence. Reliable settlers were taken not only from the genuinely Frankish parts of the empire, but also from various other peoples, individuals and groups, who had also proved to be reliable. So we find Alamanni, Frisians and even a number of Slavs. Historians have termed this policy as 'Frankish state colonization' with 'military colonists', although not all of the royal *liberi homines* had military functions.[2]

As a period of new territorial expansion and effective administrative and military reorganization, the eighth and ninth centuries under the Carolingian kings were also a period of extensive settlement planning, as an expression of spatial organization. An element of planning was the introduction of standard holdings – *mansus* (Lat.) or *huba* (*hufe*) (O. German).[3]

Under Charlemagne the Frankish empire reached its largest expansion. Saxony, in the north-west, was conquered, and the same happened to the Langobardian kingdom (Lombardy in upper Italy). The subjugation of the Saxons took as long as thirty years and royal core regions had to be established to keep Saxony under control. The empire was divided among Charlemagne's three grandsons. In the eastern part, which was to become Germany, the Carolingian dynasty died out, and in AD 919 a new royal line was elected from the Saxonian ducal family, the Ottonians, named after their favourite name Otto. They continued the Carolingian policy, especially in the eastern border region against the Slavs and the Hungarians. In the ensuing medieval centuries the central power of the royal state diminished and regional feudal forces began to become stronger and stronger, creating independent principalities. During the twelfth to thirteenth centuries, especially, the margraves in the eastern marches continued the expansive policy based on planned colonization with regular villages, the models of which they took from the Carolingian and Ottonian

[2] The discussion on the '*Fränkische Staatskolonisation*' (Frankish state colonization) and the *liberi homines* is best presented by J. Schmitt, *Untersuchungen zu den Liberi Homines der Karolingerzeit*, Europäische Hochschulschriften, European University Papers, ser. 3, vol. 83. F. Schneider, W. Schlesinger, Th. Meyer and H. Dannenbauer should be named as the main advocates of this conception.

[3] The most recent contribution to the original of the *hufe* is by W. Schlesinger, 'Die Hufe im Fränkenreich', in H. Beck, D. Denecke and H. Jankuhn (eds), *Untersuchungen zur eisenseitlichen und frühmittelalterlichen Flur in Mitteleuropa und ihrer Nutzung*, I. Abhandlungen der Akademie der Wissenschaften in Göttingen, Philologisch-Historische Klasse, 3rd ser., vol. 115 (Göttingen, 1979), pp. 41–70.

military border colonies along the former Saxon and Slavonian frontier. The famous *Angerdorf* and *Straßendorf* settlements with their regular *Gewannflur* east of the Elbe river were no new inventions at all but a continuation of settlement models already well established by the eighth to tenth centuries.

The remainder of this chapter is divided into two main sections. In the first section, planned settlements of the Carolingian period of the eighth and ninth centuries are presented and analysed. They were created by royal administration in the north-eastern border region of the empire against the Saxons and Slavs and, after the conquest of Saxony, in a region of long-lasting insurgence. In the second section, a *palatium* (palace), as the typical royal administrative centre, is shown to have been the core of a whole settlement system consisting of functional service settlements, which in many respects conform to the regulations of Charlemagne's *capitulare de villis* for the administration of the royal villas or manors. Excellent examples are offered by the palace systems established under the Carolingian kings in Upper Hesse and Southern Saxony. These systems can be identified by their place-names, which indicate the former functions of the settlements.

Carolingian Military Colonization

The first example of military colonization is taken from the endangered region along the Saxon border in the north-east. Between the Harz hills in the west and the Saale river in the east a spur of Saxon territory projected into the Frankish province of Thuringia. This dukedom had been brought back under Carolingian mastery around AD 700. Inroads by the Saxons from the north through the Harz–Saale corridor made it strategically necessary to push them back and close that gap. In AD 743 the Mayor of the House Karlmann conquered the southern part of this corridor, which was called Hassegau or Hochseegau, along with the Saxon stronghold Hochseeburg (figure 12.1). It must have been Karlmann who, after having occupied and confiscated the whole Hassegau, completely reorganized the region by transforming it into a colony of soldier–farmer villages with castles as foci and, additionally, of villages settled by unfree bondsmen.[4] This military settlement system can easily be identified by royal and ecclesiastical charters of the eighth and ninth centuries. A register of the royal abbey of Hersfeld dating from the second part of the ninth century

---

[4] R. Wenskus, 'Der Hassegau und seine Grafschaften in ottonischer Zeit', in *Beiträge zur niedersächsischen Landesgeschichte*, pp. 42–60.

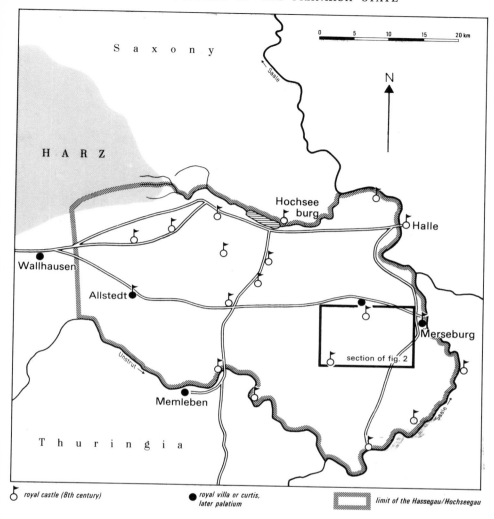

royal castle (8th century)

royal villa or curtis, later palatium

limit of the Hassegau/Hochseegau

FIGURE 12.1 *The Hassegau: an eighth-century Frankish military frontier province against the Saxons*
Source: Based on W. Hessler, *Mitteldeutsche Gaue des frühen und hohen Mittelalters* (East Berlin, 1957).

names nineteen castles and about 240 villages and hamlets belonging to these castles – *cum viculis suis et omnibus locis ad se pertinentibus* – which had to pay the royal tithe – *decimationes dare debent* – which was then in usufruct of the monastery. The tithe had been granted to Hersfeld by Charlemagne a century before, in AD 780.[5] In that earlier charter, it is stated that the tithe came from the Hassegau, which was then divided into two counties, one under Alberic, the other under Marcoard, and the tithe had to be paid by

[5] *Urkundenbuch der Reichsabtei Hersfeld*, vol. 1, edited by H. Weirich, Veröffentlichungen der Historischen Kommission für Hessen und Waldeck, 19(1) (Marburg, 1936), donation *ad annum* 780, no. 14, tithe register (late ninth century) no. 37.

253

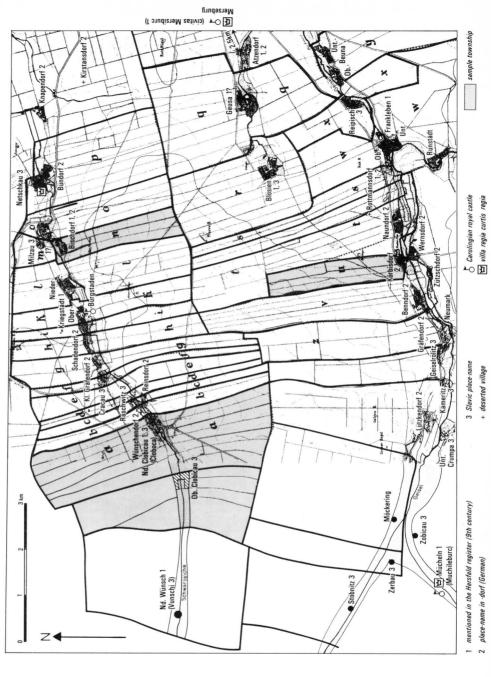

1 mentioned in the Hersfeld register (9th century)

2 place-name in -dorf (German)

3 Slavic place name

+ deserted village

⚲⚲ Carolingian royal castle

▣ villa regia curtis regia

sample township

'*ingenum hominibus*' – by free men – and to be delivered to the castles. Obviously they belonged to the special class of military colonists, soldier–farmers, mentioned earlier (p. 250). Combining the two documents, we can state that free men living in hamlets and villages that were grouped around castles, with about ten to fifteen villages forming a castle unit, had to pay a tithe to the royal administration represented by the two counts and, of course, the intermediate ranks in charge of the individual castles. The actual number of hamlets and villages of the Hassegau is larger than 240, which means that other villages existed with peasants of different legal status.

The late Dr Oskar August from Halle (German Democratic Republic), who died in 1985, studied a large number of those villages, based on cadastral maps of 1710.[6] He was able, by a special method of retrogressive analysis, to reconstruct the original *Hufen* units from the parcels into which the *Hufen* had been split in the course of time.[7] Four sample villages will be presented and analysed in detail; the first two maps from Dr August's private archives, combined into one (figure 12.3), are published here for the first time. The historico-genetic interpretation given by the present author differs partly from August's opinion, which will be indicated below. The location of the villages is given on figure 12.2, which presents a cross-section through the Hassegau (see figure 12.1).

The cross-section contains two rows of villages, with the important castle of Merseburg to the east and the castle of Muchileburc (Müncheln) to the west; both are mentioned in the Hersfeld register. The hamlet of Burgstaden, the name of which indicates the former presence of a castle, might have been the place of another eighth-century castle, which according to Küstermann could have been the so far unidentified *Herburgoburg* of the Hersfeld register.[8] Figure 12.2 reveals several features of planning:

1   The townships form two rows of parallel elongated rectangles, some even strip-like, with the streams of Geisel and Schwarzeiche as axes. The individual townships extend over 4–5 kilometres in length; their width varies from only a few hundred metres to 1.5 kilometres.[9] There can be no

---

[6] *Merseburger Matrikelkarten 1710–1728*, 7 vols folio (cadastral survey of the Chapter of Merseburg, unpublished, Archiv Kulturhistorisches Museum Merseburg); copies of the two Klobikau drawn by O. August.

[7] A description of Oskar August's method is given by H.-J. Nitz, 'Zur Rekonstruktion primärer Plansiedlungsstrukturen der mittelalterlichen Kolonisation mit Beispielen aus dem Waldviertel und der Niederlausitz', in S. Kullen (ed.), *Aspekte landeskundlicher Forschung* (Festschrift H. Grees), Tübinger Geographische Studien 90 (Tübingen, 1985), pp. 156–61.

[8] O. Küstermann, 'Altgeographische und topographische Streifzüge durch das Hochstift Merseburg', *Neue Mitteilungen aus dem Gebiet historisch-antiquarischer Forschungen*, vol. 16 (Halle, 1883), p. 219. Quotations from documents referring to villages of the Merseburg region are taken from Küstermann's work.

[9] Regional occurrences of parallel strip parishes is also known in England. Samples from Lincolnshire were presented in the conference papers of N. Brooks (taken from D. M. Owen, 'Parishes and chapelries

FIGURE 12.2 *Strip-shaped townships of the Hassegau (cross-section of figure 12.1)*
Source: A. Meitzen, *Siedelung und Agrarwesen*... (Berlin, 1895), Atlas, Anlage 115a; western part supplemented from toposheets 1 : 25,000 by H.-J. Nitz.

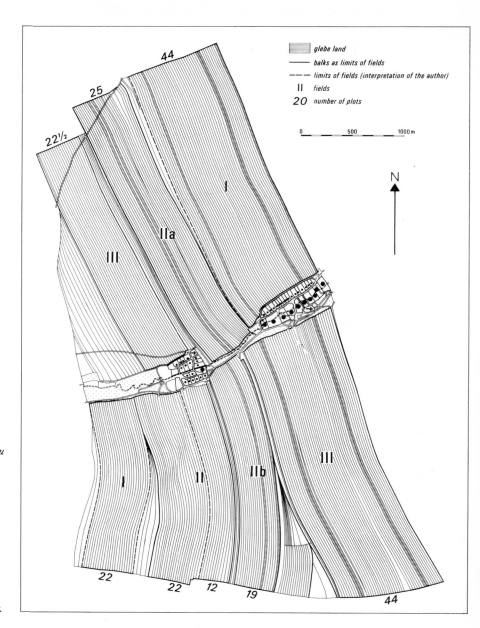

FIGURE 12.3 *Nieder-Klobikau and Ober-Klobikau (for location see figure 12.2): early medieval settlement and field structure*
Reconstruction of the early medieval field-pattern by O. August, based on the field maps of 1710 and 1846; interpretation of the original layout of the villages and the three-field systems by H.-J. Nitz.

in Kesteren', in P. H. Sawyer (ed.), *Medieval Settlement: Continuity and Change* (London, 1976); see also J. Insley, 'Field-names and the Scandinavian settlement of England', in R. Schützeichel (ed.), *Giessener Flurnamen-Kolloquium 1. bis 4. October 1984.* Beiträge zur Namenforschung, Neue Folge, Beiheft 232 (Heidelberg, 1985), p. 152, map 'Cliff parishes divided on the lines of the High Dyke'. Another sample from the Vale of the White Horse, Oxfordshire, is shown by D. Hooke (chapter 6 above). According to B. K. Roberts, *Rural Settlement in Britain* (Folkstone, 1977), 'such regular patterns, found in Lincolnshire, Yorkshire, Berkshire and Wiltshire, to cite but four areas, are surely indicative of something more deliberate, more conscious, than merely centuries of adjustment' (p. 94).

doubt that the very regular layout of the township boundaries must have resulted from a planned allocation.

2   The place-names are of German and Slavic origin. The former in their large majority (17 out of 22) bear the suffix *-dorf* (the equivalent of the Scandinavian *-thorp*), a common suffix since the eighth century; only three German place-names are of an earlier type: Kriegstädt (ninth-century *Cristat*), Runstädt and Frankleben (ninth-century *Franchenleba*), which refers to Franks who must have replaced the earlier inhabitants, but retained the suffix of the older place-name '*-leba*'. At least fourteen place-names are of Slavic origin. Both ethnic groups show no difference in township size. In the southern row, the two communities form separate village groups, in the Schwarzeiche valley they are mixed.

3   Eight or possibly ten of the 40 villages are mentioned in the Hersfeld register (figure 12.2). At least four of them bear Slavic place-names. This underlines the fact that in military settlements of this region under the Carolingians no difference existed between the two communities: German as well as Slavic settlers were brought in and given townships of various sizes, depending on the size of the individual groups.

Not all the villages were established at the same time, i.e. around AD 740–50. Dr August has traced the creation of the village Naundorf (literally 'new *dorf*'), which must have taken place only after 1040, when King Henry III gave to a noble layman five *mansi regales* along with five unfree families located between *Geruuartesdorf* (Körbisdorf) and *Radauuassendorf* (Rottmannsdorf). As the receiver of the grant had held it earlier as a fief, it cannot have been completely under wood before this date; at least a small settlement must already have existed, possibly a demesne worked by the unfree people. The grant was immediately transferred to the bishop of Merseburg, who must have founded the new village. Only a single Clobica (Klobikau) is mentioned in the ninth-century Hersfeld register, but in AD 979 there existed two Clobica. The second may only have come into existence in the early tenth century. Two of the villages bear the place-name Gräfendorf (literally 'count's village'); they probably served for the remuneration of the count.

The first two of the four samples – Ober- and Nieder-Klobikau (Upper and Lower Klobikau) – represent villages with large townships, the other two – Bischdorf and Körbisdorf – are hamlets, each with a knight's demesne. Klobikau and Bischdorf (*Biscofesdorf*) belonged to the 240 hamlets and villages that paid the royal tithe to castles; the latter, for unknown reasons, was named after a bishop connected with Hersfeld Abbey, who can only have been the Abbot Lullus who at the same time was archbishop of Mainz.

Analysis of Ober- and Nieder-Klobikau

The Field Pattern   Figure 12.3 presents August's reconstruction of the primary *Hufen* units. The parallel strip plots extend unbroken from the villages to the township boundaries in the north and the south, with a maximum extension of almost 3 kilometres in Nieder-Klobikau. The width of the individual strip is 20–21 m. The arable of each township consists of three fields, given in Roman numerals as I, II and III. In Ober-Klobikau, field I and field III contain twenty-two strips each, excluding the wedge-shaped parcels. In field III, the twenty-two strips are clearly bounded by parallel balks. Field II consists of thirty-four strips, which I have split into twenty-two and twelve respectively. This deviation in number will be discussed further below.

In Nieder-Klobikau, the original three fields again are clearly demarcated by balks and wedge-shaped plots of shorter extension. Each of the three fields contains forty-four plots, twice the number of the neighbouring Ober-Klobikau. Field II consists of two separate parts, with twenty-five strips on the northern side and nineteen in the south. August, in his unpublished interpretation, writes that in 1710 the total sum of the then mostly fragmented *Hufen* was forty-six including the wedge-shaped areas, which in his interpretation date back to before AD 979. From the location of the four *Hufen* belonging to the glebe (before AD 1121, in which year they were recorded for the first time), we can clearly conclude the rules of a regular distribution of the lands of each *Hufe* in the three fields. The four *Hufen* of the glebe had four strips in each of the three fields. Hence each individual *Hufe* consisted of three strips, one in each field. The same was the case in Ober-Klobikau (according to August). The size of the *Hufe* was 10.7 hectares in Ober-Klobikau and 16.4 hectares in Nieder-Klobikau.

The total of sixty-six *Hufen* in both villages can, for the largest part, be traced back to the ecclesiastical proprietors of the Middle Ages. In AD 1058, the bishop of Merseburg bought a *praedio* of eight *mansos* at *Clobecke* for the chapter of the cathedral. In AD 1121, the abbey of Wimodeborch (Wimmelburg) was confirmed in its possessions at *Clobico*, which consisted of $47\frac{1}{2}$ *mansi* and four *mansi* of the village church. In AD 1470, the head canon of the cathedral of Merseburg bought four *mansi* at Ober-Klobikau from Otto and Bernhard, two noblemen of Kötzschen. It is only in 1710 that the remaining *Hufen* are reported: one of the village church of Ober-Klobikau and $1\frac{1}{2}$ 'free' *Hufen* of private property.[10] Unfortunately August

---

[10] Küstermann, 'Altgeographische und topographische Streifzüge', pp. 270–8. Dr Oskar August, in his unpublished interpretation, thought that the four *hufen* of the glebe were included in the $47\frac{1}{2}$ and formed part of the eight *hufen* of the chapter of the cathedral, but in the present author's view this cannot be maintained in respect to the text of the charters. They have to be counted separately, and both Clobica have to be taken as one unit.

has not identified the four *Hufen* that were the property of the head canon of Merseburg cathedral, derived from a noble family. They might have consisted of the twelve strips to the south of Ober-Klobikau (the excess strips of field II), which could have formed a separate three-field system.

What was the legal status of the medieval inhabitants of the two Klobikau? One Clobica is included in the late ninth-century Hersfeld register as one of the villages of which, from AD 780, *free* men payed a royal tithe to the abbey. In AD 979, King Otto II exchanged property with Hersfeld Abbey: he gave fifty *mansi mediae mensurae* (*Hufen* of medium size), located in five different villages, including *Clobica et item Clobica* (Klobikau and the other Klobikau). These fifty *mansi* were given *cum familiis et mancipiis, utriusque sexus*, with their *unfree* peasants.[11] Consequently, in the Clobicau of AD 780 and of the late ninth century there must have lived free as well as unfree peasants, unless we assume that the unfree peasants came in later or that the free ones were reduced in status. Assuming two categories in the eighth/ninth century, with unfree peasants working on *mansi mediae mensurae*, it can be concluded that the free men of a higher social status held larger units because they had to serve as farmer–soldiers in castles and to pay tithe to the king. We may even suppose that the *mancipii* had to work for the free men. If the author's argument is a sound one, then the size of the larger free man's holding should have been *double* that of the unfree *mansus mediae mensurae*, which would mean *two* strips in each field, a holding of 33 hectares.

The argument of original two-*Hufen* units may also be strengthened by the fact that the larger properties of the eleventh to fourteenth centuries consisted of a multiple of two *Hufen*: four and eight. We may even assume that these large units of four and eight *Hufen* were originally possessed by higher ranks of the Carolingian military force.

The Layout of the Villages   There are no documents giving the number of free and unfree bondsmen who would have had house lots (tofts) of different size in the village. In the map of 1710, Nieder-Klobikau consists of two rows of tofts, the narrower ones north of the village road and some of larger size in the opposite row along the brook, a location which may be looked at as more favourable, with its access to water and grassland. In the northern row, seventeen or eighteen narrow tofts can be identified. If they were those of the original one-*Hufe* farms, the opposite row could have contained the larger double-*Hufen* units (and, may be, one unit of four and one of eight *Hufen*). The rows of tofts form a regular street village. The eleventh-century church is located outside the toft rows to the south of the village. This clearly indicates the earlier origin of the street village.

---

[11] *Monumenta Germaniae Historica. Diplomata regum et imperatorum Germaniae tomi II. Pars prior. Ottonis II. diplomata* (Hanover, 1888), p. 218, no. 191, *ad annum* 979.

The three fields fit so surprisingly well into the township boundaries that one must arrive at the conclusion that both the fields and the boundaries were created at the same time – for the earliest Clobica in the mid-eighth century. All the villages of the region show exactly the same pattern. We cannot avoid the assumption that this type of settlement, together with its field pattern, was created in the eighth century. In respect to common pasture, the fields of 1710 leave no space for this at all. The excellent soil (loess with high humus content) permitted the conversion of every piece of land into arable. Commons may have existed earlier in the more distant sections of the long strip fields closer to the township boundaries, but there are no indications at all as to their former extent.

In the author's view, this very regular and almost standardized village, field and township pattern, along with the dominance of the place-names in -dorf, can only be understood as having been created under one single planning institution, and the only one allotting land in the region during the eighth and ninth centuries was the royal administration. During the tenth-century and even earlier, many villages were given away by the crown as grants and fiefs to various ecclesiastical and lay grantees.

Analysis of Bischdorf and Körbisdorf

The other two sample villages may give some idea of the upper stratum of the eighth-century *ingenum homines*, which one should expect in the hierarchy below the counts. Bischdorf and Körbisdorf (*Biscofesdorf* and *Gerwartesdorf*) (see figure 12.2) are representatives of the many narrow townships containing only a small number of *Hufen* (figure 12.4). August, in his retrogressive analysis, arrived at eleven peasant *Hufen* and one knight's farm at Körbisdorf, and eight peasant *Hufen* and one knight's farm at Bischdorf.[12] Although both villages belong to different settlement groups (figure 12.1), their pattern is almost the same: the peasants' *Hufen* hold 9.5 and 9.3 hectares in total in Körbisdorf and Bischdorf respectively. Again, there are three parallel fields, with each *Hufe* having one strip in each field. The settlements are of hamlet-size – *viculus* is the term used in the ninth-century register – consisting of only nine and twelve tofts respectively. These are arranged along and around a blind alley, with the knight's farm at the dead end. If 9–10 hectares was the size of an unfree *mancipia*-holding, as in Ober-Klobikau, then the peasants of Bischdorf (which was among the villages with free men of the eighth/ninth century) cannot have belonged to this status group. The only one suitable for such a position

[12] O. August, 'Untersuchungen an Königshufenfluren bei Merseburg', in P. Grimm (ed.), *Varia Archaeologica* (Festschrift W. Unverzagt), Deutsche Akademie der Wissenschaften zu Berlin, Schriften der Sektion für Vor- und Frühgeschichte, vol. 16 (Berlin, 1964), esp. pp. 375–94.

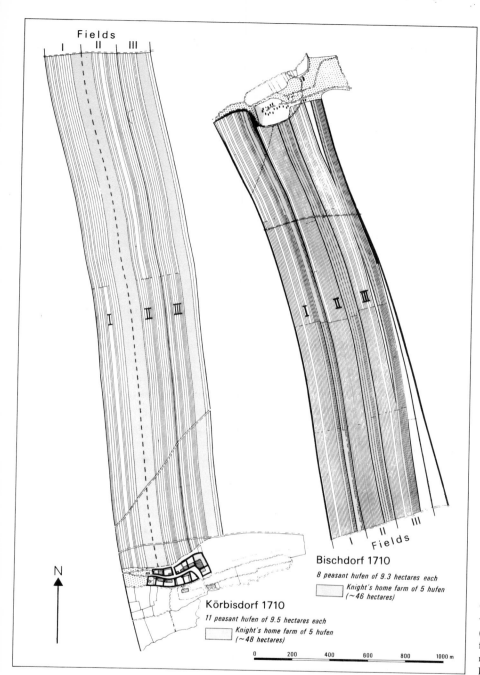

Fields
I II III

I II III

I II III

Fields
I II III

Bischdorf 1710

8 peasant hufen of 9.3 hectares each

☐ *Knight's home farm of 5 hufen (~46 hectares)*

Körbisdorf 1710

11 peasant hufen of 9.5 hectares each

☐ *Knight's home farm of 5 hufen (~48 hectares)*

N

0   200   400   600   800   1000 m

FIGURE 12.4 *Körbisdorf and Bischdorf around 1710 (for location see figure 12.2)*
Source: O. August, 'Untersuchungen an Königshufenfluren bei Merseburg', in P. Grimm (ed.), *Varia Archaeologica* (Berlin, 1964), figures 59 and 62, with permission of the Akademie der Wissenschaften der DDR, Zentralinstitut für Alte Geschichte und Archäologie, with additions by H.-J. Nitz (shading of the knights' home farms, reconstruction of the medieval village layout of Körbisdorf).

could have been the holder of the large five-*Hufen* unit. As his holding of 46 hectares is clearly larger than the double-*Hufen* unit of Clobica (33 hectares), which the author attributed to the average free man, we may conclude that the holder of the five-*Hufen* unit belonged to a medium military rank. The holders of the unfree *Hufen* of the hamlets might have been obliged to work for him.

Royal curtis with ringfort, hamlets and fields with a regular sequence of holdings: A Structure of Frankish Occupation Forces' Settlement in Northern Saxony in the Early Ninth Century

The second sample region in which royal Frankish settlement planning can be traced is located between the lower Weser and Elbe rivers. It is part of the north-west German Geest region, with only medium to poor sandy soils; in pre-modern times, in addition to dung, the soil had to be manured by raw humus scraped from the heather that surrounded the individual villages in large tracts. This economy meant the limitation of the arable to small, isolated, so-called *Esch* fields and a limited number of farmsteads. The settlements were only of hamlet size. Earlier students of historico-genetic settlement research[13] believed they had identified a type of settlement that directly originated from the 'West Germanic' tribal society of the early centuries of the first millennium, based on a clan-like structure (*Eschgenossenschaft*) and one that had – as a formal settlement structure – survived to the eighteenth-nineteenth century under the harsh environmental conditions of the Geest landscape, which did not permit growth. Social and technical features, it was claimed, resulted in a special field pattern of long parallel strips representing shares of the members of the *Eschgenossenschaft*, who were even seen by some as having functioned as the joint owners of a plough: the heavy wooden mould-board plough necessitated the formation of long narrow strips as ridges with furrows in between. Müller-Wille termed this 'archaic' settlement type as *Drubbel*. The Anglo-Saxons, it was believed, took this system from the Continent to England.

This historico-genetic interpretation can no longer be maintained. Settlement archaeology has revealed that 'Celtic' block fields predominated in the late Iron Age.[14] Although the origin of many *Drubbel* may remain

---

[13] Most influential were W. Müller-Wille, 'Langstreifenflur und Drubbel', *Deutsches Archiv für Landes- und Volksforschung*, 8 (1944), pp. 9–44, and G. Niemeier, 'Gewannfluren. Ihre Gliederung und die Eschkerntheorie', *Petermanns Geographische Mitteilungen*, 90 (1944), pp. 57–74. For English readers a good introduction into this concept is given by H. Uhlig, 'Old hamlets with infield and outfield systems in Western and Central Europe', *Geografiska Annaler*, 43 (1961), pp. 285–312. A collection of the most influential articles has been published by H.-J. Nitz (ed.), *Historisch-genetische Siedlungsforschung* (Darmstadt, 1974), pp. 187–388.

[14] Compare the comprehensive study of M. Müller-Wille, *Eisenzeitliche Fluren in den festländischen Nordseegebieten*, Landeskundliche Karten und Hefte der Geographischen Kommission für Westfalen, series: Siedlung und Landschaft in Westfalen, 5 (Münster, 1965).

open,[15] research in the Elbe–Weser region by K. Mittelhäuser, E. Köster[16] and the present author[17] in connection with previous historical research has shown that groups of settlements of the *Drubbel* and *Esch*-type originated in the post-Saxon period of Frankish military occupation and colonization. Mittelhäuser in 1953 was the first to observe several important features indicating planning, in a settlement group west of Soltau (see figure 12.5):

1   a regular sequence of holdings in the strip layout of the arable;

2   in several cases, regularities in the spatial arrangement of the tofts, some grouped in a circle, some in a row (see figure 12.5b);

3   place-names in *-loh* (with the same root as the OE *lēah*), 'a wood or clearing in the wood'; for example, Grauen (figure 12.5a) < Gravenloh = 'the count's *loh*'.

This, as well as other groups of hamlets, had as their (historical) centre a large isolated farm with compact block field plots separated from the strip fields of the surrounding hamlets. Three of these central farms bear the place-name 'Königshof' (literally 'the king's farm'). In figure 12.6 the 'Königshof' Sittensen, as well as the isolated farm 'Adiek', has a small ringfort (German: *Ringwall* or *Burgwall*) adjacent to the farmstead. Archaeological excavations of a substantial number of these fortifications (twenty in total, in a region 90 km by 90 km) have shown that they date back to the ninth to eleventh centuries.[18] Their establishment in the early ninth century is to be seen in connection with the Carolingian military occupation of the region and the foundation of Frankish settlements in response to repeated Saxon insurgences, especially in AD 792, 797 and 804, which resulted in the deportation of numerous Saxon families, the implantation of Frankish colonists, and the distribution of land among the king's nobility, including *fideles Saxones* (loyal Saxons), as was reported in the Imperial Annals of the time.[19] Along with these strategic measures,

---

[15] For the state of discussion in the early 1970s, see H.-J. Nitz, 'Langstreifenfluren zwischen Ems und Saale – Wege und Ergebnisse ihrer Erforschung in den letzten drei Jahrzehnten', in *Siedlungs- und Agrargeographische Forschungen in Europa und Afrika* (Festschrift G. Niemeier), Braunschweiger Geographische Studien 3 (Braunschweig, 1971), pp. 11–34.

[16] K. Mittelhäuser, 'Über Flur- und Siedlungsformen in der nordwestlichen Lüneburger Heide', in *Festschrift zur Feier des 75 jährigen Bestehens der geographischen Gesellschaft zu Hannover*, Jahrbuch der Geographischen Gesellschaft zu Hannover (1953), S. 236–53; E. Köster, *Historisch-geographische Untersuchungen des Orts- und Flurgefüges zweier Dörfer im Kreise Rotenburg (Wümme)*, Rotenburger Schriften, Sonderband 24 (Rotenburg, 1977).

[17] The present author has meanwhile extended research on regions adjoining those studied by K. Mittelhäuser and E. Köster. First results are presented in this chapter.

[18] K. Weidemann, 'Frühmittelalterliche Burgen im Land zwischen Elbe- und Wesermündung', in *Führer zu vor- und frühgeschichtlichen Denkmälern*, vol. 30, Das Elbe–Weser–Dreieck 2 (Mainz, 1976), pp. 165–211.

[19] For example, '*Karlus in Saxoniam Francos conlocat, Saxones inde educens cum uxoribus et liberis, id est tertium hominem*', *Annales Laurissenses Minores. Monumenta Germaniae Historica. Scriptores*, vol. 1 (Hanover,

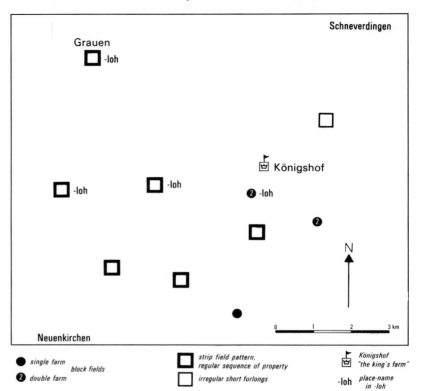

FIGURE 12.5a *King's farm (Königshof) and a group of villages with regular sequence of strip fields (Weser-Elbe region, west of Soltau)*

churches were founded, generally in connection with royal castles. This was the case at Sittensen (figure 12.6), where the church was consecrated to St Dionys, a typical 'Frankish' saint along with St Martin.

Königshof, ringfort and peasant settlements with distinct features of regularity can be seen as a coherent complex of Carolingian state colonization. This interpretation is underlined by the fact that the peasants in these settlement groups were given a special 'free' status: they were members of a special jurisdiction of their own called *Freibann* (literally 'free jurisdiction'), and the members were named 'free men', the same term as in the Hassegau. Actually the *Freibann* jurisdictions of the late Middle Ages are only relics of much larger groups of free men who, in the course of time, changed their status by self-tradition to ecclesiastical and lay lords. Even

---

1826), p. 119, no. 29; '*Aestate autem in Saxoniam ducto exercitu omnes, qui trans Albiam et in Wihmuodi habitabant, Saxones cum mulieribus et infantibus transtulit in Franciam*', *Annales regni Francorum, ad annum* 804, edited by R. Rau, *Quellen zur karolingischen Reichsgeschichte*, 1 Teil, *Ausgewählte Quellen zur deutschen Geschichte des Mittelalters*, vol. 5 (Darmstadt, 1955), p. 78; and in the same source *ad annum* 809 (p. 92), that the emperor '*per Galliam et Germaniam homines congregasset*' to man a new *civitas*, Esesfeld, north of the Elbe river.

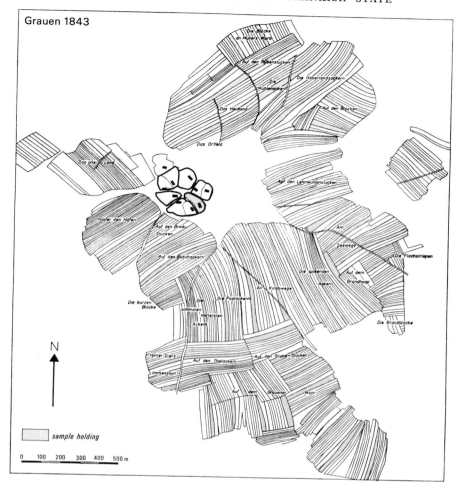

Grauen 1843

N

sample holding

0   100   200   300   400   500 m

FIGURE 12.5b   *Grauen: a sample village from the area of figure 12.5a, with regular sequence of strip plots and circular arrangement of tofts*
Source: Field map of 1843.

the king lost his interest in their military services, due to the change in military organization.[20]

Functional Settlement Systems around Frankish Royal Centres

Royal palaces (Lat. *palatium*; German *Pfalz*) were the fortified residences of the king where he or his representatives could reside and hold the diets or do administrative work. Quite a number of palaces existed in the empire and the king travelled from one to the next all the year round, though not

[20] R. Wenskus, 'Die soziale Entwicklung im ottonischen Sachsen im Lichte der Königsurkunden für das Erzstift Hamburg-Bremen', in L. Fenske, W. Rösener and Th. Zotz (eds), *Institutionen, Kultur und Gesellschaft im Mittelalter* (Festschrift J. Fleckenstein) (Sigmaringen, 1984), pp. 501–14.

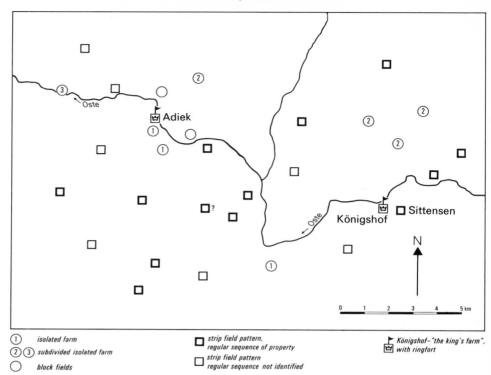

FIGURE 12.6a *Two king's farms with ringforts as centres of a group of villages with regular strip-field pattern (north-east of Bremen)*

all of them were actually visited; the individual kings had preferences for particular palaces (and royal monasteries, which also served this purpose) which they visited more frequently (and others not at all).

According to historical documents and archaeological research, a *palatium* consisted of the royal residence, an assembly hall and a church, and some minor buildings. In general, the whole complex was fortified to form a large castle and was located, if possible, on a hill. *Civitas* or *urbs* were alternative Latin terms for the fortified *palatium*. In many cases, a market developed nearby.

The second central functional element of the royal complex was the *villa regia* or *curtis regia*, the royal demesne. Its arable land comprised 100 or 200 hectares. Villages with bonded unfree and – more rarely – free tenants who had to render labour services for the demesne were grouped around it. This was the same pattern as in the average feudal estate, but in general the royal complex was larger in extent.

While the average feudal estate was able to produce everything in the demesne and in its peasant villages, the higher demand of the royal *palatium* seems to have necessitated special arrangements. As laid down in

266

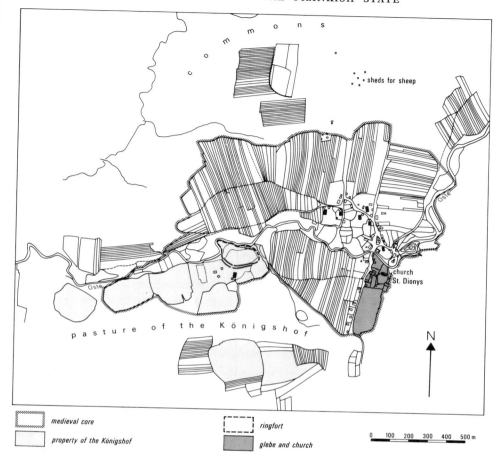

the *capitulare de villis*,[21] a manual for the administration of the large royal villas in the reign of Charlemagne, the typical royal estate consisted of several specialized branches which, as is shown below, were located in separate functional settlements.

1 The stud with special officers called *poledrarii*, who had to care for the herds of mares and stallions and to send the fresh saddle horses to the palace in November (§§ 13–15).

2 The forest administration under *forestarii* (§§ 10, 36, 62), who naturally had to be stationed in or near the forest in special settlements. They had to take care of the extensive royal forests, which were used for the hunt of the king and his high-ranking

[21] K. Gareis (ed.), *Die Landgüterordnung Kaiser Karls des Großen (Capitulare de villis vel curtis imperii)* (Berlin, 1895); quotations below are from this edition.

officers. They were also used for extensive pig-raising on acorns, and last, but not least, for clearing new arable land (§ 36), both by people from the royal manor and from nearby lay-manors. These forest uses had to be controlled according to the royal regulations.

3 The royal *luci* (in vulgar tongue called *brogili* (§ 46), the Old German *brugil*, *bruel*) was an enclosed preserve for the retention of all kinds of hunting animals for the immediate use of the palace and for this reason was located close to it.[22] Although *bruel* was the term used in West and South Germany, in northern Hesse and Saxony the term was *hagen*, the same as the Old English *haga* and, perhaps, the Norman *haia* of the *Domesday Book*, which may have been used, according to Dr Della Hooke, with the same meaning: 'a strong fence associated with the retention and probably with the capture of game animals'.[23] The *bruel* or *hagen* of the royal palace also contained special buildings.

4 There was a large demand for timber and fuel wood in the palace and the demesne, which had to be supplied sometimes from distant forests. Section 62 mentions *lignaria*, which can be translated as places for wood working, timber and fuel yards from which *materia* (timber) and, for example, *faculae* (torches) and *axilae* (shingles) had to be supplied to the centre.

5 Mills (§ 62), which could have been located close to the demesne, but which were also found at separate places with a stream or river of strong current; this sometimes drove even groups of mills, which gave rise to mill settlements of their own.

6 For the supply of iron and other metals mines, foundries and hammer-works were needed. They are mentioned in § 62 as *scrobes*, *plumbaricia* and *ferraria*.

7 Markets (*mercata*, § 62) seem to have developed more or less independently, though under the protection and control of the royal centre, and for these and mercantile reasons they were frequently located close to the palaces. Specialized handicrafts (§ 45) seem to have been located in the demesne or in the outer parts of the palace fortifications or in spatial connection with the market village close to the palace.

To demonstrate the functional settlement system of a royal *palatium* and its *villa regia*, two examples from Upper Hesse are presented: the royal centres of Amöneburg and Homberg, situated between Frankfurt and Kassel

---

[22] K. Hauck, 'Tiergärten im Pfalzbereich', in *Deutsche Königspfalzen. Beiträge zur ihrer historischen und archäologischen Erforschung*, vol. 1. Veröffentlichungen des Max-Planck-Instituts für Geschichte, 11(1) (Göttingen, 1963), pp. 30–74.

[23] D. Hooke, *The Anglo-Saxon Landscape: The Kingdom of the Hwicce* (Manchester, 1985), pp. 159–63, quotation p. 160.

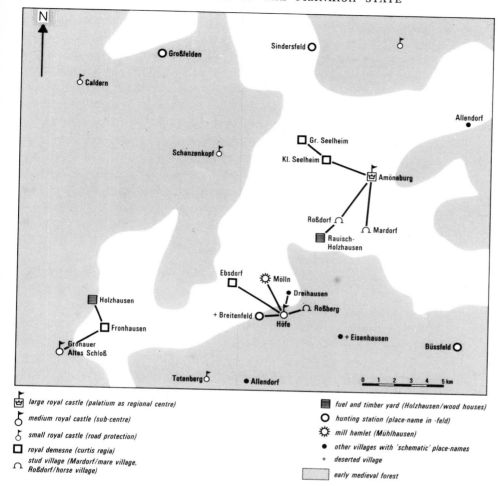

FIGURE 12.7 *Early medieval functional settlement systems around the royal centre of Amöneburg (Upper Hesse, west of Marburg)*

(figures 12.7 and 12.8 respectively). Not all the settlements existing in the eighth/ninth century are shown on the maps, only those with functional place-names. Which were the functional places of the *palatium* system?

1 The royal castle Amöneburg was referred to in AD 721 as *locus Hamanaburch*; it was managed by two Frankish officers, the brothers Bettic and Deorulf, who were at that date visited by Bonifatius-Winfred, an Anglo-Saxon monk working as a missionary in Germany.[24] Homberg is not mentioned in charters as a royal castle, but it must have belonged to the royal *fisci* recorded in AD 782 in a charter of Charlemagne.[25] Büraburg to

---

[24] Quotations of early records referring to the places are taken from *Historisches Ortslexikon des Landes Hessen, Regierungsbezirk Kassel*, edited by Hessisches Landesamt für geschichtliche Landeskunde (Marburg, 1973–80).

[25] K. Heinemeyer, 'Homberg in Hessen. Die Anfänge einer hessischen Stadt in ihrer Landschaft', *Zeitschrift des Vereins für hessische Geschichte und Landeskunde*, 90 (1984/5), pp. 17–42, esp. p. 20. The first

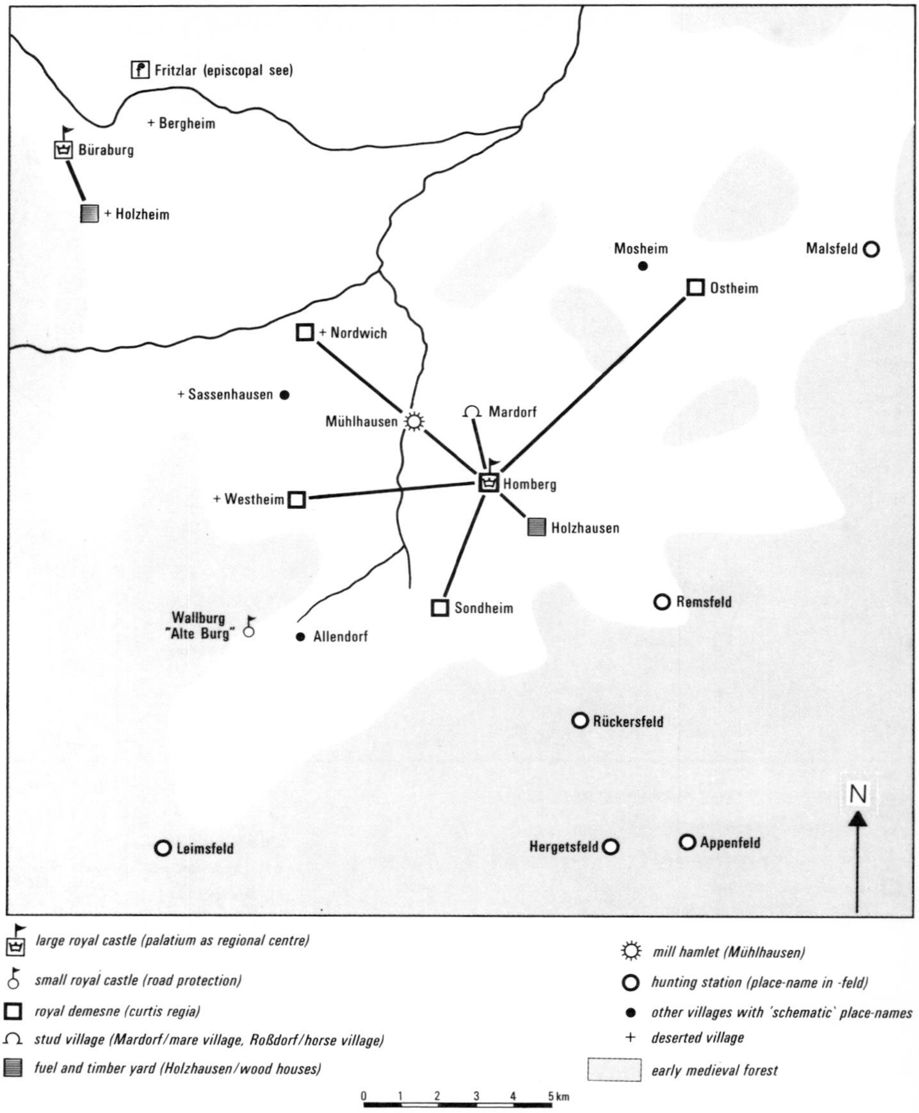
Fritzlar (episcopal see)
+ Bergheim
Büraburg
+ Holzheim
Mosheim
Malsfeld
Ostheim
+ Nordwich
+ Sassenhausen
Mardorf
Mühlhausen
Homberg
+ Westheim
Holzhausen
Sondheim
Remsfeld
Wallburg "Alte Burg"
Allendorf
Rückersfeld
N
Leimsfeld
Hergetsfeld
Appenfeld
large royal castle (palatium as regional centre)
small royal castle (road protection)
royal demesne (curtis regia)
stud village (Mardorf/mare village, Roßdorf/horse village)
fuel and timber yard (Holzhausen/wood houses)
mill hamlet (Mühlhausen)
hunting station (place-name in -feld)
other villages with 'schematic' place-names
deserted village
early medieval forest
0 1 2 3 4 5 km

FIGURE 12.8 *Early medieval functional settlement systems around the royal centre of Homberg (Upper Hesse, south of Kassel)*

to identify Homberg and the surrounding villages as a royal complex was O. Bethge in his famous article 'Fränkische Siedelung in Deutschland, auf Grund von Ortsnamen festgestellt', *Wörter und Sachen*, 6 (1914), pp. 58–83, p. 76 referring to Homberg. Bethge drew attention to the fact that groups of place-names around Frankish royal centres are frequently formed in a 'schematic' or 'bureaucratic' way, avoiding personal names as prefix and taking topographical, descriptive and functional terms instead, e.g. Nordheim, Westheim, Steinheim ('Stoneham'), Mülhausen ('Mill-houses'), Bergheim ('Hillham'), Talheim ('Valeham'), Langenfeld ('Longfield'). Place-names after cardinal points, especially, were interpreted by Bethge as given by the royal Frankish administration, which he could prove in many cases from royal charters.

the north-west of Homburg was an even more important castle. The Amöneburg complex is connected with two secondary castle centres – the ringfort 'Höfe' (eighth/ninth century) near Dreihausen in the south and 'Gronauer Altes Schloß' of the same age.[26]

2   All the castles were coupled with royal *curtes*: Amöneburg with Seelheim, Höfe with Ebsdorf and Gronauer Altes Schloß with Fronhausen. Each 'couple' constitutes the core of a royal manorial complex or *villa*. Together they may have formed what was in contemporary sources called a *fiscus*. The place-name of the two Amöneburg *curtes* indicates their function – Groß*seel*heim and Klein*seel*heim (the large and small Seelheim): compounded with the suffix -*heim* (OE -*hām*), *seel* is derived from the Old German *seli*, 'belonging to the lord's demesne'. Großseelheim was the head demesne and Kleinseelheim a branch demesne.[27] The place-name Fronhausen is derived from Old German *fro*, 'the lord'. The Homberg *curtis* is thought to have formed part of the palace settlement, with the *palatium*-castle on the hill and the *curtis* below. Four villages named after the cardinal points, Westheim, Sondheim (Southham), Ostheim and Nordwich, may have served as branch demesnes, as they were by their names clearly oriented to Homberg.[28]

3   Roßdorf, Mardorf and Roßberg were the stud settlements: Mardorf is literally 'mare village' (-*dorf* = -*thorp*), and Roßdorf is 'horse village', probably for the stallions and the saddle horses.[29]

4   There are three Holzhausen – literally 'wood houses' or, more correctly, 'houses for woodwork' – which were connected with Homberg, Amöneburg–Höfe, and Fronhausen. They were the locations of the *lignaria* of the *capitulare* mentioned above, the timber and fuel yards where, among other things, torches and shingles were fabricated. The older royal castle Büraburg to the north-west of Homburg had its Holzheim ('woodham'); surprisingly, around this castle the other functional place-names are missing.

5   Special mill settlements, not just single mills, are indicated by the two place-names 'Mühlhausen' near Homberg and Mölln (in the late Middle

[26] The present state of archaeological research on Carolingian castles in Hesse is drawn together in H. Roth ande E. Wamers (eds), *Hessen im Frühmittelalter. Archäologie und Kunst* (Sigmaringen, 1984).

[27] Recorded at Seleheim in AD 750/779. The demesne contained in AD 1015: 3 *territoria* (fields of the demesne), 78 *hufen*, 3 mills and a church.

[28] Bethge, 'Fränkische Siedelung in Deutschland', p. 76; Heinemeyer, 'Homberg in Hessen', p. 20. So far archaeological evidence for a royal Carolingian castle is absent, but mainly due to the fact that the place Homberg cannot yet be properly excavated.

[29] Roßdorf and Mardorf, as well as Seelheim and Holzhausen, near Amöneburg AD 750/779, are part of the property of a royal official (count?) who donated it to the Abbey of Fulda, but the donation at Roßdorf was cancelled by Charlemagne. This undoubtedly indicates that these places were part of the royal *fiscus*. Mardorf (Homberg) in AD 782 was a royal villa. At Holzhausen, Mosheim ('Moss' *hām*) and Mardorf near Homberg, *liberi homines* are mentioned, which, according to Heinemeyer (see note 25 above), were members of higher ranks of 'free men' (p. 23).

Ages 'Mulen' and 'Mulenum'), which was connected to the royal *curtis* at Ebsdorf.

6   A deserted village east of Ebsdorf/Höfe is named 'Eisenhausen' (literally 'iron houses'), which must have been a place of iron production with the *scrobes* and *ferraria* of the *capitulare*.

7   On the fringe or in the interior of the eighth/ninth-century forest there are groups of individual villages bearing place-names in *-feld*. In modern German (and even since the late Middle Ages) *-feld* means 'field'. In the early Middle Ages, however, the meaning must have been different, because although numerous new villages established in the forests also had their arable fields only a few were given place-names with the suffix *-feld* which would make no sense if this suffix really meant 'arable'. In north-west Germany and in the Netherlands, an old and different meaning of *feld* survived into the nineteenth century: *Feld* or *Veld* meant 'treeless heath' as well as a natural or man-made clearing in the forest. The OE *feld* has the same meaning of 'open land'.[30]

The historian Paul Höfer in his article on 'The rule of the Franks in the Harz region' offered a quite convincing explanation of the *-feld* place-name based on historical and geographical evidence.[31] He observed that the Ottonian kings had several important hunting stations in the Harz mountains; some even had the rank of hunting palaces, where the kings used to reside for weeks. All of them had place-names in *-feld*. As was typical for the 'official' (bureaucratic) naming of places, the prefixes were derived from topographical and descriptive features and very rarely from personal names: for example, Bodfeld on the stream Bode and Lengefeld, 'long *feld*', From this and from the geographical concentration of the place-names in *-feld* in the medieval royal Harz forest (figure 12.9), Höfer concluded that at that time a *feld* had the specific meaning of a clearing with a royal hunting station. Figure 12.9 shows the garland of royal palaces around the Harz and in it the numerous *feld* hunting-stations.

This explanation corresponds very closely to the author's interpretation of the functional settlement system around the royal *palatia*–castles of Amöneburg and Homberg. All of the *-feld* settlements are located in the ninth-century forest or on its fringe, where they could function as hunting stations and foresters' posts, as was to be concluded from the functions of the *forestarii* of the *capitulare*. They constituted the outermost elements of the functional settlement system of a royal *villa* or *fiscus* with the *palatium*–castle at its centre.

It would be beneficial to extend research on this topic to other early

---

[30] Hooke, *The Anglo-Saxon Landscape*, p. 45.
[31] P. Höfer, 'Die Frankenherrschaft in den Harzlanden', *Zeitschrift des Harzvereins*, 40 (1907), pp. 115–79.

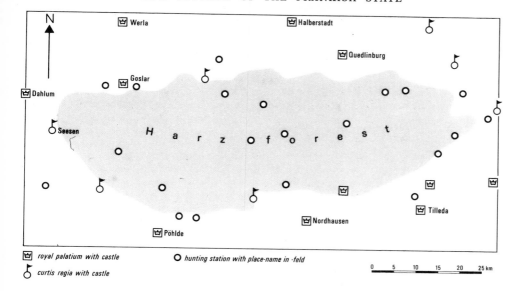

royal palatium with castle   O hunting station with place-name in -feld

curtis regia with castle

0   5   10   15   20   25 km

FIGURE 12.9   *The royal Harz forest with its hunting stations*

medieval royal or princely core regions around known central palaces and castles. For centres of this type in Poland, Bohemia and Hungary it is a well-established fact that service settlements were connected with the royal or ducal centres, villages of specialized trades forming a functional settlement system even more elaborate than that of the Carolingian state. This may be explained by the fact that these states were even more centralized and 'bureaucratic' than those in the west.[32]

[32] One of the latest contributions to this theme is the work of Karol Modzelewski, *Organizacja gospodarcza pánstwa Piastowskiego X–XIII wiek* (The economic organization of the state of the Piast dynasty of the tenth to thirteenth centuries). Polskiej Akademii Nauk (Polish Academy of Sciences), Instytut Historii Kultury Materialnej, Zakład Narodowy im. Ossolińskich, Wyd. PAN. (Bratislava, 1975); reviewed by W. Schich in *Zeitschrift für Ostforschung*, 27 (1978), pp. 21–24. For Bohemia, see D. Trestik and B. Krzemiénska, 'Zur Problematik der Dienstleute im frühmittelalterlichen Böhmen', in F. Graus and H. Ludat (eds), *Siedlung und Verfassung Böhmens in der Frühzeit* (Wiesbaden, 1967), pp. 70–103.

13

Systems of Agriculture in Central Europe up to the Tenth and Eleventh Centuries

HELMUT HILDEBRANDT

Until now, the question has not been completely answered as to which agricultural systems had been developed in Central Europe up to the time of the early High Middle Ages (AD 1050–1100). For one reason, there are too few literary sources; for another, there have been only a limited number of palaeobotanical studies since the 1960s which have helped to close some gaps in the state of research. Quite often the interpretation of all these sources is rather difficult. Only one or two components of the field systems have become obvious through documents and registers and, in many cases, the references do not deal with cropping systems as such. Sometimes research has to rely on analogies as well as any kind of retrospective interpretation of late medieval and early modern sources, especially from recently settled areas or remote, and therefore less changed, regions. Such conclusions, however, will always be precarious to a certain degree. Even terms like *celga*, *campus*, and so on, which seem to indicate a common-field arrangement in early medieval times, have obviously been used in that sense only since the High and Late Middle Ages (AD 1050–1300; 1300–1500). They must have changed their meaning towards the familiar one some time previously. The first use of these terms in Carolingian sources, therefore, does not fix the date before which this kind of cultivation must have come into existence. By contrasting palaeobotanical findings with results and hypotheses from the study of literary sources one can at least check the present teachings. However, even palaeobotanical methods are stretched to their limits by some principal questions, such as those concerning common fields, fallow and arable–grassland rotation. For these and other reasons, only some hypotheses of present-day research can be considered as proven; others are still hypothetical and therefore controversial.

A three-field system with winter crop, summer grain and fallow has definitely been in use in some parts of Central Europe since the early Middle Ages (the eighth to tenth centuries). Winter crops were mainly rye, spelt and a small amount of wheat. Barley, and especially oats, made up the summer grain. The third year's fallow served for the restoration of the soil and as pasture.

Such a three-field system has been proved for south-western Germany as early as AD 763 by a charter of the monastery of St Gallen, mentioning the typical three-times-a-year ploughing of the fields. In spring, a tenant had to plough one acre of the abbey's land for the summer grain. Another acre had to be ploughed first in June, that is in the fallow, and a second time in autumn for the winter crop. He was also supposed to sow the winter crop on the second acre: '*in primum ver arata iurnalem unam, et in mense iunio brachare alterum, et in autumno ipsum arare et seminare*'.[1] Only a little later, in about AD 795, tenants in a settlement in the canton of Berne had to reap certain fields of the same size of both winter crop and summer grain: '*ut per annis singulis. . . duas anzingas, unum autumnalem et alium estivalem, illos segare et intus trahere*'.[2] This indicates three-field crop rotation for the northern parts of Switzerland.

Concerning Rhinehessia, in the northern Upper Rhine area there is an instruction of AD 793 which also strongly suggests a three-field system. Every year tenants had to plough and sow for two kinds of crops, probably a winter crop and a summer grain: '*ut singulis annis duos fructus arare debeat et seminare*'.[3] Furthermore, some parts of the *Weißenburger Urbar* dating back to the ninth and tenth centuries document three-field crop rotation in the Upper Rhine area. According to this register of the Weißenburg Abbey in Lower Alsatia, tenants had to plough either in spring and autumn, or in spring, in June, and in autumn: '*in autumno iurnales II arare debet et in verno similiter*';[4] '*in mense iunio VII arare debent iurnales III, in autumno similiter, in verno II*'.[5] The rents of the ninth and tenth centuries registered in the abbey's inventory do not contrast with these three-times-a-year ploughing services typical of three-field crop rotation. In only one village were there farms belonging to the monastery that paid as annual rent the winter crop and summer grain in the proportion of one to two. This ratio occurred in three-course systems as well: '*de frumento modius I, de avena modii II*'.[6] If they were not on share-cropping, the Weißenburg tenants usually had to pay a rent of one to three bushels of oats only. This rent was not typical of three-course rotation. But the Weißenburg inventory also registers considerable amounts of grain as mill rents. Consequently three was winter-crop growing too, because very often winter corn was the usual mill rent. In one

---

[1] H. Wartmann (ed.), *Urkundenbuch der Abtei St Gallen*, vol. 1 (Zurich and St Gallen, 1863–1917), no. 39.

[2] Ibid., no. 140.

[3] K. Glöckner (ed.), *Codex Laureshamensis*, vol. 2, Arbeiten der Historischen Kommission für den Volksstaat Hessen (Darmstadt, 1929–36, reprinted 1963), no. 936.

[4] C. Zeuss (ed.), *Traditiones Possessionesque Wizenburgenses* (Spirae, 1842), no. 17.

[5] Ibid., no. 65.

[6] Ibid., no. 56.

case, the abbey's list even expressively mentions '*molendina VI, inde veniunt de sigale modii CL*', that is a rent of rye.[7] Most of these winter crops are obviously the recompense for milling, which means that they were grown by tenant farmers. This winter crop and the rent of oats, both mentioned in the abbey's register, seem to represent the tenant's three-field cropping system. Thus in the northern parts of the Upper Rhine area, the manor farms and the tenant farms must have had, at least to a certain degree, a similar cropping system in the ninth and tenth centuries.

The Weißenburg Abbey seems to have been satisfied mostly with a rent of oats and to have dispensed with the more expensive winter crops. The reason for this surprising fact might be as follows: the rent of oats reflects an older period of Central European rural economy and food production, in which rye did not yet play the most important part as bread grain. As far as is known from documents and palaeobotanical studies, winter cropping, especially rye, had not been widespread in Central Europe before the later Early Middle Ages; until then farmers cultivated mainly summer grains.

There are also some interesting ninth- and tenth-century sources relating to north-eastern France and the western Eifel. For instance, there is the *Polyptyque de l'Abbé Irminon* of the abbey of St Germain de Prés in Paris, the *Polyptyque de l'Abbaye de Saint-Remis de Reims*, and a register of the Prüm monastery. Here, in the ninth century the tenants' services and the monastic fields were divided according to winter crop and summer grain, the one or the other crop, both crops, or either of two crops: '*ad hibernaticam sationem . . . ad estivaticam sationem; ad hibernaticum . . . ad tramisem; una satio . . . alia satio; ambas sationes; utrasque sationes; in unaquaque satione; per singulas sationes*'.[8] Furthermore, according to a charter of an abbot Ramericus, in about AD 1000 tenants had to plough three times a year, namely for winter crop, fallow and oats, which was the summer grain: '*tres coroweias, ad galcheras, ad remotiones, ad avenas*'.[9] According to the abbey of St Vincenz at Metz, the dates of these services '*in tribus sasonibus, quando colitur terra*' were '*in festo S. Joh. et . . . in festo Martini et . . . in adnuntiatione S. Marie*', which means 24 June (fallow), 11 November (winter crop) and 25 March (summer grain).[10]

In this context, the following references concerning two manor farms of St Amand Abbey near Tournai, in the ninth century, are also to be considered. The arable size of the first one was 30 *bunaria* (1 *bunarium* = 3

---

[7] Ibid., no. 56.

[8] M. B. Guérard (ed.), *Polyptyque de l'Abbé Irminon* (Paris, 1844), passim; M. B. Guérard (ed.), *Polyptyque de l'Abbaye de Saint-Remis de Reims* (Paris, 1853), passim; J. Schwab (ed.), *Rheinische Urbare*, vol. 5: *Das Prümer Urbar*, Publikationen der Gesellschaft für rheinische Geschichtskunde, vol. 20 (Düsseldorf, 1983), no. XLV, p. 202.

[9] Guérard (ed.), *L'Abbé Irminon*, appendix, p. 353, no. XIX.

[10] Ibid., p. 650, n. 10; G. Schröder-Lembke, 'Zur Flurform der Karolinger Zeit', *Zeitschrift für Agrargeschichte und Agrarsoziologie*, 9 (1961), p. 145.

or 4 acres). Ten of these were seeded with 40 bushels of winter crop and ten with 60 bushels of summer grain, because this was seeded more densely. The last 10 *bunaria* remained fallow: '*seminatur ad hibernaticum bunaria X de modiis XL et ad tremissem bunaria X de modiis LX. Bunaria X interiacent*'.[11] The arable land of the other farm registered in the abbey's list in the ninth century consisted of 48 *bunaria*, 16 of which were seeded with winter crop and 16 with summer grain.[12] With regard to the remainder there is no entry, but being exactly one-third of the total these 16 *bunaria* must have been the fallow land at the side of the winter crop and summer grain. All these references prove three-course rotation.

In the tenth and eleventh centuries, the arable of an abbey north-west of Worms consisted of 14 acres for the one crop and $7\frac{1}{2}$ acres for the other crop, minus some *ancingas*: '*ad unam sationem iurnales XIIII, ad aliam sationem VII et dimidium, exceptis ancingis*'.[13] This manor farm's arable land was divided into two portions for two different crops (*sationes*) in a proportion of almost exactly two to one. In the almost double-sized *satio* there were 7 acres of winter crop and 7 acres of fallow. It is quite logical to include the fallow in the winter-crop fields, since its function in a three-course rotation is that of the land to be seeded with the next winter crop. Accordingly, the ninth-century register of Saint Germain de Prés also states double plough service for winter-sown crops, fallow included: '*arat ad hibernaticum perticas II, ad tramisum perticam I; . . . arat ad hibernaticum perticas IV, ad tramisum perticas II*'.[14] In this reference, it means that the abbey's arable land within the village territory near Worms was subdivided into three cropping-units of about 7 acres each for three-course rotation.

The next reference also confirms a three-course rotation. For about AD 1100 the so-called *Eppelsheimer Hofrecht* mentions landed property of the convent St Salvator at Metz, in a village north-west of Worms, which had to be ploughed three times a year. The first portion measured 55 acres, the second 52 acres and the third 51 acres. Each of ten tenants had to plough one day for each crop; the remainder was ploughed by the manor's plough: '*sunt ibi croade III, una iugerum LV, altera LII, tercia LI . . . Sunt ibi infra potestatem X mansi, unusquisque mansus facit diem I in croada ad unamquamque sationem, et quod remanet, dominico aratro fit*'.[15] The subdivision of landed property in three parts of almost the same size is very typical of a farm organized by three-course rotation. Only such a cropping system can plausibly explain why three portions are mentioned here instead of the total of 158 acres. This conclusion is supported by the expression

---

[11] Guérard (ed.), *L'Abbé Irminon*, éclaircissement, p. 925, XIX, no. 3.
[12] Ibid., p. 926, XIX, no. 4.
[13] D. Bonin (ed.), *Urkundenbuch der früheren freien Reichsstadt Pfeddersheim* (Frankfurt, 1911), no. 4.
[14] Guérard (ed.), *L'Abbé Irminon*, passim.
[15] L. Baur (ed.), *Hessische Urkunden*, vol. 5 (Darmstadt, 1860–73), no. 1.

'ploughing services for each crop'. The subdivision into three slightly varying portions might be caused by a common-field system. If there were not yet such field orders, these variations in size might be explained by the number and the different sizes of parcels of the demesne.

As far as it is known, in the tenth century there were three-field systems with winter crop, summer grain and fallow, especially in some early-settled areas, from the northern parts of Switzerland and southern Germany up to the north-east of France and Belgium (see figure 13.1). The three-course rotation is documented as early as the eighth and ninth centuries in the south, in the central parts, and in the north of this region: that is, in areas far apart from each other. Therefore its spread in the Early Middle Ages (AD 700–1050) is probably the result of processes that developed independently of each other rather than of innovation and diffusion from one single centre. The three-field system as an innovation in agriculture seems to have arisen in Central Europe in the Early Middle Ages. Manorial registers from the ninth to eleventh centuries, pollen diagrams, and preserved grains indicate the prevalence of spring-sown oats and barley from the Alps to the North Sea until well into the Early Middle Ages. According to these sources, rye, which became typical of three-course rotation, gradually has prevailed as the winter grain only since the ninth and tenth centuries. Until then, winter wheat was of little importance in Central Europe and spelt, which had been more common in Roman times and remained so in north-eastern France into the Early Middle Ages, was even on the decline. The typical three-field system, with its near-balance of winter crop and summer grain, could only arise in the old-settled areas in the Early Middle Ages, when the winter-crop component had become approximately equal to the summer grains. This was caused mainly by the increase in the cultivation of rye. Before the tenth century, there is no equivalent to the rather common or predominant winter crops mentioned in high and late medieval corn registers.

This change in Central European cereal cultivation during the course of the ninth and tenth centuries and at the beginning of the High Middle Ages can be proved by palaeobotany and also by a few indications in documents and rent books of that time.[16] In the charters of the Bavarian bishopric of Freising,[17] up to about AD 830, a hide is a farm of undefined

[16] K.-E. Behre, 'Zur mittelalterlichen Plaggenwirtschaft in Nordwestdeutschland und angrenzenden Gebieten nach botanischen Untersuchungen', *Untersuchungen zur eisenzeitlichen und frühmittelalterlichen Flur in Mitteleuropa und ihrer Nutzung. Abhandlungen der Akademie der Wissenschaften in Göttingen, philologisch-historische Klasse*, 3rd ser., no. 116, pt 2 (Göttingen, 1980), pp. 30–44; U. Willerding, 'Anbaufrüchte der Eisenzeit und des frühen Mittelalters, ihre Anbauformen, Standortverhältnisse und Erntemethoden', *Untersuchungen zur eisenzeitlichen und frümittelalterlichen Flur*, 3rd ser., no. 116, pt 2 (1980), pp. 126–96.
[17] Th. Bitterauf, *Die Traditionen des Hochstifts Freising*, vol. 1 (München, 1905–9).

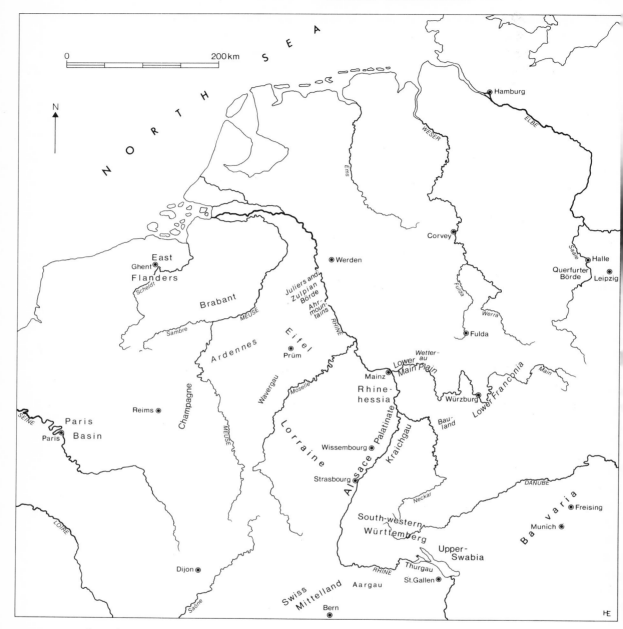

FIGURE 13.1 *Approximate distribution of three-field cultivation in Central Europe in the tenth century. Italic print denotes supposed or likely locations.*

size, whereas a standard hide (*hoba legalis*) becomes more frequent afterwards.[18] This new hide of the ninth and tenth centuries, which replaced the old type, is not only a farm, but is also a field size of 45 acres, 15 acres of each crop and fallow; in the latter part of the tenth century: '*hoba legalis, id*

[18] A. Hömberg, *Grundfragen der deutschen Siedlungsforschung*, (Berlin, 1938), VIII, pp. 54–8.

est in tribus plagis iugera XV; id est in unaquaque aratura iugera XV.[19] Not only do standard hides, or hides of about that size, become more frequent in the ninth and tenth centuries, but farms with a number of acres (*iugera*) that can be divided by three are also on the increase. Both standard hides and a number of acres that can be divided by three are, as Hömberg rightly said, obviously a consequence of the introduction of three-field cultivation, at first very likely without common fields.[20] Consequently, the three-field system increased gradually in this Bavarian area only from the ninth or tenth century during a longer period of transition. Tenants got the field sizes to correspond completely with three-course rotation by exchanging small parts of the arable, and this is well recorded in many barter documents.

Furthermore, there is the evidence in the two registers of the abbey of Werden (on the river Ruhr) dating from about AD 880 and AD 900.[21] Hömberg showed that in the late ninth century Werden Abbey changed the payment of corn rents towards a more or less standardized barley-unit, independent of the actual corn-growing system of its tenant farms in the various Westfalian regions with Werden agricultural properties.[22] In the register of about AD 900, the rents are listed more or less unitarily in the form of barley quantities or barley values, whereas in the older of the two registers dating from about AD 880 some regions can still be differentiated according to their main crops. This means that before AD 880 these areas had to deliver mainly oats or mainly barley or mainly rye, and consequently the fields were measured in this early historical period corresponding to the quantities of oats or barley or rye that were used for sowing.

Both the payment of summer grains in the older register of AD 880 and the more or less corresponding field-measurement system, based upon the amount of barley or oat seed required, document forms of corn-growing before the great increase in winter-crop cultivation. These older conditions, as far as they were still in existence, were covered by the newly introduced barley unit in the later register of about AD 900. The Werden monastery possibly had to introduce a standardized corn-rent unit because on its land cereal cultivation methods went through continuous changes at that time. The continual increase in winter-sown rye caused a constant change in cultivation which, without a standardized rent unit, would have meant a perpetual change in paying rents. The register of *c.* AD 900 reflects the

---

[19] Bitterauf, *Die Traditionen des Hochstifts Freising*, vol. 1, nos 1180, 1305.

[20] Hömberg, *Grundfragen der deutschen Siedlungsforschung*, p. 57.

[21] R. Kötschke (ed.), *Rheinische Urbare*, vol. 2: *Die Urbare der Abtei Werden a.d. Ruhr, A. Die Urbare vom 9.–13. Jahrhundert*, Publikationen der Gesellschaft fur Rheinische Geschichtskunde, vol. 20 (Düsseldorf, 1906, reprinted 1978).

[22] A. Hömberg, 'Münsterländer Bauerntum im Hochmittelalter', *Westfälische Forschungen*, 15 (1962), II, pp. 32–6.

introduction of the new barley unit. Therefore the innovation of a rental system, based only on barley, may have been the reason why a new register was written only twenty years after the previous one.

This revisal of the rental system was probably caused primarily by a change in the existing cultivation of crops, a fact that Hömberg overlooked in his research.[23] Special indications of the changing crop-cultivation system can be seen in the older register of about AD 880 in some marginal notations concerning particular rent entries. These marginal notations mean that, despite the fact that a set value for rent payment existed in the form of barley, other kinds of payment were possible, namely in whatever crops were cultivated. Thus a Werden tenant then was also allowed to pay '*in aliis*' or '*in quo potest*'.[24]

Still other indications for such an innovation process lasting into the High Middle Ages are included in a rental book of Corvey Abbey, on the river Weser, dating from the eleventh century.[25] For some regions in the north-western lowlands of Germany, where later on rye was almost exclusively cultivated – the so-called permanent rye cultivation – this Corvey register still documents a number of rather different forms of corn-rent paid by tenants, namely:

1   only rye;
2   mainly rye and some oats;
3   mainly rye and some barley;
4   mainly rye and some spring crop (barley and oats);
5   rye and spring crops two to one;
6   rye and barley two to one;
7   rye and oats one to one or nearly one to one;
8   rye and barley one to one;
9   oats and rye two to one;
10   mainly oats and some rye;
11   only oats.

The great number of these varieties of rents indicates a change. It shows that in spite of the obvious tendency towards rye cultivation, spring crops had not yet disappeared there in the corn-growing system of the eleventh century. Permanent rye cultivation in these lowlands therefore could not have been in existence at that time to such an extreme extent.

Consequently, for the north-western German lowlands it can be assumed that a longer period of transition, from the spring-crop cultivation of the Early Middle Ages to the permanent growing of rye in the later

[23] Ibid., pp. 32–6.
[24] Ibid., p. 34.
[25] H. H. Kaminsky (ed.), *Studien zur Reichsabtei Corvey in der Salierzeit*, Veröffentlichungen der Historischen Kommission Westfalens, vol. 10 (Köln and Graz, 1972), pp. 195–222, passim.

Middle Ages and Early Modern times (AD 1300–1500; after 1500), must have existed, despite some findings in pollen analysis that apparently indicate the opposite.[26] A three-field system with winter crop, summer grain and fallow, or a four-field system with winter crop, fallow, summer grain and fallow, or an infield–outfield system with rye in the inner area and oats or barley in the outer area, can all be considered as possibilities during this period of transition.

On the other hand, in some mountainous areas bordering on the southeast of the lowlands the corn-rents given to Corvey Abbey in the eleventh century consisted more or less completely of summer grains, mainly oats.[27] In this region at that time, most of the tenant farms paid a relatively large amount of oats, together with only 3 bushels of rye. Furthermore, a few payments of only oats, or of barley and winter crop in a proportion of two to one or three to one, have also been recorded there. This dominance of payments in oats in the abbey's rent book indicates a possible use of arable-grassland rotation. In this context, the same thing can be said concerning a singular entry, referring to a ploughing service only for spring sowing. On the other hand, another singular reference in the Corvey register, recording a twice-a-year ploughing service, namely in the spring and in the autumn, documents perhaps the beginnings of three-course rotation.[28]

In Central Europe, the amount of winter-sown crops is not equivalent to summer grains until well into the Early Middle Ages. Most likely, there was no such thing as three-field cultivation from Roman times onward. The agricultural historian Schröder-Lembke, who analysed Roman sources, came to the same conclusion.[29] She, too, considers three-field systems with winter crop, summer grain and fallow as an innovation of the Franconian era.

Two passages in Pliny deal with Germanic–Celtic cereal production during the Roman Iron Age.[30] According to Pliny's *Historia Naturalis* (18, 44), written in the first century AD, 'oat is the main disease in corn, and the barley degenerates into oat in such a way that the oat itself counts as a kind of corn, inasmuch as the races of Germany grow crops of it and live entirely on oatmeal porridge': '*primum omnium frumenti vitium avena est, et hordeum in eam degenerat, sic ut ipsa frumenti sit instar, quippe cum Germaniae populi serant eam neque alia pulte vivant*'. This prevalence of summer grains does not fit with three-field systems, but rather with arable–grassland rotation.

---

[26] Behre, 'Zur mittelalterlichen Plaggenwirtschaft', pp. 32–5.
[27] Kaminsky, *Studien zur Reichsabtei Corvey*, passim.
[28] Ibid., pp. 197–8. § III.
[29] G. Schröder-Lembke, 'Römische Dreifelderwirtschaft?', *Zeitschrift für Agrargeschichte und Agrarsoziologie*, 11 (1963), pp. 25–33.
[30] J. C. Plinius Secundus, *Naturalis Historia*, edited by H. Rackham, the Loeb Classical Library, vol. 5 (London and Cambridge, Mass., 1950).

In the second passage (that is in *Historia Naturalis* 18, 49), Pliny reports that the winter crops of the Treverer race on the lower Moselle had been nipped by an extreme frost three years previously. The Treverers had sowed again in March and the harvest had been quite bounteous: '*nec recens subtrahemus exemplum in Treverico agro tertio ante hunc anno compertum: nam cum hieme praegelida captae segetes essent, reseverunt etiam campos mense Martio uberrimasque messes habuerunt.*' The possibility of compensating for the losses of winter-sown corn by the cultivation of spring-sown grains is astonishing to Pliny. Such a thing was unknown in Italy and was therefore reported as a curiosity. In the Treverer region the destruction of seeds by frost was certainly not a singular event in that particular year, but afflicted large parts of the whole winter-corn production. Without any doubt the Treverers therefore needed large quantities of summer grains quickly for a second seed. The full extent of the winter-corn losses can be guessed at by the fact that Pliny reported the event and by the rich harvest of summer grains ('*uberrimas messes*'). Reserves of summer grains for such an emergency require large-scale or even dominant summer-grain cultivation in the Treverer territory. Thus Pliny's passage is not a contradiction of the one mentioned above and of the palaeobotanical findings; rather, it means that summer-grain cultivation dominated.

In this context, Schröder-Lembke and Jäger were mistaken in assuming that summer-grain cultivation was not usual in Roman Gaul at that time, but was only a makeshift for winter-crop losses.[31] Pliny's *Historia Naturalis* (18, 49) does not prove a cultivation system dominated by winter crops, as Jäger thinks, but one dominated by summer grains. In Pliny's times, the Treverers did grow winter crops besides summer grains, but not in an almost balanced ratio typical of three-field systems. This extract from Pliny therefore does not prove Roman origins of early medieval three-field systems in Central Europe.

Another question besides that of crop rotation concerns how cropping was organized. A three-field system can be run individually on each parcel of land or it can be communally regulated in common fields. According to the present state of research, a fully developed common-field system did not come into being until the beginning of the High Middle Ages, that is in the tenth century at the earliest. So far such terms as *zelga*, *aratura*, *satio*, *campus* and *pars* in charters and registers of the eighth to tenth centuries have been interpreted as common fields, but in fact they only refer to the type of culture or tillage, that is winter crop, summer grain and fallow.[32]

---

[31] Schröder-Lembke, 'Römische Dreifelderwirtschaft?', p. 32; H. Jäger, 'Bodennutzungssysteme (Feldsysteme) der Frühzeit', *Untersuchungen zur eisenzeitlichen und frümittelalterlichen Flur*, no. 116, pt 2, p. 211.

[32] H. Hildebrandt, *Studien zum Zelgenproblem, Untersuchungen über flürlichen Anbau aufgrund methodenkritischer Interpretationen agrargeschichtlicher Quellen, dargestellt an Beispielen aus dem deutschsprachigen Raum*. Mainzer Geographische Studien, 14 (Mainz, 1980), X, pp. 196–235.

Most probably these terms were not used for certain topographical parts of the arable land with common-field cropping.

In AD 789, a tenant farmer of the St Gallen Abbey in Seen in the canton of Zurich had to plough one acre of the demesne for each kind of tillage as usual: '*unaquaque zelga unum iuchum arare, sicut mos in domnico arare*',[33] and, according to a similar instruction of AD 791, at Spaichingen in Württemberg one acre of each kind of tillage had to be ploughed and then sowed with the manor's seed: '*in unaquaque aratura iurnale unum arare et cum semine nostro siminare*'.[34] These tenants did not have to plough or sow in each rotation unit, that is common field, but for each crop or each kind of grain in a three-field system. A tenant's duty was measured in accordance with the three categories of winter crop, summer grain and fallow. For the abbey, as the owner of the arable land, it did not matter whether the ploughing and sowing was done in scattered parcels or in common fields.

Bavarian documents of the tenth and eleventh centuries seem to use these terms with the same meaning. In these references, the size of a standard hide is defined as 15 acres in three or in each *aratura* or *plaga*.[35] In this connection *aratura* or *plaga* can hardly mean 'common field', because such an ideal, totally equal allotment of different farms' parcels in three common fields, did not occur even in mature common-field systems of later days. Without regard to common fields a hide, however, could be divided into three equal portions for three-course rotation. It could therefore be defined in this way, too.

From the turn of the Early to the High Middle Ages, common-field systems spread gradually over Central Europe. As was the case with three-course rotation, this seems to have occurred by independent development at different places rather than by spread from a single centre. Since then, such Latin terms as *zelga* and *campus* or the German terms *Feld* and *Flur* have been used in the sense of common fields. Originally, however, they obviously meant only arable as such, or a certain type of tillage in general. Later on in the High Middle Ages, when common fields became the rule for corn-growing within the infields in these areas, the meaning of *zelga*, *campus* and so on changed to 'common field' in the modern sense. These terms therefore cannot be used as a proof of early medieval common-field cultivation.[36]

Furthermore, in contrast to Jäger's views, subdivision of the arable with fragmented holdings (as was partly the case as early as Carolingian times) and the necessity to use fallow land as pasture do not necessarily prove the

---

[33] Wartmann, *Urkundenbuch der Abtei St Gallen*, vol. 1, no. 120.
[34] Ibid., no. 130.
[35] See p. 000 above.
[36] Hildebrandt, *Studien zum Zelgenproblem*, pp. 232–5.

existence of common-field systems.[37] For until well into Early Modern times many arable lands with fragmented holdings were not cultivated in common fields, despite the fact that many parcels were not accessible by paths, and despite grazing on fallow land. Some of these arable lands were never organized in common fields or they only formed a large number of small, isolated units with the same tillage.[38]

Neither is it possible to prove the hypothesis that common fields in early-settled areas of southern Germany developed from the small territories of Merovingian communities.[39] The early common fields were supposed to have been formed here during the seventh century in a reform by consolidation. This caused many of these small settlements to be deserted. It has been said that since the seventh century the original Merovingian units had been used as common fields within the larger consolidated territories of communities. Indeed, there were such consolidations in southern Germany in that period, as archaeological findings indicate, but there is no such correspondence of medieval or early modern common fields and these Merovingian territories.

Finally, one cannot infer the antiquity of common-field cultivation in Central Europe from fences mentioned in Germanic Codes. These fences were obviously not common-field fences. Their only function was to protect seeded fields from game and cattle on common land. There are no other indications of common-field systems in these Germanic Codes.

Recent studies, especially in late-settled areas, have shown that crop rotation as one component of the three-field system is obviously older than common-field orders.[40] Wherever the development of cereal production is reflected in written sources, it can be seen that in most cases three-field systems with common fields had been preceded for some time by three-field cultivation on single parcels of land. Quite often between these two periods there was a time of transition with only rudimentary common fields. In this stage of development, small parts of the arable, for instance furlongs, were cultivated alike. Obviously, little by little, neighbouring parcels were added to these miniature common fields and thus they grew into real common fields. Retrospectively, one can assume the existence of such older preforms before the medieval – eleventh and twelfth centuries, – cultivation in large common fields. Therefore Thirsk is probably right in her opinion that in England, too, fully-fledged common-field systems with

[37] Jäger, 'Bodennutzungssysteme (Feldsysteme) der Frühzeit', pp. 217–18.

[38] See, for example, M. Döppert, 'Frühneuzeitliche Feldsysteme im Schlitzer Land', *Archiv für hessische Geschichte und Altertumskunde*, Neue Folge, 43 (1985), pp. 58–68.

[39] W. Müller, 'Namen – Zelgen – Gräber – Markungen. Ein vorläufiger Beitrag zur alemannisch-fränkischen Besiedlungsgeschichte', *Ludwigsburger Geschichtblätter*, 19 (1967), pp. 71–89.

[40] See, for example, Döppert, 'Frühneuzeitliche Feldsysteme im Schlitzer Land', pp. 48–68 and Hildebrandt, *Studien zum Zelgenproblem*, pp. 196–235.

common fallow pasture are the result of step-by-step development.[41] Conditions for such a development were especially good in the High Middle Ages, when the population increased considerably; as a consequence, there was a lack of pasture, farms had to be subdivided, and many parcels were no longer linked to field-paths.

Besides the increasing three-field system, either regularly conducted or unordered, arable–grassland rotations were still widely spread in Central Europe in the tenth and eleventh centuries. Such systems were very common and provably existed into the Late Middle Ages or even Early Modern times as forerunners of three-course rotation. With regard to some areas of Bavaria, for instance, oats dominate in high and late medieval rent registers.[42] In such regions, arable–grassland rotation with the renting of oats is also very likely for preceding periods. The same arable–grassland rotation with payment of oats can be proved by sources for recently settled areas. Therefore retrospective analogy is justifiable. Most likely there was the same cultivation system in older-settled areas in early medieval times before the beginning of three-course rotation. Furthermore, in later medieval times in some regions the size of parcels was measured by the amount of oats needed to seed them. This also points towards early medieval cereal production based on arable–grassland rotation and dominated by oats, for winter crops, as far as it can be seen, were in most cases used to measure the field sizes, where they were part of the cropping system. Both oat-dominant rents and the measurement of the fields by oats can be considered as indications of arable–grassland rotation, especially in regions with high precipitation and heavy soils. The sentence '*arva per annos mutant et super est ager*' in Tacitus' *Germania* (chapter 26)[43] seems to be correctly interpreted in the sense of arable–grassland rotation.[44] The question, however, remains as to whether early medieval arable–grassland rotation goes back without a break to the first century AD.

In Central Europe, the transition from the later Early Middle Ages to the High Middle Ages was a period of change in cereal cultivation. The principal phenomenon was a trend towards the cultivation of winter crops and, at the same time, a reduction of the summer grains, which had dominated until then. In the end there were the two extremes of continual winter-crop systems, on the one hand, and arable–grassland rotation, mainly based on summer grains, on the other hand. An almost balanced

---

[41] J. Thirsk, 'Zur genetischen Siedlungsforschung in Grossbritannien mit besonderer Berücksichtigung der Siedlungsgeschichte', unpublished paper (Trier, April 1984).

[42] G. Schröder-Lembke, 'Zum Zelgenproblem', *Zeitschrift für Agrargeschichte und Agrarsoziologie*, 17 (1969), p. 50.

[43] C. Tacitus, *De Origine et Situ Germanorum*, edited by H. Furneaux and J. G. C. Anderson (Oxford, 1952).

[44] See also Jäger, 'Bodennutzungssysteme (Feldsysteme) der Frühzeit', p. 215.

proportion of winter crops and summer grains is then reached in three-field systems. Both kinds of grains were also part of so-called 'free systems', in which they changed with or without fallow in a free rotation. Such systems are presumed to be very old too. The same is probably true for infield–outfield systems, for there are ninth-century sources mentioning parts of the arable of the same manor farm, which are partly measured by winter-crop seed and partly by seeded summer grains.[45] Since the second half of the tenth century, in many areas in the lowlands of north-western Germany the growing of spring crops had gradually been replaced by a one-field system, with continuous rye cultivation and turf-fertilization. Only now and then was this winter-crop growing suspended by a summer-grain or fallow year. Until the ninth century, however, it was mainly barley besides oats and fallow years that was typical of the cereal production in these regions. This is mainly proved by palaeobotany.[46]

In some Upper and Middle Rhine regions and in some villages in the Lower Main area, the development towards winter crops was almost as extreme as in the north-western lowlands. Roughly since the eleventh century there was a two-field rotation in these areas, which was organized with or without common fields and consisted of rye and fallow. Spring-sown grains replaced the fallow only now and again. Written sources concerning these areas, like the Weißenburg Abbey's register, either prove three-field rotation or they indicate arable–grassland farming until the tenth and eleventh centuries.[47] This two-field system is for the first time well supported by a register of AD 1200 in which tenants' payments are only made in rye and parcels of the arable of farms are listed under two common fields only.[48] Probably the earliest indication of such a field system is a service instruction of the eleventh century delivered in the *Lorscher Codex* concerning Weinheim, near Heidelberg. Here, tenants had to plough for winter crops only, which had to be seeded on St Remigius, that is 1 October. This means that they only had to plough the fallow land in June and a second time on 8 September: '*III iugera arat omni anno ad seminandum cum dominico semine. Arare debet in mense Iunio atque iterum in natuitate Marie, ut sit seminatum in missa S. Remigii.*'[49]

[45] Schwab, *Rheinische Urbare*, vol. 5, no. LV, p. 218. See also L. Kuchenbuch, *Bäuerliche Gesellschaft und Klosterherrschaft im 9. Jahrhundert Studien zur Sozialstruktur der familia der Abtei Prüm*, Vierteljahrsschrift für Sozial- und Wirtschaftsgeschichte, Beihefte no. 66 (Wiesbaden, 1978), p. 100, and n. 13.

[46] Jäger, 'Bodennutzungssysteme (Feldsysteme) der Frühzeit', pp. 207–8; Behre, 'Zur mittelalterlichen Plaggenwirtschaft', passim. See also p. 279 above.

[47] H. Hildebrandt, 'Zum Problem der rheinischen Zweifelderwirtschaft', *Mainzer Naturwissenschaftliches Archiv*, 16 (1977), pp. 7–34.

[48] H. Beyer, L. Eltester and A. Goerz (eds), *Urkundenbuch zur Geschichte der jetzt die Preussischen Regierungsbezirke Coblenz und Trier bildenden mittelrheinischen Territorien*, vol. 2 (Coblenz, 1860–5), pp. 365 ff.

[49] Glöckner, *Codex Laureshamensis*, vol. 3, no. 3669.

There is perhaps even a third kind of field system showing a tendency towards winter crops. About AD 1300, for example, tenants in the Alemannian area paid rent and tithe of winter crops and summer grains in the proportion of two to one. In some regions, the proportion was even three to one or four to one. Here winter crops, that is bread grains, were mainly spelt and rye; oats dominated as the main spring crop. In historical research, this high medieval prevalence of winter corn within a three-course rotation in common fields has so far been believed to be a relic of an older early medieval two-field rotation with only rye and fallow.[50] Nevertheless, these dominant winter-crop rentings and tithings seem to be the expression of special types of three-field rotation. Due to the tendency to grow winter crops, spelt and rye – instead of summer grains – were partly taken also as the second crop. This occurred, for instance, in two of three, in one of two, in one of three, or in one of four, succeeding three-year rotation units. In the Alemannian area, the tendency did not go any further towards one-sided winter-crop cultivation in the High Middle Ages, for people obviously knew very well from decreasing harvests and diseases in plants that spelt as a kind of wheat – in contrast to the rye of the one-field system in north-western Germany – is not so compatible with itself. Therefore farmers probably regarded an intermediate summer corn besides the fallow as being necessary. Moreover the risk of a winter-crop failure caused by frost could then have been another reason for continuing summer-grain cultivation to a certain extent as well. Such three-field systems with prevailing winter crops have also been proved for other Central European regions as the main type of corn-growing during the Late Middle Ages and Early Modern times.

In Central Europe, the later Early Middle Ages and the beginning of the High Middle Ages were a time of change with regard to cereal growing. Common-field cultivation developed from small preforms and then spread out more and more. Winter crops as bread grains – that is mainly rye and spelt – established themselves in various field systems. The degree to which they replaced summer grains differed from one region to the other. Three-course rotation spread rather widely, obviously because of, amongst other reasons, its near-balance of winter crops and summer grains, which lessened the risks of crop failures even in poor climatic conditions. Such three-field systems offered the best chance to compensate for winter-crop failures by frost or drought losses of summer grains.

Winter-crop cultivation had been increasing from the late Early Middle Ages, and in the High Middle Ages it was adopted even more because the growth in population and the development of towns caused a rising demand for bread grains. Field systems based on winter corn became quite

[50] Schröder-Lembke, 'Zum Zelgenproblem', pp. 49–50.

profitable because of the higher market value of such crops; in the High Middle Ages their price must have been about twice as high as that of summer grains. Therefore, and because of its combination with vine-growing, two-field cultivation in the Rhine and Main areas was superior to three-field systems, despite its larger annual fallow land of about 50 per cent of the arable. Even the *Esch* one-field cultivation of rye in north-western Germany was a quite competitive farming system, although it does not seem to have been very intensive because of its large common lands used as additional fields for turf-cutting.

After the turn from the Early to the High Middle Ages, with the tendencies discussed, no new field systems were introduced in the High Middle Ages itself, as far as is known. Those cultivation forms in use until then merely spread out more or less. It was only in the Late Middle Ages and Early Modern times that the classification of cropping systems was enlarged again by a new tendency towards the cultivation of summer grains.

14

Anglo-Saxon England and the Origins of the Modern World Economy

RICHARD HODGES

Historians of the modern world tend to make two sweeping statements about the Middle Ages. First, it is commonly asserted that the lineage of the modern world system can be traced back to the so-called 'Commercial Revolution' of the eleventh century. Secondly, the roots of this eleventh-century economic take-off (to use terms employed by historians of the eighteenth century) are frequently said to have significant implications for development policy in the Third World. The trouble with these two statements is that each embodies gravely over-simplified historical analysis which would be considered quite unacceptable if it were applied to later medieval or modern times. In this chapter, it is my intention to make statements of a comparably sweeping scale about the first millennium AD, which I believe might be more consistent with historical research about the second millennium. As will be clear, recent archaeological research will be used not only to consider these major issues, but also to shed a little light upon the European context of 1066 and *Domesday Book*.

Let me begin with the makings of the modern world. Fernand Braudel has brilliantly charted the unfolding rhythms of time through this millennium.[1] One of his principal models is what he describes as world economies – the making of the human race into a single market. Immanuel Wallerstein has elaborated Braudel's idea by devising world empires and world systems.[2] The empires, to put it succinctly, are connected through a centralized political body, while the systems involve collections of territorial entities bound together through economic interaction with core zones and peripheries. One of the most stimulating uses of this model is by Eric Wolf in his book, *Europe and the People without History*, in which the origins of the modern world are traced not in western terms (a moral race, as he calls it), but from the standpoint of those peoples who have been more than often manipulated by western history.[3] Wolf's book examines

[1] F. Braudel, *Capitalism and Material Life 1400–1800* (London, 1984).
[2] I. Wallerstein, *The Modern World-System* (London, 1974); R. Hodges, *Primitive and Peasant Markets* (Oxford, 1988).
[3] E. R. Wolf, *Europe and the People without History* (Berkeley, CA, 1982).

the Braudelian sequence of world economies as each affects Third World communites. The past, as he points out, involves 'both the people who claim history as their own and the people to whom history has been denied'; together they 'emerge as participants in the same historical trajectory'.[4] In recent years, however, the bald simplicity of dependency theory, as the Braudel–Wallerstein–Wolf thesis is termed by anthropologists and development economists, has come under attack from anthropologists and archaeologists. In a seminal essay, Carol Smith has argued that world systems may be altered through their connections with communities on their peripheries.[5] Likewise, Colin Renfrew has devised the concept of peer-policy interaction to account for the formation of complex political units, largely independent of wider, dominant relations.[6] Renfrew sees patchwork quilts of territories pulling each other along together. In many respects, this model complements the world-systems approach by focusing upon the mediation between polities and the wider world of which they are a part.

Concepts such as these invoke a good deal of suspicion from archaeologists and historians of the medieval period. But, as I hope to illustrate, Anglo-Saxon history, like European history, should not be treated in isolation in terms set out by our sources. Modern behavioural approaches to the past drawing upon anthropology and sociology as well as history are urgently required to avoid the often apt caricature of medieval history in *1066 and All That*. Modern approaches based upon the fullest appreciation of the multi-disciplinary sources at our disposal invariably afford us a greater consciousness of our own world situation.

1066 is not merely the date of a convenient battle; it roughly marks the first flowering of the European economy and the emergence of a distinctive medieval culture. But what triggered this 'take-off'? The answer, of course, must be sought in the preceding millennium: in the world of antiquity and the so-called Dark Ages. In seeking answers, historians have often been held to ransom by what Marx termed vulgar history – by written sources which, for the most part, served the ideological motives of the elite and offer a poor sample of economic and sociological measurements upon such issues as market and state development.[7] The people denied history, to paraphrase Wolf, seldom figure in the first millennium. Moreover, it is hardly surprising to discover that many twentieth-century historians have approached early medieval sources with a mental framework that owes a

[4] Ibid., p. 23.

[5] C. A. Smith, 'Local history in global context: social and economic transitions in Western Guatemala', *Comparative Studies in Society and History*, 26 (1984), pp. 193–228.

[6] C. Renfrew and J. F. Cherry (eds), *Peer-Polity Interaction and Sociopolitical Change* (Cambridge, 1986).

[7] Discussed in M. P. Leone, 'Some opinions about recovering mind', *American Antiquity*, 47 (1982), pp. 742–60, esp. pp. 753–7.

good deal to Adam Smith's analyses of the Industrial Revolution.[8] That is, the role of the market and the place of the town are held to constitute important, if not pre-eminent features of the period. Let me illustrate this point rather baldly using Robert S. Lopez's famous book, *The Commercial Revolution of the Middle Ages*, as an example.[9]

Lopez, of course, begins with the barbarians and follows the world of antiquity into a darkened gloom in which there existed (I quote) 'self-centred agriculture'.[10] Demographic growth, however, alters this state of affairs, being the prime motor of agricultural progress, and then agricultural progress being the prerequisite of the Commercial Revolution. Hence, Lopez argues in the wake of Pirenne, Bloch, Ganshof and Duby that 'the revolution took off from the manor'.[11] Nevertheless, he emphasizes the harshness of subsistence, mindful, one suspects, of classical and medieval civilization. 'Above all', he says, 'medieval Europe had little room for investment over and above preservation of life'.[12] So how were matters altered? He traces the answer to the Jews and Italians – to traders like the Venetian Doge Justinian Partecipazio in AD 829, who had assets amounting to 1,200 silver pounds and was paving the way for a new bold future filled with merchant venturers. This future began to be realized in the tenth century, according to Lopez, when 'Italy was ready – more ready than in the heyday of the Roman Empire. No doubt her towns had become smaller and poorer, but they had broken loose from agrarian moorings that had held them back in antiquity.'[13] In common with many historians, Lopez depicts these towns as places where merchants and citizens were taking control, while traditional lords carved out rural resource bases. So Lopez asserts: 'These unique political and social circumstances enabled the Italian towns to react to the stimulus of demographic growth and agrarian revival more promptly than did the rest of Europe.'[14] Lopez believes that 'by releasing agrarian income for investment in business and by making credit operations more flexible the Commercial Revolution had moved two stumbling blocks that impeded economic growth in antiquity'.[15] 'The business fever, when it came, left almost no-one untouched.'[16] Thus, he deduces 'to pry the circle open, the Commercial Revolution needed the collaboration of producers and consumers everywhere, the merchants

---

[8] Discussed by A. Wrigley, 'Urban growth and agricultural change', *Journal of Interdisciplinary History*, 15 (1985), pp. 683–728.

[9] R. S. Lopez, *The Commercial Revolution of the Middle Ages* (Englewood Cliffs, NJ, 1971).

[10] Ibid., p. 56.

[11] Ibid., p. 56.

[12] Ibid., p. 59.

[13] Ibid., p. 66.

[14] Ibid., p. 67.

[15] Ibid., p. 79.

[16] Ibid., p. 67.

providing the spark, the whole society offering the fuel'.[17] 'Without pursuing our comparisons any further, we may state that the European commercial revolution was a unique phenomenon, the unexpected result of a chain reaction that began almost accidentally in a few peripheral towns of Italy.'[18]

This brief synopsis of Lopez's model offers some flavour of what might be termed the prehistory of the American Dream. It represents to a considerable extent the kind of history Eric Wolf set out to challenge. Lopez's model ascribes much to an entrepreneurial spirit that slipped the shackles of its classical and barbarian past to create the spirit of western democracy. If I caricature it slightly, it is because the model has been incorporated by Walt Rostow in his highly influential tracts on development theory, in which the mystery of economic take-offs in Third World countries have been scrutinized in these early medieval terms.[19]

It would be most misleading and improper to assert that Lopez's model is universally accepted by historians of this period. Variations on this theme, though, have been proposed by mainstream historians and Marxists restricted by the sources – or, rather, by the unquantified sample of written information – available on this critical period. I should like at this point, of course, to assert that archaeology now changes this situation; I would, however, be exaggerating. Nevertheless, the archaeological sources offer an alternative and complementary data base, which as a sample is comparable at its best to the written evidence.[20] Using some of the archaeological data, therefore, let me offer some draft notes on this sweeping theme to illustrate the potential that exists in the material record for rewriting the history of this formative period.

Wallerstein defines the Roman system as a world empire: a community with a core and peripheries, which were connected by a highly centralized political and economic system.[21] Archaeology now vividly documents the collapse of this system with the third-century crisis of Italy soon reaching northern England, for example, like a wave, manifesting itself most emphatically in the reduction of peasant settlements. The data to illustrate this point are coming to light in field surveys in areas as different as the Fens[22] and the Peak District.[23] Archaeology indicates that the removal of the political superstructure left Britain, for example, rather as if it had been

---

[17] Ibid., p. 84.

[18] Ibid., p. 57.

[19] W. Rostow, *The Stages of Economic Growth* (Cambridge, 1960).

[20] R. Hodges, 'Method and theory in medieval archaeology', *Archaeologia Medievale*, 9 (1982), pp. 7–38.

[21] Wallerstein, *The Modern World-System*.

[22] P. Hayes, personal communication.

[23] R. Hodges and M. Wildgoose, 'Roman or native in the White Peak, Derbyshire', *Derbyshire Archaeological Journal*, 101 (1981), pp. 42–58.

hit by a holocaust (albeit lasting beween three and four generations) – a political vacuum practising subsistence agriculture.[24] Early fifth-century Britain is not unusual; the same circumstances overtook most of central Italy by the early to mid-seventh century.[25] Put in other terms, the old Roman core had shifted to Constantinople for a brief spell, placing the western imperial provinces in economic jeopardy after the mid-fourth century.[26] Stupendous demographic adjustments are a feature of this shift. Hence, in the West, to judge from the numerous deserted villas and farms discovered in recent field surveys, the landscape was depopulated, whereas in Greece and Palestine, for example, rural populations increased to serve the burgeoning maritime cities.[27] The barbarian migrations must be considered as a consequence of these great changes, but the archaeology of the Anglo-Saxons, Franks, Ostrogoths and Lombards in their migratory phase barely exists. Instead, since the nineteenth century there has been a tendency to attribute finds from subsequent periods to these ethnic groups. These finds, however, mostly from cemeteries, most frequently relate to the Roman collapse as it approached its nadir. A strong case exists for regarding these ethnically distinctive rural objects as features of groups seeking to accentuate their identity for political purposes as new territorial configurations were being made.

This one-dimensional picture deceptively reduces the complex rhythms connecting many parts of Europe in this period. Let me illustrate this point with one critical example. The final collapse of the late antique world in the Mediterranean can be phased as follows: (1) inland zones collapsed in the sixth century; (2) coastal littorals collapsed by about AD 640.[28] Meanwhile, a North Sea political and economic nucleus was evidently taking shape from the very end of the fifth century. Dutch settlement surveys and environmental research confirm James's thesis on the Franks: a new settlement expansion phase was under way in this region.[29] This coincides with the ubiquitous destruction of prestige goods in the mortuary rite wherein gifts

[24] R. Hodges, *The Anglo-Saxon Achievement* (London, 1988).

[25] R. Hodges, 'San Vincenzo al Volturno and its region between the 5th and 11th centuries', in R. Hodges and J. Mitchell (eds), *San Vincenzo al Volturno*, British Archaeological Reports, International series –S252 (Oxford, 1985), pp. 259–73.

[26] K. Randsborg, *First Millennium* (Cambridge, forthcoming).

[27] See, for example, J. L. Bintliff and A. M. Snodgrass, 'The Cambridge/Bradford Boeotian expedition: the first four years', *Journal of Field Archaeology*, 12 (1985), pp. 123–61.

[28] R. Hodges and D. Whitehouse, *Mohammed, Charlemagne and the Origins of Europe* (London, 1983); R. Hodges, J. Moreland and H. Patterson, 'San Vincenzo al Volturno, the kingdom of Benevento, and the Carolingians', in C. Malone and S. Stoddart (eds), *Papers in Italian Archaeology IV, Part iv, Classical and Medieval Archaeology*, British Archaeological Reports, International series –S246 (Oxford, 1985), pp. 261–85; Hodges, 'San Vincenzo al Volturno and its region'.

[29] W. Willems, 'Romans and Batavians, a regional study in the Dutch Eastern River area, I', *Berichten van de Rijksdienst voor hat Dudheidkundig Bodemonderzoek*, 31 (1981), pp. 7–218; E. James, 'Cemeteries and the problems of Frankish settlement in Gaul', in P. H. Sawyer (ed.), *Names, Words and Graves: Early Medieval Settlement* (Leeds, 1979), pp. 55–90.

were evidently given to the gods and thereby removed from worldly circulation.[30] This mortuary rite appears to have stimulated the need for prestige goods, giving rise to far-flung trade networks as the classical market-based system of production and distribution had disappeared in this part of Europe.[31] The poetry and history of this period strongly suggest that this prestige-goods exchange was formulated upon prehistoric principles of gift exchange. Yet it must be remembered that these exchange routes reached to the Mediterranean basin, where market-based commerce was to exist for another century or more.[32] The mechanics of this trade are beyond the scope of this chapter, but the complex pan-European pattern of economies needs to be borne in mind as we assess the part played by the so-called barbarians.

Now let us turn to the post-classical circumstances. Archaeological investigations in most parts of Western Europe indicate the existence of tribal economies in the seventh and eighth centuries. Nevertheless the Church represented a powerful link with the world of antiquity in social and economic terms.[33] The role of the Church, indeed, cannot be disentangled from the next stage in the development of the North Sea zone in the later seventh century. The Church almost certainly encouraged the shift from a gift-based society to the beginnings of commodity production. In England, for example, the Church was first associated with conspicuous long-distance exchange of prestige goods between c. AD 590 and 630, but the collapse of the Mediterranean connections in the 630s and the social competition resulting from this led to investment in territoriality.[34] The English landscape took shape in this century, as the Church revived the concept of commodity production, from which as a major landowner it was bound to profit. In my view, *The Tribal Hidage*, the first written laws and land charters, and the Middle Saxon shuffle of settlements (to use Andrew Selkirk's phrase) are all expressions of this new economic initiative.[35]

The most significant new direction arising as a consequence of commodity production was the creation of urban centres like Dorestad and Hamwic. These places incorporated facilities for traders in prestige-goods exchange, but recent investigations show that their real purpose was to centralize regional production and exchange. The switch from gold to silver currency is a further indication of this shifting economic complexion.

---

[30] Cf. C. A. Gregory, *Gifts and Commodities* (London, 1982).

[31] R. Hodges, *Dark Age Economics* (London, 1982), pp. 29–31.

[32] Ibid, pp. 31–9; U. Nasman, 'Vendel period glass from Eketorp II, Öland, Sweden, *Acta Archeologica*, 55 (1984), pp. 55–116.

[33] J. Goody, *The Development of the Family and Marriage in Europe* (Cambridge, 1983).

[34] Hodges, *The Anglo-Saxon Achievement*.

[35] C. J. Arnold and P. Wardle, 'Early medieval settlement patterns in England', *Medieval Archaeology*, 25 (1981), pp. 145–9; M. Welch, 'Rural settlement patterns in the early and middle Anglo-Saxon period', *Landscape History*, 7 (1985), pp. 13–26.

But we must beware: Europe in AD 700 was a patchwork quilt of territories, most of which were constrained by their histories from developing urban communities.

The archaeology of the English emporia indicates that Wessex may have been more socially advanced than the other English kingdoms. Hamwic, the West Saxon emporium spread over 45 hectares and possessing a population of several thousands, was a unique late seventh- or early eighth-century phenomenon, while in Kent, London, East Anglia and perhaps Northumbria a traditional prestige-goods exchange functioned at elite compounds rather than at a planned town. Urban development was similarly restricted within the Frankish kingdoms, while in Italy the history of coinage as well as other aspects of production and distribution emphasizes the peculiar isolation of the peninsula. The Italian economy had completely collapsed by the mid-seventh century, and other than in Rome a primitive society existed rather similar to that of fifth-century Britain.[36]

Lopez describes agriculture in this period as self-centred and he stresses the harshness of subsistence. This Victorian view of Dark Age economics is neither consistent with Massimo Montanari's extensive documentary studies of early medieval food production (in Italy), nor the archaeological evidence.[37] Using the latter, I have challenged Marshall Sahlins's view that the original affluent society was palaeolithic; instead I believe it was created in these early medieval times.[38] Faunal and palaeobotanical analyses for Anglo-Saxon, Frankish and Lombardic sites depict a healthy surfeit of protein.[39] Palaeopathological analyses reinforce the point: women, in particular, were living longer and were taller in stature.[40] Lopez, like so many historians, confuses the harshness of subsistence farming in modern peasant societies, where there exist high populations and repressive taxation systems, with these medieval circumstances, where the populations were fantastically low and taxation was minimal because the political system itself was primitive.

Lopez, again like many historians, looks to demographic growth as the prime motor of agricultural progress. The archaeological evidence challenges this thesis and serves to underscore our ignorance of reproduction strategies in tribal societies. Recent surveys of two great monastic territories in central Italy – at Farfa and San Vincenzo al Volturno – as well

[36] Hodges and Whitehouse, *Mohammed, Charlemagne and the Origins of Europe.*
[37] M. Montanari, *L'Alimentazione Contadina nell' Alto Medioevo* (Naples, 1979).
[38] M. Sahlins, *Stone Age Economics* (London, 1974); Hodges, *Dark Age Economics*, pp. 130–50.
[39] W. Prummel, 'Early medieval Dorestad: an archaeological study', *Excavations at Dorestad 2, Berichten van de Rijksdienst voor het Oudheidkundig Bodemonderzoek* (Amersfoort, 1983).
[40] A. Nelson, 'A study of stature, sex and age ratios and average age at death from the Romano-British to the late Anglo-Saxon period' (unpublished MA thesis, University of Sheffield, 1985).

as surveys throughout Western Europe show that agricultural expansion is a tenth- and eleventh-century phenomenon.[41] Archaeology, however, provides an interesting new dimension on the Carolingian period, which may offer a clue to what was happening.

Elsewhere in examining the Pirenne thesis I have described the Carolingian renaissance in terms of long-distance trade.[42] I attempted to show that the Carolingian elite were seeking silver from the Baltic – silver ultimately derived form the Abbasid Caliphate – to furnish their economic and political policy. This model can be revised in the light of more recent research. First, the trade route to the Danes handled by the Frisians to obtain Arabic and Baltic resources may have been mirrored by the route from central Italy via the Beneventans to the Aghlabid kingdoms of the Maghreb, where similar resources were to be found. A. O. Citarella and H. M. Willard in a recent study describe how the abbey of Monte Cassino acquired Arabic treasure from the Beneventan elite, who sold cereals to the Aghlabids in ports like Gaeata, Naples and Salerno as well as in North Africa.[43] The wealth of Monte Cassino in the Carolingian age is now demonstrated by the excavations of its sister monastery, 50 kilometres away at San Vincenzo al Volturno.[44] These excavations illustrate the huge expansion of critically-placed monasteries in this period, and the overt display of Carolingian renaissance culture to manipulate, it must be presumed, the Beneventans.[45] Secondly, recent research on commodity production in the Carolingian world emphasizes the great technological developments occurring in this short time-period, as classical methods were reinstituted. Techniques such as lime-based cement-mixing were reintroduced to many parts of Western Europe, making it now possible to construct great abbeys. Likewise metal technology, pottery technology, glass technology and, in all probability, agrarian technology were developed to promote a more efficient use of resources (see chapter 12 above).[46] But this technology was controlled by the elite within the empire, as the contrasting excavations at San Vincenzo and one of its dependent villages, Vacchereccia, illustrate.[47] The monastery was equipped with a great range of items made using

[41] T. Leggio and J. Moreland, 'Recognizione nei dintorni di Farfa 1985: resconto preliminare', *Archaeologia Medievale*, 13 (1986), pp. 333–44; C. Wickham, 'The terra of San Vincenzo al Volturno in the 8th to 12th centuries: the historical framework', in Hodges and Mitchell (eds), *San Vincenzo al Volturno*, pp. 227–58.

[42] Hodges and Whitehouse, *Mohammed, Charlemagne and the Origins of Europe*.

[43] A. O. Citarella and H. M. Willard, *The Ninth Century Treasure of Montecassino* (Montecassino, 1983).

[44] Hodges and Mitchell (eds), *San Vincenzo al Volturno*.

[45] Hodges et al., 'San Vincenzo al Volturno, the kingdom of Benevento'.

[46] Hodges, 'San Vincenzo al Volturno and its region'; R. Hodges, *The Hamwih Pottery*, Council for British Archaeology Research Report 37 (London, 1981); J. Moreland, 'A monastic workshop and glass production at San Vincenzo al Volturno, Molise, Italy', in Hodges and Mitchell (eds), *San Vincenzo al Volturno*, pp. 37–60.

[47] Hodges et al., 'San Vincenzo al Volturno, the kingdom of Benevento'.

classical/medieval technology; the village appears to have been self-sufficient and primitive. The Carolingian elite may have traded scientific information. The iron-smelting furnace at Ramsbury (possibly a royal estate), the mortar-mixers at Northampton, the new building concepts to be seen at Repton and Wing, and the introduction of the penny made from a flan are a few of the many Anglo-Saxon illustrations of this exchange.[48] New technology would have enabled the elite to increase production, much as Lopez anticipated. But the archaeology reveals an interesting paradox about the question of surplus and investment.

In the Carolingian polity – the seat of these great economic and technological programmes – the investment advanced inefficiently. The scale of the empire necessitated, as the philosopher Thomas Hobbes noted, the Church performing the role of Charlemagne's legions.[49] The Church welded this great entity together. Hence much of this investment was sunken into ideological instruments like the monastery at San Vincenzo, where the excavations have revealed a half-hectare eighth-century Benedictine house transformed into a five-hectare small town from c. AD 800 to 840. Like many monasteries, the investment was made to gain monastic support for the Carolingian regime. In other words, the investment was put into a political entity. Little effort was made at this time to develop the monastery's territory or to increase its working population. Of course, agricultural and commodity production was increased in some parts of the ninth-century continental Europe, as surveys in the eastern Rhenish territories indicate (see chapter 12 above), but these programmes were evidently insufficient to safeguard the long-term aspirations of the Carolingian dynasty, especially when its long-distance relations with the Baltic and North Africa began to falter in the 820s and 830s. However, the archaeological evidence from England and Beneventum shows not only the assimilation of the technological, cultural and political implications of the Carolingian renaissance, but also the economic implementation which was surely in Charlemagne's mind. Storage buildings are a new feature of ninth-century compounds at North Elmham, Raunds and Wicken Bonhunt – to name three examples.[50] Similarly, I excavated the earliest medieval storage pits of mid-ninth-century date in Italy at Santa Maria in Civitàৗ – an episcopal settlement in Beneventum.[51] In sum, it is tempting to argue that the political circumstances beyond the Carolingian frontiers enabled these elites to imitate the renaissance, but in their own way. Thus, regional

[48] J. Haslam, 'A middle Saxon iron smelting site at Ramsbury, Wiltshire', *Medieval Archaeology*, 24 (1980), pp. 1–68; J. Williams, 'From "palace" to "town": Northampton and urban origins', in P. Clemoes (ed.), *Anglo-Saxon England*, vol. 13 (1984), pp. 113–36.

[49] T. Hobbes, cited by J. A. Hall, *Powers and Liberties* (Oxford, 1985), p. 121.

[50] Hodges, *The Anglo-Saxon Achievement*.

[51] R. Hodges, G. Barker and K. Wade, 'Excavations at D85 (Santa Maria in Civitàৗ)', *Papers of the British School at Rome*, 48 (1980), pp. 70–124.

commodity exchange was beginning to flourish in mid-ninth-century England. Hamwic in the ninth century, in my opinion, had become principally a regional centre, as had London, Ipswich and York – manifestations of the developing political system in which controlled commodity exchange could be deployed to political advantage rather than to undermine centralized authority.[52] The fate of Europe, in fact, was to rest upon the influence of the Franks beyond their boundaries, because the collapse of the Carolingian polity invoked a sharp reaction in those outer (peripheral) territories dependent upon it.

Klavs Randsborg and I have attempted to show how the end of Carolingian trade is related to the Viking and Saracen raids.[53] The chronology of the decline of the emporia and the pattern of Anglo-Saxon and Frankish coin-finds in Scandinavia provide a telling measure of this period. Moreover, we have postulated that the political economies of the Anglo-Saxons were stable enough to withstand the Carolingian collapse, but this was not so in Denmark, Norway and the Maghreb. The Saracen and Viking menace, therefore, was a consequence, not a cause of change. However, the central question is what impact did these pagans make upon the territories they raided? Were their raids and invasions as disruptive as we have been led to believe by our monastic sources?

Archaeology offers some interesting new evidence on this matter. First, in Braudelian terms, Anglo-Scandinavian England experienced an industrial revolution in the Alfredian and Edwardian period after the Danish settlement. The archaeology of the English towns and their production–distribution networks leaves us in no doubt that the concepts in mind at c. AD 800 were being efficiently implemented after c. AD 900. In other words, regional development under state control was successfully enacted to the great advantage of the West Saxon dynasty. Lopez, like many continental historians, failed to identify this extraordinary English phenomenon, largely because it was so insular. The West Saxon achievement was the logical conclusion of Charlemagne's aspirations. I would wholeheartedly concur with Wormald when he writes 'England, like all European nations, was founded in a "dark age"; we shall never quite understand how. The main objection to belief in the inevitability of English unification is that it is all too easy. It is virtually incredible that what did not happen until long afterwards in countries that were initially subjected to a single political authority should have happened automatically in a country that was not.'[54]

---

[52] Hodges, *The Anglo-Saxon Achievement*.

[53] Hodges, *Dark Age Economics*, pp. 150–61; K. Randsborg, 'Les activités internationales des Vikings: raids ou commerce?', *Annales*, 36 (1981), pp. 862–8.

[54] P. Wormald, 'Bede, the Bretwaldas and the origins of *Gens Anglorum*', in P. Wormald (ed.), *Ideal and Reality in Frankish and Anglo-Saxon Society* (Oxford, 1983).

By contrast, as Wormald indicates, most-Carolingian Europe was slow to develop. The Rhineland may have followed the West Saxon pattern, but the few excavations in Dutch and French towns show that urban expansion evolved slowly during the tenth and eleventh centuries (see, for example, Galinie, on the Neustrian capital at Tours).[55] Likewise, excavations in the north Italian towns of Brescia, Ferrara and Verona demonstrate that urban expansion occurred at about AD 1000.[56] It is too soon to challenge Lopez's model as far as the development of an urban revolution is concerned, but elements of his post-Carolingian scenario need to be refined. First, plentiful rural archaeology reveals that village development in West Germany and Italy (*incastellamento*) occurred during the second half of the tenth century.[57] *Incastellamento*, for example, was in many respects a conscious attempt by landlords to implement those Carolingian policies that were first attempted in the eastern Frankish territories. Yet, at the Benedictine monastery at San Vincenzo al Volturno, for example, the tenth-century monastery was a ramshackle place, while successive abbots set about investment in their *terra*. (The same is almost certainly true of neighbouring monasteries like Farfa and Monte Cassino.) Only when the investment in agrarian development was beginning to reap dividends after *c.* AD 1000 was the monastery rebuilt.[58] Hence, I would postulate a sequence that begins with agrarian investment, which generated a new rural reproductive strategy, which in turn broadly stimulated regional market development. The slow expansion of the West European economy in contrast to England reflects the divisive political legacy of the Carolingians. At about the turn of the millennium the archaeology confirms the familiar historical viewpoint that Europe was advancing at differential rates in response to its Carolingian heritage, drawing upon its underdeveloped resources for differing political needs. What happened next cannot be precisely defined, but again the archaeology offers some clues.

About AD 1025 a Byzantine merchant ship sank off the coast of Turkey at Serçe Liman. George Bass's underwater excavations of this vessel have shown that this was a cargo ship taking glass scrap from Syria to a glassworks in Byzantium.[59] To judge from several small cargoes of pots, the

---

[55] H. Galinié, 'Excavations in Tours', in B. Hobley and R. Hodges (eds), *The Rebirth of Towns in the West*, Council for British Archaeology (London, 1988).

[56] B. Wade-Perkins, 'The rebirth of towns in North Italy', in Hobley and Hodges (eds), *The Rebirth of Towns in the West*.

[57] W. Janssen, 'Some major aspects of Frankish and medieval settlement in the Rhineland', in P. H. Sawyer (ed.), *Medieval Settlement: Continuity and Change* (London, 1976), pp. 41–60; R. Comba and A. Settia (eds), *Castelli: Storia e Archeologia* (Cuneo, Regione di Piemonte, 1984).

[58] C. Wickham, 'Monastic lands and monastic patrons', in R. Hodges (ed.), *San Vincenzo al Volturno*, (London, forthcoming).

[59] G. Bass and F. H. van Doorninck, 'An 11th-century shipwreck at Serçe Liman, Turkey', *International Journal of Nautical Archaeology*, 7 (1978), pp. 119–32; F. H. van Doorninck, *International Journal of Nautical Archaeology*, 11 (1982), pp. 7–11.

ship had already come from Egypt and had called in at a southern Turkish port. The Serçe Liman wreck is an image of those medieval entrepreneurial beginnings to which Lopez alludes. A comparable image can be found at Pisa, where polychrome maiolicas similar to some of those found in the Serçe Liman wreck were set into the façades of the maritime port's new churches. The study of these pots by Berti and Tongiorgi, like that of the pottery from recent excavations by David Whitehouse at Otranto in the heel of Italy (currently being examined by members of the British School at Rome), show emphatically that the trans-Mediterranean trade exploded into life at this time.[60] Excavations of Tuscan villages like Montarrenti, Rocca San Silvestro and Scarlino show that the first timber village structures were rebuilt in stone during the course of the eleventh century or early in the twelfth century, and already a few of their inhabitants were in receipt of Islamic and Byzantine maiolicas.[61] These discoveries bear out the point made by Lopez: the integration of town and country, which had hindered classical antiquity, was being overcome.

Trans-European connections bringing large volumes of trade goods at this date do not exist. The silks from late Saxon London, like Anglo-Saxon pennies in Italy, are difficult to quantify.[62] These were still small-scale commercial affairs. In a similar category, we may include the little black woman found in the eleventh-century cemetery at North Elmham. I cannot resist quoting Calvin Wells's inimitable interpretation of this skeleton:

why she is here, is equally elusive. Perhaps she was indeed a full-time branded slave girl. Perhaps she was a waif bought by a local magnate who hoped that the charm of this little black pearl would give him status as a collector of living Faberge jewels by titillating the curiosity of his neighbours. Or maybe she was the fancy of a merchant bringing home 'A souvenir from Cordoba' for his wife; or even a thegnly effort at keeping up with the Caliphs.[63]

In fact, the Commercial Revolution, as Lopez describes it, appears, to judge from the archaeology, to have comprised a number of inter-regional zones which by the end of the century were welded into a unified system. For example, southern England and northern and western France developed mercantile connections in the second quarter of the eleventh century which were to be of great importance in later medieval centuries. This, at least, is the thrust of the ceramic and coin evidence from Exeter,

[60] G. Berti and L. Tongiorgi, *I Bacini Ceramici Medievali delle Chiese di Pisa* (Rome, 1982); D. Whitehouse, personal communication.

[61] R. Francovich, *Scarlino II: Scavi 1979–93* (Florence, forthcoming); R. Francovish, 'Tuscany in the Dark Ages', in K. Randsborg (ed.), *First Millennium* (Rome, forthcoming).

[62] F. Pritchard, 'Late Saxon textiles from the City of London', *Medieval Archaeology*, 28 (1984), pp. 46–76.

[63] C. Wells, 'The human bones', in P. Wade-Martin, *North Elham*, vol. 2. *East Anglian Archaeology*, 9 (1980), pp. 247–374.

Southampton and St Malo.[64] Similarly, Alan Vince has shown that London's trade with the Continent took off at this time, after a period in which it had been concerned solely with regional commercial connections.[65] It is no coincidence, therefore, that Hartwig Ludtke, in his study of Schleswig's pottery, attributes the beginnings of Rhenish Pingsdorf in the Baltic Sea port to the eleventh century.[66] These painted tablewares are a harbinger of the great commercial relations which over the following centuries underscore the Hanseatic League. North Sea towns like London, Yarmouth, Norwich, Lund, Medemblik, Oslo and Ribe exhibit artefactual connections which grow to immense proportions in the twelfth and thirteenth centuries.

The beginnings of Braudel's modern world economy, therefore, can be traced to the political configurations of post-Carolingian Europe. This must be related to the reception of traders from the then burgeoning Indian Ocean mercantile system in the Middle East at ports where ships like that which perished at Serçe Liman were welcomed. Nevertheless, as Wormald demonstrates, England was in some ways a special case. Its wealth was based upon two centuries of strong government, which made it an attractive conquest for the Normans. It was an altogether different proposition to the southern Italian and Sicilian territories, which in AD 1066 were being annexed by the mighty Robert Guiscard. *Domesday Book* like the early twelfth-century *Catalogus Baronum* – its Italian equivalent – is a manifestation of the Norman desire to capitalize upon their conquest and to develop their resources more efficiently. The steady expansion into marginal landscapes following close upon these two great fiscal surveys reflects the will to expand production as the embryonic inter-regional networks of Western Europe became steadily more integrated. A great debate now surrounds the social implications of his strategy. Some historians believe the feudal relations placed increasing restraints upon the peasantry; other historians speculate upon the expedient governmental policies of the Normans, as they sought to get the best out of their conquests. The archaeology of the twelfth-century European peasantry remains too slight to be informative on this matter, but by the thirteenth century we are in safer territory. The Commercial Revolution most emphatically incorporated all parts of society in a fashion that was never achieved under the Roman Empire. This fact is plain in any archaeological survey of almost any part of Europe. Why this happened in the medieval West when it did

---

[64] R. Hodges and A. Mainman, 'The Saxo-Norman imported pottery', in J. P. Allan, *Medieval and Post-Medieval Finds from Exeter, 1971–1980* (Exeter, 1984), pp. 13–18.

[65] A. Vince, 'The Saxon and medieval pottery of London: a review', *Medieval Archaeology*, 29 (1985), pp. 25–94.

[66] H. Ludtke, 'Die mittelalterliche Keramik von Schleswig', *Ausgrabungen in Schleswig. Berichte und Studien*, 4 (Neumünster, 1985).

not happen in a classical antiquity or in the East, and its implications for the modern world, are currently attracting a good deal of discussion. The answers must be traced not to the elite, of whom so much has been written, but to those eleventh- and twelfth-century peasants denied history who, according to Lopez, fuelled this commercial achievement. In short, critical questions stand in need of archaeological research.

In this chapter I have presented an alternative to Lopez's model. Necessarily, I have surveyed the archaeological sources much as he and others have summarized the written data base. The two sources are both comparable and complementary. The archaeological evidence, however, invites us to consider what happened, as opposed to what certain authors wished their readers to believe to have happened. The world systems' approach leads us to focus upon the decline and fall of classical antiquity; on the rise of the Carolingian polity in conspicuous imitation of the earlier Roman Empire; on the late ninth-century Viking/Saracen raids; and on the beginnings of a Europe of nation-states linked by common commercial aspirations from the eleventh century onwards. This approach naturally compresses the past into one dimension and fails to account for the creation of such connections or the role of those on the periphery in determining the histories of the core. It amounts to only one rhythm of this age. The other rhythm may be formulated as the struggle between peer groups each seeking their own identity, and from time to time roped into larger all-embracing space–time dynamics. This holistic approach invites us to be cautious of Lopez's version of the European Miracle, especially if its implications are destined to be enshrined in modern development theory. The archaeology has the important feature of measuring the behaviour of the rich and poor, as well as compelling us to focus upon production and distribution as aspects of political evolution. We must be critical of reading what we wish to find into the past. Nevertheless, each age creates its own perspective of the past. It is my contention that we are still fascinated by a Victorian diorama of the Dark Ages, which inevitably must be almost entirely reconsidered. Quite what the story will be in a hundred years hence I do not know, but sufficient of this European take-off is documented already to caution us that Third World countries absorbing western technology today are not merely incorporating a physical or economic product, but social attitudes forged over a very long time.

Glossary

ancingas (*andecinga*)   (L.) plot of arable belonging to the lord's demesne, allotted to one particular serf for cultivation

banleuca   area of jurisdiction

berewick   dependent farm of a multiple estate; a detached portion of inland or demesne, which was usually geographically separate from the manor of which it formed a part, but which was owned as far as its soil was concerned by the lord of the manor

cadestre   system of territorial organization upon which taxation or tribute was levied

caput   (L.) head manor

ceaster   (OE) a city (often used to refer to a walled Roman town)

cella memoria   (L.) a tomb in a late Roman (extra-mural) cemetery

ceorl   (OE) a peasant

colonia   (L.) chartered town often with a nucleus of retired army veterans in its population. There were four *coloniae* in Britain

curia   (L.) archbishop's court

demesne   land held in lordship

dominium   (L.) lordship

enceinte   area of a Roman town within the wall; (York) Anglo-Scandinavian area

ferding   a quarter hundred

fief   feudal benefice, territory held in fee (initially sufficient to support a mounted soldier, later held in return for military service)

fieldbook   a survey of all the strips or lands in a field system, commonly giving the name of the owner and area. Listed by furlong and field

furlong   a group of lands lying together and cultivated as a sub-unit of a field. The acreage varied widely according to the local topography. Also a standard measure of 40 perches or 220 statute yards

geld   a tax levied according to hidage over most of the country, but in East Anglia vills paid so many pence for every pound due from the hundred

hide   unit of fiscal assessment. Originally 'the land of one family', possibly based upon arable land with appurtenances; later, a specific area of land; in Northamptonshire it has been shown to consist of ten or more yardlands

hundred   a territorial grouping based upon the concept of 100 hides, but of variable composition

insula (L.) rectangular block of property in a Roman town

land smallest unit of cultivation, about a rood in area, forming an elongated strip about 200 yards long

lathe an early territorial unit in Kent, often with vast common pastures and displaying economic unity

leet petty folk court, beneath a hundredal court; a jurisdictional and an economic unit consisting of a number of vills, the one aspect was emphasized by the possession of a common and a non-manorial court, the other by extensive intercommoning rights appertaining to all these vills.[1]

lete one or more vills grouped for the payment of geld and other tax burdens; a subdivision of a hundred in East Anglia

liberty a territory free from direct royal control; a privileged district exempt from a sheriff's jurisdiction

margrave German title of some princes of the Holy Roman Empire, originally of the military governor of a border province

minster church mother church, originally staffed by a team of priests, serving a territory that often contains ancillary churches

monasterium (L.) monastery or minster

multiple estate a unit of territory of unified ownership and management, but consisting of a number of discontiguous parts

open field an area of open arable land divided into furlongs and strips; usually several hundred acres in extent and cropped and fallowed as a whole unit

ora (OE) a coin of Danish origin

parish an area of ecclesiastical administration dependent on and served by a particular church

parochia (L.) territory of a minster church

pievi (I.) Italian mother churches, normally with centralized baptismal rights

principia (L.) centrally placed headquarters in a Roman fortress

rape a division of a hundred in south-eastern England (in Norman times often a unit of a military nature)

regio (L.) a district focused on an early Anglo-Saxon royal estate

rihtscriftscire (OE) properly assigned district of a confessor, parish

small virgate a yardland

sokeland land which physically belonged to the men seated on it, but which nevertheless carried certain liabilities to services and dues which were to be rendered to the lord of the manor to which it was appendant

territorium (L.) territory; Roman administrative territory

tithe one-tenth of the annual increase of the produce of the soil, a render initially due to the mother church

township a pre-Norman unit of settlement regarded as a community; sometimes became a parish, but usually a sub-unit of a parish (later it was often referred to as a tithing). Frequently possessed its own settlement nucleus and field system. An area of common agricultural unity based on a particular field system. It is

---

[1] I. H. Adams, *Agrarian Landscape Terms: a Glossary for Historical Geography*, Institute of British Geographers (London, 1976), p. 74, citing D. C. Douglas, *The Social Structure of Medieval East Anglia* (Oxford, 1927), p. 212.

often equivalent to the vill, but the latter term is more usually used to refer to the taxation unit, whereas the township tends to be used to refer to the physical fabric of a community, in terms of its fields, buildings, woods and rivers

villa integre　(L.) lete, a subdivision of a hundred in East Anglia

villa regalis　(L.) king's/royal vill

villa regia　(L.) royal vill

virgate　the fourth part of a hide; (Northamptonshire): sometimes called the large or Domesday virgate

wergild　(OE) compensation, value of a man's life

witan　(OE) group of councillors who met regularly at an assembly called a *witenagemot* to exercise government

yardland　a unit of tenure designed to support a peasant farm. (Northamptonshire): a standard medieval holding consisting of about 60 lands scattered uniformly over the whole field system. The acreage was variable from village to village, but 25 acres was common

Index